Advances in Spatial Science

The Regional Science Series

This series contains scientific studies focusing on spatial phenomena, utilising theoretical frameworks, analytical methods, and empirical procedures specifically designed for spatial analysis. Advances in Spatial Science brings together innovative spatial research utilising concepts, perspectives, and methods relevant to both basic science and policy making. The aim is to present advances in spatial science to an informed readership in universities, research organisations, and policy-making institutions throughout the world.

The type of material considered for publication in the series includes: Monographs of theoretical and applied research in spatial science; state-of-the-art volumes in areas of basic research; reports of innovative theories and methods in spatial science; tightly edited reports from specially organised research seminars. The series and the volumes published in it are indexed by Scopus.

More information about this series at http://www.springer.com/series/3302

Bianca Biagi • Alessandra Faggian •
Isha Rajbhandari • Viktor A. Venhorst
Editors

New Frontiers in Interregional Migration Research

Springer

Editors
Bianca Biagi
Department of Economics and Business
University of Sassari-CRENoS-GSSI
L'Aquila, Italy

Alessandra Faggian
Social Sciences
Gran Sasso Science Institute
L'Aquila, Italy

Isha Rajbhandari
Department of Economics
University of Puget Sound
Tacoma, Washington, USA

Viktor A. Venhorst
Faculty of Spatial Sciences
Department of Economic Geography
University of Groningen
Groningen, The Netherlands

ISSN 1430-9602 ISSN 2197-9375 (electronic)
Advances in Spatial Science
ISBN 978-3-030-09349-5 ISBN 978-3-319-75886-2 (eBook)
https://doi.org/10.1007/978-3-319-75886-2

Printed on acid-free paper

This Springer imprint is published by the registered company Springer International Publishing AG part of Springer Nature.
The registered company address is: Gewerbestrasse 11, 6330 Cham, Switzerland

To my beloved mother and the privilege I had to be her daughter.

Bianca Biagi

To my parents, because too often we do not give enough credit to the people we love the most.

Alessandra Faggian

To my dear parents.

Isha Rajbhandari

To the wonderful Neeltje, Eva and Sam.

Viktor A. Venhorst

Preface

This book focuses on the new challenges in interregional migration research. Currently, the scale of analysis is shifting from a macro to a more micro level. The availability of extensive micro data on individual migrants allows researchers to revisit the role of different migration drivers by population subgroups (e.g. by education and ethnicity) and include life cycle and contextual considerations (e.g. entering education or the labour market, working in growing industries, moving thanks to, or in spite of, existing networks). At the same time, the availability of longer time series and longitudinal data is crucial in studying the role migrants play in promoting regional resilience, for instance in regions hit by the recent economic crisis or by natural disasters; in reducing core-periphery disparities, which is a central issue in economic development studies; and in the longer term effects of Brexit.

The aim of the book is to establish the state of the art in interregional migration research and to identify routes forward. It updates and revisits the main academic debates on interregional migration, as well as presenting new emerging lines of investigation and a forward-looking research agenda. It presents original work spanning from in-depth discussion of recent theoretical advances to cutting-edge empirical analyses.

This ambitious agenda would have not been possible without the inspiring contributions of world-leading academics who submitted their original work to this book. The editors are grateful for their contributions and look forward to continue shifting research frontiers with them in the decades to come.

Department of Economics and Business, University of Sassari-CRENoS-GSSI, L'Aquila, Italy — Bianca Biagi
Social Sciences, Gran Sasso Science Institute, L'Aquila, Italy — Alessandra Faggian
Department of Economics, University of Puget Sound, Tacoma, WA, USA — Isha Rajbhandari
Faculty of Spatial Sciences, Department of Economic Geography, University of Groningen, Groningen, The Netherlands — Viktor A. Venhorst

Contents

List of Contributors

Andrea Ariu Economics Department, Ludwig-Maximilians-Universität Munich and IFO, Munich, Germany

CRENOS, Cagliari, Italy

Kathryn Benier School of Social Sciences, Monash University, Clayton, VIC, Australia

Bianca Biagi Department of Economics and Business, University of Sassari-CRENoS-GSSI, L'Aquila, Italy

Roberta Comunian Culture, Media and Creative Industries, King's College London, London, UK

Jonathan Corcoran Queensland Centre for Population Research, School of Earth and Environmental Sciences, The University of Queensland, St Lucia, QLD, Australia

Daniel Crown Department of Agricultural, Environmental, and Development Economics, The Ohio State University, Columbus, OH, USA

Kathryn R. Dotzel US EPA Office of Transportation and Air Quality, Ann Arbor, MI, USA

Alessandra Faggian Social Sciences, Gran Sasso Science Institute, L'Aquila, Italy

Ugo Fratesi Politecnico di Milano, Milano, Italy

Margherita Gerolimetto Department of Economics, Ca′ Foscari University of Venice, Venezia, Italy

Arthur Grimes Motu Economic and Public Policy Research, Wellington, New Zealand

Victoria University of Wellington, Wellington, New Zealand

Timothy Jaquet Department of Agricultural, Environmental, and Development Economics, The Ohio State University, Columbus, OH, USA

Sarah Jewell Department of Economics, University of Reading, Reading, UK

Santtu Karhinen Finnish Environment Institute and Department of Economics, Oulu Business School, University of Oulu, Oulu, Finland

Stefano Magrini Department of Economics, Ca′ Foscari University of Venice, Venezia, Italy

Philip McCann Sheffield University Management School, The University of Sheffield, Sheffield, UK

Mark Partridge Department of Agricultural, Environmental, and Development Economics, The Ohio State University, Columbus, OH, USA

Jinan University, Guangzhou, China

Gran Sasso Science Institute, L'Aquila, Italy

Marco Percoco Università Bocconi, Milano, Italy

Isha Rajbhandari Department of Economics, University of Puget Sound, Tacoma, WA, USA

Jaakko Simonen Department of Economics, Oulu Business School, University of Oulu, Oulu, Finland

Cindy Smart Boston Consulting Group, Sydney, NSW, Australia

Rauli Svento Department of Economics, Oulu Business School, University of Oulu, Oulu, Finland

Wilbur Townsend Motu Economic and Public Policy Research, Wellington, New Zealand

Viktor A. Venhorst Faculty of Spatial Sciences, University of Groningen, Groningen, The Netherlands

Chapter 1
Editorial: New Frontiers in Interregional Migration Research

Bianca Biagi, Alessandra Faggian, Isha Rajbhandari, and Viktor A. Venhorst

1.1 Data and Theory: Tortoise and Hare, or Leap-Frogging?

Research on interregional migration has taken great strides in the last decades. Data quality has improved considerably, with micro-level data increasingly available. This has allowed researchers to link substantive background data, pertaining to a broad variety of life domains, to information on past migration trajectories, as well as current movements. Such data is now not only available for Western economies, but also for some developing and transition economies.

Also, what is generally referred to as "Big Data," i.e. large scale data collected often as a result of the regular proceedings of running a business or government service, coupled with increased computing power, allows researchers to visualize even minute migration patterns, sometimes in real time. In addition, availability of large-scale surveys and the increased accessibility to Census-like registry datasets, has enabled the field to focus on much more finely-defined "regions," moving from

B. Biagi (✉)
Department of Economics and Business, University of Sassari-CRENoS-GSSI, L'Aquila, Italy
e-mail: bbiagi@uniss.it

A. Faggian
Social Sciences, Gran Sasso Science Institute, L'Aquila, Italy
e-mail: alessandra.faggian@gssi.it

I. Rajbhandari
Department of Economics, University of Puget Sound, Tacoma, WA, USA
e-mail: irajbhandari@pugetsound.edu

V. A. Venhorst
Faculty of Spatial Sciences, Department of Economic Geography, University of Groningen, Groningen, The Netherlands
e-mail: v.a.venhorst@rug.nl

B. Biagi et al. (eds.), *New Frontiers in Interregional Migration Research*,
Advances in Spatial Science, https://doi.org/10.1007/978-3-319-75886-2_1

country or state level data to smaller areas, sometimes even reaching the level of neighbourhoods within municipalities.

The level of specificity that was previously the domain of targeted case studies, can now be achieved in more general and generalizable quantitative research designs. This in itself is pushing forward the research frontier in the field. However, new challenges arise.

On the data side, for instance, while the existing large registries have the advantage of providing large samples for more sophisticated quantitative models, researchers are dependent on the measurements, questions and definitions of the data supplying agencies. One has to "make do" with what is available. Tax offices collect strictly what is needed in order to execute their tasks. Visa registers may only contain very limited amounts of background information. This might sometimes be in contrast with state-of-the-art operationalisations, theoretical grounding of variables and fine-tuning of survey techniques the field has brought forth. Secondly, this seemingly endless level of potential empirical precision also requires matching theoretical frameworks. It is easy to fall in the trap of data mining without having clear testable hypotheses grounded in theory. Even when the theoretical background is well specified, it becomes even more fundamental to specify, at the very beginning of a project, what is the most adequate spatial and temporal scale for analysis.

1.1.1 Setting the Agenda

These developments bring us to the main focus of the book. Given the new developments in "Big Data" availability and other new data sources geo-coded at a finer spatial scales, what are the new challenges for researchers and policy makers in the field of interregional migration? How did researchers deal with these new challenges? What kind of theoretical and empirical advances in the field of interregional migration were made possible, and which new policies options were identified by these new "Big Data"? And conversely, which data advances are due to our improved theoretical understanding of the migration phenomena? In which ways can we develop our understanding of migration via sharper conceptualisations of what constitutes migration?

In answering these questions, we will also look at how new research on interregional migration dealt with the concurrent economic and financial crisis, which impacted interregional migration in multiple ways by widening regional disparities and youth unemployment in lagging regions and exacerbating the existing periphery-core dynamics. We will also seek to uncover the relationship between migration patterns and the rather new and fashionable concept of regional "resilience." Are regions resilient because of migrants or are migrants moving to resilient regions? And what are the characteristics of the migrants moving to more resilient regions? The answers to these questions will help the field shed light on the future impacts of events such as Brexit and the heterogeneous effects dynamics in globalization on countries around the world.

1.1.2 Overview

This book is structured in three main parts, preceded by this editorial. This editorial does not seek to provide complete summaries of the chapters incorporated in this book. Rather, our intensive discussion of their contents is intended, firstly, to identify what we have come to refer to as the frontier in interregional migration research: where do leading authors in the field envisage this line? How have they dealt with the challenges of working on the edge? Secondly, we hope our discussion will maximize the accessibility of this book to wide readership. We conclude our discussion with a round-up of the advances and challenges as identified in the chapters in this volume.

Part I provides an in-depth discussion of the current theoretical state-of-the-art, in direct relation to advances in data availability, as well as the impact of institutional innovation and policy shocks. We investigate to what extent data, societal trends and theory have interacted to produce the current knowledge on migration research. Based on this, challenges and knowledge gaps are identified.

Part II is an overview of migration research so far in three different geographical, institutional and historical contexts: the US, Europe and Oceania. The interrelation between theory, data collection and institutional and policy shocks is addressed. A contribution on the recent refugee crisis in Europe is also included.

In Part III, we present four empirical contributions using world-leading registry and survey data, combining individual background characteristics and contextual information. This sheds light on the extent to which we are able to learn from studying migrants in their contexts, and from applying new and more heterogeneous conceptualisations of mobility.

1.2 Part I: Shifting the Theoretical Frontier, New Data and New Questions?

1.2.1 Chapter 2: Theoretical Advances on Interregional Migration Models

Bianca Biagi and Kathryn R. Dotzel

In Chapter 2, the authors map the innovation over time of internal migration studies from 1970s onwards. This results in an appraisal of current internal migration research, and the identification of gaps in the literature. Even though research into internal migration has, over time, been characterized as multidisciplinary, the main contributions to migration research in the first half of the twentieth century stem from advances in labour economics and the analysis of economic disparities between regions. Here, migration is studied as a labour market clearing mechanism. More recently, even within the field of economics, but certainly also beyond, the various perspectives on migration have multiplied, but little attempt has been made to integrate these streams. Thanks to its multidisciplinary nature, the phenomenon of migration and its determinants has been, and continue to be, studied intensively. Yet, there has been less attention to the impact of migration on both sending and receiving areas, as well as the individual and family life course. The development of theory, in particular the view on what constitutes the "migrant" (skilled worker, consumer with a love of variety, member of a household), goes hand in hand with advances in the availability of suitable data.

Stemming from the predominantly economic focus on migration, most of the work that was published in the 1970s focused on the role of economic disparities between regions and their consequences on the direction and composition of migrant flows. The scientific debate centred on the analysis of gross flows and the development of gravity equations, considering both origin and destination characteristics. Migration in this setting was positioned more and more as a form of spatial job search, with differences noted between the US and Europe: labour market adjustment in the US appears indeed more migration centred, whereas in Europe, labour force participation decisions play a more important role.

Economic disparities however did not fully account for the empirical patterns in migration as well as migration outcomes: individuals did not seem to always move in the expected direction, and economic disparities did not dissipate, even in the face of substantial migration flows. Driven by the increased availability of micro and longitudinal data, the authors note, theory evolved in the 1980s and 1990s in the direction of what are generally referred to as "equilibrium approaches" as opposed to the "disequilibrium approaches" based on economic disparities. Migrants are now more thought of as consumers, who are willing to accept pay cuts in return to local "untradeable" amenities. Also, gradually, there is a shift in the unit of analysis as such, with the migrant no longer considered as a solitary unit, but part of a family, with total family utility being maximized.

Much debate ensued in the literature, as to which of these "antagonists," as the authors call them, is the dominant determinant in migration flows. Arguably, this debate is still ongoing, with temporal shocks, as well as fundamental changes in the population composition at least partially driving the empirical results. The economic crises in the first decades of the twenty-first century, coupled with population aging and the resulting shifts in migration flows towards more amenity rich destinations continues to fuel the debate.

Therefore, the authors conclude, the focus in migration literature in the 2000s and onwards has therefore been on heterogeneity: migrants are no longer considered as solitary rational economic agents. They are family members, they are part of networks in sending and receiving countries, they may have previous experience of their destination areas, they have skillsets which may be generic or specialist in nature, they are in a certain phase of their lives; all of which are relatively important determinants of migration. But, as the authors continue, this heterogeneity is also vitally important when considering individual and regional outcomes.

In addition to this increased attention for migrant heterogeneity, the authors advocate an explicit consideration of the spatial context in which migration decisions take place and in which migration goals and outcomes are to be realized. This point is supported by the other contributions in this book. Likewise, the authors call attention to the international dimension: the social and family dimension of these flows remains somewhat under-researched as is the angle of (effects on) developing economies. This blind spot regarding cross-border commuting will be revisited in Part II of this book.

1.2.2 *Chapter 3: Determinants and Consequences of International Migration*

Andrea Ariu

In the third chapter, Andrea Ariu delves deeper into the issues surrounding migration in relation to its effects on sending and receiving economies. The author commences with a brief yet thorough exposition of the canonical gravity model. Its flexibility in explaining zero flows, migrant heterogeneity and selectivity, and inclusion of (heterogeneous) migration costs, but perhaps most importantly, it can be tailored to take dynamics in the characteristics of "third option" destinations into account. Changes in the attractiveness in alternative destinations may impact the likelihood of moving from one region to a particular other region.

The recent literature is surveyed, leading to what can effectively be described as a blue print model. The literature has advanced from applying typically interregional income differentials to studying the effects of diasporas, expectations and policies on migration flows. Interestingly, some of these more recent approaches have advanced as a result of access to registries such as data on VISA waivers to study the effects of policy shocks. As such, well over five decades after its inception, the gravity approach is still "shifting frontiers."

New challenges lie ahead however. As noted also by Biagi and Dotzel in the preceding chapter, there is still much debate on the effects of migration on sending and receiving countries regions. Ariu notes that much of the literature on the effects on sending regions is theoretical in nature. This literature starts from the assumption that migration is selective, and that typically the higher skilled have an incentive to be migratory, implying that lagging regions may experience "brain drain." Ariu sketches the development in this literature, as it moved from free market economics to a focus on the negative consequences of human capital loss and onwards to potential positive effects on sending economies: it is considered that the likelihood of access to good opportunities abroad result in investment in education at home, thereby increasing the skill levels in the sending economy. Also, remittances receive more and more attention. More recently effects on institutions are considered as well as impacts on democratic traditions. Yet, Ariu points out, even though it is clear from this literature that migration may have positive effects on sending economies, it is still unclear to what extent this balances the negative effects.

In contrast, Ariu discusses how the debate on migration effects on destination countries and regions has been rather more lively in the last decades. The effect of immigration on the wages of the native workforce remains a source of considerable debate. The main theoretical point is to what extent the migrant workforce complements or substitutes the native workforce. Ariu notes that this puzzle has methodological consequences too: location choice of migrants is likely to be endogenous to these issues. Over the years, various identification strategies have been applied in the literature, including the comparison of migrant outcomes to only those native workers similar in terms of education and work experience. Overskilling of migrants is another issue that has received attention. Methodologically, the literature has seen advances as increased availability of data allows the application of instrumental variable techniques or matching on observables. Here, as such, theoretical advances are not data driven. Rather, the improvement of data allows for better testing of existing questions.

Ariu proposes some advances, building on the questions and opportunities raised earlier in this chapter. Improved data allows existing and improved questions to be answered: migrant and native workforce characteristics and firm characteristics can now be included allowing for better identification strategies. The question of impact on sending and receiving economies is ultimately one of the actual activities and contributions of migrant and native workers. It will help arrive at establishing complementarities and substitutions. Limited geographical coverage is a continuing challenge however, preventing cross-country comparisons. This holds for analyses spanning different specific localities within countries, for example the urban environment.

Overall, new data sources may inspire new questions, as Biagi and Dotzel note, but additionally Ariu demonstrates that even the classic migration frameworks continue to pose questions that only now we are coming close to answering.

1.3 Part II: State of the Art and Future Challenges in Migration Research Around the World

1.3.1 Chapter 4: State of the Art and Future Challenges of Interregional Migration Empirical Research in North America

Isha Rajbhandari and Mark Partridge

In the field of interregional migration research, the United States provide an interesting, if not to say the benchmark case. Even though migration rates have declined over the last decades, the US population has been consistently highly mobile. Furthermore, there have been fundamental changes in the migration trends. This chapter provides an analysis of the extant literature on these trends. Furthermore, it also investigates to which extent climate change and the ensuing shocks have been incorporated in this literature.

The earlier literature on US migration was predominantly based on regional level analysis, due to the lack of micro data. The authors note that this presents a risk, in the sense that individual heterogeneity is disregarded and migration outcomes may be overstated. For example, an unemployed person may exhibit a very different response to the unemployment rate in a potential destination than an employed person.

Major trends were nonetheless identified: a decline in the urban areas as a destination and sizeable migration to the south and west regions in 1970s. This sparked the debate on the relative importance of economic versus non-economic characteristics, which arguably continues to this day. Proponents of equilibrium approach assume that total personal utility is ultimately constant across space and across all spheres of life. Empirical evidence for the US was found to be in line with this: migrants flow towards areas with favourable weather, even if this implies trading off employment or wages. Other authors found that the availability of jobs continued to be a leading determinant of migration. Furthermore, employment growth was occurring in amenity rich regions, so this suggested at least an indirect effect of amenities.

Great strides forward were made when micro data was applied to migration research. Analysis focused on the actual decision making unit and the role of one's position in the life cycle. This type of research remained scarce before the 2000s but it was certainly consequential. For example, it became generally recognized that age is of prime importance, not only in terms of migration likelihood, but also in terms of destination choice. Another crucial dimension is the skill profile of the mobile.

Post 2000s, the literature demonstrates a further decline in migration propensities, although there is some stabilization visible. Also there are stronger flows towards suburbs. As the debate continues between the importance of amenity-led growth relative to the availability of job opportunities, some studies offer a somewhat more reconciliatory view. For example, firm are thought to locate close to where they suspect their workforce might be interested in living: in or near growing cities with ample services. Retirees continue to exhibit alternative patterns. Employment growth is reported for amenity rich areas, as well as suburbs, which is partially the result of aging population inflow and spending. A more recent literature notes how the higher skilled concentrate in areas which are already skilled, increasing regional disparities.

Even though a sizeable body of literature has assessed the direct consequences of climate related disasters, both recent and long past, the authors argue that this literature is theoretically uninformed, and has thus far failed to correctly incorporate the adaptive elements in migration behaviour. The negative effects of disasters are amply documented, but there is little consideration for the fact that, in particular, regions which are currently found to be attractive destinations are also more prone to experience climate change induced events. Furthermore, the costs are understated in the sense that no account is made for the extent of differences in the resiliency of the stayers and movers for these areas. Will the remaining population be able to cope? Conversely, adaptive behaviour is not accounted for: new technology may help shape migration flows in ways that reduce the costs of climate change.

The authors close by noting that problems of the past may yet return: in spite of the increased availability of micro data, as new topics emerge researchers may still have to rely on regional analyses as the existing sources may still prove lacking. State-to-state differences in data collection, a disregard of emerging topics, and limited insight in the occupational effects of migration are among the data challenges that the authors note.

1.3.2 Chapter 5: State of the Art and Future Challenges of Interregional Migration Empirical Research in Europe

Margherita Gerolimetto and Stefano Magrini

Gerolimetto and Magrini start with an exposition on the differences between European migration flows and those in the United States. It is noted that Europeans tend to be less migratory and the authors point towards the relatively higher transaction costs associated with migration across countries in Europe. But the motivations behind migration differ as well, with the disequilibrium framework, focusing on economic disparities between regions, appearing slightly more dominant in Europe, even though the flows are thin. The equilibrium framework, focusing more on non-economic "untradeable" characteristics of regions, appears to apply more and more to the United States.

This is noteworthy, as the freedom of movement of people and goods is fundamental in the institutional setup of the European Union (EU) and has been receiving attention in the various programmes the EU is running, such as initiatives under Horizon 2020. The authors describe how the fundamental freedoms have, up to a certain extent, always been at odds with continued protectionist actions, referred to as transitional measures, on the part of certain member states, especially in those years when EU expansion was on the cards. It was believed by many that the opening of borders with new member states would have detrimental effects on home labour markets. Perhaps in spite of these measures, EU enlargement between 2004 and 2009 has had substantial effects on, in particular, East-West migration, which doubled, if not tripled. West-East flows remained rather stable, however, which is parallel to what we see in terms of the global North-South flows, as pointed out by Percoco and Fratesi in Chapter 6. Overall, however, the size of these migrants streams remained rather modest in size.

This leads to the question to what extent alternative forms of mobility are applied by the Europeans, and furthermore which alternative forms of mobility ought to be considered more by research. The authors first discuss (cross-border) commuting. Access to commuting hubs helps regions deal with economic shocks: it is relatively easy to shift the workforce from one opportunity to the next. Similar flows have been found to take place across international borders, in which case commuting becomes a viable alternative to international migration. Indeed commuting flows have been found to respond to broadly the same economic disparities as do migration flows.

The authors also consider forced migrants and refugees, in comparison to international migrants and their impact on the receiving labour markets. Even though limited impacts on host labour markets are generally reported, the underlying question goes beyond mere integration of foreign workers in labour markets: the flows are acute and concern the preparation of institutional, economic and intelligence systems in order to enable both host communities as well as migrants. In that light, and also related to commuting as an alternative clearing mechanism, the authors note that, apart from a rich body of literature on EU interregional migration, an integrated cross-border perspective is lacking.

1.3.3 Chapter 6: The Geography of Asylum Seekers and Refugees in Europe

Marco Percoco and Ugo Fratesi

Percoco and Fratesi focus on what is generally referred to as the refugee crisis: the sudden increase in influx of refugees from war-ridden Middle East which has lead to a steady increase of refugees since the early 2010s, but took off from 2014 onwards. Their goal is to review the main institutional and political factors influencing the debate over the spatial distribution of refugees in Europe.

In the outset, their perspective is more historical. Nonetheless, depending on the composition of the refugee flow, or the degree of involvement of receiving countries in the crisis that causes the refugee flow, responses in the receiving countries have varied considerably. For more recent events, it is difficult to establish impact. However, the authors cite work studying the impact of Jewish professors entering the US economy particularly in terms of economic outcomes, as well as public opinion. Even though the impact was positive, a large share of the public remained sceptical of the new arrivals.

History may be repeating itself, even in the face of ever increasing international migration streams. The authors note how over the last decades apart from North-South flows, all global flows have increased. In terms of impact on receiving economies, migrant heterogeneity is playing a key role. A number of studies is cited which have used policy shocks as natural experiments and drawn careful conclusions about the impact of the arrival of specific migrant types. These impacts are mixed, and depend on, for example, the extent to which the inflow is embedded in suitable policies and investments. All in all, the authors note that the evidence on the impact of refugees is scarce. Perceptions about refugees and migrants in general differ considerably between inhabitants of different countries, seemingly depending on their own position in the migration trail.

The authors continue with a presentation of recent figures on locations and routes of refugee migration. Only after 2014 has the number of positive status decisions been higher than the rejections. Differences between EU countries hinge in part on their position relative to the migrant routes and therefore, the composition of the inflow, and in part on differences in their legal systems. Concerning the routes, there appears to be a network factor, in the sense that others will follow where previously fellow countrymen have succeeded. But more importantly perhaps, some routes have been widely documented as being particularly perilous.

Location choices, routing, and composition of the migrant and refugee populations influence the attitudes of Europeans towards refugees. The authors provide an intensive discussion on the mechanisms at work here. Descriptive results indicate that indeed opinions differ between Europeans in different countries. The exact location of refugees in receiving countries plays a central role: location choice has been highly institutionalized, with in some cases regions allowed to bid up to host refugees. There are economic impacts, as well as impacts on public opinion.

This then leads to an agenda of issues that according to the authors are so far somewhat under-researched. In particular, this concerns the interactions, in terms of economic and social impacts, and local innovation spillovers of refugees and the actual location they end up in, but also their wellbeing as a result of being in these specific locations. Data is scarce on this intersection of characteristics, partially due to cultural and political sensitivities that continue to surround the topic.

1.3.4 Chapter 7: State of the Art and Future Challenges of Interregional Migration Empirical Research in Oceania

Kathryn Benier and Jonathan Corcoran

Benier and Corcoran investigate migration policies in Australia and New Zealand and their effect on drivers and consequences of migration. They do so from an essentially historical perspective, comparing patterns of immigration policies between Australia and New Zealand as the two main immigration destinations in Oceania.

Many parallels exist between the two countries. Migration was needed to build the nations, the authors begin. Infrastructure needed to be build and labour was needed. Along with these motivations, the authors note that an idea of a white Australia was put into policy as well. While there were no such formal policies in New Zealand, it was preferred. The composition of these early groups of immigrants is well known: mostly from Great-Britain (including convicts in the earlier waves) and Ireland, Germany, America and China during and after the gold rush of the 1850s. Inflow into Australia continued to hail from predominantly the UK, with the government actively setting goals for population increase. Explicit references to a

White Australia were not removed from policies until the 1970s, to be replaced by criteria based on personal characteristics such as occupational groups. Similar changes were implemented in New Zealand.

Such criteria put both countries in the position to benefit from "brain gain" processes. The authors continue their exposition by looking into the specifics of the settlement of these migrants within these countries, covering urban-rural migrations, interstate migration and trans-Tasman moves. What transpires from their discussion is first and foremost that suitable data, which is sufficiently finely grained in temporal and spatial sense, and provides detailed background information on the migrants, is lacking. The lack of data, to a certain extent, prevents a thorough analysis of migrant outcomes in relation to their location choices within the destination countries. Nevertheless, based on the available literature, it is clear that an urban-rural dichotomy is a reality among migrants just like the native populations. Interstate migration is predominantly studied using census data, which obscures the view on personal characteristics. Trans-Tasman migration is a rather one sided affair, with moves towards Australia starting to outnumber moves towards New Zealand by a significant margin from the mid-1970s.

Overall, the authors note that the current trends in the literature, focusing on non-economic determinants are therefore somewhat difficult to pick up on in Oceania. In particular, investigating migrants in their eventual destinations is proving difficult. This is also noted by Smart et al., who, in their chapter on ethnic and economic determinants of location choice of migrants in New Zealand, note that proper investigation of careers and mobility patterns and subsequent location decisions is difficult. Yet, the eventual location is the place in which impact materialises, so this is a significant blind spot. The authors call for more attention to place based policies with an eye to continued regional development. Also, there is no real insight in the effectiveness of the selective immigration policies as information on the longer term career patterns for migrants is lacking.

1.4 Part III: Shifting the Research Frontiers: The Interaction of Migrants, Their Backgrounds, Contexts and Impacts

Part III presents empirical applications, touching on some of the frontiers identified in Parts I and II of this book. Each of the following chapters exploits extensive background information on either the migrant, or the context in which they find themselves, be that the industrial setting or the regional characteristics. These chapters demonstrate how improved data helps answer new questions, but also helps to comprehensively revisit the classic questions.

1.4.1 Chapter 8: Inter-regional and Inter-sectoral Labour Mobility and the Industry Life Cycle—A Panel Data Analysis of the Finnish High Technology Sector

Jaakko Simonen, Rauli Svento, Santtu Karhinen, and Philip McCann

Simonen et al. revisit the labour market approach to migration, in which mobility is considered as a labour market clearing mechanism. In their chapter, they do so from a novel angle by relying on the detailed Finnish employer-employee matched registry data to study inter-regional job mobility in direct relation to inter-sectoral mobility. Importantly, they analyze trends in these different adjustment mechanisms in the context of the high-technology industry life cycle. Clearly, if an industry is growing and potentially shrinking later on, this will necessarily entail a degree of inter-regional and inter-sectoral mobility of existing workers. Next to the explicit setting in the industry life-cycle, this finely grained conceptualisation of mobility may also serve to provide new insights.

Labour mobility has been demonstrated in earlier research to be a key mechanism for knowledge transfer. In that sense, attracting labour is not only important in filling vacancies in a growing industry. The influx of highly skilled workforce in regions and in industries located in these regions, in particular if these new workers bring along with them related but relevant new skills, will serve to further propel the receiving industry. The authors note that this is particularly true for the high-technology sector.

Between the early 1990s and the early 2000s employment in the high-technology sector in Finland has seen a remarkable increase, more than doubling in size in regions such as Oulu in the north of Finland. The authors consider five possible pathways for workers in the high-technology sectors: no change in firm, region or sector, a change of firm within the same region and high-tech sector, or combinations of either inter-regional or inter-sector mobility. The authors argue that taking this heterogeneity on board is vital in properly understanding worker mobility.

Overall, mobility of any type is increasing with total industry size. The growth of high-technology industry is accompanied by a growing number of workers experiencing some degree of mobility. However, as the phase of stabilization sets in after 2001, total labour mobility drops off at first, only to recover slightly after 2004. The initial drop-off is associated in particular with a decrease in the share of inter-industry mobility (within the same region), but also less frequent changes in both sector and region. In absolute sense, intra-regional mobility, within the same sector is and remains the most important.

The authors seek to explain these patterns using a regional approach where the share of high-technology workers is modelled using regional explanatory variables. In assessing the factors that are typically associated with labour mobility, the authors find that they serve to explain mobility during the growth phase of the high-technology industry rather well. In contrast, no structural explanations could be offered for inter-regional mobility during the stabilization phase. Moreover, the authors stress that high-technology worker mobility comes in many shapes. These need to be accounted for in order to further our understanding of what drives them.

1.4.2 Chapter 9: Ethnic and Economic Determinants of Migrant Location Choice

Cindy Smart, Arthur Grimes, and Wilbur Townsend

Smart et al. study the case of immigrant location choice in New Zealand to arrive at a fresh assessment of the wider question on the importance of regional economic determinants versus non economic determinants. In particular, they seek to assess the role of ethnic networks in destination regions.

New Zealand provides a particularly interesting case to study this question. Migrant location choice in countries with directly adjacent neighbours will likely be affected by the location of these borders. New Zealand's closest neighbours, on the other hand, are 1800 km away.

The authors commence their study with a comprehensive analysis of network effects, in terms of their role in migrant location choices. The authors elaborate on how these networks and the externalities associated with them are not necessarily positive. Even though they may help new incomers find work and reduce migration cost, the negative externalities due to increased competition for jobs, adverse selection of low productivity workers, and decreased incentive to assimilate may outweigh the positive effects. Therefore, other explanations for clustering of migrants are examined such as herd effects and the presence of gateway cities. Herd effects amount to migrants copying the behaviour of other migrants, hence potentially leading to an outcome other than the one that would have materialized under full information. This in turn could lead to lower importance of economic factors. A gateway city is the first point of contact with the transport or mobility system in a country. As migrants pass through, they may decide to stay.

We can therefore think of these factors as behavioural in nature, but they are clearly related to economic considerations. The authors continue to outline these links in this chapter. It is noted that higher skilled migrants might be more free to locate where they wish, as they may be less dependent on networks. In spite of this, clustering is still observed, and therefore the prevalence of culture over economics remains difficult to establish. Recruitment behaviour of firms may also be important, as this will cause workers to co-locate, on the grounds of working for the same firm.

In the international literature, other factors which are considered are language, education levels, and the role of relocation behaviour. Command of the local language increases one's chances of work. However, mastering a language may be too costly for some, which would lead them to locate in areas where unemployment is high: they have lower chances on employment regardless. Education works in broadly the same manner: the extent to which migrants need to cluster in order to use local networks depends critically on the extent to which they are able to go their own way. Relocation serves to decrease concentration, as migrants improve their information position they may seek out better options elsewhere in the country.

As noted earlier, New Zealand, as a result of its geographical setting, provides an interesting case to study the relative importance of migrant networks versus regional economic considerations. Additionally the authors note that immigration policy, focusing on attracting high skilled migrants with good command of English, as more elaborately described in the chapter by Benier and Corcoran, may lead to a somewhat lower extent of clustering than would be observed in other countries.

The empirical analysis relies on the 2013 New Zealand Census confidentialised unit record file. From a descriptive analysis of migrants in New Zealand regions the authors conclude that in particular migrants hailing from the Pacific Islands, and also migrants with an Asian, Middle-eastern, and African background tend to cluster more. However, clustering is slightly higher for those with a higher educational degree, which is in contrast with the expectations previously described. Location quotients are applied to establish regional patterns in migrant location choices. Here the authors note that these groups cluster in Auckland, which supports the gateway hypothesis. Other groups, such as migrants with a Western background, locate in higher amenity regions.

The authors proceed to model location choice, following the conditional logit approach. Their preferred specification uses a lagged industry-specific regional wage variable, regional fixed effects, and interactions with a variable which measures the share of people with the same origin as the migrant. They find that both the share of people from the same birth country as well as the regional wage affect location choice positively. The authors note that the role of wages is in contrast with the recent patterns in the US, where amenities have been found to be of greater importance. A number of interactions are significant. Migrants with degrees are focused on areas with a high return to their skills and if one is bilingual networks matter less. Both findings are in line with expectations. However, long-term stayers are found in areas with a larger diaspora, which contrasts the relocation hypothesis, even though the authors note that this is difficult to establish in a cross-sectional study.

Overall, this chapter demonstrates similar patterns in ethnic clustering as shown elsewhere. The importance of wages is a deviation to recent results from other countries, such as the US. Furthermore, it demonstrates considerable heterogeneity among migrant groups. The extent to which ethnic networks are exerting either positive or negative effects on migrant outcomes cannot really be seen in isolation from economic characteristics of regions and background characteristics of migrants. In particular, the higher skilled seem to cluster to a higher extent than theory would predict. This is important not only for their own outcomes, but arguably also for the way these networks function for new incomers.

1.4.3 Chapter 10: 'Young, Talented and Highly Mobile': Exploring Creative Human Capital and Graduates Mobility in the UK

Roberta Comunian and Sarah Jewell

As we have seen, in the migration literature there is considerable attention for the migration patterns and outcomes for the higher skilled. One group that has come under particular focus are those working in creative occupations, who are considered to be in key positions to exert their skills on the economy. The process of selection and entry into these occupations is thus of great interest, also in terms of the spatial mobility that is associated with it.

Comunian and Jewell look into migration patterns of graduates and the extent to which there is a relation between the shape of the spatial trajectory going from their domiciles, their university regions and, ultimately, the location of their job. From the preceding chapters we know that it is the combination of migrant skills and the surroundings in which they settle which ultimately strengthens their outcomes. The authors consider that this is particularly true for young, recent graduates, making their way into the creative fields. Job opportunities are thinly spread, in particular for graduates in creative topics. This in turn may limit their migration options. They are likely to return home due to lack of alternatives, relying on local support networks. Home, however, may not be the place where the return on the investment in their education is maximized. Interestingly, the authors take a more longitudinal approach which allows for the time needed to settle into the labour market. This accounts for potentially longer search times for the creative graduates, looking for creative occupations.

The authors compare graduates in creative fields to other graduates in terms of their migration trajectories, the likelihood of landing a creative job, their wage rate and their job satisfaction. From the descriptive analysis it transpires that graduates in creative fields are less likely to be in full-time employment and more often self-employed. Unemployment rates are higher, too. In terms of their migration trajectories, they are somewhat more likely to be university stayers. Return migration (back to domicile) is observed often as well, along with students in Humanities. Also, it is demonstrated that job outcomes vary with migration trajectories. Repeat movers, who could be considered the most mobile, do better in terms of job outcomes.

Modelling the type of migration behaviour, it is notable that, after controlling for personal characteristics, creative graduates are more likely to stay in their university regions and less likely to be a non-migrant, relative to all other groups of graduates. Being a graduate in a creative topic increases your chances of landing a creative job, relative to being a business student, and more so than being in one of the STEM fields or in humanities. Generally speaking, late migrants, university stayers, and repeat migrants are more likely to land a creative job than non-migrants. However, within the group of creative graduates, in particular repeat movers find a good match in a creative job. Return migrants on the other hand, are less likely to find a creative job. So, even though creative graduates are more likely to stay in their university regions, this does not make them more likely to work in their fields.

In terms of salary, the creative graduates are considerably less successful than their counterparts in other fields. Likewise, they score lower on career satisfaction. Overall, there is little difference between return migrants and non-migrants in terms of salaries. However, among creative graduates, in particular repeat migrants do better than those in other trajectories whereas return migrants once more do less well.

The authors note therefore that much of what happens to recent graduates applies up to a certain extent to creative graduates, when it comes down to the general characteristics (demographics, grades). However, the process of matching and the extent of having to apply spatial search in order to land a creative job differs between these different groups of graduates. Creative graduates do not do as well as other graduates in terms of economic returns, which is not necessarily related to ending up in creative jobs, as STEM graduates in particular do rather well in these occupations. What this chapter furthermore demonstrates is that this is a longer term struggle too.

1.4.4 Chapter 11: Interregional Migration and Implications for Regional Resilience

Daniel Crown, Timothy Jaquet, and Alessandra Faggian

Crown, Jaquet and Faggian look at interregional migration from the angle of resilience. To what extent are the factors that make regions interesting destinations for migrants also responsible for making these areas resilient, or, in other words, helping these areas to recover from negative shocks? Migration here is conceptualized as a conduit through which the regional economy can adjust. But, as it is demonstrated elsewhere in the book, mobility can take different forms and destinations depending on the circumstances a potential migrant finds him or herself in. The industry life-cycle, the presence of a network in the destination area, and one's own skill profile help to shape migration decisions and outcomes. In this chapter, the perspective of the business cycle is added: does a migrant destination choice hinge on the general economic state of affairs? Migration rates in the US have been steadily declining since the 1980s, but particularly so during recessions, the authors note. What does that imply for migration in relation to resilience?

The authors proceed in modelling separately the county-by-county migration flows using a Poisson model, and two versions of regional resilience, using employment growth and a resilience measure based on the relative distance between actual employment and the level predicted if local industries grow at the national level. These models are then estimated using the same set of explanatory variables, for two time periods ("normal" and "recession and recovery"). The explanatory variables include the share of population over 65, the median house price and labour demand shocks. Interestingly, the authors apply clustering to arrive at a measure of (dis-)

similarity of counties in terms of their industrial structure. This measure allows the authors to shed light on the the extent to which migrants move to areas that are similar to their current region during a crisis. Arguably, similar regions will experience similar economic shocks, so moving between similar regions will not help individual migrants improve their situation, not will it help to balance the economic situation.

Indeed, the results from the migration model suggest that migrants are not completely free in terms of moving towards areas which have industries with a more fortuitous profile. Migrants are less likely to move to counties with a different industrial structure during a recession. The authors note that adjustments in human capital needed for such a transition to be successful, are not easy to make. Looking at resilience, the authors note that the industry structure seems to matter most during times of recession. Migration is entered in the resilience models as well, even though the authors note that it is likely endogenous, and it appears that migrant inflows are positively related to resilience. The authors conclude that migration and resilience are related predominantly through industry structure, with compensating effects from migration during recessions found to be somewhat wanting. Destination choice changes between periods of growth and recession, but much more finely grained data, among others in terms of time specificity, would shed better light on the dynamics of migrant decision making.

1.5 Round-Up and Conclusions: Shifting Frontiers and Setting the Agenda

We conclude this editorial with a brief round-up, across the chapters, of the state-of-the-art and future challenges in the field of interregional migration.

This book has started out in Part I with an in-depth discussion of the state of the art in theory in relation to not only societal change but also data availability. In the advent of new data sources becoming available, this leads to questions whether future advances in this field will be primarily data driven, theory driven or whether in fact new local and global migration shocks will steer the field. Even in the face of new data sources and (economic) shocks, excellent theory will remain important, or become even more important, with increasing complexity in data sources and institutional settings.

Secondly, a recurring theme in this book is that true understanding of the drivers of migration, and furthermore the impact of migrants on sending and receiving economies cannot be achieved if we remain unable to study the migration backgrounds of individuals. This implies that better, preferably longitudinal, data at the micro level of individual migrants is needed. From this book it transpires that such data should at least be able to help us identify the extent to which networks in sending and receiving economies are actively used in different phases of the migrant life course and the extent to which the skills embodied in the migrant are in fact complementary to, in particular, the host economy. Furthermore, the context in which migrants operate is dynamic in itself. Public opinion, institutional settings, industry life cycles and the economic circumstances all have their own dynamic and potentially time specific impacts on migrant outcomes. In this light, data needs to be sufficiently spatial and temporally fine-grained.

Third, in general non-economic determinants and outcomes have been noted as (increasingly) important in migrant destination choices and outcomes. This is due in part to changes in population composition due to aging, but arguably also links to the improved information position of migrants. The challenge here is the sheer breadth of information these non-economic determinants could encompass. Even from this volume alone a broad range of factors, which might be considered attractive to migrants, has emerged, ranging from cultural amenities to safety.

Fourth, this book has presented examples of what can be learned when mobility is conceptualised in different ways. New forms of mobility may serve to replace migration. Commuting, even across borders, has been discussed in this light. This book has presented examples of the benefits of analysing more finely grained (combinations of) migratory and non-migratory trajectories that workers can engage in if spatial job search is necessary. Temporary moves constitute a third example of mobility that is difficult to capture, but present many individuals with the opportunity to solve complex location puzzles. Yet, these forms may exactly be where the new frontier in migration research is to be found.

Fifth, the role of time is often overlooked. This book demonstrates that there is great added value of being able to account for settling-in time, search durations, and adaptive processes in migration research. Clearly, achieving this is riddled with challenges as retrospective as well as panel designs come with their own opportunities and difficulties. Likewise, measuring phenomena consistently across geographical contexts has proven difficult. Measuring consistently over time will be no different.

Lastly, the cross border perspective is lacking in many approaches. Statistical offices more often than not are "blind across the border." In mapping out migrant histories this presents clear challenges. But, furthermore, life courses become more and more complex. Interregional and international mobility comes in many shapes and sizes with work and residency spread out across multiple locations. Mobile workers rely on new ways to combine work and life. If our conceptualisation of these life domains does not follow suit, we risk loosing sight of at least part of the life setting of this group. Potentially, with an eye to a future with further individualisation of life courses, this means we are loosing sight of the most interesting migrant sub-group.

Part I
Shifting the Theoretical Frontier, New Data and New Questions

Chapter 2
Theoretical Advances on Interregional Migration Models

Bianca Biagi and Kathryn R. Dotzel

Abstract The purpose of this chapter is twofold. First, we aim to give a general overview of the main innovations, decade-by-decade, of internal migration studies from the 1970s until today. The second purpose is to highlight existing empirical research focused on interregional migration and gaps in the literature that must be addressed in the future.

Keywords Interregional migration · New economic geography · Gravity model · Equilibrium · Disequilibrium · Spatial agglomeration · Endogenous growth

2.1 Overview of the Literature on Interregional Migration

Since the late nineteenth century, interregional migration has been explored across multiple disciplines, including sociology, demography, geography, and economics. In the late 1800s, the geographer Ravenstein (1885) conducts what is most often credited as the first systematic study on interregional migration. In addition to

---

Some of the material included in this chapter is based upon the MPhil Dissertation by Biagi (2014).

This work is not a product of the United States Government or the United States Environmental Protection Agency. The author is not doing this work in any governmental capacity. The views expressed are her own and do not necessarily represent those of the United States or the US EPA.

B. Biagi (✉)
Department of Economics and Business, University of Sassari-CRENoS-GSSI, L'Aquila, Italy

GSSI, L'Aquila, Italy
e-mail: bbiagi@uniss.it

K. R. Dotzel
US EPA Office of Transportation and Air Quality, Ann Arbor, MI, USA

B. Biagi et al. (eds.), *New Frontiers in Interregional Migration Research*, Advances in Spatial Science, https://doi.org/10.1007/978-3-319-75886-2_2

using British Census Data to analyze nativity and place of residence of the population, during this period Ravenstein formulates seven 'Laws of Migration' (see Box 2.1), most of which have been confirmed by subsequent research. Box 2.2 defines the different types of interregional migration that have received attention by researchers.

Box 2.1 Ravenstein's Laws of Migration

First Law. *We have already proved that the great body of our migrants only proceed a short distance, and that there takes place consequently a universal shifting or displacement of the population, which produces "currents of migration" setting in the direction of the great centres of commerce and industry which absorb the migrants.*

In forming an estimate of this displacement we must take into account the number of natives of each county which furnishes the migrants, as also the population of the towns or districts which absorb them.

Second Law. *It is the natural outcome of this movement of migration, limited in range, but universal throughout the country, that the process of absorption would go on in the following manner:*

The inhabitants of the country immediately surrounding a town of rapid growth, flock into it; the gaps thus left in the rural population are filled up by migrants from more remote districts, until the attractive force of one of our rapidly growing cities makes its influence felt, step by step, to the most remote corner of the kingdom. Migrants enumerated in a certain centre of absorption will consequently grow less with the distance proportionately to the native population which furnishes them, and a map exhibiting by tints the recruiting process of any town ought clearly to demonstrate this fact.

Third Law. *The process of dispersion is the inverse of that of absorption, and exhibits similar features.*

Fourth Law. *Each main current of migration produces a compensating counter-current.*

Fifth Law. *Migrants proceeding long distances generally go by preference to one of the great centres of commerce or industry.*

Sixth Law. *The natives of towns are less migratory than those of the rural parts of the country.*

Seventh Law. *Females are more migratory that [sic] males.*

Source: Ravenstein (1885, pp. 198–199)

Box 2.2 Types of Interregional Migration

The United Nations defines 'migration' as 'a move from one migration-defining area to another (or a move of some specific minimum distance) that was made during a given migration interval and that involved a change of residence' and, in turn, a 'migrant' as an individual who has participated in this process at least once (United Nations 1970).

The literature on human migration is vast and can be loosely divided into studies focused on interregional and international migration. While the latter group of research always considers movements between countries, the definition of 'region' varies across interregional migration studies. As noted by Faggian et al. (2017, p. 4), 'the most appropriate definition of regional scale depends on the determinant or consequence under investigation' as well as 'practical issues, such as data availability, geography, or laws governing mobility'. In general, interregional migration studies focus on either administrative regions (e.g., US states or counties) or functional regions (e.g., local labour markets, travel to work areas) (Faggian et al. 2017).

While the interregional migration literature is typically associated with moves at the sub-national (i.e., internal) level, interregional studies that consider movements between countries (such as the NUTS 1 administrative region in Europe) also exist, blurring the distinction between interregional and international migration. At the sub-national level, the economic literature considers two main types of internal migration, which are distinguished by migratory distance: (1) residential mobility (also known as 'local mobility') and (2) proper internal migration. As explained by Borjas (2000, p. 1), 'residential [mobility] occurs when the household (or person) changes its place of residence by moving from one neighbourhood to another within the same local area' while 'internal migration occurs when the household moves across larger geographically distinct units—such as counties, metropolitan areas, states or provinces—but remains within the same country'. Thus, by this definition, internal migration implies a change of both residence and job, while a movement that does not involve a job change can simply be described as residential mobility.

Migrants are further characterized by their history of migration and employment status in their destination region. 'New migrants' are individuals who move for the first time, while 'repeat migrants' have moved at least once in the past (Kau and Sirmans 1976). Individuals who move back to their place of birth belong to a special subcategory of repeat migrants known as 'return migrants' (Vanderkamp 1971)[1]. Migration that occurs with a job in hand in the destination region is called 'contracted migration'. On the contrary, migration

(continued)

[1]DaVanzo (1978) defines repeat and return migrants as 'chronic migrants'.

Box 2.2 (continued)

that occurs before the job search process in the destination region (i.e., after the move) is called 'speculative migration'. In the former case, relocation is assumed to be the result of the search process; in the latter case, relocation is part of the search process itself (Molho 1986).

Migration propensity is additionally linked to established social relationships with past migrants in the destination region. 'Chain migration' occurs when 'prospective migrants learn of opportunities, are provided with transportation, and have initial accommodation and employment arranged by means of primary social relationships with previous migrants' (MacDonald and MacDonald 1964, p. 82). Regional economist Edgar M. Hoover connects chain migration to a 'beaten-path effect', which he defines as the tendency of some migrants to target destinations in which they already have friends or relatives (Hoover 1971).

The advent of work on interregional migration in the economic literature can be traced to John Richard Hicks, who concludes in 1932's *The Theory of Wages* that economic opportunities are the main determinant of migration. However, the modern rise of interregional migration as a separate stream of economic research can mainly be credited to studies by labour economists focused on the spatial allocation of workers. In the field of economics, human migration has been investigated by international, labour, urban, and regional economists, including proponents of Paul Krugman's 'new economic geography' theory (Krugman 1991). Although each of these economic fields considers the role of space on the drivers and impacts of migration, few attempts have been made to link their distinct but closely connected research streams, including parallel developments from internal and international migration studies.

Since the 1970s, many literature reviews have focused on the theoretical models of interregional migration and its determinants (i.e., drivers), consequences (i.e., impacts), and prospects for academic research have been published. Key examples of these are provided in Table 2.1. It is worth noting that while the determinants of interregional movements have been widely studied, the consequences of these moves remain an emerging area of interest for researchers [see Faggian et al. (2017) for a contemporary review of the extant literature on the impacts of interregional migration of high-skilled migrants].

Another notable characteristic of interregional migration studies is their overwhelming focus on the United States, which is characterized by relatively high rates of internal migration in comparison to other developed countries. To date, North America remains the most studied continent. During the period 1970–1971, 17.9% of US residents moved internally, of which 11.4% moved within the same county and 6.5% moved between counties. Since the early 1960s, the major direction of migration has generally shifted from rural-to-urban regions to urban-to-rural regions

Table 2.1 Literature reviews on interregional migration since the 1970s

Author(s)	Year	Main economic field	Type of migration	Focus	Countries	Publication
Greenwood	1975	Urban, regional	Internal	Determinants, consequences	US	*Journal of Economic Literature*
Greenwood	1985	Urban, regional	Internal	Determinants, consequences	US and some EU countries	*Journal of Regional Science*
Molho	1986	Labour	Internal	Models	US and UK	*Scottish Journal of Political Economy*
Greenwood, Mueser, Plane, and Schlottmann	1991	Urban, regional	Internal	Models, determinants	US and some EU countries	*The Annals of Regional Science*
Greenwood	1997	Urban, regional	Internal	Determinants	Various countries	*Handbook of Population and Family Economics*
Greenwood and Hunt	2003	Urban, regional	Internal	Determinants (focus is on early studies), models (mainly spatial)	US and UK	*International Regional Science Review*
Cushing and Poot	2004	Urban, regional, international	Internal, international	Models, determinants, consequences, public policies	Various countries	*Papers in Regional Science*
Greenwood	2014	Urban, regional	Internal	Determinants (focus is on economic opportunities)	US and UK	*Handbook of Regional Science*
Graves	2014	Urban, regional	Internal	Models, determinants (focus is on amenities)	US	*Handbook of Regional Science*
Faggian, Rajbhandari, and Dotzel	2017	Urban, regional	Internal	Consequences (focus is on high-skilled migrants)	Various countries	*Regional Studies*

(Greenwood 1985). Only recently has the rate of sub-national migration in the United States begun to stagnate: between 2008 and 2009, internal migrants included approximately 12.1% of the US population, of which 8.4% of moved within the same county, and 3.7% moved between counties.[2] In contrast, European countries have long been characterized by very low rates of internal migration. Based on calculations by Cheshire and Magrini (2006), net internal migration in the United States is 15 times greater than in Europe when moves between sub-regions of comparable size are considered.

The purpose of this chapter is to explore the decade-by-decade evolution of the main theoretical approaches to modelling interregional migration. While the main focus will be on breakthroughs related to internal movements, given the overlap between the interregional and international migration literature, contributions related to between-country movements will also be discussed when relevant. The aim of this chapter is not to provide an exhaustive review of the extant literature on interregional migration, but to more generally discuss the main innovations, applications, and theoretical approaches, decade-by-decade, of internal migration studies from the 1970s[3] (Sect. 2.2), 1980s (Sect. 2.3), 1990s (Sect. 2.4), and twenty-first century (Sect. 2.5). A second purpose is to highlight potential steps forwards and remaining challenges that must be addressed in the literature (Sect. 2.6).

2.2 The 1970s

During the 1970s, one of the main purposes of studies on interregional migration (and more specifically, internal migration) was to demonstrate the role played by disparities in economic opportunities between regions (Greenwood 1975). Migrants were expected to originate from regions with relatively low wages and high unemployment rates and move to regions with relatively high wages and low unemployment rates (Hicks 1932; Greenwood and Hunt 2003). Due to the paucity of microdata during this decade, the majority of studies were macroeconomic in nature and employed cross-sectional models. Scholars additionally debated whether it was preferable to model net or gross migration rates and how best to solve issues of endogeneity resulting from use of regional characteristics as explanatory variables in internal migration analysis (Muth 1971).

Lack of availability of microdata additionally made it difficult to investigate how personal characteristics influence migration decisions, as predicted by the human

[2]U.S. Census Bureau, Current Population Survey, Annual Geographical Mobility Rates, By Type of Movement: 1947–2009. See also the contribution by Partridge (2010).

[3]For a discussion of pre-1970s studies, see Greenwood and Hunt (2003).

capital model of migration developed by Sjaastad (1962) in the early 1960s.[4] Sjaastad (1962), as well as Lowry (1966), incorporates behavioural considerations into the classic gravity model approach to interregional migration, which assumes that migrants are rational individuals who select the destination that maximizes the difference between the expected benefit of the move and the cost of moving. Such extended versions of the gravity model have been described as 'modified gravity models'. In modified gravity models, distance between the individual's origin and destination region enters as a driver of the rational decision to move (Greenwood 1969; Greenwood and Sweetland 1972). 'Systemic gravity models', introduced by Alonso (1978), represent a further advancement of the gravity model approach during the 1970s. In these models, migrant flows between each pair of regions depend on characteristics of the two regions in addition to characteristics of all other potential destination regions.

2.2.1 *Microeconomic Analysis of the Drivers of Internal Migration*

One of the most significant findings of applied microeconomic research during this period is the failure of unemployment to fully explain internal migration decisions. In the late 1970s, DaVanzo (1978)[5] publishes one of the most influential studies on the topic. One significant finding from her analysis, which focuses on the United States, is that families whose household heads are unemployed are more likely to move than families whose heads are employed. The role of unemployment on migration decisions is analysed more in-depth by microeconomic and macroeconomic researchers during the following decades. Another fundamental theoretical and applied contribution using microdata during the 1970s is the work of Mincer (1978) on the role of family relationships in migration. He finds that (1) married individuals are less likely to move than those who are single or separated or divorced; (2) employment of the wife in a married two-parent family reduces the

[4]Sjaastad (1962) applies the concept of human capital, as defined by Becker (1962), to migration decisions. Sjaastad's approach is called the 'endogenous human capital model of migration', because the individual is viewed as rational and perfectly informed regarding how to invest in education and acquire skills in order to maximise future lifetime utility (in the form of income and job satisfaction) and whether and how to migrate based on this initial investment. Migration will take place in the case where discounted expected returns in earnings are the highest.

[5]DaVanzo uses longitudinal data on households from the Panel Study of Income Dynamics (PSID). Specifically, she models 'a sample of 1605 white couples living in the United States whose marriages were intact in 1971 and 1972 and whose [household] heads were not students, retired, or in the military service in 1971' (DaVanzo 1978, p. 506). Mincer (1978) offers theoretical models of the migration decision from a family perspective for the United States. The empirical findings used to support theoretical models utilize data from a variety of sources including U.S. Census Current Population Reports and other Census samples, U.S. Bureau of Labor Statistics National Longitudinal Surveys (NLS), and Coleman-Rossi (C-R) microdata samples.

likelihood that the family will migrate; and (3) higher education of the husband increases the likelihood that the family will migrate. The described contributions by DaVanzo (1978) and Mincer (1978) are additionally significant due to their focus on family utility rather than individual utility, a novelty in migration studies at the time. The attention paid to the impact of employment status on migration during the 1970s reflects a more general focus on determinants rather than consequences of migration during this period.

2.3 The 1980s

The major advances in interregional migration analysis in the 1980s can largely be attributed to increased availability of micro- and longitudinal data (Greenwood 1985). One of the most significant breakthroughs of this period can be credited to urban economists, who, in the late 1970s and early 1980s, offer an alternative theory for the cause of persistent regional economic disparities as well as the role of place-based amenities in migration decisions (Greenwood 1985). The main novelty of this approach, now referred to as the 'equilibrium model' of migration, was its interpretation of individual spatial utility and regional economic opportunities. Before this decade, 'disequilibrium models' of migration were considered the only paradigm for understanding interregional migration processes.

2.3.1 Disequilibrium and Equilibrium Models of Migration

Disequilibrium models of migration (Muth 1971; Greenwood and Hunt 1984) assume that interregional economic disparities reflect the utility differential and, thus, interpret interregional migration as an almost entirely economic phenomenon and 'by product' of employment search. In other words, they posit that homogenous individuals react to regional disequilibria in wages and unemployment rates by moving to areas with relatively high wages and relatively low unemployment rates; this process continues until the interregional wage equilibrium is restored and the utility of homogenous individuals across regions is equalised. However, disequilibrium models of migration assume that labour markets are slow to adjust due to imperfect information and 'sticky wages'. Thus, labour market disparities persist over time.

Alternatively, the neoclassical literature makes a case for the so-called equilibrium models of migration. Equilibrium migration models (Graves 1980, 1983; Graves and Linneman 1979; Knapp and Graves 1989) conceptualize an alternative view of migration drivers based on the assumption that individuals prefer living in places with abundant natural amenities (i.e., favourable climate conditions) and, therefore, must be economically compensated for living in places characterized by low levels of natural amenities (i.e., disamenities). Conversely, individuals are willing to accept lower wages to live in places with more abundant amenities (and higher house prices). The theoretical background for equilibrium models is provided by studies on urban quality of life[6] and 'compensating differentials' (Rosen 1979; Roback 1982; Blomquist et al. 1988[7]), which assume that the price of location-specific amenities is capitalized into local wages and rents.[8] The urban economist Paul Graves (1976, 1980) applies this theory to interregional migration.

From a macroeconomic perspective, interregional differences in wages are interpreted as partial compensation for spatial variations in non-tradable, non-economic factors. Consequently, interregional wages are not expected to equalize if space remains non-homogeneous in terms of amenities. This implies that economic opportunities act as compensating differentials and interregional wage disparities signal differences in place-based amenities (but *not* differences in the utilities of homogeneous individuals, which are equalized across regions). In such models, individuals migrate when endogenous conditions (e.g., household life cycle) or exogenous conditions (e.g., price or supply of amenities, degree of regional economic development, income) specific to the individual change and alter the level or type of amenities demanded. In the 1980s, disequilibrium and equilibrium approaches are viewed as antagonistic, triggering a debate which intensifies in the early 1990s.

2.3.2 Migration and Job Search Theory

Another major area of research that emerges during this decade applies 1970s job search theory as an alternative to the neoclassical models of migration. This approach relaxes the two main assumptions of existing labour models: (1) potential migrants are operating on perfect information, and (2) migration results from wage differentials across regions.

Job search theory argues that individuals seek out employment opportunities in a dynamic sequential process that takes place in the context of imperfect information and uncertainty. As explained by Mortensen (1984, p. 7), in the sequential job search process, 'the worker is viewed as sampling wage offers one at time and deciding on the basis of the sample obtained to date whether or not to stop the search or to continue'. Jobs are appraised by workers one at a time, and the size of the sample is a

[6]See Lambiri et al. (2007) for a contemporary review of the quality of life literature in economics and, more specifically, urban economics.

[7]The interpretation of regional differentials as 'compensating differentials' in wages and housing rents is due to Roback (1982).

[8]The microeconomic foundation for this theory is supplied by Rosen in an earlier paper (1974) and is based on the economic theory of revealed preferences and Lancaster's (1966) new approach to consumer theory. Lancaster argues that consumers of heterogeneous commodities have preferences for each characteristic of the final good; therefore, they purchase a set of characteristics rather than a set of goods, per se. The final price of the heterogeneous goods embodies the implicit price of each specific characteristic. Rosen (1979) proposes the hedonic pricing method for calculating the implicit price of the quality of life in US cities, which is embodied in housing rents.

random variable that depends on the 'stopping rule' (Mortensen, p. 7). A key goal of the job search literature is to determine the 'optimal stopping rule' (Molho[9] 1986, p. 402). Migration studies apply this framework to examinations of two types of movements: those that occur following, i.e., ex post, the search process and with a job in hand (known as 'contracted migration'); and those that occur before, i.e., ex ante, the job search process (known as 'speculative migration') (Molho 1986). In the contracted case, moving is the *result* of the job search process, while in the speculative case, it is part of the search process itself.[10]

2.3.3 *Unemployment and Migration: Advances During the 1980s*

This decade is also characterized by a persistent interest in applied research on the relationship between unemployment and migration. Following the seminal work of DaVanzo (1978) in the 1970s, contributions by Schlottmann and Herzog (1981) for the US; Hughes and McCormick (1985, 1987), Molho (1986), and Pissarides and Wadsworth (1989) for the UK; and Van Dijk et al. (1989) for the US and the Netherlands are published in the 1980s. These studies notably model out-migration without accounting for the effect of economic conditions in destination regions.

Overall, the literature finds that individual unemployment and regional unemployment rate may have differing effects on out-migration. Specifically, studies confirm that in Europe and the United States, unemployed individuals are more likely to migrate than employed ones. Pissarides and Wadsworth (1989, p. 43) note that when 'all economic effects are combined, there is evidence that there is a statistically significant flow in the "right" direction', i.e., 'gross outflows from high unemployment...and low wage regions are higher than gross outflows from other regions'. In their study, the authors observe that in the UK during the periods of 1976–1977 and 1983–1984, when the unemployment rate was high, the probability of migration decreased. This suggests that 'the response to economic incentive is reduced [in periods of] high unemployment' (Pissarides and Wadsworth 1989, p. 43). Hughes and McCormick (1985), from their own examination of the United Kingdom, attribute this result to the linkage between unemployment and housing tenure. More specifically, in the presence of an active council house system, which exists in the United Kingdom, the probability of migrating is lower for council tenants compared to other tenants or owner-occupiers.

Van Dijk et al. (1989) argue that unemployment rate can be considered as an indicator of labour market 'tightness', meaning that a higher rate of unemployment

[9]Molho (1986) reviews existing theories of migration with specific attention paid to job search models, human capital approaches, and gravity models. A main contribution of this review is the formal representation of the human capital approach of Sjaastad (1962), which is presented in his seminal article without formalisation.

[10]For a clear explanation of job search models, see Faggian (2014).

could alternatively encourage or discourage out-migration. In the latter case, a high unemployment rate in the origin region could discourage movement if the potential mover believes he will remain unemployed in the destination region. The authors additionally find that in the United States, a higher unemployment rate increases out-migration, while the opposite effect is observed in the Netherlands. This difference is attributed to the distinct role of labour market institutions in the two countries. The more efficient institutional system (and subsidies program) in the Netherlands encourages contracted migration and less risky behaviour (i.e., less moves prior to the job search process) compared to the United States, where migrants are more likely to make risky decisions regarding job search and movements are mostly speculative.

2.4 The 1990s

The 1990s are characterized by many steps forward in both applied and theoretical interregional migration research, such as: (1) the consideration of amenities as a migration determinant; (2) more in-depth analysis of the effect of unemployment rate on migration decisions, including in times of recession; and (3) applied research on the process of self-selection in internal migration based on age and skills, which paves the way for studies on the economic impacts, i.e., consequences, of migration in the destination regions. As in the previous decade, the 1990s were met with an increase in the availability of micro- and longitudinal data.

2.4.1 Equilibrium and Disequilibrium Models and the Role of Amenities

In the early 1990s, there was intense debate between proponents of the disequilibrium and equilibrium approaches to migration (Evans 1990, 1993; Greenwood et al. 1991; Graves and Mueser 1993). The main point of the contention was the 'adjustment speed' of markets. Supporters of equilibrium models of migration argued that markets are efficient enough to quickly compensate for changes in utilities across space, and, hence, any exogenous change in income will be restored and compensated quickly through migration. In contrast, proponents of disequilibrium models argued that firms' capital stock, regional housing stock, and workers (i.e., potential migrants) are slow to respond and adjustments take a very long time. If the markets fail to compensate (or compensate only in very long run), evaluations of amenities will report biased results.

The majority of studies in this area focus on the United States and aim to find support for equilibrium (versus disequilibrium) approaches to migration. Greenwood et al. (1991) analyze all US states and District of Columbia for the period 1971–1988 and uncover evidence that some states were in equilibrium at the time, while others were not. When in equilibrium, state net migration is zero (or very close to zero) and differences in wages and rents are capitalized into the availability of amenities or disamenities. It is worth noting that the debate surrounding which theoretical model prevails in advanced economies (i.e., whether differences in wages and rents reflect differences in utilities across space) remains unresolved in this decade. However, as will be discussed in Sect. 2.5, the 2000s see a resurgence of the topic for both US and European regions.

2.4.2 Unemployment and Migration: Advances During the 1990s

The non-linear relationship between migration and average regional unemployment rate continues to be one of the main focuses of researchers, including labour economists, in the 1990s. Using macroeconomic data, Jackman and Savouri (1992) study the case of bilateral gross migration flows in 19 UK regions for the 1975–1989 period and propose a function that explains migration as a special case of hiring. This function assumes that total hires in the labour market represent the strongest determinant of aggregate migration. In periods of recession, regional unemployment differences increase due to increased out-migration of the unemployed and decreased in-migration caused by the 'crowding-out effect' of locally unemployed job seekers. As Westerlund (1997) explains in his study of gross migration flows in Sweden between 1970 and 1989, 'a given level of unemployment in a regional labor market is not likely to produce the same effect on migratory behavior in situations where there are ten unemployed for every vacant job as in situations where the number of vacancies equals the number of unemployed in the region' (p. 56). Many empirical applications use employment growth as a proxy for the job vacancy rate. Faini et al. (1997) confirm that the impact of regional unemployment on mobility is non-linear for the case of Italy; more specifically, only long-distance migration responds to regional unemployment rates.

2.4.3 Self-Selection in the Process of Migration

Another key contribution of this decade is the work by Borjas et al. (1992), who analyse self-selection of internal migrants in the US based on Roy's[11] (1951) distribution of earnings model. While the Hicks-Sjaastad approach (Hicks 1932; Sjaastad 1962) predicts that interregional differences in income, discounted by the cost of migration, produce 'unidirectional migration flows' towards regions with

[11]Roy's model analyses occupational choice for heterogeneous skill levels; in 1992, Borjas et al. apply the model to migration analysis for the first time.

higher wages, the Roy model predicts that this effect depends on spatial mismatches between skills and their rewards (Borjas et al. 1992, p. 160). Specifically, migration responds to regional differences in the return to skills, in addition to mean income, and these differences determine the skill composition of migration flows. The final impact of migration depends on the size as well as the skill composition of these flows.

Using data from Longitudinal Survey of Youth for the period 1979–1986, Borjas et al. (1992) determine that US states export different types of workers in terms of skill level, i.e., some states export workers of higher ability while others export workers of lower ability. Migration decisions ultimately depend on the spatial mismatch of skills in the sense that individuals will move towards regions that better reward their own skills. As such, high-skilled workers are more likely to migrate from states where the return to skills and wage disparities between high-skilled and low-skilled workers are relatively low, while unskilled workers are more likely to migrate from states in which skill prices as well as skill-level wage disparities are relatively high. This means that, on average, skilled migrants move to places with higher wage dispersion, while unskilled migrants move to places with lower wage dispersion. Using the Roy model, Borjas et al. (1992) extend the Hicks-Sjastaad approach by considering comparative advantage based on skill level as a determinant of migration. Their work has a large influence on applied research considering the regional impacts of immigration in the first decade of the 2000s.

2.5 The 2000s

In recent years, the topic of migration has received ample attention by scholars and researchers. The major advancements are, among others, the topics of disequilibrium and equilibrium migration, the role of amenities in high human capital migration (including graduate migration), and migration analysis from the perspective of new economic geography as well as institutional economics.

2.5.1 Equilibrium/Disequilibrium and the Role of Amenities: The State of the Art

Recent empirical evidence in favour of the spatial equilibrium hypothesis for the US is provided by, among others, Glaeser and Gottlieb (2008), Winters (2009) and Partridge et al. (2012). Glaeser and Gottlieb (2008) consider the high rate of interregional labour mobility in the US as initial evidence for the validity of equilibrium models: approximately 45% of Americans migrated internally between 1995 and 2000. Secondary evidence for spatial equilibrium results from their analysis of the standard deviation of wages across metropolitan areas, even after controlling for years of schooling as an indicator of human capital. Glaeser and Gottlieb (2008) find that differences in human capital explain approximately 50% of the variance in regional wage levels. However, they determine that even when controlling for human capital characteristics, wage differences persist; therefore, if spatial equilibrium bears out, such differences should be offset by high costs of living and low amenities. Additional evidence in favour of spatial equilibrium includes the large positive correlation between income per capita and house prices across metropolitan areas; the large positive correlation between the log of price index and the log of income per capita; and the negative, though small, correlation between mean January temperature and real wages.

Winters (2009) analyses the relationship between regional wages and prices in the US to determine whether workers are fully compensated for cost of living differences. Using microeconomic data on earnings and individual characteristics from the 2006 Current Population Survey (CPS) of the U.S. Census, he empirically tests a wage equation in which hourly wages are regressed on a set of individual characteristics, the general price level, and regional amenity levels. He interprets the coefficient on the log of the price index as the wage–price elasticity, and, following quality of life literature [see Roback (1982) and, more recently, Shapiro (2006)], divides the general price level in each city into housing and non-housing prices. Winters (2009) ultimately finds that the elasticity between wages and the general price level across cities is equal to one when data on rents is used instead of housing prices. This outcome can be considered as additional evidence in favour of spatial equilibrium in the United States: when the coefficient on the price level is equal or close to one, it indicates that workers are fully compensated for differences in prices across cities. Partridge et al. (2012), studying internal migration in the United States between 2000 and 2008, uncover a persistent slowdown in gross and net migration, which can be interpreted as a signal of spatial equilibrium. However, the authors highlight the need for further research on this topic.[12]

In Europe, the situation seems rather different compared to the United States. Empirical research shows that the European populations tend to be rather immobile. Regional net migration in the United States is 15 times greater than in Europe when similarly-sized geographic regions are compared (Cheshire and Magrini 2006). However, these differences are not limited to degree of mobility. Evidence from Europe suggests that interregional migration is driven primarily by a disequilibrium mechanism in which, allowing for life-cycle effects (Fielding 1992; Plane and Heins 2003), migration is mainly a response, albeit a slow one, to spatial differences in economic factors such as wages and employment opportunities (Faggian and McCann 2009). In Europe, natural amenities such as favourable climate do not affect migration to the extent that is found in the United States. Cheshire and Magrini (2006) investigate the role of amenities in migration using a cross-section of 121 large city regions, or Functional Urban Regions (FURs), in the European Union (specifically, the EU12). Because of limited availability of migration data,

[12]Ferguson et al. (2007), analysing population change for 2400 Canadian communities, conclude that amenities prevail as drivers of migration for youth, young adults, and elderly cohorts.

they use the population growth rate between 1980 and 2000 in each of the FURs as an endogenous variable. Regressing economic and climate variables[13] on population growth, they find that estimated coefficients on natural amenities are insignificant, while coefficients on economic opportunities are positive and significant. However, when population growth within the individual EU countries is considered, the impact of climate is positive and stronger than that of economic opportunities. Cheshire and Magrini (2006) conclude that these results indicate that for EU countries natural amenities matter, but only for sub-national migration. Conversely, Alecke et al. (1999) and Etzo (2011) confirm the role of favourable economic conditions in the destination region as a migration driver in Germany and Italy, respectively. Biagi et al. (2011) conclude that economic variables impact migration in Italy only for long distance moves (mainly in the south-to-north direction) and find some evidence of spatial equilibrium for the case of short distance migration.

In a recent paper, Rodríguez-Pose and Ketterer (2012) investigate interregional migration for 133 European regions (in the EU12) over the period 1990–2006.[14] In addition to economic and climate conditions, they consider a large set of variables including measures of social externalities and place-based regional variables such topography (natural and physical landscape characteristics) and cultural, historical, and identity-type variables (aesthetic, recreational, cultural, and artistic landscapes). Unlike Cheshire and Magrini (2006), they find that natural amenities significantly affect the relative attractiveness of sub-national territories across the European Union, ultimately concluding that place-based migration preferences exist in Europe as they do in the United States.

2.5.2 *The Role of Amenities Revisited*

Up to this point, the described macroeconomic studies have considered the effects of amenities on migration flows in general. Conversely, Glaeser et al. (2001) specifically investigate the role of urban versus natural amenities for high human capital individuals in the US and find that even in situations in which cities or regions are economically homogenous, it is disparities in urban amenities rather than natural amenities across regions that play a role in attracting high human

[13]Cloud cover, minimum temperature, mean temperature, maximum temperature, and wet days.

[14]They use a combination of NUTS1 and NUTS2 data instead of the FURs used by Cheshire and Magrini (2006). According to Rodríguez-Pose and Ketterer (2012, p. 536), using administrative data on regions as a whole allows them 'to capture the impact of different (non-urban) land cover variables on migrants' place-based utility and hence provide an opportunity to study not only the amenity-related pull of city–regions, but also that of more peripheral (or rural) areas.

capital migrants.[15] Workers with higher education and human capital are expected to choose locations with high wages that are also pleasant to live in, in terms of amenities.

The analysis of migration drivers based on level of human capital is one of the main directions of migration studies in the 2000s. In his seminal work, Richard Florida (2002a, b) suggests that cultural amenities such as movie theatres, bars, museums, art galleries, restaurants, and 'trendy' shops, along with tolerant and open-minded inhabitants, play a significant role in attracting the so-called 'creative class'. According to Florida (2004), creativity is not necessarily a by-product of educational attainment; rather, creative people are highly innovative and highly mobile, are able to find original solutions to problems through the development of novel ideas and technologies, and their presence is associated with higher urban growth. The creative class is therefore identified by the kind of jobs individuals hold rather than their formal education. Florida has since been criticized on a number of grounds: because the concept of the creative class overlaps with that of human capital (Glaeser 2005; Hansen and Niedomysl 2009); because the creative class includes a very diverse set of occupations (Markusen 2006), including jobs that are not rewarded with higher wages such as those filled by 'bohemian graduates'; and, finally, because there is rather mixed empirical evidence on the importance of the creative class for regional economic performance (Hansen and Niedomysl 2009; Boschma and Fritsch 2009; Marrocu and Paci 2012). In regards to migration drivers, Boschma and Fritsch (2009)—analysing movements of the creative class in Denmark, England and Wales, and Finland, among other countries[16]—find that job opportunities, as well as cultural and recreational amenities, are more important than tolerance and openness of the local population for attracting migrants. Hansen and Niedomysl (2009), from their interregional migration study of the creative class in Sweden, similarly conclude that the so-called 'people climate' of the destination region has less of an impact on migration than predicted by Florida's creative class theory.

The recent chapter on spatial equilibrium in labour markets published by Philip Graves (2014) in the *Handbook of Regional Science* highlights the importance of continued investigations of the role played by amenities and their ultimate impact on local rents and wages in interregional migration studies. The presence of amenities affects both utilities of households and production functions of firms (i.e., there are amenities that are beneficial, neutral, and detrimental for households and, similarly, amenities that are beneficial, neutral, and detrimental for firms), and the prevailing combination of the type and quality of amenities in a region will determine local wages and rents (Graves 2014, p. 21, Fig. 2.1). Therefore, the final effect of amenities on internal migration is much more complex than expected by former studies, and more research is needed in this area.

[15]Some scholars have pointed out that cities and regions are at the centre of innovation since they foster the interactions between workers and firms (Jacobs 1969). A fundamental role in the innovation process is played by production externalities of human capital accumulation (Lucas 1988). Some studies demonstrate that cities or regions with better educated people grow faster than others (Glaeser et al. 1995).

[16]Their dataset includes more than 500 regions in total.

2.5.3 Migration in New Economic Geography Models

Since the seminal work of the Nobel Prize economist Paul Krugman (1991) and the advent of new economic geography (NEG), mainstream economics has recognized the impacts of distance, agglomeration economies, and economies of scale on migration decisions. From an empirical point of view, NEG models are very similar to gravity models; the difference between the two is that NEG models are supported by economic theory. In the NEG view, individual welfare depends on the variety of goods consumed locally (McCann 2013).

Krugman (1991) considers spatial agglomeration as a cumulative process à la Hirschman (1958) based on two main centripetal forces (Crozet 2004; McCann 2013). The first of these encompasses 'backward linkages', i.e., demand externalities that affect the location choice of firms. In the presence of economies of scale and transportation costs, firms prefer to locate in regions with high demand for their products. The second force includes 'forward linkages', or cost externalities that affect the location of workers. Because of their preference for consuming a variety of goods, workers prefer to locate in large manufacturing regions where minimal transportation costs lower the cost of consumption (and living). The preferences of individuals and firms for centralized markets fosters agglomeration, which, in turn, fosters regional productivity. Therefore, in core regions, the price index of manufactured goods is lower because the majority of goods are produced locally, while in remote regions, it is higher because the majority of goods are imported from distant locations. Holding nominal wages constant, real wages are expected to be higher in core regions and lower in peripheral ones, since in core regions a larger variety of goods are available to consumers at lower prices. Therefore, the price index of manufactured goods is negatively related to their market potential. Hence, transport costs and consumer preferences for variety trigger a 'core–periphery' type of development in which firms and capital generally concentrate in larger regions. If transportation costs were at or near zero, the advantages of agglomeration would almost disappear (McCann 2013).

The application of the NEG framework to the analysis of migration flows is a rather recent development, with the priority of such studies being to investigate the existence of the forward linkage[17] or to predict the distribution of labour in specific regions or countries.[18] In empirical models (Crozet 2004; Paluzie et al. 2009), the share of migrants moving towards a given region has been found to depend negatively on its distance from the origin region [a proxy for transportation costs and other types of costs such as psychological costs à la Sjaastad (1962)] and depend positively on (1) the probability of employment in the region (à la Harris and Todaro 1970); (2) the expected nominal wage; and, finally, (3) the market potential of the

[17]Crozet (2004) analyses European Countries and Pon et al. (2007) investigate the case of Spain.

[18]Both Kancs (2010) and Kancs and Kielyte (2010) analyze and predict migration in the enlarged European Union after integration.

region, measured by the price index of a collection of traded manufactured goods. The latter is used as an indicator of market potential and is expected to be the strongest migration driver, validating the impact of the forward linkage. The main limitation of such models is that they consider only economic drivers of migration and completely neglect other types of push and pull factors such as amenities.

2.5.4 *The Role of Social and Family Capital in Migration Decisions*

According to one stream of economic analysis, institutions such as social and family capital play a significant role in shaping economic performance. The concept of social capital was established by political scientists (Banfield 1958; Putnam 1993; Fukuyama 1997) and sociologists (Bourdieu 1985; Coleman 1988; Portes 1998).[19] While many researchers study the effects of social capital and how it can persist over time,[20] little work has been dedicated to the role of family capital, particularly in the context of migration.

In some countries, individuals prefer to live close to their original family, which may affect attitudes towards migration. Whether family ties ultimately have a positive or negative effect on migration is a matter that researchers must investigate further. Excluding the seminal work of Mincer (1978), only recently has the topic received attention by researchers. Alesina and Giuliano (2007, 2010), studying 78 countries worldwide, find that geographic mobility is lowest where family ties are strongest. Belot and Ermisch (2009) find that proximity to friends negatively affects migration decisions in the United Kingdom. In the case of the US, Spilimbergo and Ubeda (2004) highlight that black US workers tend to be less mobile than white US workers due to stronger relationships with family members, on average. David et al. (2008) find that the relative immobility of European labour (mainly in southern Europe) can be explained by the concept of 'local social capital', defined as an intrinsic attachment by Europeans to their country of origin. Home ownership can play a role as well: studies demonstrate that home ownership is correlated positively with the presence of social capital (Winter 2000). Glaeser et al. (2002) find that homeowners are relatively less mobile and normally live in places with higher social capital. Moreover, presence of social or family ties may boost migration to regions by increasing the amount of information available to the

[19]The economist Loury (1977) analyses social capital as one of the main attributes contributing to the accumulation of human capital.

[20]For a comprehensive look at the role of social capital in institutions and the labour market, see: http://www.socialcapitalgateway.org/publications/papers

migrant and decreasing the cost of migration.[21] On this regard, Rainer and Siedler (2012, p. 3) find that the existence of family and relatives in West Germany is a predictor of the 'migration hazard rate' for East Germans.

A number of studies indicate that social and professional networks may impact the extent to which migrants contribute to local productivity. For example, in a study examining the interregional mobility of inventors in Western Europe and Scandinavia, Miguélez and Moreno (2013) find that migrant inventors support growth in their destination economy through collaborations with inventors in their origin region. Skilled migrants may also contribute to knowledge transfer between regions if, in the future, initial moves inspire similar moves by members of the migrants' professional networks. Trippl (2013, p. 1567) determines that this is the case for the sub-national labour mobility of 'star scientists' (she refers to this process as the 'follower phenomenon'). The following section provides a more in-depth examination of impacts of migration by migrant skill level.

2.5.5 Consequences of Interregional Migration: The Dimension of Skills

The 2000s have been met with a growth in the number of studies focused on the consequences (i.e., impacts) of interregional migration, building upon the seminal work of Greenwood (1975). Many of these studies distinguish migrants by skill level, with special focus paid to the impacts of moves of high-skilled individuals. Topics and outcomes of interest include endogenous growth, changes in labour market conditions, and the role of incentives for acquiring skills and education.

High human capital migration has the potential to support scientific advancements and the diffusion and creation of knowledge in destination regions. The assumption that increased productivity and technological development is spurred by growth in regional stock of human capital underlies 'endogenous growth theory' (Solow 1957; Romer 1986, 1987; Lucas 1988; Jones 2009). Many studies conducted in recent years examine related impacts of sub-national labour mobility (Power and Lundmark 2004; McCann and Simonen 2005; Eriksson 2011; Boschma et al. 2014). For example, in their analysis of the interrelationship between internal flows of university graduates and innovation outcomes in the UK, Faggian and McCann (2009) find evidence that regional patenting productivity, particularly in high technology industries, is positively affected by influxes of skilled workers. More recently, Timmermans and Boschma (2014) find that interregional labour flows positively impact firm productivity in destination regions when migrants possess skills that are related, but not identical, to those of existing employees.

[21] As stated at the beginning of the chapter, studies on the impact of social network-related 'chain migration' and 'beaten path migration' emerged at the beginning of the 1960s and 1970s with work by MacDonald and MacDonald (1964) and Hoover (1971).

Migrant skill level has also become a key consideration in studies focused on the impact of migration on labour market conditions, particularly in the case of immigration. Behrens and Sato (2011) build upon contributions by Ottaviano and Peri (2006, 2008) by proposing that influxes of workers from a given skill group result in two counteracting effects on wages in destination regions. First, by definition, the in-migration of workers with a specific set of skills (e.g., low-skilled workers, high-skilled workers) increases the regional supply of these workers, depressing within-group wages and increasing the wages of the other worker groups (known as the 'negative skill endowment effect'). Second, regional productivity of workers in a given skill group is positively affected by the in-migration of workers from the same skill group. Since workers are imperfect substitutes, in-migration is assumed to increase the range of available skills (known as the 'positive skill externality effect'). Thus, the ultimate impact of migration on wages for a given skill group in destination regions is ultimately determined by (1) 'the rate at which in-migration increases the diversity of available skills in the economy' and (2) 'the [skill] composition of the immigrant flow' (Behrens and Sato 2011, p. 7). Behrens and Sato's (2011) model is notable because it allows for analysis of migration on wages in the long run, when 'native' workers can acquire new skills, as well as in the short run, when the skill endowment of the existing population is taken as fixed.

When examining how wages of low- and high-skilled workers in destination regions respond to in-migration in the short run, Behrens and Sato (2011) conclude that wages increase in response to influxes of workers from the opposite skill group, supporting earlier findings by Borjas (2003) for the case of US immigration. Additionally, wages of workers will decrease[22] in response to the in-migration of workers from the same skill group only if the migrants are adequate substitutes for existing workers or if regional factor payments to the skill group account for a sufficiently small share of total factor payments.[23] In the long run, in-migration increases the share of skilled workers and the wage differential between low- and high-skilled workers; if the expansion in the collective range of skills in the region (for low- and high-skilled migrants) is net positive, wages of both high-skilled and low-skilled workers and the average wage will increase.

The dimension of skills has also been addressed in studies focused on the relationship between internal migration and regional labour market *disparities* in recent years. As already described in this chapter, the neoclassical, i.e., equilibrium, approach of the 1980s assumes that differences in wages and employment across

[22]A number of studies (Friedberg 2001; Moretti 2004; Dustmann et al. 2005) in this decade find evidence that migration results in within-group wage increases in the destination region for the case of high-skilled workers or uncover weak or insignificant effects (Ciccone and Peri 2006; Islam and Fausten 2008).

[23]In this case, 'the additional competition in the factor market is not offset by a sufficient increase in high skilled labor productivity' (Behrens and Sato 2011, p. 11).

regions are mitigated through migration, since when 'the labour market is flexible and competitive and mobility costs are not too high, workers tend to move from high to low unemployment regions in search of better labour market prospects' (Granato et al. 2015, p. 515). However, when the focus is on the moves of high-skilled workers, who tend to select into migration, internal migration may reinforce labour market disparities, challenging neoclassical assumptions (Suedekum 2004; Kanbur and Rapoport 2005). As explained by Arntz et al. (2014, p. 1734), 'the more unequal employment is spread across the regional workforce, the more a region attracts an increasingly skilled inflow of migrants'.

A recent contribution by Granato et al. (2015), which examines the impact of labour mobility on interregional wage differences in Germany, provides support for the argument that the neoclassical model of migration fails in its predication of convergence of labour market conditions across regions when migrants' skills are not assumed to be homogenous. Granato et al. (2015) determine that, although internal moves of low- and medium-skilled workers in Germany support convergence, college graduate migration *increases* wage differences between regions due to assumed complementarities between high- and low-skilled labour. More specifically, they argue that the marginal product of unskilled labour in destination regions increases in response to the in-migration of skilled workers, which, in turn, raises demand for unskilled labour, decreasing the unemployment rate for this skill group. In contrast, the out-migration of skilled workers from origin regions lowers the marginal productivity and demand for unskilled labour in these regions. Fratesi and Percoco (2014) obtain comparable results for high-skilled interregional migration in Italy.

The channels through which the out-migration of high-skilled individuals impact origin regions remains an underexplored area of research in the interregional context. Kanbur and Rapoport (2005) argue that one way in which high human capital immigration (or, simply, the opportunity to emigrate if highly skilled) alters regional human capital stock is by incentivizing education and skill acquisition in origin regions. Many studies in the 2000s find evidence of this effect for international movements (Beine et al. 2001, 2008, 2011; Stark and Wang 2002; Stark 2004; Docquier and Rapoport 2012).

High-skilled out-migration can also deplete regions of their human capital base, i.e., through 'brain drain' (Bhagwati and Hamada 1974; McCulloch and Yellen 1977). Although existing studies focus on international moves, Faggian et al. (2017, p. 135) note that 'one expects negative consequences of out-migration of high-skilled individuals on the origin economy to be of a similar or even greater magnitude [compared to the international case], as interregional migrants face lower barriers to migration relative to their international counterparts'. This is a topic that deserves further attention in the interregional migration literature in the future.

2.6 Conclusions and Future Challenges

The present chapter highlights the main advances of interregional migration research since the 1970s. The last 15 years have produced substantial developments and many new challenges that must be addressed in future research. Much work needs to be done using microdata to model migration flows by level of human capital, type of occupation, age, and gender. The non-linear role of distance as well as more complex spatial models according to type of migration flow deserve increased focus by scholars as well (see LeSage and Pace 2008). More attention needs to be paid to the role of social and family capital in migration in addition to relevant developments in the immigration literature; to date, the quantity of studies addressing these topics are increasing. Specifically, there has been a rise in the number of studies on the consequences of international redistribution of human capital for developed countries.[24] However, more collaboration between scholars focusing on international and interregional migration are needed [see also Cushing and Poot (2004) for more information related to this matter]. Finally, additional applications focused on emerging economies should be pursued, such as recent work by Aroca and Rodrìguez (2013) on migration issues in Latin American countries.

References

Alecke B, Mitze T, Untiedt G (1999) Internal migration, regional labour market dynamics and implications for German East-West disparities – results from a panel VAR. Ruhr economic papers #96

Alesina A, Giuliano P (2007) The power of the family. NBER working paper 13051, and IZA 2750

Alesina A, Giuliano P (2010) The power of the family. J Econ Growth 5:93–125

Alonso W (1978) A theory of movements. In: Hansen N (ed) Human settlement systems: international perspectives on structure, change and public policy. N. M. Hansen, Cambridge

Arntz M, Gregory T, Lehmer F (2014) Can regional employment disparities explain the allocation of human capital across space? Reg Stud 48(10):1719–1738. https://doi.org/10.1080/00343404.2014.882500

Aroca P, Rodrìguez J (2013) Population distribution and internal migration issues in LAC. In: Cuadraro-Roura JR, Aroca P (eds) Regional problems and policies in Latin America. Springer, Berlin

Banfield EC (1958) The moral basis of a backward society. Free Press, Chicago, IL

Becker GS (1962) Investment in human capital: a theoretical analysis. J Polit Econ 70(5):9–49

Behrens K, Sato Y (2011) Migration, skill formation, and the wage structure. J Reg Sci 51(1):5–30. https://doi.org/10.1111/j.1467-9787.2010.00682.x

Beine M, Docquier F, Rapoport H (2001) Brain drain and economic growth: theory and evidence. J Dev Econ 64(1):275–289. https://doi.org/10.1016/S0304-3878(00)00133-4

[24]According to Borjas (1999), by the end of the 1990s, 9% of the population of Austria and Germany and 6% of the population of France was foreign-born.

Beine M, Docquier F, Rapoport H (2008) Brain drain and human capital formation in developing countries: winners and losers. Econ J 118(528):631–652. https://doi.org/10.1111/j.1468-0297.2008.02135.x

Beine M, Docquier F, Oden-Defoort C (2011) A panel data analysis of the brain gain. World Dev 39(4):523–352. https://doi.org/10.1016/j.worlddev.2010.03.009

Belot M, Ermisch J (2009) Friendship ties and geographical mobility: evidence from Great Britain. J R Stat Soc Ser A Stat Soc 172:427–442

Bhagwati J, Hamada K (1974) The brain drain, international integration of markets for professionals and unemployment: a theoretical analysis. J Dev Econ 1(1):19–42. https://doi.org/10.1016/0304-3878(74)90020-0

Biagi B (2014) Drivers of interregional migration flows: jobs or amenities? University of Southampton, Southampton

Biagi B, Faggian A, McCann P (2011) Long and short distance migration: the role of economic, social and environmental characteristics. Spat Econ Anal 6:111–131

Blomquist GC, Berger MC, Hoehn JP (1988) New estimates of quality of life in urban area. Am Econ Rev 78:89–107

Borjas GJ (1999) Economic research on the determinants of immigration, lesson for European Union. World Bank technical paper, 438

Borjas GJ (2000) The economic progress of immigrants, NBER chapters. In: Issues in the economics of immigration. National Bureau of Economic Research, Cambridge, MA

Borjas GJ (2003) The labor demand curve is downward sloping: reexamining the impact of immigration on the labor market. Q J Econ 118(4):1335–1374. https://doi.org/10.1162/003355303322552810

Borjas GJ, Bronars SG, Trejo SJ (1992) Self-selection and internal migration in the United States. J Urban Econ 32:159–185

Boschma RA, Fritsch M (2009) Creative class and regional growth: empirical evidence from seven European countries. Econ Geogr 85:391–423

Boschma R, Eriksson RH, Lindgren U (2014) Labour market externalities and regional growth in Sweden: the importance of labour mobility between skill-related industries. Reg Stud 48(10):1669–1690. https://doi.org/10.1080/00343404.2013.867429

Bourdieu P (1985) The forms of capital. In: Richardson JG (ed) Handbook of theory and research for the sociology of education. Greenwood, New York

Cheshire P, Magrini S (2006) Population growth in European cities: weather matters but only nationally. Reg Stud 40:23–37

Ciccone A, Peri G (2006) Identifying human-capital externalities: theory with applications. Rev Econ Stud 73(2):381–412. https://doi.org/10.1111/j.1467-937X.2006.00380.x

Coleman JS (1988) Social capital in the creation of human capital. Am J Sociol 94:S95–S120

Crozet M (2004) Do migrants follow market potentials? An estimation of a new economic geography model. J Econ Geogr 4:439–458

Cushing B, Poot J (2004) Crossing boundaries and borders: regional science advances in migration modelling. Pap Reg Sci 83:317–338

DaVanzo J (1978) Does unemployment affect migration? Evidence from micro data. Rev Econ Stat 6:504–514

David Q, Janiak A, Wasmer E (2008) Local social capital and geographical mobility. A theory, Documentos de Trabajo 248, Centro de Economía Aplicada, Universidad de Chile

Docquier F, Rapoport H (2012) Globalization, brain drain, and development. J Econ Lit 50(3):681–730. https://doi.org/10.1257/jel.50.3.681

Dustmann C, Fabbri F, Preston I (2005) The impact of immigration on the British labour market. Econ J 115(507):F324–F342. https://doi.org/10.1111/j.1468-0297.2005.01038.x

Eriksson RH (2011) Localized spillovers and knowledge flows: how does proximity influence the performance of plants? Econ Geogr 87(2):127–152. https://doi.org/10.1111/j.1944-8287.2011.01112.x

Etzo I (2011) The determinants of the recent interregional migration flows in Italy: a panel data analysis. J Reg Sci 51(5):948–966
Evans AW (1990) The assumption of equilibrium in the analysis of migration and interregional differences: a review of recent research. J Reg Sci 30:515–531
Evans AW (1993) Interregional equilibrium: a transatlantic view. J Reg Sci 33:89–97
Faggian A (2014) Job search theory. In: Fischer M, Nijkamp P (eds) Handbook of regional science. Springer, Heidelberg
Faggian A, McCann P (2009) Human capital, graduate migration and innovation in British regions. Camb J Econ 33:317–333
Faggian A, Rajbhandari I, Dotzel KR (2017) The interregional migration of human capital and its regional consequences: a review. Reg Stud 51(1):128–143
Faini R, Galli G, Gennari P, Rossi F (1997) An empirical puzzle: falling migration and growing unemployment differentials among Italian regions. Eur Econ Rev 41:571–579
Ferguson M, Ali K, Olfert MR, Partridge MD (2007) Voting with their feet: jobs versus amenities. Growth Change 38:77–110
Fielding AJ (1992) Migration and social mobility: South East England as an escalator region. Reg Stud 26:1–15
Florida R (2002a) The rise of the creative class. Basic Books, New York
Florida R (2002b) The economic geography of talent. Ann Assoc Am Geogr 92:743–775
Florida R (2004) Cities and the creative class. Routledge, London
Fratesi U, Percoco M (2014) Selective migration, regional growth and convergence: evidence from Italy. Reg Stud 48(10):1650–1668. https://doi.org/10.1080/00343404.2013.843162
Friedberg RM (2001) The impact of mass migration on the Israeli labor market. Q J Econ 116(4):1373–1408. https://doi.org/10.1162/003355301753265606
Fukuyama F (1997) Social capital and the modern capitalist economy: creating a high trust workplace. Stern Bus Mag 4(1):1–16
Glaeser EL (2005) Review of Richard Florida's the rise of the creative class. Reg Sci Urban Econ 35:593–596
Glaeser EL, Gottlieb JD (2008) The economics of place-making policies. Brook Pap Econ Act 39:155–239
Glaeser EL, Scheinkman J, Shleifer A (1995) Economic growth in a cross-section of cities. J Monet Econ 36:117–143
Glaeser EL, Kolko J, Saiz A (2001) Consumer city. J Econ Geogr 1:27–50
Glaeser E, Laibson D, Sacerdote B (2002) An economic approach to social capital. Econ J 112:437
Granato N, Haas A, Hamann S, Niebuhr A (2015) The impact of skill-specific migration on regional unemployment disparities in Germany. J Reg Sci 55(4):513–539. https://doi.org/10.1111/jors.12178
Graves PE (1976) A re-examination of migration, economic opportunity, and the quality of life. J Reg Sci 12:107–112
Graves PE (1980) Migration and climate. J Reg Sci 20:227–237
Graves PE (1983) Migration with a composite amenity: the role of rents. J Reg Sci 23:541–546
Graves PE (2014) Spatial equilibrium in labor markets. In: Fisher MM, Nijkamp P (eds) Handbook of regional science. Springer, Berlin
Graves PE, Linneman P (1979) Household migration: theoretical and empirical results. J Urban Econ 6:383–404
Graves PE, Mueser P (1993) The role of equilibrium and disequilibrium in modelling regional growth and decline; a critical reassessment. J Reg Sci 33:69–84
Greenwood MJ (1969) An analysis of the determinants of geographic labour mobility in the United States. Rev Econ Stat 51:189–194
Greenwood MJ (1975) Research on internal migration in the United States. J Econ Lit 13:397–433
Greenwood MJ (1985) Human migration: theory, models and empirical studies. J Reg Sci 25:521–544
Greenwood MJ (1997) Internal migration in developed countries. In: Rosenzweid MR, Stark O (eds) Handbook of population and family economics. Elsevier Science, Amsterdam, pp 647–720

Greenwood MJ (2014) Migration and labour market opportunities. In: Fisher MM, Nijkamp P (eds) Handbook of regional science. Springer, Berlin

Greenwood MJ, Hunt G (1984) Migration and interregional employment redistribution in the United States. Am Econ Rev 74:957–969

Greenwood MJ, Hunt G (2003) The early history of migration research. Int Reg Sci Rev 26(1):3–37

Greenwood M, Sweetland D (1972) The determinants of migration between standard metropolitan statistical areas. Demography 9:665–681

Greenwood MJ, Mueser PR, Plane DA, Schlottmann AM (1991) New directions in migration research: perspectives from some North American regional science disciplines. Ann Reg Sci 25:237–270

Hansen HK, Niedomysl T (2009) Migration of the creative class: evidence from Sweden. J Econ Geogr 9:191–206

Harris JR, Todaro MP (1970) Migration, unemployment and development: a two-sector analysis. Am Econ Rev 60:126–142

Hicks JR (1932) Theory of wages. Macmillan, New York

Hirschman AO (1958) The strategy of economic development. Yale University Press, New Haven

Hoover EM (1971) An introduction to regional economics. Alfred A. Knopf, New York

Hughes GA, McCormick B (1985) Migration intentions in the UK: which households want to migrate and which succeed. Econ J 95(Suppl):113–123

Hughes GA, McCormick B (1987) Housing markets, unemployment and labour market flexibility in the UK. Eur Econ Rev 31:615–645

Islam A, Fausten DK (2008) Skilled immigration and wages in Australia. Econ Rec 84:S66–S82. https://doi.org/10.1111/j.1475-4932.2008.00485.x

Jackman R, Savouri S (1992) Regional migration in Britain: an analysis of gross flows using NHS central register data. Econ J 102:1433–1450

Jacobs J (1969) The economy of cities. Random House, New York

Jones BF (2009) The burden of knowledge and the "Death of the Renaissance Man": is innovation getting harder? Rev Econ Stud 76(1):283–317. https://doi.org/10.1111/j.1467-937X.2008.00531.x

Kanbur R, Rapoport H (2005) Migration selectivity and the evolution of spatial inequality. J Econ Geogr 5(1):43–57. https://doi.org/10.1093/jnlecg/lbh053

Kancs D (2010) Labour migration in the enlarged EU: a new economic geography approach. J Econ Policy Reform 14:171–188

Kancs D, Kielyte J (2010) European integration and labour migration. EERI research paper series EERI_RP_2010_27. Economics and Econometrics Research Institute (EERI), Brussels

Kau JB, Sirmans CF (1976) New, repeat and return migration: a study of migrant types. South Econ J 43:1144–1148

Knapp TA, Graves PE (1989) On the role of amenities in models of migration and regional development. J Reg Sci 29:71–87

Krugman P (1991) Increasing returns and economic geography. J Polit Econ 99(3):483–499

Lambiri D, Biagi B, Royuela V (2007) Quality of life in the economic and urban economic literature. Soc Indic Res 84:1–25

Lancaster K (1966) A new approach to consumer theory. J Polit Econ 74:132–157

LeSage JP, Pace KR (2008) Spatial econometric modelling of origin-destination flows. J Reg Sci 48:941–967

Loury GC (1977) A dynamic theory of racial income differences. In: Wallace PA, La Mond AM (eds) Women, minorities, and employment discrimination. Heath, Lexington, MA, pp 153–186

Lowry I (1966) Migration and metropolitan growth: two analytical models. Chandler, San Francisco

Lucas RE Jr (1988) On the mechanics of economic development. J Monet Econ 22:3–42

MacDonald JS, MacDonald LD (1964) Chain migration ethnic neighborhood formation and social networks. Milbank Mem Fund Q 42:82–97

Markusen A (2006) Urban development and the politics of a creative class: evidence from the study of artists. Environ Plan A 38:1921–1940
Marrocu E, Paci R (2012) Education or creativity: what matters most for economic performance? Econ Geogr 88:369–401
McCann P (2013) Modern urban and regional economics, 2nd edn. Oxford University Press, Oxford (OUP Catalogue)
McCann P, Simonen J (2005) Innovation, knowledge spillovers and local labour markets. Pap Reg Sci 84(3):465–485. https://doi.org/10.1111/j.1435-5957.2005.00036.x
McCulloch R, Yellen JL (1977) Factor mobility, regional development, and the distribution of income. J Polit Econ 85(1):79–96. https://doi.org/10.1086/260546
Miguélez E, Moreno R (2013) Research networks and inventors' mobility as drivers of innovation: evidence from Europe. Reg Stud 47(10):1668–1685. https://doi.org/10.1080/00343404.2011.618803
Mincer J (1978) Family migration decisions. J Polit Econ 86:749–773
Molho IT (1986) Theories of migration: a review. Scott J Polit Econ 33:396–419
Moretti E (2004) Estimating the social return to higher education: evidence from longitudinal and repeated cross-sectional data. J Econ 121:175–212
Mortensen D (1984) Job search and labor market analysis. Working paper no. 594. Northwestern University, Center for Mathematical Studies in Economics and Management Science
Muth RF (1971) Migration: chicken or egg? South Econ J 37:295–306
Ottaviano GIP, Peri G (2006) The economic value of cultural diversity: evidence from US cities. J Econ Geogr 6(1):9–44. https://doi.org/10.1093/jeg/lbi002
Ottaviano GIP, Peri G (2008) Immigration and national wages: clarifying the theory and the empirics. NBER working paper #14188. Available at: http://www.nber.org/papers/w14188
Paluzie E, Pons J, Silvestre J, Tirado D (2009) Migrants and market potential in Spain over the 20th century: a test of the new economic geography. Span Econ Rev 11:243–265
Partridge MD (2010) The dueling models: NEG vs. amenity migration in explaining US engines of growth. Pap Reg Sci 89:513–536
Partridge MD, Rickman DS, Olfert MR, Kamar A (2012) Dwindling U.S. internal migration: evidence of a spatial equilibrium or structural shifts in local labor markets? Reg Sci Urban Econ 42:375–388
Pissarides C, Wadsworth J (1989) Unemployment and the inter-regional mobility of labour. Econ J 99:739–755
Plane DA, Heins F (2003) Age articulation of U.S. inter-metropolitan migration. Ann Reg Sci 37:107–130
Pon J, Paluzie E, Silvestre E, Tirado DA (2007) Testing the new economic geography: migrations and industrial agglomerations in Spain. J Reg Sci 47:289–313
Portes A (1998) Social capital: its origins and applications in modern sociology. Annu Rev Sociol 24(1):1–24
Power D, Lundmark M (2004) Working through knowledge pools: labour market dynamics, the transference of knowledge and ideas, and industrial clusters. Urban Stud 41(5–6):1025–1044. https://doi.org/10.1080/00420980410001675850
Putnam RD (1993) Making democracy work. Princeton University Press, Princeton
Rainer H, Siedler T (2012) Family location and caregiving patterns from an international perspective. Popul Dev Rev 38:337–351
Ravenstein EG (1885) The laws of migration. J R Stat Soc 48:167–235
Roback J (1982) Wages, rents, and the quality of life. J Polit Econ 90:1257–1278
Rodríguez-Pose A, Ketterer TD (2012) Do local amenities affect the appeal of regions in Europe for migrants? J Reg Sci 52:535–561
Romer PM (1986) Increasing returns and long-run growth. J Polit Econ 94(5):1002–1037. https://doi.org/10.1086/261420
Romer PM (1987) Growth based on increasing returns due to specialization. Am Econ Rev 77(2):56–62

Rosen S (1974) Hedonic prices and implicit market: product differentiation in pure competition. J Polit Econ 82:34–55
Rosen S (1979) Wage-based indexes of urban quality of life. In: Mieszkowsky P, Straszheim M (eds) Current issues in urban economics. Johns Hopkins University Press, Baltimore
Schlottmann A, Herzog H (1981) Employment status and the decision to migrate. Rev Econ Stat 63:590–598
Shapiro JM (2006) Smart cities: quality of life, productivity, and the growth effects of human capital. Rev Econ Stat 88:324–335
Sjaastad LA (1962) The costs and returns of human migration. J Polit Econ 70:80–93
Solow RM (1957) Technical change and the aggregate production function. Rev Econ Stat 39(3):312–320
Spilimbergo A, Ubeda L (2004) Family attachment and the decision to move by race. J Urban Econ 55:478–497
Stark O (2004) Rethinking the brain drain. World Dev 32(1):15–22. https://doi.org/10.1016/j.worlddev.2003.06.013
Stark O, Wang Y (2002) Inducing human capital formation: migration as a substitute for subsidies. J Public Econ 86(1):29–46. https://doi.org/10.1016/s0047-2727(01)00104-9
Suedekum J (2004) Selective migration, union wage setting and unemployment disparities in West Germany. Int Econ J 18(1):33–48. https://doi.org/10.1080/1351161042000180629
Timmermans B, Boschma R (2014) The effect of intra- and inter-regional labour mobility on plant performance in Denmark: the significance of related labour inflows. J Econ Geogr 14:289–311
Trippl M (2013) Scientific mobility and knowledge transfer at the interregional and intraregional level. Reg Stud 47(10):1653–1667. https://doi.org/10.1080/00343404.2010.549119
United Nations (1970) Methods of measuring internal migration, manual IV. United Nations, New York
Van Dijk J, Folmer H, Herzog HW, Schlottmann AM (1989) Migration and labour market adjustment. Kluwer, London
Vanderkamp J (1971) Migration flows, their determinants and the effects of return migration. J Polit Econ 79:1012–1031
Westerlund O (1997) Employment opportunities, wages and international migration in Sweden 1970–1989. J Reg Sci 37:55–73
Winter I (2000) Towards a theorized understanding of family life and social capital. Australian Institute of Family Studies, Melbourne
Winters JV (2009) Wages and prices: are workers fully compensated for cost of living differences? Reg Sci Urban Econ 39:632–643

Chapter 3
Determinants and Consequences of International Migration

Andrea Ariu

Abstract This chapter provides a simple overview of the canonical model of international migration, discusses the consequences of migration on both sending and receiving countries and draws some considerations on future research prospects for the international migration literature.

Keywords International migration · Models · Empirics

3.1 Introduction

International migration increased from 75 millions in 1960 to 211 millions in 2010. While apparently huge, these numbers represent respectively only 2.5% and 3.1% of the world population (Brücker et al. 2013). This means that most of the people on the planet live in the countries in which they were born and only a tiny minority decides to leave. This is mostly because the process of migration is very costly, thus offsetting its benefits. On the one hand, this is the result of migration restrictions, transport costs and relocation costs (which include finding a new job, possibly learn a new language, etc.). On the other hand, the uncertainty involved makes risk averse people decide to stay rather than leaving. Indeed, if we take into account people that would like to leave their country, the amount of world migrants could get up to 20% (Docquier et al. 2014). South-South migration represents the majority of actual migration stocks (44%). North-North migration accounts for 18% of stocks and is stable over time. South-North migration represents the most dynamic component of migration with an increase from 10% in 1960 to 33% in 2010. Most of migrants are male and college graduate, but female migration is increasing substantially in recent years. The most popular destination is US, with about 20% of immigration stocks

A. Ariu (✉)
Economics Department, Ludwig-Maximilians-Universität Munich, Munich, Germany

IFO, Munich, Germany

CRENOS, Cagliari, Italy
e-mail: andrea.ariu@econ.lmu.de

B. Biagi et al. (eds.), *New Frontiers in Interregional Migration Research*,
Advances in Spatial Science, https://doi.org/10.1007/978-3-319-75886-2_3

Ozden et al. (2011). Both the size and the dynamics of migration pose serious policy issues on countries and raise questions on the possible liberalization effects of migration.

In this chapter, we first analyze the determinants of the migration choice, by highlighting both the theoretical approach to the problem and the main determinants identified by the literature; second, we discuss the main consequences of migration for both receiving and sending countries. Finally, we draw some considerations on future research prospects for the international migration literature.

3.2 Why Do People Migrate?

In this paragraph we first outline the theoretical framework to think about migration determinants and then review the main forces underlying the migration decision identified in the literature.

3.2.1 *The Canonical Model*

All the models since Sjaastad (1962) and then Borjas (1987) suppose that the choice of migration depends on the comparison between the benefits from remaining in the origin country with those from migrating in a foreign country (net of the migration cost). This approach found a general consensus in the literature and has become the reference to model the migration flows. In particular, the Random Utility Model of migration allows the researcher to start from the choices of individual agents to country-pair migration flows. Using this approach, we compare the utility of an individual i staying in the origin country j (where j denotes one of the countries among the set J) versus the utility of migrating in country k (with $k \in J$ and $k \neq j$). The first can be expressed as:

$$U_{jj}^{i} = w_{jj} + \varepsilon_{jj}^{i}$$

where the double script jj indicates respectively the origin and the destination. w_{jj} represents a deterministic component of utility including all the variables that are observed by the econometrician (such as wages, diasporas, etc.) and ε_{jj}^{i} is an individual-specific stochastic component of utility representing the specific tastes of the perspective migrant with respect to the migration choice. If instead the individual i decides to migrate to k, his utility can be written as:

$$U_{jk}^{i} = w_{jk} - c_{jk} + \varepsilon_{jk}^{i}$$

where c_{jk} represents the cost of moving from j to k. If $U_{jk}^{i} > U_{jj}^{i}$, the individual decides to migrate. If instead $U_{jk}^{i} < U_{jj}^{i}$, the person remains in her origin country j. The stochastic term ε^i_{jk} is a key determinant in the choice of migrating or not and allows different individuals to take different choices. Most of the literature assumes this random component to follow an independent and identically distributed Extreme Value Type-1 distribution. Under this assumption, the probability for the individual i to migrate from j to k can be written as:

$$Pr\left(U^i_{jk} > U^i_{jj}\right) = \frac{e^{w_{jk}-c_{jk}}}{\sum\limits_{h \in J} e^{w_{jh}-c_{jh}}}$$

where h indicates all the possible alternative countries (including the origin) in the set J.[1] By indicating with M_{jk} the number of people deciding to migrate and by diving it for the number of people deciding to stay, M_{jj} we get:

$$\frac{M_{jk}}{M_{jj}} = \frac{e^{w_{jk}-c_{jk}}}{e^{w_{jj}}}$$

by taking the log, this expression becomes like a gravity equation:

$$log\left(\frac{M_{jk}}{M_{jj}}\right) = \left(w_{jk} - w_{jj}\right) - c_{jk}$$

both origin, destination and bilateral characteristics explain the migration rates from j to k. This means that all the usual forces of the gravity equation can be condensed in this expression. For example, we expect migration flows to increase in the wage of the destination country and decrease in the wage of the origin country. Moreover, bilateral factors such as distance affect the choice. This theoretical framework has several advantages:

- **it explains zeroes:** if no person living in j has that $U^i_{jk} > U^i_{jj}$, then $\frac{M_{jk}}{M_{jj}} = 0$ and we can observe a zero migration flow between j and k. This is a frequent situation in the data: 60% of all corridors are indeed empty (Ozden et al. 2011).
- **it explains migrants selection:** on the one hand, people having different ε can decide different locations or not to migrate, so, not everybody makes the same choice. In this sense the model can explain the selection into migrating or not. On the other hand, the model can be modified to have two types of individuals, for example low and high-skilled. These categories of migrants can react differently to migration costs and the benefits present in the destination country. This allows us to model the so-called "positive selection of migrants", which refers to the fact

[1]Please refer to McFadden (1984) for more details about the properties of the distribution and for a complete treatment of the derivation of this expression. Just to provide the intuition, this expression says that for individual i the choice of migrating to country k provides him more utility than any other possible destination $h \neq J$ and is also higher than the choice of staying in j. This derivation is possible only under the assumption that the choice of one destination does not depend on the characteristic of the others.

that migrants tend to be the most skilled among the pool of potential migrants. In other words, this framework allows us to model why emigrants have a higher education than people that decide to remain in the origin country.

- **it embeds migration costs into the migration choice:** both geographical and policy variables can determine the choice of the migrant.
- **it can be tailored to account for the multilateral resistance to migration:** by relaxing the assumption on the irrelevance of irrelevant alternatives (IIA), it is possible to take into account the effect that a third country can have on the migration flow between *j* and *k*. The idea is that the choice of a potential migrant from j when considering to relocate to *k* can be influenced also from the characteristics of all the other destinations. This means that the choice is not relative just to the two countries j and k but also relative to all the others. This concept was developed in the trade literature by Anderson and van Wincoop (2003), and the intuition is that trade flows between two countries depend also on what other countries are trading with each other. Bertoli and Fernández-Huertas Moraga (2013, 2015) derive the model in this context and develop adequate estimation procedures to deal with this issue in a migration setting.

The most important drawback of using this framework is that it is only a partial equilibrium framework and it does not allow for a proper analysis of the welfare consequences of migration, both for the receiving and sending countries. Therefore, while it explains quite well migration flows across countries along all north and south corridors, other models should be used to capture the general equilibrium effects of migration and make a proper accounting of the welfare effects. Unfortunately, on that side there is no consensus on how to model the welfare consequences and in Sect. 3.3 we limit ourselves to the analysis of the consequences of migration for both receiving and sending countries without entering into the details of the frameworks used.

3.2.2 Migration Determinants

Having presented the building block of the model, we discuss now what is usually included into the net benefits of migrating $w_{jk} - w_{jj}$ and the migration costs c_{jk}. This means that we are going to take into account all the determinants of migration flows identified by the literature.

- the most important factor for migration decision is the per-capita income difference between two countries, especially for high-skilled. Grogger and Hanson (2011) show that 58% of the variation in the stock of migrants is explained by differences in per-capita income levels between two countries. Most of the papers use a logarithmic specification to model the relation between migration flows and income (Mayda 2010; McKenzie et al. 2014; Bertoli and Fernández-Huertas Moraga 2013, 2015; Bertoli et al. 2011; Ortega and Peri 2012) while Grogger and Hanson (2011) assume that w_{jk} depends linearly on income per capita. In most cases the income per capita is proxied by the GDP per capita, thus implicitly assuming that all migrants earn the same in the destination country. However, more recent papers tried to solve this issue by looking at post-tax earnings (Grogger and Hanson 2011), by looking at income specific earnings (Belot and Hatton 2012), or by using wages rather than earnings (Beine et al. 2011) adjusted by the observed productivity of migrants in the destination (Ariu et al. 2016).

- the second most important factor influencing migration flows is represented by the diasporas. At least one third of the variation in migration flows is explained by the existence of migration diasporas in the destination country (Beine et al. 2014). In particular, gravity models find that on average, a 10% increase in the bilateral migration stock is associated to a 4% increase in the bilateral migration flow (Beine et al. 2011; Bertoli and Fernández-Huertas Moraga 2013; Beine and Parsons 2012). This means that people that migrated already to a country can help perspective migrants by offering information and local help. Therefore, diasporas can lower the cost of migrations.
- Expectations can influence migration flows. People do not only look at current possible earnings in both origin and destination, but they also form expectations about future income growth. For example, Bertoli et al. (2013) have shown that variations in the yields on 10-year government bonds successfully explain migration decisions.
- Migration policies can also alter migration flows. Direct evidence is present in Beerli and Peri (2015), in which they quantify the effect of the implementation of the EU-Swiss free movement of people agreement using quasi-natural experiment. In particular, the relaxation of Swiss restrictions led to a 4% increase in the number of foreign workers in Switzerland. More indirect tests use VISA waivers (Bertoli and Fernández-Huertas Moraga 2013), VISA policies (Bertoli and Fernández-Huertas Moraga 2015; Beine and Parsons 2012), multilateral agreements such as Shengen (Grogger Hanson 2011; Beine et al. 2013) or immigration reforms (Ortega and Peri 2012).

3.3 Consequences for Sending Countries

As highlighted in the introduction, most of the increase in migration of the last 50 years comes from migrants from poor countries relocating to rich countries (Ozden et al. 2011). Moreover, most of these flows are represented by high-skilled. This outflow represents an important loss of human capital and it is usually referred as "Brain Drain". The literature analyzing the Brain Drain is mostly theoretical and it experienced three main waves which concentrated on the economic consequences of brain drain Docquier and Rapopport (2012).

The first wave dates back to the 1960s. These theoretical contributions were based on trade frameworks and pointed towards the beneficial effects of free migration for the world economy. In this type of setting, the predictions for the sending countries were uncertain or neutral. The loss associated to the reduction in the human capital stock was counterbalanced by remittances (Grubel and Scott 1966; Johnson 1967; Berry and Soligo 1969). A second wave of literature instead focused more on the negative aspects of the human capital loss. Introducing in their frameworks various types of frictions, such as domestic labor market rigidities, resulted in negative consequences for the poor countries. By letting the high-skill leave, rich countries could become even richer by exploiting the human capital formed in the developing one (Bhagwati and Hamada 1974; McCulloch and Yellen 1977). The third wave of papers identified under which circumstances the Brain Drain can have positive consequences for sending countries. These include a possible increase in productivity of the sending country (Mountford 1997), increase the returns to human capital investment and increase the average human capital level (Stark et al. 1997; Stark and Wang 2002; Vidal 1998; Beine et al. 2001), decrease the returns to rent-seeking (Mariani 2007). Finally, an important number of papers analyzed the determinants and the consequences of remittances. In particular, migrants can help their families in the origin countries by sending them part of their income. The effects of such flows on the origin country of the migrant are still debatable due to the difficulty to isolate the effect of remittances from all the other shocks that can influence the economy of a country. Faini (2007) provides a nice review of these results. More in general, the literature focusing on the economic consequences of emigration on origin countries lacks empirical evidence on the consequences and mechanisms behind the brain drain. The main problem is that is it difficult to disentangle the effect of emigration from that of other confounding factors. Therefore, in the absence of a clean natural experiment, the literature remained mostly on the theoretical side.

More recent contributions left a bit aside the pure economic perspective to focus instead on the effect of emigration on institutions. For example, Spilimbergo (2009) shows that migrants educated in democratic countries are able to promote democracy in their home country. Similarly, Docquier et al. (2016) find a positive causal effect of emigrants on the quality of institutions. In particular, they find that over the period 1975–2000 unskilled emigration positively impacted institutional quality in origin countries using different indicators of democracy and economic freedom. Batista and Vicente (2011) constructed an experiment in Cape Verde to understand the influence of migration on the demand for political accountability. They find that migrants and return migrants that have been exposed to more democratic countries have a stronger bias on political accountability. Finally, Barsbai et al. (2017) use a quasi natural experiment to show that emigration towards democratic countries influenced electoral outcomes and political preferences in Moldova. They use the Russian financial crisis in 1998 which led a consistent part of the population to leave the country and they use variation in political ideologies and democratic traditions to analyze destination-specific political spillovers of emigration. They find that communities with a larger emigration towards more democratic countries shifted votes away from the Communist Party while those that had a strong emigration towards Russia increased their support to the Communist Party. These papers show that the exposure to more democratic values thank to migration can: (i) change the voting behavior of the migrant and (ii) have spillovers over the families and communities in the origin countries. Therefore, besides the loss of human capital, origin countries experience an inflow of new ideas from abroad that can have positive effects also on the economic side.

The lesson from these papers is that besides brain drain represents a loss of human capital and has bad short term economic consequences, in the medium and long run emigration can have also positive outcomes both in terms of growth and development, but also in terms of institutional quality. Still it remains uncertain what is the net effect of both negative and positive mechanisms.

3.4 Consequences for Destination Countries

The debate over the consequences on the destination countries has been the most lively in the past 10 years. On the one hand, Borjas (2003), Borjas (2017) and Monras (2015) show that the impact of immigration on wages is small but negative. On the other hand, there is extensive evidence that the effects of immigrants on wages and employment of natives is negligible or even positive (e.g. Card (1990, 2001), Ottaviano and Peri (2012), Beerli and Peri (2015), Foged and Peri (2016)). Still, there is no consensus on the effect of migrants on wages, however, most of the literature argues in favor of negligible or even positive effects of immigration. Very broadly, Borjas (2003), Borjas (2017) argue that following an increase in the supply of migrants which are in the same education-experience group should affect the wages of natives because the labor demand curve is negatively sloped. Other studies instead point at the imperfect substitutability of migrants and natives. For example Peri and Sparber (2009) show that immigrants specialize in different tasks than natives, thus complementing the native labor force. In general, the lack of consensus raises because of different views on the substitutability or complementarity between migrants and natives, which also leads to different estimation strategies and results. The resolution of this puzzle is also tricky due to the endogeneity raising from the non-random location choices of migrants.

Focusing on the first issue, the problem comes from the comparability between immigrants and natives. On the one hand, Borjas et al. (1996) argue that immigrants should be compared with natives of the same experience and education. This approach implicitly assumes perfect substitutability across migrants and natives within the same experience and education. On the other hand, Ottaviano and Peri (2012) and Manacorda et al. (2012) assume that they can be imperfect substitutes within the same experience-education cell. This comes from the observation that even if migrants have the same education level and experience of natives, they tend to be employed in occupations that have a skill content that is lower than that of natives (Mattoo and Neagu 2008). Therefore, an high-skilled migrant could potentially end up in a low-skilled job. The estimation strategy following these choices leads to opposite results: Borjas et al. (1996) find small but negative effects while Ottaviano and Peri (2012) and Manacorda et al. (2012) find that immigrants do not have any effect on natives and very small negative effects on previous immigrants.

This second set of results can be explained by the fact that immigrants tend to specialize in different occupations with respect to natives Peri and Sparber (2009). Therefore, they do not really compete for the same jobs, even if they share the same education and experience.

Focusing on the second issue, most of the studies rely on an instrumental strategy that uses the interaction of historical presence of immigrants across regional labor markets with aggregate flows changes. This method allows to compute reasonably exogenous changes in the supply of migrants, thus solving the endogeneity problem related to the allocation of migrants across space. This approach has been first proposed by Altonji and Card (1991) and it is also called "shift-share instrument" and has been extensively used in many papers (e.g. Card 2001; Peri and Sparber 2009; Dustmann et al. 2013). The underlining assumption is that the repartition of migrants in the past is not correlated with the current demand for immigrants. A more hybrid approach is to use a synthetic control group employed for example in Borjas (2017) and Peri and Yasenov (2015). This technique constructs a comparison group using a weighted average of possible control units; in this way, the technique allows the researcher to compare the treated group to an optimally chosen control. Few other studies have exploited exogenous episodes of supply increases, such as the return of French expatriates from Algeria (Hunt 1992), the collapse of the Soviet Union (Borjas and Doran 2015; Friedberg 2001) or the return of Germans from Romania and Bulgaria (Glitz 2012). Other approaches rely on the random allocation of refugees across space (Foged and Peri 2016) or the exploitation of policy changes which have some regional and time variation (e.g. the Swiss-EU agreement in Beerli and Peri (2015) or the Czech-German commuting policy for cross-border workers in Dustmann et al. (2017)).

3.5 Future Prospects

The main limitation to the development of the international migration literature has been the lack of data. Most of the first contributions were purely theoretical and only with the database developed by Docquier and Marfouk (2006) the literature could test many of the theoretical findings and find new patterns to analyze. The data is based on the Censuses of OECD countries and there is information on the migration stocks of foreign born by origin country for the years 1990 and 2000. This dataset was then refined to disentangle the education and gender dimensions and it has been updated with information for the year 2010.[2] The availability of these data led the field to find new cross-country evidence on migration, its determinants and consequences. One limitation of the cross-country data is that it is impossible to analyze the heterogeneity of the migration flows and it is hard to find a plausibly exogenous variation to make causal inference. Recently some datasets at the individual level

[2]See Brücker et al. (2013) for more information on the latest version of the data.

have become available for some regions and countries. This increased the opportunities for clean identification strategies. However, they are usually limited in their geographical coverage. So, it is harder to make cross-country analyses and to test the external validity of the results.

These new data have several advantages. First, they allow a more precise definition the labor markets, thus allowing researcher to focus on cities and districts rather than regions. Second, the many sources of variation allow the researchers to have cleaner identification strategies and to study the mechanisms leading to some results. Third, these data can be linked with information on firms. This employer-employee data can allow researchers to study reallocation of workers both across firms within regions, but also within firms. This opens a totally new perspective since it allows researchers to understand the role of migrants in the production processes of the firm and their contribution to productivity and growth at the micro level. For example, recent papers find that immigrants have positive effects on the productivity of the firm (Ghosh et al. 2014; Ruffner and Siegenthaler 2016; Mitaritonna et al. 2017). Many other questions can be answered using these micro data. For example it would be possible to study more in depth the substitutability versus the complementarity of migrants with native workers. It would be possible to understand wage dynamics and the reallocation of workers under different shock scenarios, such as trade liberalization and demand shocks. Finally, Ottaviano and Peri (2013) point also at the city as a new frontier for the migration literature to understand the impact of migration on agglomeration economies. This is because migrants are different than the destination population and in this offers new opportunities and threats that are worth exploring. On the one hand, migrants tend to be positively selected (i.e. they tend to be more skilled than the origin population) and they own a set of skills, tasks and values that is different from that of natives. This brings new opportunities for firms and local markets that can expand thanks to the new varieties of knowledge, capabilities and products or services. On the other hand, this poses challenges at the level of spatial congestion and social assimilation. Both positive and negative effects can now be explored in detail and provide contributions that span across different fields of economics, such as urban economics, economic geography and international trade, just to mention some.

3.6 Conclusion

In conclusion, the literature on international migration has been flourishing in the recent years especially thanks to the increased availability of new and more detailed data. While there is a consensus on the theoretical tools to be used, there are still some debates on the empirical implementation and on the results. This especially applies to the research focusing on the impact of immigrants on wages and employment of natives. These new datasets are allowing researchers to discover new mechanisms behind migration and the literature is evolving towards having cities and firms as the focus of analysis. Therefore, there is a natural shift from a more macro approach to micro which allows researchers to understand better the heterogeneity behind aggregate flows and to account more finely for winners and losers of the migration phenomenon. However, this comes at the expenses of the generality of the results which can rarely be compared across countries and regions due to the limited geographical coverage of these new datasets.

References

Altonji JG, Card D (1991) The effects of immigration on the labor market outcomes of less-skilled natives. In: Immigration, trade, and the labor market, NBER chapters. National Bureau of Economic Research, Cambridge, MA, pp 201–234

Anderson JE, van Wincoop E (2003) Gravity with gravitas: a solution to the border puzzle. Am Econ Rev 93(1):170–192

Ariu A, Docquier F, Squicciarini M (2016) Governance quality and net migration flows. Reg Sci Urban Econ 60:238–248

Barsbai T, Rapoport H, Steinmayr A, Trebesch C (2017) The effect of labor migration on the diffusion of democracy: evidence from a former Soviet Republic. Am Econ J: Appl Econ 9(3): 36–69

Batista C, Vicente PC (2011) Do migrants improve governance at home? Evidence from a voting experiment. World Bank Econ Rev 25(1):77–104

Beerli A, Peri G (2015) The labor market effects of opening the border: new evidence from Switzerland. NBER working papers 21319. National Bureau of Economic Research, Cambridge, MA

Beine, M. and Parsons, C. (2012). Climatic factors as determinants of international migration. CESifo working paper series 3747. CESifo Group, Munich

Beine M, Docquier F, Rapoport H (2001) Brain drain and economic growth: theory and evidence. J Dev Econ 64(1):275–289

Beine M, Docquier F, Ozden C (2011) Diasporas. J Dev Econ 95(1):30–41

Beine, M., Bourgeon, P., and Bricongne, J.-C. (2013). Aggregate fluctuations and international migration. CESifo working paper series 4379. CESifo Group, Munich

Beine M, Bertoli S, Moraga JF-H (2014) A practitioners' guide to gravity models of international migration. Working papers 2014-03. FEDEA, Madrid

Belot MVK, Hatton TJ (2012) Immigrant selection in the OECD. Scand J Econ 114(4):1105–1128

Berry AR, Soligo R (1969) Some welfare aspects of international migration. J Polit Econ 77(5): 778–794

Bertoli S, Fernández-Huertas Moraga J (2013) Multilateral resistance to migration. J Dev Econ 102:79–100

Bertoli S, Fernández-Huertas Moraga J (2015) The size of the cliff at the border. Reg Sci Urban Econ 51(C):1–6

Bertoli S, Moraga JF-H, Ortega F (2011) Immigration policies and the ecuadorian exodus. World Bank Econ Rev 25(1):57–76

Bertoli S, Brücker H, Moraga JF-H (2013) The European crisis and migration to Germany: expectations and the diversion of migration flows. Working papers 2013-03. FEDEA, Madrid

Bhagwati J, Hamada K (1974) The brain drain, international integration of markets for professionals and unemployment: a theoretical analysis. J Dev Econ 1(1):19–42

Borjas G (1987) Self-selection and the earnings of immigrants. Am Econ Rev 77(4):531–553

Borjas GJ (2003) The labor demand curve is downward sloping: reexamining the impact of immigration on the labor market. Q J Econ 118(4):1335–1374

Borjas GJ (2017) The wage impact of the marielitos: a reappraisal. Ind Labor Relat Rev 70(5): 1077–1110

Borjas GJ, Doran KB (2015) Cognitive mobility: labor market responses to supply shocks in the space of ideas. J Labor Econ 33(S1):S109–S145
Borjas GJ, Freeman RB, Katz L (1996) Searching for the effect of immigration on the labor market. Am Econ Rev 86(2):246–251
Brücker H, Capuano S, Marfouk A (2013) Education, gender and international migration: insights from a panel-dataset 1980–2010. Technical report, Mimeo, Norface Research Programme on Migration
Card D (1990) The impact of the mariel boatlift on the miami labor market. Ind Labor Relat Rev 43(2):245–257
Card D (2001) Immigrant inflows, native outflows, and the local labor market impacts of higher immigration. J Labor Econ 19(1):22–64
Docquier F, Marfouk A (2006) International migration by educational attainment (1990–2000). In: Ozden C, Schiff M (eds) International migration, remittances the brain drain. Palgrave Macmillan, New York, pp 151–199
Docquier F, Rapoport H (2012) Globalization, brain drain, and development. J Econ Lit 50(3): 681–730
Docquier F, Peri G, Ruyssen I (2014) The cross-country determinants of potential and actual migration. Int Migr Rev 48(1):37–99
Docquier F, Lodigiani E, Rapoport H, Schiff M (2016) Emigration and democracy. J Dev Econ 120(C):209–223
Dustmann C, Frattini T, Preston IP (2013) The effect of immigration along the distribution of wages. Rev Econ Stud 80(1):145–173
Dustmann C, Schnberg U, Stuhler J (2017) Labor supply shocks, native wages, and the adjustment of local employment. Q J Econ 132(1):435–483
Faini R (2007) Migration and remittances. The effects on the origin country. Revue d'economie du developpement 15(2):153–182
Foged M, Peri G (2016) Immigrants' effect on native workers: new analysis on longitudinal data. Am Econ J: Appl Econ 8(2):1–34
Friedberg RM (2001) The impact of mass migration on the Israeli labor market. Q J Econ 116(4): 1373–1408
Ghosh A, Mayda AM, Ortega F (2014) The impact of skilled foreign workers on firms: an investigation of publicly traded U.S. firms. CReAM discussion paper series 1442, Centre for Research and Analysis of Migration (CReAM), Department of Economics, University College London
Glitz A (2012) The labor market impact of immigration: a quasi-experiment exploiting immigrant location rules in Germany. J Labor Econ 30(1):175–213
Grogger J, Hanson GH (2011) Income maximization and the selection and sorting of international migrants. J Dev Econ 95(1):42–57
Grubel HB, Scott AD (1966) The international flow of human capital. Am Econ Rev 56(1–2): 268–274
Hunt J (1992) The impact of the 1962 repatriates from Algeria on the French labor market. Ind Labor Relat Rev 45(3):556–572
Johnson H (1967) Some economic aspects of the brain drain. Pak Dev Rev 7(3):379–411
Manacorda M, Manning A, Wadsworth J (2012) The impact of immigration on the structure of wages: theory and evidence from Britain. J Eur Econ Assoc 10(1):120–151
Mariani F (2007) Migration as an antidote to rent-seeking. J Dev Econ 84:609–630
Mattoo A, Neagu IC, Özden C (2008) Brain waste? Educated immigrants in the US labor market. J Dev Econ 87(2):255–269
Mayda A (2010) International migration: a panel data analysis of the determinants of bilateral flows. J Popul Econ 23(4):1249–1274
McCulloch R, Yellen JL (1977) Factor mobility, regional development, and the distribution of income. J Polit Econ 85(1):79–96

McFadden D (1984) Econometric analysis of qualitative response models. In: Griliches Z, Intriligator M (eds) Handbook of econometrics, vol 2. Elsevier, Amsterdam
McKenzie D, Theoharides C, Yang D (2014) Distortions in the international migrant labor market: evidence from Filipino migration and wage responses to destination country economic shocks. Am Econ J: Appl Econ 6(2):49–75
Mitaritonna C, Orefice G, Peri G (2017) Immigrants and firms' productivity: evidence from France. Eur Econ Rev 96:62–82
Monras J (2015) Immigration and wage dynamics: evidence from the Mexican peso crisis. IZA discussion papers 8924, Institute for the Study of Labor (IZA)
Mountford A (1997) Can a brain drain be good for growth in the source economy? J Dev Econ 53(2):287303
Ortega F, Peri G (2012) The effect of income and immigration policies on international migrations. Migr Stud 1(1):47–74
Ottaviano GIP, Peri G (2012) Rethinking the effect of immigration on wages. J Eur Econ Assoc 10(1):152–197
Ottaviano G, Peri G (2013) New frontiers of immigration research: cities and firms. J Reg Sci 53(1): 1–7
Ozden C, Parsons CR, Schiff M, Walmsley TL (2011) Where on earth is everybody? The evolution of global bilateral migration 1960–2000. World Bank Econ Rev 25(1):12–56
Peri G, Sparber C (2009) Task specialization, immigration, and wages. Am Econ J: Appl Econ 1(3): 135–169
Peri G, Yasenov V (2015) The labor market effects of a refugee wave: applying the synthetic control method to the mariel boatlift. NBER working papers 21801. National Bureau of Economic Research, Cambridge, MA
Ruffner J, Siegenthaler M (2016) From labor to cash flow? The impacts of abolishing all immigration restrictions for EU workers on Swiss firms. Technical report, Mimeo, ETH Zurich
Sjaastad L (1962) The costs and returns of human migration. J Polit Econ 70(5):80–93
Spilimbergo A (2009) Democracy and foreign education. Am Econ Rev 99(1):528–543
Stark O, Wang Y (2002) Inducing human capital formation: migration as a substitute for subsidies. J Public Econ 86(1):29–46
Stark O, Helmenstein C, Prskawetz A (1997) A brain gain with a brain drain. Econ Lett 55(2):22734
Vidal J-P (1998) The effect of emigration on human capital formation. J Popul Econ 11(4):589–600

Part II
State of the Art and Future Challenges in Migration Research Around the World

Chapter 4
State of the Art and Future Challenges of Interregional Migration Empirical Research in North America

Isha Rajbhandari and Mark Partridge

Abstract This book chapter offers an overview of the literature on the determinants of U.S. interregional migration trends. With its particularly high rates of internal migration, the United States serves as an interesting case study for analyzing regional migration trends. The contributions highlight the migration trends that are specific to the country and include in-depth discussions about the various factors that have shaped them over time. The aim of the book chapter is to provide a comprehensive review that not only accounts for the previous research, but also incorporates recent developments in migration literature. One of the important contributions of the book chapter is its discussion on the linkages between migration and climate change in the U.S. The chapter also identifies the current gaps in the literature and suggests possible novel avenues for future research on interregional migration.

Keywords Interregional migration · Climate-related migration · Determinants of migration · Equilibrium · Disequilibrium

4.1 Introduction

The United States is one of the world's most mobile countries, which makes it an interesting case study when examining migration trends. The high rate of U.S. migration has resulted in a flexible labor market (Obstfeld and Peri 1998) and significant regional growth differentials (Partridge 2010; Partridge et al. 2012).

I. Rajbhandari (✉)
Department of Economics, University of Puget Sound, Tacoma, WA, USA
e-mail: irajbhandari@pugetsound.edu

M. Partridge
Department of Agricultural, Environmental, and Development Economics, The Ohio State University, Columbus, OH, USA

Jinan University, Guangzhou, China

Gran Sasso Science Institute, L'Aquila, Italy
e-mail: partridge.27@osu.edu

B. Biagi et al. (eds.), *New Frontiers in Interregional Migration Research*,
Advances in Spatial Science, https://doi.org/10.1007/978-3-319-75886-2_4

According to a 2009 report by the U.S. Census Bureau, about 20% of the population changed residences each year in 1960s. Even though the migration rate has declined, the report finds that about 13% of the population has annually changed residence since 2000 (Partridge 2010). During the 1970s and 1980s, the South, Southwest, and Rocky Mountain regions experienced high rates of in-migration from the Great Lakes states and the Northeast region, traditionally considered as the core region of the country (Partridge 2010). This shift in the interregional migration trend has been attributed to the lagging job growth in agricultural, mineral extraction, and heavy manufacturing industries in the core region and a corresponding increase in job opportunities in the South and West (Greenwood 1985; Rappaport 2007). The observed migration pattern is also consistent with amenity-led migration (Graves 1979) to places endowed with high levels of natural amenities such as warm climate, pleasant landscape, lakes/oceans, and mountains (Partridge 2010), resulting in positive population growth in both rural and urban areas. The willingness of households to migrate serves as a primary driver of regional shifts in labor supply (Chen and Rosenthal 2008). Nevertheless, U.S. migration trends have undergone several key changes, most of which have been documented and analyzed in the migration and regional literature.

Studies show that migration in the U.S. is selective in nature. In their review of the existing research on internal U.S. migration, Greenwood (1975) states that 'migration is selective of the younger, better-educated, and more high-productive workers' (p. 415). Similarly, a more recent contribution by Molloy et al. (2011) shows how the average propensity to migrate internally increases with education (Faggian et al. 2017). Increased availability of micro-data has allowed researchers to better analyze the migration behaviors of highly educated individuals such as graduates, scientists, and inventors (Faggian and Franklin 2014; Winters 2011b). Literature on elderly mobility has also received special attention because the migration trends and determinants of the elderly is different from other demographic groups (Graves and Knapp 1988). Studies find that elderly migrants prefer locations with low taxes on property, estate, inheritance, and school (Gale and Heath 2000; Walters 2002). In addition, the extant literature focuses on studying the economic and non-economic determinants of migration (Greenwood 1985; Graves 1979), reversal of migration flows from metropolitan to nonmetropolitan areas (McGranahan et al. 2010; Rupasingha et al. 2015), declining rates of economic migration (Partridge et al. 2012; Kotkin 2009), and commuting (Baum-Snow, 2010; Lee et al. 2006).

The main objective of this chapter is to provide a review of the extant literature on the determinants of U.S. interregional migration, while highlighting the prominent migration trends. The chapter also identifies the current gaps in the literature and suggests possible extensions for future work. It focuses on reviewing recent developments in migration research that are missing from previous reviews such as Greenwood (1975) and Faggian et al. (2015). One of the contributions is that it includes climate-related migration research that highlights the linkages between climate change and U.S. migration, and identifies the associated challenges. The geographic scope of the review is limited to the U.S. subnational regions, though at times, we compare these contributions with relevant studies in Europe and Australia.

While international migration is also an important migration feature, a discussion of the international migration literature is beyond the scope of this review. Most of the contributions discussed in this chapter examine migration trends of the general populace. Existing literature on high-skilled migration is discussed separately from the general population migration because of its intrinsic peculiarities and differences (Faggian et al. 2017), as well as its important link to regional economic growth.

The chapter is organized as follows. The second and third sections review the past (pre-2000) and current (post-2000) contributions on the determinants of interregional migration in the U.S. The fourth section reviews literature on climate change migration. The last section concludes and discusses current gaps in the literature, while providing possible avenues for future research.

4.2 Past Literature

Historically, U.S. migration literature has mostly been focused on analyzing the economic and non-economic determinants of interregional migration. The debate on whether job opportunities and income, or alternatively, amenities have a greater influence on internal migration has been central to the extant literature. Well-renowned economists Michael Greenwood and Philip Graves have played crucial roles in influencing the literature to gradually develop along the two distinct lines (Graves 1980). The unprecedented decline in percentage of U.S. population residing in the metropolitan areas, coupled with increased migration to the South and West in the 1970s, stimulated the interest in amenity-based migration in the U.S.

The spatial equilibrium model of migration, represented by Graves and Linneman (1979) and Polachek and Horvath (1977), posits that market rents and wages adjust so as to leave utility constant across space. In this case, migration occurs to facilitate an adjustment to a new equilibrium and is a result of changes in demand for location-specific amenities (Graves 1980). Graves (1980) demonstrates that when income levels and unemployment rates are taken into account, certain climatological amenity variables such as heating and cooling degree days, annual temperature variance, relative humidity, and wind speed are important in explaining net population migration during the 1960s (Greenwood and Hunt 1989). Using post-1970 Census data, Beale (1977) finds that non-metropolitan counties were growing more rapidly than metropolitan counties, thus providing empirical support to the spatial equilibrium model of migration (Graves 1980).

Several other theoretical and empirical studies have found climate to be an important determinant of net migration in the 1960s and 1970s (Cebula and Vedder 1973; Graves and Linneman 1979; Graves and Mueser 1993; Krumm 1983; Schachter and Althuas 1993). These studies, mostly conducted at the metropolitan statistical area (MSA) level of analysis, argue that income and unemployment differences across cities reflect not the real utility differentials, commonly assumed in the literature, but rather the compensation required for spatial indifference that account for the changes in the demand for location-specific goods such as climate

(Graves 1980). In their seminal work, Roback (1982) demonstrates that the value of amenities is capitalized in both the wages and rents. The empirical evidence shows that the combination of low wages in the West in the 1970s and extremely high growth rates of population suggest that the regional differences in earnings can be largely accounted for by regional differences in local amenities.

On the contrary, the proponents of the disequilibrium model of migration view the system as initially being out of equilibrium, leading to income and employment differentials across space (Greenwood 1985). These differentials encourage migration from low-income to high-income regions, and subsequently reduce the differences. In this model, jobs and wages are considered to be more important than location-specific amenities in explaining net migration. Using migration data derived from a 1% sample of all persons employed in Social Security-covered jobs from 1958 to 1975 at the level of Bureau of Economic Analysis economic areas (BEA), Greenwood and Hunt (1989) find a positive and significant impact of rate of employment growth on net metropolitan migration, whereas, the impact of amenity variables is mostly insignificant. Contrary to Graves (1979, 1980), this study finds no obvious relationship between increasing importance of location-based amenities and rising real incomes. Nonetheless, to the extent that migrants are attracted to job opportunities and jobs are growing rapidly in amenity-rich areas, Greenwood and Hunt (1989) hypothesize that amenity variables might indirectly influence migration.

Numerous studies such as DaVanzo (1978, 1983), Porell (1982), and Herzog and Schlottmann (1984) find that interregional wage differentials play an important role in influencing migration in the U.S. Porell (1982) compares the relative importance of economic versus quality of life factors in explaining migration at the MSA-level over the 1965–1970 period. The study finds migration to be more responsive to economic factors, even though quality of life factors are also important. Similarly, DaVanzo (1978) uses the Panel System of Income Dynamics (PSID) data to find that families whose heads are looking for work are more likely to move than families whose heads are not looking. Likewise, Herzog and Schlottmann (1984) use the 1970 Census Public Use Micro data Samples (PUMS) to conclude that unemployment doubles the likelihood of interstate labor force migration.

Although migration models are typically formulated based on the behavioral foundations of individuals and under the individual utility maximization framework, aggregate data at the state- and county-level are frequently employed to estimate these models (Greenwood 1975, 1985). Age, education, income, employment status, and race are personal characteristics that could significantly influence migration (Greenwood 1975). Therefore, including only origin and destination characteristics such as median age, median number of years of schooling, mean income, mean January temperatures, and unemployment rates to proxy for individuals characteristics of the migrants could lead to biased results because they do not account for the heterogeneity in the demographic and socioeconomic characteristics of the migrants and the stayers (Greenwood et al. 1991). Assuming that migration frequently involves change in occupation and/or industry of employment, aggregate-level analysis that attributes increases in earnings entirely to change in location can overstate the returns to migration (Greenwood 1975). Likewise, higher unemployment rates differentially influence migration of unemployed individuals relative to their employed counterparts, which is not apparent in studies that attempt to explain migration using aggregate data (Greenwood 1985).

In the past literature, limited attention was paid to the role of personal characteristics on migration decisions due to the aggregate nature of available data. The use of aggregated data could bias the effect of personal characteristics which are important determinants of an individual's decision to migrate (Greenwood 1985; Navratil and Doyle 1977). Nonetheless, the availability of individual-level data has allowed several studies to use micro-data to estimate the impact of personal characteristics on migration behavior, thereby improving focus on the decision-making unit i.e. family, household, or individual (DaVanzo 1978, 1983; Herzog and Schlottmann 1984). The longitudinal nature of these datasets, to some extent, also permit the study of significant life-cycle influences on migration decisions (Greenwood 1985). Polachek and Horvarth (1977) use PSID data to emphasize the importance of life-cycle phenomena and family considerations on migration decisions. Likewise, studies can account for the influence of past migration experiences on current migration decisions, as well as assess the returns to migration (Greenwood 1985). However, prior to the 2000s, individual-level analysis was at its beginning stages with migration being defined over a period of time, and consequently, studies could only assess the importance of life-cycle variables within a cross-sectional framework (Greenwood 1985).

An important consequence of life-cycle considerations was the recognition that age is one of the strongest empirical predictors of geographical mobility behavior (Plane 1993). Studies have found that the effects of economic opportunity differentials on migration decline sharply with age (Morgan and Robb 1981). The authors find that the impact of relative income and employment growth on migration is the highest for individuals within the 25–34 year-old age group. Likewise, Graves (1979) finds that while areas with higher income attract more whites between the ages of 25–35 years, the effect drops significantly for individuals over 35 years of age.

Elderly migrants have received considerable attention in the U.S. migration literature because their migration trends and determinants are different from other demographic groups (Graves and Knapp 1988). In their work, Graves (1979) and Graves and Regulska (1982) show that retirement leads to an increase in amenity-led migration relative to active workers. Since the retired elderly are not competing in the labor markets, they tend to prefer locations where a larger percentage of the amenity values are capitalized in labor markets relative to land markets (Graves and Knapp 1988; Graves and Waldman 1991). Migrants above the age of 65 years are attracted to areas with warm climates, coastal location, large elderly populations, relatively many residents of the respondent's own race, high median home values and income taxes, and low property taxes, poverty rates, and public school expenditures (Newbold 1996; Walters 2002; Clark and Hunter 1992; Assadian 1995; Gale and Heath 2000). Using 1990 Census micro-data, Newbold (1996) finds that elderly individuals above 65 years of age are likely to leave states with low per capita Medicare expenditures, low population, cold winters, and relatively few residents of the respondent's own race. Likewise, Walters (1994) finds that mild winters and clear summers are the most attractive destination characteristics for the elderly in the U.S.

In the U.S., elderly migrants congregate within a few key destinations, mainly Florida, Arizona, and California, which experience demographic, economic, and cultural changes over a relatively short period of time (Bean et al. 1994; Deller 1995; Rice and Pepper 1997; Sastry 1992). Elderly migration increases the geographic concentration of older population in these destinations, which could influence the composition of public goods and services, and therefore requires special attention. High wealth and increased expenditures in the form of health care and demand for local services from the retired elderly could create a multiplier effect and contribute to increased regional growth in the destination. Serow and Haas (1992) estimate the direct and indirect effects of retirement migration in western North Carolina and find that every dollar spent by migrants in the local economy generated nearly another dollar of total economic outputs through increased employment and spending by labor force participants. They find the economic effects to be greatest in labor-intensive sectors of the economy.

4.3 Current Literature

The internal migration flow in the U.S. is amongst one of highest in the world. However, the rate has been declining in recent decades, with the decline becoming more apparent at the end of the 1990s (Partridge et al. 2012). The decline in interregional migration could suggest that the U.S. has entered an era that favors 'new localism' (Kotkin 2009) and increased rootedness (Cooke 2011). The post-2000 period has seen a significant decline in domestic migration rates (Rupasingha et al. 2015). Figure 4.1 uses the U.S. Census data on migration to demonstrate the decline in the geographical mobility rates across counties and across states, respectively, from 2000 to 2015.

As seen in Fig. 4.1, the migration rates across counties and states in the U.S. follow a similar trend and have been steadily declining over time. The decline is steeper between 2004 and 2008, after which the migration rates have remained steady but low. Even though the direction of migration flows in the U.S. has historically been from nonmetropolitan to metropolitan areas, in the recent decades, the direction has reversed, with more people moving from metropolitan areas to nonmetropolitan areas (Rupasingha et al. 2015). About 220,000 more people moved to nonmetropolitan areas from metropolitan areas than the reverse between 1995 and 2000 (Rupasingha et al. 2015). Figures 4.2 and 4.3 below show the migration inflows between metropolitan and non-metropolitan areas, and principal cities and suburban areas, respectively.

Figure 4.2 demonstrates the migration inflows in metropolitan and non-metropolitan areas from 2000 to 2014. Contrary to the literature, the figure depicts a higher number of people migrating to metropolitan areas compared to nonmetropolitan areas. One of the reasons could be that the definition of metropolitan areas changes over time. The new metro definitions often include what were fast

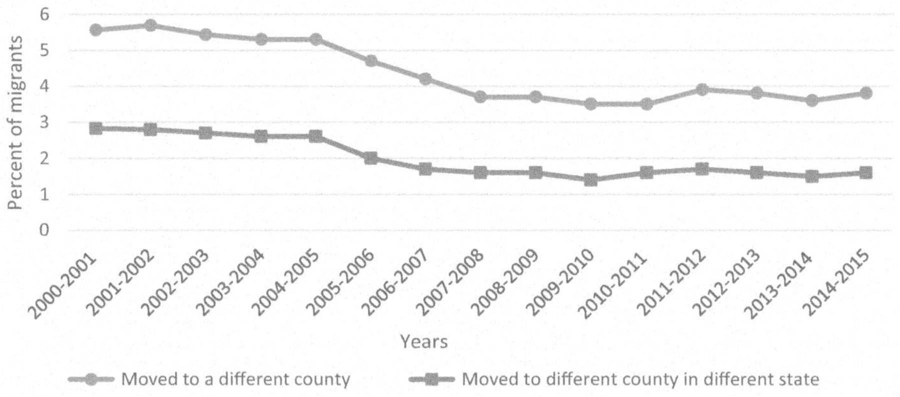

Fig. 4.1 Annual Gross Migration Rates: 2000–2015. Source: U.S. Census Bureau, Current Population Survey, Table A-1. Annual Geographical Mobility Rates, By Type of Movement: 1947–2015, available at: http://www.census.gov/population/socdemo/migration/tab-a-1.pdf (accessed April, 2017)

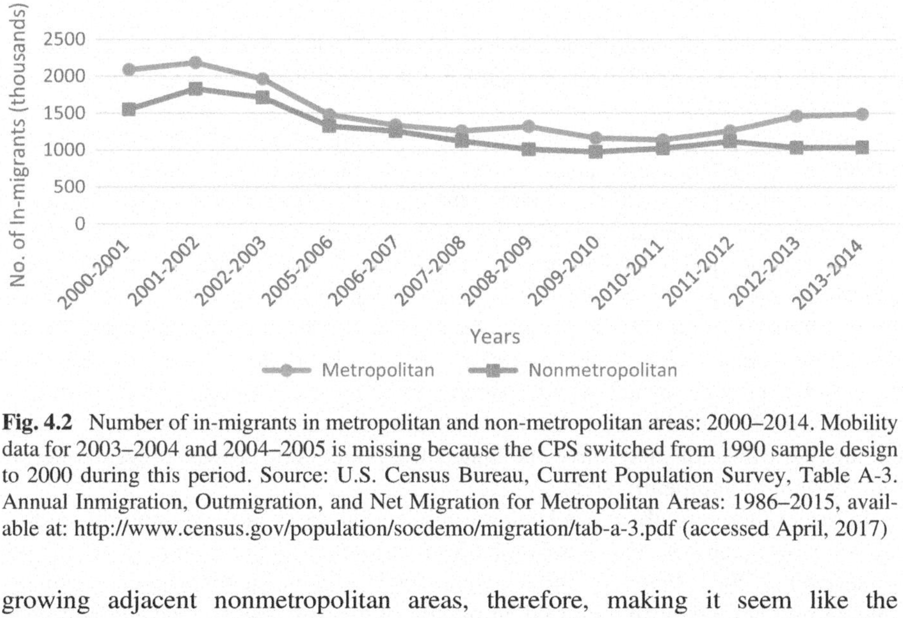

Fig. 4.2 Number of in-migrants in metropolitan and non-metropolitan areas: 2000–2014. Mobility data for 2003–2004 and 2004–2005 is missing because the CPS switched from 1990 sample design to 2000 during this period. Source: U.S. Census Bureau, Current Population Survey, Table A-3. Annual Inmigration, Outmigration, and Net Migration for Metropolitan Areas: 1986–2015, available at: http://www.census.gov/population/socdemo/migration/tab-a-3.pdf (accessed April, 2017)

growing adjacent nonmetropolitan areas, therefore, making it seem like the remaining nonmetropolitan areas are losing population. To provide a better idea about the distribution of population within the metropolitan areas, Fig. 4.3 separates the migration inflows to metropolitan areas between the urban core and the suburban areas from 2000 to 2014. The figure clearly depicts that more people are migrating to the suburban areas than the urban core of the metropolitan areas. This shows that suburbanization has positively influenced the movement of people to areas adjacent to the urban core and allowed for the expansion of metropolitan areas. Additionally,

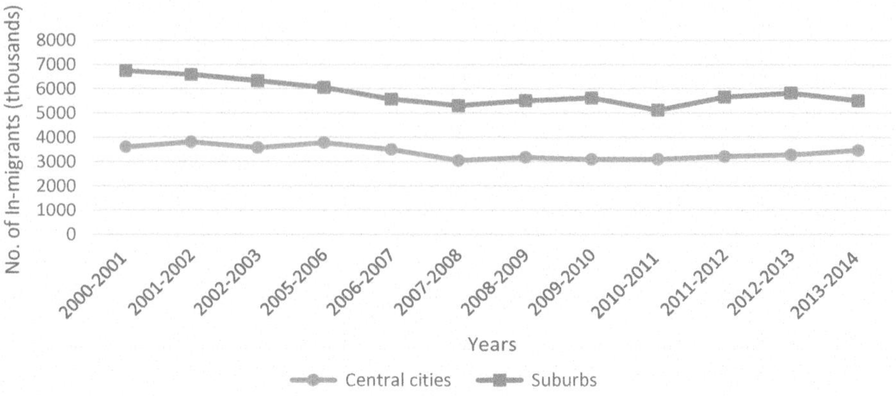

Fig. 4.3 Number of in-migrants in central cities and suburbs: 2000–2014. Mobility data for 2003–2004 and 2004–2005 is missing because the CPS switched from 1990 sample design to 2000 during this period. Source: U.S. Census Bureau, Current Population Survey, Table A-3. Annual Inmigration, Outmigration, and Net Migration for Metropolitan Areas: 1986–2015, available at: http://www.census.gov/population/socdemo/migration/tab-a-3.pdf (accessed April, 2017)

the figure depicts an increasing trend of people moving away from central cities. Similar to Fig. 4.1, both Figs. 4.2 and 4.3 also highlight the declining trend in U.S. migration flows.

The debate on whether economic or non-economic characteristics have a greater influence on the interregional migration trends in the U.S. is ongoing. Recent research highlights three main theoretical frameworks that explore U.S. interregional migration in the twentieth century, namely agglomeration/new economic geography (Tabuchi and Thisse 2002; Glaeser and Resseger 2010), job opportunities (Storper and Scott 2009; Scott 2010), and amenity migration (Graves 1979, 1980). Partridge (2010) explores the accuracy with which the three models can predict the actual interregional migration trends over the last four to five decades. The results show the actual growth patterns to be most consistent with amenity-led migration as the initial factor behind growth, although agglomeration economies and cumulative causation may have facilitated the population growth process once it took hold in high-amenity areas.

In recent literature, there has been a significant increase in the number of studies focusing on amenities and quality of life as important determinants of migration (Glaeser et al. 2001; Partridge and Rickman 2003). U.S. households are increasingly valuing weather's contribution to their quality of life, especially since the latter half of the twentieth century (Cragg and Kahn 1999; Costa and Kahn 2003). Rise in income levels over a certain threshold has allowed people to consider amenities in their location decisions, leading to increased valuation of nice weather as a consumption amenity and consequently, increased weather-related movements (Rappaport 2007). Therefore, areas with higher winter temperature are positively correlated with population growth whereas areas with higher summer temperature and humidity are negatively correlated with population growth (Rappaport 2007;

Poston et al. 2009). Similarly, vicinity to the ocean as a proxy for coastal amenities and USDA amenity index as a proxy for natural amenities have been extensively used in migration studies (Faggian and Franklin 2014; Nelson 2009; Partridge et al. 2008, 2010, 2012). Partridge et al. (2008) uses county growth patterns from 1950 to 2000 to quantify the economic significance of amenity migration. Their work indicates that amenity-led growth results in population growth in the peripheral areas of the country, with typical nonmetropolitan areas gaining about 32% population over the study period.

In contrast, Storper and Scott (2009) argue that job availability and not household amenities determine U.S. regional dynamics. The authors reject the notion that households sort based on their quality of life. Scott (2010) uses fractional-response regression models to assess the differential impacts of local economic structure, employment opportunities, and amenities on the destination choices of engineers from 1994 to 1999. At least in the case of engineers of working age, the author finds that local economic structure and job opportunities play the dominant role in determining their locational choices. However, the results suggest that warmer winters have some positive impact on the locational choices of engineers who are retired or close to retirement, although the magnitude of the effect is significantly smaller relative to that of job opportunities.

Studies have attempted to reconcile the disparity in views regarding the importance of economic and non-economic determinants of migration. Chen and Rosenthal (2008) use panel of quality of life and business environment measures from 1970 to 1990 to measure whether households move for amenities or job opportunities. They find that firms prefer large and growing cities, and workers, especially those with high human capital, migrate to cities with improving quality of business environments. On the contrary, they find that areas with improving quality of life and consumer amenities tend to differentially attract retirees, which is consistent with the life course and migration literature (Plane and Heins 2003; Etzo 2008).

Nonetheless, research suggests that the importance of economic and non-economic factors might vary over time and across space. Sasser (2010) examines the role of labor market conditions, per capita income, and housing affordability in determining domestic migration at the state level from 1977 to 2006. All three measures, though significant, vary in importance and magnitude over time. Labor market conditions and per capita incomes have had the greatest impact on state-level migration, with housing affordability playing a secondary role. However, since the late 1980s, the importance of housing affordability has increased considerably, while the importance of the other two variables has decreased (Sasser 2010). This is consistent with recent studies exploring the importance of employment and housing affordability on migration across metropolitan areas (Bluestone 2006; Sum et al. 2007). Studies find that natural amenities are playing a smaller role in population redistribution in the 2000s relative to the 1990s (Partridge et al. 2012; Rickman and Rickman 2011). Additionally, economic factors are dominant in determining the migration flows during recessions and energy shocks (Partridge and Rickman 2003). In their work, Partridge and Rickman (2003) find that for energy producing regions and manufacturing-intensive Rustbelt states, economic factors are dominant whereas, in the Sunbelt states, amenities are dominant.

Outside the U.S., however, the debate between economic and non-economic determinants is not as prominent in the literature. Studies do not find amenities to be a major factor in determining migration. For example, Ferguson et al. (2007) find that in Canada, amenity migration is not dominant, although Polèse (2009) suggests that this trend might be changing in parts of British Columbia and in communities of Atlantic Canada. Similarly, Cheshire and Magrini (2006) find evidence that amenity migration has not played a prominent role in influencing migration flows across countries in Europe. They argue that language and cultural barriers play an important role in limiting amenity-led migration in the region.

In the last decade, the number of studies analyzing the migration behavior of high-skilled individuals such as graduates, scientists, engineers, and inventors has increased dramatically (Faggian and McCann 2006, 2009a; Faggian et al. 2017; Zucker and Darby 2007). The two main reasons motivating this surge include the important role of high-skilled individuals for local economic growth (Glaeser and Shapiro 2003; Simon and Nardinelli 2002; Whisler et al. 2008) and the availability of micro-level data on highly educated individuals that has allowed researchers to incorporate personal characteristics in their empirical analyses (Faggian et al. 2017). Considering that greater proportions of high-skilled households are positively correlated with employment growth in cities (Glaeser and Shapiro 2003; Simon and Nardinelli 2002), researchers are highly interested in studying the migration decisions of high-skilled individuals (Faggian and McCann 2009b; Gottlieb and Joseph 2006; Scott 2010).

High-educated households tend to migrate to places with high quality business environments (Chen and Rosenthal 2008). Highly skilled and educated individuals earn an urban wage premium, which makes it beneficial for them to migrate to urban areas (Bacolod et al. 2009). This is specifically pronounced for young and highly educated individuals, and demonstrates their desire to gain higher returns on their human capital investment through higher wages (Chen and Rosenthal 2008; Elvery 2010; Plane and Jurjevich 2009; Winters 2011a). Betz et al. (2016) examines the net migration patterns of bachelor and post-graduate degree holders across U.S. metropolitan areas. The results suggest that agglomeration is the predominant driver of human capital migration after 2000. The authors find some evidence that in the 1990s, the growth of 'smart' industries had a significant impact on attracting high-educated workers. In contrast, Adamson et al. (2004) find that amenities play an important role in attracting highly educated individuals to metropolitan areas in the U.S. The study also finds that skill-based productivity factors are essential for attracting high-skilled individuals, specifically to the larger metropolitan areas.

The existing stock of human capital in an area can also play an important role in attracting and retaining a high-skilled workforce (Berry and Glaeser 2005; Waldorf 2009; Whisler et al. 2008). The knowledge and productivity spillovers from the initial share of educated workers increases the productivity and wages of other educated workers, thereby incentivizing them to migrate to areas with more highly educated workers (Moretti 2004). Cities with higher initial shares of college-educated workers experience greater increases in the proportion of college-educated workers residing there (Berry and Glaeser 2005). Even though the study is specific to the human capital migration prior to 2000s, it provides important insights into the divergence of human capital across cities. Likewise, Winters (2011b) examines the relationship between human capital and population growth for nonmetropolitan counties in the U.S. between 1995 and 2011. They find that in-migration of students enrolled in higher education explains most of the relationship between human capital and nonmetropolitan migration. This suggests that the stock of human capital only increases net migration to nonmetropolitan areas that have access to higher education institutions. Smart cities are becoming more educated over time in part because they are able to retain recent graduates from local universities, who had originally moved there to pursue higher education (Winters 2011a). Yet, Betz et al. (2016) find that university graduates are avoiding metropolitan areas with high initial shares of university graduates since 2000, probably due to more labor supply competition. Rather, they appear to be most attracted to more populated metropolitan areas with better opportunities for labor matching.

While increased access to detailed data on highly educated individuals has contributed to improved studies on interregional migration behavior of high-skilled individuals in several European countries and Australia, equivalent studies in the U.S. have been limited due to restricted data availability (Faggian et al. 2017). Nonetheless, access to some individual-level datasets such as the Scientists and Engineers Statistical Data (SESTAT) system from the National Science Foundation, with longitudinal data on education and employment of the college-educated science and engineering workforce in the U.S., and the Integrated Postsecondary Education Data System (IPEDS) from the National Center for Education Statistics, with data on postsecondary institutions, have increased recent research on high-skilled migration (Faggian et al. 2017).

The migration literature has often identified the presence of a rural-urban wage disparity, with the wages in the urban areas being higher than in the rural areas, as an important pull factor for individuals to move to urban areas from rural areas (Muhlenkamp and Waldorf 2008). Research has found migration to be an effective mechanism for redistributing population from rural to urban areas (Ambinakudige and Parisi 2015). Nonetheless, there is concern over whether the prevalent urban-rural wage disparity is contributing to brain drain in the rural areas by attracting young and highly educated individuals from rural areas to higher paying jobs in the urban areas. Muhlenkamp and Waldorf (2008) show that rurality of the place of work has a strong and significant negative impact on an individual's income, especially among the young and highly educated workforce in Illinois, Indiana, Ohio, and Iowa. Their results suggest that individuals working in rural areas earn 15% less than those who work in the most urban areas, *ceteris paribus*, which encourages educated individuals to migrate to urban areas for higher wages.

Given that there are significant differences between the rural and urban areas, rural to urban migration has played a prominent role in the U.S. migration literature. However, since the early 1970s, the direction of migration has often been from urban to rural areas (Rupasingha et al. 2015). Researchers have proposed several hypotheses to explain why more people and firms are moving to nonmetropolitan areas. First, amenity-based migration could play an important role in influencing migration to high-amenity nonmetropolitan areas (Gottlieb and Joseph 2006; McGranahan et al. 2010; Rappaport 2007). Second, suburbanization allowed metropolitan areas to expand or people to move to areas adjacent to metropolitan areas. Population growth in nonmetropolitan areas may depend on the proximity to urban areas, which allows for rural-to-urban commuting (Cromartie 1998; Partridge et al. 2008; Partridge et al. 2010a). Rupasingha et al. (2015) show that while natural amenities are a strong predictor of internal migration flows in the U.S., the effect in nonmetropolitan counties may be diminishing over time. The study also finds that migration responds to agglomeration economies, even in nonmetropolitan counties, thereby suggesting that nonmetropolitan areas require some threshold of agglomeration to attract and retain migrants.

Sprawling urban areas have resulted in a large number of rural areas being closely tied to suburban and urban areas within commuting distances. Even though commuting patterns within the U.S. have not been as extensively studied compared to Europe, they have important implications for local economic growth (Findeis et al. 2009; Partridge et al. 2010a). Goetz et al. (2010) utilizes network science to analyze commuting patterns and understand how they influence local economic growth. The results suggest that counties receiving a greater mass of in-commuters experience faster economic growth for their residents. On the contrary, counties experiencing a greater mass of out-commuters are associated with significantly lower economic growth. The results are consistent with similar studies conducted in other countries such as UK (Green 2007), Germany (Patuelli et al. 2009) and Canada (Shearmur and Motte 2009).

According to a report by the American Community Survey, commutes accounted for less than 20% of all trips taken in 2009. With changing economic structure due to the decentralization of jobs and residences from the central cities, shifts in commuting flows could effectively reflect how the employment growth and locations are changing over time and space (Lee et al. 2006). Present evidence indicates that commuting flows have changed from primarily being within-central city to becoming within-suburb (Baum-Snow 2010). Some studies show that changes in economic structure, as well as declines in city transport cost due to construction of highways, have allowed commuters and firms to spread out while maintaining similar levels of productivity (Baum-Snow 2010). However, Fallah et al. (2012) find that more dense U.S. metropolitan areas have higher levels of productivity, all else constant. Lee et al. (2006) investigate the historical changes in economic structure, and the spatial distribution of jobs and community patterns with respect to increasing suburbanization in U.S. cities. The study shows a strong growth of suburban areas relative to central cities, increased urbanization economies in suburban areas, and a significant increase in total commuting flows, with increasing commuting trips ending in the suburbs and declining trips ending in the central cities.

4.4 Climate Change and Migration

Natural hazards such as droughts, floods, tornadoes, hurricanes, and other natural hazards pose substantial costs to the society in terms of physical and economic damage. According to the report by National Oceanic and Atmospheric Administration, in 2011 the United States set a new record of weather-related disasters due to an unprecedented number of tornadoes in the Southeast, heavy flooding in the Ohio Valley, and record droughts and fires in Texas (Schultz and Elliott 2013). The increase in frequency and scale of such hazardous events, along with growing concern over the impacts of global climate change, has resulted in increased scholarly attention to the implications of natural hazards on demographic processes, including migration (Elliott 2015; Pais and Elliot 2008; Groen and Polivka 2010; Gutmann and Field 2010; Hugo 2011; Hunter 2005; Hunter and Nawrotzki 2016). Most of the empirical research on climate-change migration has focused on housing, labor, and agricultural markets.

The existing literature defines the research on natural hazards and migration using two main dimensions. Some studies explain the relationship based on how migration influences social vulnerability that affects individuals' ability to prepare for or recover from environmental hazards (Cutter et al. 2008; Emrich and Cutter 2011; Johnson and Krishnamurthy 2010; McLeman 2009). Another dimension utilizes information on how acute or chronic natural hazards influence migration patterns, which include outmigration, as well as return migration to disaster areas after a short- and long-term departure (McLeman and Smit 2006; Fussell et al. 2010; Gutmann and Field 2010). Shumway et al. (2014) creates an environmental hazards impact index to examine how migration varies among sets of counties that are differently exposed to environmental hazards from 2000 to 2010. The study finds that counties that experience the highest impacts lose income as a result of both net outmigration and income loss through out-migrants having higher incomes than in-migrants.

In order to understand how climate change effects human migration behavior in the U.S., researchers use case studies approaches to analyze the impacts of recent and historical natural calamities such as the Dust Bowl in the Great Plains, Hurricane Katrina in New Orleans, and *sea-level rise* on Holland Island in the Cheasapeake Bay. Severe drought in the U.S. Great Plains from 1931 to 1939 led to massive soil erosion and drastic reductions in soil productivity causing tremendous dust storms to drift across Colorado, Kansas, Oklahoma, and Texas (and even further North into the Great Plains), which is popularly referred to as the Dust Bowl (McLeman et al. 2014). Studies (Gutmann et al. 2005; Gutmann and Field 2010; Hornbeck 2012) utilizing population movements from the Dust Bowl to explore the association between environment and migration find that severe loss in agricultural productivity results in high rates of outmigration from areas with high levels of unemployment and agricultural employment (Hunter and Nawrotzki 2016).

The impact of rising sea levels on migration is widely recognized as an important consequence of climate change (Hauer et al. 2016). The Cheasapeake Bay in the

U.S. has experienced significant relative sea-level rise, which triggered the abandonment of Holland Island in the 1900s (Gibbons and Nicholls 2006). Using a case study approach, Gibbons and Nicholls (2006) explore the relationship between sea-level rise and island abandonment. Their results suggest that while sea-level rise was the underlying driver for abandonment, the socioeconomic consequences of outmigration reduced the viability of the island's community, eventually leading to abandonment. The results from the study highlight the need for multifaceted response to the threat of rising sea-levels (Barnett and Adger 2003).

A substantial body of migration research has emerged from the U.S. Gulf Coast's experience with Hurricane Katrina (Pais and Elliot 2008; Frey et al. 2007; Fussell et al. 2010; Hori and Schafer 2010; Hunter and Nawrotzki 2016; Sastry 2009). These studies discuss the short- and medium-term impacts of natural disasters on household mobility decisions. Some Louisiana parishes directly hit by the hurricane experienced vast population changes (Hori and Schafer 2010), while other parishes experienced population increases, due to both disaster-related displacement and longer-term migration trends. Research on return migration show significant disparities by race and socioeconomic status. In the wake of the hurricane, New Orleans has become more white, older, more educated, less poor, and has fewer renters (Frey et al. 2007; Groen and Polvika 2010). Likewise, the hurricane disproportionately impacted black and low-income residents of the city (Brunsma et al. 2007; Pais and Elliot 2008; Fussell et al. 2010; Hartman and Squires 2006; Logan 2006). The racial and ethnic implications are applicable to other natural hazard scenarios in the U.S. Persistent racial and ethnic inequalities increase vulnerability and exposure of minorities to local natural hazards, making them more susceptible to displacement and permanent outmigration (Elliott et al. 2010; McLeman and Smit 2006).

While existing literature on the impacts of climate change on the U.S. economy generally find significantly negative effects, they typically do not account for firm and household migration decisions as the primary adaptive responses to climate change. Research that does not consider adaptive responses such as migration and adoption of innovative technology tend to overestimate the costs of climate change (Kahn 2015). Given the high rates of internal mobility in the U.S. and the potential for greater frequency of major climatic changes including hurricanes, storms, droughts, flooding, and heat waves, the migration patterns of households and firms can be expected to change as they relocate to areas with higher profits and utility. However, results from the current migration models predict that households and firms would move to locations that will experience the most severe effects of climate change, which seems implausible if the climate forecasts are accurate (Partridge et al. 2017). Thus, more research is needed in understanding when climate change will become a tipping point—e.g., we know that people will not keep flowing into South Florida if it is underwater and we know that residents of South Florida will relocate. It is these types of *offsetting* adaptive effects that need to be considered when examining the costs of climate change to the no-climate change counterfactual.

The existing climate change migration literature is problematic because it is more data mining rather than based on a theoretical model (especially the spatial equilibrium approach is needed). It also relies on migration patterns and equilibrium behavior from the late twentieth and early twenty-first century that will unlikely be applicable for future flows as climate change becomes more apparent. Its use of past climate data omits key climatic factors that will likely affect future migration trends (Feng et al. 2015; Kahn 2015; Partridge et al. 2017). The lack of a good theoretical foundation could lead to misguided conclusions based on past trends that imply increased preference of households and firms for hot weather and other future adverse weather events (Kahn 2015). Specifically, since the mid-twentieth century, Americans have been consistently moving to warm Sunbelt locations and coastal areas that will experience the bulk of the adverse climatic events such as heat waves and drought. This migration behavior will likely reverse itself and it is important to determine when the new thresholds will be met.

Climate change also reflects a non-marginal change (which is why it is important). But that means that future weather experiences will typically fall outside the range of past experiences—potentially making predictions based on past data extremely inaccurate. As discussed in the previous sections, researchers currently rely on climate measures such as average daily-high January or July temperature, number of precipitation days, or temperature variations, which, although work well in explaining climatic migration responses since World War II, are incomplete measures for analyzing the effects of potentially large and catastrophic changes due to climate change on future migration trends (Feng et al. 2015; Partridge et al. 2017). Therefore, there is an urgent need to develop better measures of climatic conditions associated with climate change and use these measures to better assess the tipping points where the migration patterns will reverse. Some examples will be how to categorize an area's susceptibility to hurricanes or rising sea levels and measures for catastrophic drought (e.g., in which water use restrictions in an area greatly inhibit residents' willingness to reside there).

An additional problem with the existing climate-change migration research is the difficulty in identifying a clear counterfactual. Considering that households and firms will relocate, the effects of climate change cannot be approximated by only examining how productivity is affected by climate change in their current locations (Partridge et al. 2017). A clear counterfactual will involve comparing the economic activities in the current locations without climate change to the economic activities in the future locations after households and firms have sorted as a result of climate change. For example, in order to fully analyze the costs and benefits of the Dust Bowl, one would need to compare the differences between the economic activities of residents and firms in their current locations without the Dust Bowl and future locations. Considering that many of the households and firms relocated to California in response to the Dust Bowl, it is likely that the adaptive response led to higher well-being, or in the case of global climate change, underestimated the benefits of adaptive migration. Moreover, institutions and government policy at the federal, state, and local levels could influence how climate change affects future migration and costs to the households and firms, which are also absent in the current migration models. For example, will zoning along the coast continue to be as friendly to development, increasing the costs of climate change? Similarly, will there be a moral hazard in which the governments spends funds to protect those who move into the most affected regions (e.g., building bigger and larger seawalls) that would further increase the costs of climate change?

4.5 Conclusion and Future Research Challenges

The U.S. has particularly high rates of migration, which have been essential for a flexible labor market (Obstfeld and Peri 1998), as well as advantages in innovation and growth (Crescenzi et al. 2007). The high mobility rates have generated interesting migration trends in the country, which are informative for understanding human migration behavior. Even though the migration rate has declined in the recent decades, the trends persist, making the U.S. an interesting case study for analyzing regional migration trends.

This book chapter has offered an overview of the extant literature on the determinants of interregional migration trends in the U.S. The contributions highlight the migration trends that are specific to the country and include in-depth discussions about the various factors that have shaped them over time. The aim of the book chapter is to provide a comprehensive review that not only accounts for the previous research, but also incorporates recent developments in migration literature. One of the important contributions of the book chapter is its discussion on the linkages between migration and climate change in the U.S.

Considering that migration trends within the U.S. continue to change over time, it is reasonable to believe that the studies exploring the importance of economic and non-economic determinants of migration will continue to expand. The challenge is to better understand how the relative roles of economic and non-economic factors influence migration trends and how it varies over time. Research findings depict a slightly diminishing role of natural amenities on overall migration in recent decades (Partridge et al. 2012; Rupasingha et al. 2015). Therefore, it is important to examine the extent to which migration to nice weather can be expected to continue (Rappaport 2007). Understanding this relationship is essential, given that climate change and subsequent extreme weather conditions are increasing the vulnerability of coastal areas. Therefore, moving forward, it will be challenging to predict how technological change, climate change, or even capitalization of amenities into wages and housing cost will affect future migration trends (Partridge 2010).

The migration rates in the U.S. have been low post 2000 (Sasser 2010). Studies such as Doherty (2009) and Frey (2009) posit that the financial crisis of 2009 has led to rapid declines in labor market conditions, per capita incomes, and housing affordability, and a corresponding drop in migration flows due to fewer job opportunities and less financial means to migrate, even as migration flows actually have been declining for decades and migration rates actually bottomed out since the Great Recession. In contrast, Rupasingha et al. (2015) find no significant impact of the housing crisis and Great Recession on overall gross migration flows. Since migration has important implications on regional growth, future research should examine whether the migration rates will remain low in the long-term and how that might affect regional growth differentials. Additionally, low mobility of individuals imply that jobs need to be created in areas where people live, in which case, place-based policies may be more effective for regional growth (Fletcher 2010).

Partridge et al. (2012) finds some evidence that geographical mobility is increasingly tied to occupationally-based demand shocks rather than industry-based shocks, indicating a major shift in the functioning of regional labor markets. Therefore, more research exploring the potential relationship between occupational mobility and dwindling internal migration is necessary to understand the implications on regional labor markets (Partridge et al. 2012).

Understanding the linkages between climate change and migration is important to recognize the drivers of household migration and predict how future changes in climate could influence migration trends as individuals adapt to changing conditions. A significant challenge to understanding this relationship involves integrating migration data with climate information at the regional, national, and sub-national levels (McLeman 2013). Therefore, new methods and approaches are needed that allow researchers to model migration trends influenced by climate change, predict relevant outcomes, and participate in discussions of broader policy implications. Existing research suggest that areas that are highly vulnerable to environmental hazards experience loss of both population and income, which could significantly increase their vulnerability and reduce their ability to adapt (Shumway et al. 2014). However, research is this field is relatively new. Therefore, more in-depth analyses are required to develop a better understanding of this relationship to inform policies designed to help vulnerable communities adapt to the impacts of climate change.

As previously discussed, natural disasters generally act as an environmental *push* from affected areas resulting in temporary and permanent outmigration of households (Gutmann and Field 2010; Hunter 2005). However, government and private sources provide recovery capital to assist local recoveries in the U.S. (Schultz and Elliott 2013). This influx of investment could generate economic opportunities that *pull* workers to the damaged areas (Elliott 2015). Studies find that large numbers of in-migrants enter hazard-damaged areas in search of employment during the recovery efforts (Donato et al. 2007; Elliott et al. 2010; Fussell 2009; Gotham and Greenberg 2014). The in-migration of workers raises important questions about the timing and nature of their movement, heterogeneity in the types of workers moving to these areas, impact on local skill, racial, and ethnic compositions, and its implications on the areas' adaptability to natural disasters, which are yet to be answered.

The case studies approach of natural disasters has enabled researchers to gain initial understanding of how climate change influences interregional migration in the U.S. However, by focusing on specific events and areas, these studies tend to overlook how climate change impacts overall geographical mobility (Gutmann and Field 2010). Additionally, existing climate-change migration models do not account for the adaptive responses of households and firms such as migration and adoption of innovative technology and therefore, overestimate the costs of climate change on the local economy (Kahn 2015). Technological development, government policy, and improving relative climate conditions in other parts of the country could influence how climate change affects migration and the costs incurred by households and firms (Feng et al. 2015). However, these factors are missing from the current migration models, which limit the ability of researchers to assess the overall impacts of climate change on future migration patterns. More research is needed to investigate the roles of rural-urban divide and rising income inequality on the ability of lower-income households to employ adaptive responses (Partridge et al. 2017).

Given the lack of good quality data at the global level, most of the analyses on climate-related migration is currently conducted at the regional and sub-regional level (Adamo and Izazola 2010; Gemenne 2011; McLeman 2013). The trend is likely to continue, as acquiring reliable data on climate-related migration, especially at larger scales, is a challenging undertaking. Moreover, it is extremely difficult to track displaced populations after disasters due to lack of available data, technical difficulties of collecting data in the wake of a disaster, unlimited destination options for the displaced, and the high cost associated with tracking (Hori and Schafer 2010). Surveys such as the 2006 Louisiana Health and Population Survey and Displaced New Orleans Residents Pilot Study have been conducted for hazard-damaged areas, allowing researchers to analyze the relationship between environmental hazard and demographic change. However, these datasets have limited information on most housing and economic outcomes which restrict any in-depth analyses of the disasters (Hori and Schafer 2010).

At the national level, the U.S. has a few micro-level data sources with migration data. The American Community Survey (ACS) and Current Population Survey (CPS) are annual sample datasets, which include information on migrants' geographical locations, education, and economic and demographic characteristics at the individual-level and can be used to analyze the migration trends (Faggian et al. 2017). However, the annual estimates in the ACS are only available for areas with population higher than 65,000, with only 3- to 5-year estimates that include data at smaller geographical levels. Likewise, the CPS is a small dataset with estimates that are only reliable at the state level (Faggian et al. 2017). Additionally, the National Longitudinal Survey of Youth (NLSY) by the U.S. Bureau of Labor Statistics is a longitudinal dataset which covers the period 1979–1996. However, the dataset includes a sample of only 6000 individuals, which raises questions about the representativeness of the sample for the entire U.S. (Faggian and Franklin 2014).

While in Europe (and recently Australia), studies have focused on interregional migration of highly educated individuals, equivalent literature in the U.S. has been rather limited due to restricted data availability (Faggian et al. 2017). The census and longitudinal micro-data available in the country are not specific to high-skilled migrants. Owing to the complexity of the U.S. educational system and lack of coordination among the states for data collection, micro-data on individual students and graduates comparable to those used by Faggian et al. (2007), Faggian and McCann (2009a, b), and Venhorst (2012, 2013) for European countries and Corcoran et al. (2010) for Australia are not available for the entire U.S. (Faggian and Franklin 2014). Betz et al. (2016) do use ACS data in their assessment of university graduates. Nonetheless, with increasing access to micro-level data, recently there has been an increase in the study of high-skilled migration in the country. The Scientists and Engineers Statistical Data (SESTAT) from the National Science Foundation provide information on labor market outcomes for college graduates, however, the sample is relatively small and restricted to individuals within the science and engineering sector (Faggian et al. 2017). Similarly, the Integrated Postsecondary Education Data System (IPEDS) includes data on post-secondary institutions, but does not support consecutive-year analysis of migration (Dotzel 2017). Moreover, both the datasets are only available at the state level and cannot be used to conduct analysis at a smaller geographical level such as counties, metropolitan areas, or local labor markets (Faggian et al. 2017).

References

Adamo SB, Izazola H (2010) Human migration and the environment. Popul Environ 32:105–108
Adamson DW, Clark DE, Partridge MD (2004) Do urban agglomeration economies and amenities have a skill bias? J Reg Sci 44:201–224
Ambinakudige S, Parisi D (2015) A spatiotemporal analysis of inter-county migration patterns in the United States. Appl Spat Anal Policy 1:1–17
Assadian A (1995) Fiscal determinants of migration to a fast growing state: how the aged differ from the general population. Rev Reg Stud 25(3):301–315
Bacolod M, Blum BS, Strange WC (2009) Urban interactions: soft skills versus specialization. J Econ Geogr 9:227–262
Barnett J, Adger NW (2003) Climate dangers and atoll nations. Clim Chang 61:321–337
Baum-Snow N (2010) Changes in transportation infrastructure and commuting patterns in U.S. metropolitan areas, 1960–2000. Am Econ Rev 100(2):278–382. https://doi.org/10.1257/aer.100.2.378
Beale CL (1977) The recent shift of united states population to non-metropolitan areas, 1970–1975. Int Reg Sci Rev 2:113–122
Bean FD, Myers GC, Angel JL, Galle OR (1994) Geographic concentration, migration, and population redistribution among the elderly. In: Martin LG, Preston SH (eds) Demography of aging. National Academy Press, Washington, DC, pp 319–355
Berry CR, Glaeser EL (2005) The divergence of human capital levels across cities. Pap Reg Sci 84:407–444
Betz M, Partridge MD, Fallah B (2016) Smart cities and attracting knowledge workers: what cities attract highly educated workers in the 21st century? Pap Reg Sci 95:819–841
Bluestone B (2006) Sustaining the mass economy: housing costs, population dynamics, and employment. Paper presented at the Federal Reserve Bank of Boston's New England Public Policy Center and The Rappaport Institute for Greater Boston Conference on Housing and the Economy in Greater Boston: Trends, Impacts, and Potential Responses, May 22
Brunsma DL, Overfelt D, Picou JS (2007) The sociology of Katrina: perspectives on a modern catastrophe. Rowman and Littlefield, Lanham, MD
Cebula RJ, Vedder RK (1973) A note on migration, economic opportunity, and the quality of life. J Reg Sci 13:205–211
Chen Y, Rosenthal SS (2008) Local amenities and life-cycle migration: do people move for jobs or fun? J Urban Econ 64:519–537
Cheshire P, Magrini S (2006) Population growth in European cities: weather matters – but only nationally. Reg Stud 40:23–37
Clark DE, Hunter WJ (1992) The impact of economic opportunity, amenities and fiscal factors on age-specific migration rates. J Reg Sci 32(3):349–365

Cooke TJ (2011) It's not just the economy: declining migration and the rise of secular rootedness. Popul Space Place 17(3):193–203
Corcoran J, Faggian A, McCann P (2010) Human capital in remote and rural Australia: the role of graduate migration. Growth Change 41:192–210
Costa DL, Kahn ME (2003) The rising price of nonmarket goods. Am Econ Rev 93(2):227–232
Cragg MI, Kahn ME (1999) Climate consumption and climate pricing from 1940 to 1990. Reg Sci Urban Econ 29(4):519–539
Crescenzi R, Rodrıguez-Pose A, Storper M (2007) The territorial dynamics of innovation: a Europe–United States comparative analysis. J Econ Geogr 7:673–709
Cromartie JB (1998) Net migration in the great plains increasingly linked to natural amenities and suburbanization. Rural Dev Perspect 13:27–34
Cutter SL, Barnes L, Bery M, Burton C, Evans E, Tate E, Webb J (2008) A place-based model for understanding community resilience to natural disasters. Glob Environ Chang 18(4):598–606
DaVanzo J (1978) Does unemployment affect migration?-evidence from micro data. Rev Econ Stat 60:504–514
DaVanzo J (1983) Repeat migration in the United States: who moves back and who moves on? Rev Econ Stat 65:552–559
Deller SC (1995) Economic impact of retirement migration. Econ Dev Q 9(1):25–38
Doherty C (2009) Home prices play big role in Americans' decision to move. Wall Street Journal 2009 Real Time Economics Blog, July 14
Donato KM, Trujillo-Pagan N, Bankston C III, Singer A (2007) Reconstructing New Orleans after Katrina: the emergence of an immigrant labor market. In: Brunsma DL, Overfelt D, Picou JS (eds) The sociology of Katrina: perspectives on a modern catastrophe. Rowman & Littlefield, New York, pp 217–234
Dotzel KR (2017) Do natural amenities influence undergraduate student migration decisions? The Annals of Regional Science 59(3):677–705
Elliott JR (2015) Natural hazards and residential mobility: general patterns and racially unequal outcomes in the United States. Soc Forces 1:1723–1747
Elliott JR, Timothy JH, Sams-Abiodun P (2010) Limits to social capital: comparing network assistance in two New Orleans neighborhoods devastated by hurricane Katrina. Sociol Q 51(4):624–648
Elvery JA (2010) City size and skill intensity. Reg Sci Urban Econ 40:367–379. https://doi.org/10.1016/j.regsciurbeco.2010.05.006
Emrich CT, Cutter SL (2011) Social vulnerability to climate-sensitive hazards in the southern United States. Weather Clim Soc 3(3):193–208
Etzo I (2008) Internal migration: a review of the literature. Munic Personal RePEc Archive (MPRA) Paper No. 8783. http://mpra.ub.uni-muenchen.de/8783/
Faggian A, Franklin R (2014) Human capital redistribution in the USA: the migration of the college-bound. Spat Econ Anal 9(4):376–395
Faggian A, McCann P (2006) Human capital flows and regional knowledge assets: a simultaneous equation approach. Oxf Econ Pap 58(3):475–500. https://doi.org/10.1093/oep/gpl010
Faggian A, McCann P (2009a) Human capital, graduate migration and innovation in British regions. Camb J Econ 33:317–333
Faggian A, McCann P (2009b) Universities, agglomerations and graduate human capital mobility. Tijdschr Econ Soc Geogr 100:210–223
Faggian A, McCann P, Sheppard SC (2007) Some evidence that women are more mobile than men: gender differences in UK graduate migration behavior. J Reg Sci 47:517–539
Faggian A, Corcoran J, Partridge M (2015) Interregional migration analysis. In: Karlsson C, Andersson M, Norman T (eds) Handbook in the research of methods and applications in economic geography. Edward Elgar, Cheltenham, pp 468–490
Faggian A, Rajbhandari I, Dotzel KR (2017) The interregional migration of human capital and its regional consequences: a review. Reg Stud 51:1–16
Fallah B, Partridge MD, Olfert MR (2012) Economic growth and sprawl: evidence from a stochastic growth approach. Ann Reg Sci 49:589–617

Feng B, Partridge MD, Rembert M (2015) The Perils of modelling how migration response to climate change (Unpublished)
Ferguson M, Ali K, Olfert MR, Partridge MD (2007) Voting with their feet: jobs versus amenities. Growth Change 38:77–110
Findeis J, Brasier K, Salcedo Du Bois R (2009) Population-driven transition zones in the United States: demographic change, land use, and adjustments in the structure of agriculture. In: Goetz S, Brouwer F (eds) New perspectives on agri-environmental policies: a multidisciplinary and transatlantic approach. Taylor & Francis, Routledge, pp 13–40
Fletcher MA (2010) Few in U.S. move for new jobs, fueling fear the economy might get stuck, too. Washington Post, July 30, p A1
Frey W (2009) The great American migration slowdown: regional and metropolitan dimensions. Brooking Research Report. December, Washington, DC
Frey WH, Singer A, Park D (2007) Resettling New Orleans: the first full picture from the census. The Brookings Institution, Metropolitan Policy Program, Washington, DC
Fussell E (2009) Hurricane chasers in New Orleans: latino immigrants as a source of a rapid response labor force. Hisp J Behav Sci 31(3):375–394
Fussell E, Sastry N, VanLandingham M (2010) Race, socioeconomic status, and return migration to New Orleans after hurricane Katrina. Popul Environ 31(1–3):20–42
Gale LR, Heath WC (2000) Elderly internal migration in the United States revisited. Public Finan Rev 28(2):153–170. Section 6.2
Gemenne F (2011) Climate-induced population displacements in a 4 C + world. Philos Trans R Soc Lond A Math Phys Eng Sci 369:182–195
Gibbons SJA, Nicholls RJ (2006) Island abandonment and sea-level rise: an historical analog from the Chesapeake Bay, USA. Glob Environ Chang 16(1):40–47
Glaeser EL, Resseger MG (2010) The complementarity between cities and skill. J Reg Sci 50: 221–244
Glaeser EL, Shapiro JM (2003) Urban growth in the 1990s: is city living back? J Reg Sci 3:139–165
Glaeser EL, Kolko J, Saiz A (2001) Consumer city. J Econ Geogr 1:27–50
Goetz SJ, Han Y, Findeis JL, Brasier KJ (2010) U.S. commuting networks and economic growth: measurement and implications for spatial policy. Growth Change 41(2):276–302
Gotham KF, Greenberg G (2014) Crisis cities: disaster and redevelopment in New York and New Orleans. Oxford University Press, New York
Gottlieb P, Joseph G (2006) College-to-work migration of technology graduates and holders of doctorates within the United States. J Reg Sci 46:627–649
Graves PE (1979) A life cycle empirical analysis of migration and climate, by race. J Urban Econ 6(2):135–147
Graves PE (1980) Migration and climate. J Reg Sci 20(2):227–237
Graves PE, Knapp T (1988) Mobility behavior of the elderly. J Urban Econ 24:1–8
Graves PE, Linneman PD (1979) Household migration: theoretical and empirical results. J Urban Econ 6:383–404
Graves PE, Mueser PR (1993) The role of equilibrium and disequilibrium in modeling regional growth and decline: a critical reassessment. J Reg Sci 33(1):69–84
Graves PE, Regulska J (1982) Amenities and migration over the life-cycle. In: Diamond DB Jr, Tolley GS (eds) The economics of urban amenities. Academic, New York, pp 211–221
Graves PE, Waldman DM (1991) Multimarket amenity compensation and the behavior of the elderly. Am Econ Rev 81(5):1374–1381
Green N (2007) Functional polycentricity: a formal definition in terms of social network analysis. Urban Stud 44(11):2077–2103
Greenwood MJ (1975) Research on internal migration in the United States: a survey. J Econ Lit 13:397–433
Greenwood MJ (1985) Human migration: theory, models, and empirical studies. J Reg Sci 25(4): 521–544
Greenwood MJ, Hunt GL (1984) Migration and interregional employment redistribution in the United States. Am Econ Rev 74:957–969

Greenwood MJ, Hunt GL (1989) Job versus amenities in the analysis of metropolitan migration. J Urban Econ 25(1):1–16
Greenwood MJ, Mueser PR, Plane DA, Schlottmann AM (1991) New directions in migration research. Ann Reg Sci 25:237–270
Groen JA, Polivka AE (2010) Going home after hurricane Katrina: determinants of return migration and changes in affected areas. Demography 47(4):821–844
Gutmann M, Field V (2010) Katrina in historical context: environment and migration in the U.S. Popul Environ 31(1–3):3–19
Gutmann MP, Deane GD, Lauster N, Peri A (2005) Two population-environment regimes in the Great Plains of the United States, 1930-1990. Popul Environ 27(2):191–225
Hartman C, Squires GD (2006) There is no such thing as a natural disaster: race, class and Katrina. Routledge, New York
Hauer ME, Evans JM, Mishra DR (2016) Millions projected to be at risk from sea-level rise in the continental United States. Nat Clim Chang 6(7):691–695
Herzog HW Jr, Schlottmann AM (1984) Labor force mobility in the United States: migration, unemployment, and remigration. Int Reg Sci Rev 9:43–58
Hori M, Schafer MJ (2010) Social costs of displacement in Louisiana after hurricanes Katrina and Rita. Popul Environ 31(1–3):64–86
Hornbeck R (2012) The enduring impact of the American dust bowl: short and long-run adjustments to environmental catastrophe. Am Econ Rev 102(4):1477–1507
Hugo G (2011) Future demographic change and its interactions with migration and climate change. Glob Environ Chang 21:S21–S33
Hunter LM (2005) Migration and environmental hazards. Popul Environ 26(4):273–302
Hunter LM, Nawrotzki R (2016) Migration and environment. In: White MJ (ed) International handbook of migration and population distribution. Springer, Dordrecht, pp 465–484
Johnson CA, Krishnamurthy K (2010) Dealing with displacement: can "social protection" facilitate long-term adaptation to climate change? Glob Environ Chang: Hum Policy Dimens 20(4): 648–655
Kahn ME (2015) Climate change adaptation: lessons from urban economics. Behav Environ 5(1): 1–30
Kotkin J (2009) There's no place like home. Newsweek, 9 Oct 2009
Krumm RJ (1983) Regional labor markets and the household migration decision. J Reg Sci 23:361–376
Lee S, Seo JG, Webster C (2006) The decentralising metropolis: economic diversity and commuting in the US suburbs. Urban Stud 43(1):2525–2549
Logan JR (2006) The impact of Katrina: race and class in storm-damaged neighborhoods. Working paper. Spatial structures in the social sciences. Brown University
McGranahan DA, Wojan TR, Lambert DM (2010) The rural growth trifecta: outdoor amenities, creative class and entrepreneurial context. J Econ Geogr. https://doi.org/10.1093/jeg/lbq007
McLeman R (2009) Impacts of population change on vulnerability and the capacity to adapt to climate change and variability: a typology based on lessons from "a hard country". Popul Environ 31(5):286–316
McLeman R (2013) Developments in modelling of climate change-related migration. Clim Chang 117:599–611
McLeman R, Smit B (2006) Migration as an adaptation to climate change. Clim Chang 76:31–53
McLeman R, Dupre J, Ford LB, Ford J, Gajewski K, Marchildon G (2014) What we learned from the Dust Bowl: lessons in science, policy, and adaptation. Popul Environ 35:417–440
Molloy R, Smith CL, Wozniak A (2011) Internal migration in the United States (Discussion Paper No. 5903). Institute for the Study of Labor (IZA), Bonn
Moretti E (2004) Estimating the social return to higher education: evidence from longitudinal and repeated cross-sectional data. J Econ 121(1–2):175–212. https://doi.org/10.1016/j.jeconom.2003.10.015

Morgan JN, Robb EH (1981) The impact of age upon interregional migration. Ann Reg Sci 15(3): 31–45

Muhlenkamp A, Waldorf B (2008) Rural-urban income disparities among the highly educated. Migration and human capital. Edward Elgar

Navratil FJ, Doyle JJ (1977) The socioeconomic determinants of migration and the level of aggregation. South Econ J 43:1547–1559

Nelson JP (2009) Valuing proximity to lake and ski recreation amenities: hedonic prices for vacation rental houses at deep creek lake, Maryland, Pennsylvania State University, Department of Economics, Working Paper

Newbold KB (1996) Determinants of elderly interstate migration in the United States, 1985-1990. Res Aging 18(4):451–476

NOAA (National Oceanic and Atmospheric Administration) (2011) U.S. Sets record with a dozen billion-dollar weather disasters in one year. Available at: http://www.noaanews.noaa.gov/stories2011/20111207_novusstats.html. Accessed April 2017

Obstfeld M, Peri G (1998) Regional non-adjustment and fiscal policy. In: Begg D, VonHagen J, Wyplosz C, Zimmermann KF (eds) EMU: prospects and challenges for the euro. Blackwell, London, pp 207–259

Pais J, Elliott JR (2008) Places as recovery machines: Vulnerability and neighborhood change after major hurricanes. Social Forces 86(4):1415–1453

Partridge MD (2010) The dueling models: NEG vs amenity migration in explaining U.S. engines of growth. Pap Reg Sci 89(3):513–536

Partridge MD, Rickman DS (2003) The waxing and waning of US regional economies: the chicken-egg of jobs versus people. J Urban Econ 53:76–97

Partridge MD, Rickman DS, Ali K, Olfert MR (2008) Lost in space: population growth in the American hinterlands and small cities. J Econ Geogr 8:727–757

Partridge MD, Ali K, Olfert MR (2010a) Rural to urban commuting: three degrees of integration. Growth Change 41(2):303–335

Partridge MD, Rickman DS, Ali K, Olfert MR (2010b) The spatial dynamics of factor price differentials: productivity or consumer amenity driven? Reg Sci Urban Econ 40:440–452

Partridge MD, Rickman DS, Olfert MR, Ali K (2012) Dwindling U.S. internal migration: evidence of spatial equilibrium or structural shifts in local labor markets? Reg Sci Urban Econ 42:375–388

Partridge MD, Feng B, Rembert M (2017) Improving climate-change modeling of US migration. Am Econ Rev Pap Proc 107(5):1–6

Patuelli R, Reggiani A, Nijkamp P, Baade F (2009) Spatial and commuting networks: a unifying perspective. In: Reggiani A, Nijkamp P (eds) Complexity and spatial networks: advances in spatial science. Springer, Berlin, pp 257–271

Plane DA (1993) Demographic influences on migration. Reg Stud 27:375–383

Plane DA, Heins F (2003) Age articulation of U.S. inter-metropolitan migration flows. Ann Reg Sci 37:107–130

Plane DA, Jurjevich JR (2009) Ties that no longer bind? The patterns and repercussions of age-articulated migration. Prof Geogr 61:4–20

Polachek SW, Horvath FW (1977) A life cycle approach to migration: analysis of the perspicacious peregrinator. In: Ehrenberg R (ed) Research in labor economics. CT JAI Press, Greenwich, pp 103–149

Polèse M (2009) The wealth and poverty of regions: why cities matter. University of Chicago Press, Chicago, IL

Porell FW (1982) Intermetropolitan migration and quality of life. J Reg Sci 22:137–158

Poston DL Jr, Zhang L, Gotcher DJ, Gu Y (2009) The effect of climate on migration: United States, 1995-2000. Soc Sci Res 38:743–753

Rappaport J (2007) Moving to nice weather. Reg Sci Urban Econ 37:375–398

Rice TW, Pepper ML (1997) Region, migration, and attitudes in the United States. Soc Sci Q 78(1): 83–95

Rickman DS, Rickman SD (2011) Population growth in high amenity nonmetropolitan areas: what's the prognosis? J Reg Sci 51(5):863–879. https://doi.org/10.1111/j.1467-9787.2011.00734
Roback J (1982) Wages, rents, and the quality of life. J Polit Econ 90(6):1257–1278
Rupasingha A, Liu Y, Partridge MD (2015) Rural bound: determinants of metro to non-metro migration in the United States. Am J Agric Econ 97(3):680–700
Sasser AC (2010) Voting with their feet: relative economic conditions and state migration patterns. Reg Sci Urban Econ 40:122–135
Sastry ML (1992) Estimating the economic impacts of elderly migration: an input-output analysis. Growth Change 23(1):54–79
Sastry N (2009) Displaced New Orleans residents in the aftermath of Hurricane Katrina: results from a pilot survey. Organ Environ 22(4):395–409
Schachter J, Althaus PG (1993) The assumption of equilibrium in models of migration. J Reg Sci 33(1):85–88
Schultz J, Elliott JR (2013) Natural disasters and local demographic change in the United States. Popul Environ 34:293–312. https://doi.org/10.1007/s11111-012-0171-7
Scott AJ (2010) Jobs or amenities? Destination choices of migrant engineers in the USA. Pap Reg Sci 89:43–63
Serow WJ, Haas WH III (1992) Measuring the economic impact of retirement migration: the case of western North Carolina. J Appl Gerontol 11(2):200–215
Shearmur R, Motte B (2009) Weak ties that bind: do commutes bind Montreal's central and suburban economies? Urban Aff Rev 44(4):490–524
Shumway JM, Otterstrom S, Glavac S (2014) Environmental hazards as disamenities: selective migration and income change in the United States from 2000–2010. Ann Assoc Am Geogr 104(2):280–291
Simon CJ, Nardinelli C (2002) Human capital and the rise of American cities, 1900–1999. Reg Sci Urban Econ 32:59–96
Storper M, Scott AJ (2009) Rethinking human capital, creativity and human growth. J Econ Geogr 9:147–167
Sum A, Khatiwada I, McLaughlin J, Palma S (2007) Outmigration in Massachusetts: the links between job creation and housing prices. Center for Labor Market Studies and MassINC, Boston. June
Tabuchi T, Thisse JF (2002) Taste heterogeneity, labor mobility and economic geography. J Dev Econ 69:155–177
Venhorst VA (2012) Smart move? The spatial mobility of higher education graduates. University of Groningen Publication, Groningen
Venhorst VA (2013) Graduate migration and regional familiarity. Tijdschr Econ Soc Geogr 104: 109–119
Waldorf BS (2009) Is human capital accumulation a self-propelling process? Comparing educational attainment levels of movers and stayers. Ann Reg Sci 43:323–344
Walters WH (1994) Climate and U.S. elderly migration rates. Pap Reg Sci 73(3):309–329
Walters WH (2002) Later-life migration in the United States: a review of recent research. J Plan Lit 17(1):37–66
Whisler RL, Waldorf BS, Mulligan GF, Plane DA (2008) Quality of life and the migration of the college-educated: a life-course approach. Growth Change 39:58–94
Winters JV (2011a) Why are smart cities growing? Who moves and who stays. J Reg Sci 51: 253–270
Winters JV (2011b) Human capital and population growth in nonmetropolitan U.S. counties: the importance of college student migration. Econ Dev Q 25(4):353–365
Zucker LG, Darby MR (2007) Star scientists, innovation and regional and national immigration (Working Paper No. 13547). National Bureau of Economic Research (NBER), Cambridge, MA. http://nber.org/papers/w13547

Chapter 5
State of the Art and Future Challenges of Interregional Migration Empirical Research in Europe

Margherita Gerolimetto and Stefano Magrini

Abstract In this chapter, we review the long-standing debate on the main determinants of interregional migration in light of the most recent advancements in Europe. Given the vast amount of empirical studies on inter-regional migration in this continent, we will concentrate on some topics that appear to characterise the European context. Starting from some stylized facts regarding mobility posing particular attention to the European Union agenda and its enlargement to the New Member States in Eastern and Central Europe, we will then discuss the extent to which the change in commuting patterns can represent an alternative form of spatial labour market adjustment given the high density of urbanization characterizing Europe. Finally, we focus on forced migration, that has afflicted (and still afflicts) the area in the last few years and is still among the main concerns facing the European Union because of its many related issues.

Keywords EU enlargement · Commuting · Forced migration

5.1 Introduction

According to early migration theories (Hicks 1932; Sjaastad 1962; Greenwood 1997), migrants' decision to move is based on the expectation of reaching a higher level of utility once settled in their destination; in addition, since utility typically arises from consumption, differences in wages or other forms of incomes across territories are seen as key factors of geographical mobility. Along these lines, interregional migration follows what is often called the "disequilibrium model" (Greenwood 1975, 1985): initial disparities in wages and employment stimulate people to move so that equilibrium over space is finally restored.

An alternative view, the "equilibrium approach" to migration, stems from the work of Graves (1976, 1980, 1983), who calls into question the role of migration as a

M. Gerolimetto (✉) · S. Magrini
Department of Economics, Ca' Foscari University of Venice, Venice, Italy
e-mail: margherita.gerolimetto@unive.it; s.magrini@unive.it

B. Biagi et al. (eds.), *New Frontiers in Interregional Migration Research*, Advances in Spatial Science, https://doi.org/10.1007/978-3-319-75886-2_5

re-equilibrating mechanism. Urban and natural amenities, together with other aspects linked to the quality of life, can play a role in attracting people in a particular place (Florida 2002; Partridge 2010; Rodríguez-Pose and Ketterer 2012). According to this model, differences in wages partially counter-balance spatial variations in non-tradable non-economic factors that shape the location specific availability of amenities.

When comparing Europe and USA migration patterns, two main differences seem to emerge. Firstly, differently from USA where the level of mobility has always been rather high, in Europe the level of mobility is smaller (among the others, Decressin and Fatas 1995; Bentivogli and Pagano 1999; Puga 2002; Fidrmuc 2004) for a complex variety of reasons. Probably, the most important reason for Europeans being "geographically sticky people" (Cheshire and Magrini 2006) are the profound differences in culture, language and institutions that exist across European nations and regions. For an individual, long distance geographical mobility means a complete change of social environment: it very often involves a loss of established social networks of family and friends and the need to start again within a new social environment, with a different social security, health and school system, often combined with the need to learn a new language. These difficulties become even greater when the move involves the challenge to find a new job in an often profoundly different labour market. Moreover, because of transactions costs and housing policies,[1] movements in Europe involve a much higher costs, compared to the USA.

Secondly, there appears to be a fundamental difference between the two sides of the Atlantic with respect to the model that provides an explanation to migration flows. On the one hand, recent USA evidence documents the considerable role played by non-economic factors in shaping migration patterns in line with the prediction stemming from the "equilibrium approach" (Partridge and Rickman 2003, 2006). In Europe, in contrast, the "disequilibrium model" appears to be a more adequate theoretical explanation. Indeed, European migration flows are primarily stimulated, albeit slowly, by differences in economic opportunities across space; natural amenities, such as climate, play a much lower role in Europe than in the USA (Cheshire and Magrini 2006).

Empirical studies based on European data have documented in various ways the disequilibrium model that appears to be plausible for Europe. Just to mention a few, Bentivogli and Pagano (1999), using annual NUTS1[2] data of 11 European countries over the period 1981–1994, report that migration responds to changes in income disparities, but not to changes in (relative) unemployment rates. Faini et al. (1997) explain a decrease in the interregional migration rates within Italy in terms of the growing financial burden brought in by a change in residence. Decressin and Fatas (1995) show that the adjustment to an economic shock in Europe takes substantially more time than in USA. Fidrmuc (2004) and Huber (2004) focus on previously centrally planned economies and find that migrations do not help reducing the level

[1]Social housing is a much larger fraction of the stock in most European countries and place-specific and rent controlled housing ties people to their existing locations (Cheshire and Magrini 2006).

[2]NUTS1 are the major socio-economic regions, according to the Eurostat classification of territorial units for statistics.

of regional disparities that exists within them. Stark et al. (2009) analyse Poland during the period 1999–2005 and show that the decision to migrate was driven by an increase in relative poverty. More recently, Rodríguez-Pose et al. (2015) use net-migration data for 133 regions belonging to 12 European countries over the period 1990–2006 and show that local amenities, such as average temperature and recreation and tourism services, do appear to affect migration but only once economic factors and human capital related factors have been fully allowed for.

To sum up, the deep heterogeneity that exists both between and within European countries, compared to the USA, in terms of cultural, historical and linguistic characteristics represents a substantial migration barrier; consequently, it affects the relevance attributed to economic vs. non-economic factors in the decision to migrate (Biagi et al. 2011). In other words, the actual pattern of migration flows across Europe does not seem to conform to the predictions stemming from the equilibrium model as movements are very limited and amenities do not really play a role or, if they do, it is just to a very local extent (Cheshire and Magrini 2006) and only after economic related factors have been fully taken into account (Rodríguez-Pose and Ketterer 2012).

In light of the limited aptitude to move revealed by Europeans, a freer movement of people and goods across the member states has always been considered a key aspect of the process of building an effective European Union and, more recently, of a sustainable monetary union. The recent extraordinary flow of external migrants has further contributed to focus attention on this issue. As an example of this attention, the Europe 2020 growth strategy emphasises the efficient allocation of labour within EU as a key driver for future growth in light of the increasing challenges of globalization and rapid technological change (European Commission 2010a). Specifically, intra-EU mobility is seen as necessary to "modernise labour markets and empower people by developing their skills throughout the lifecycle with a view to increase labour market participation and better match labour supply and demand" (European Commission 2010b, p. 10). In the same vein, the 2012 Employment Package stresses that geographical labour mobility enhances "the (re)allocation of resources by acting as an adjustment mechanism for distorted labour markets whilst also enabling economies to better cope with sudden shocks". Among other things, this attention to mobility in Europe has led to the devolution of resources, both within the Seventh Framework Programme for Research (FP7) and the following Horizon 2020, aiming at studying this phenomenon and identifying policy instruments capable of favouring the achievement of the above mentioned objectives.

It is interesting to observe that the results of the empirical studies reported before, refer essentially to single nations or groups of nations that are relatively homogenous. There is a lack of studies on migration in a pan-European perspective, i.e. focusing on all state Members and not only on the states who started the process to build the European Union, ignoring the New Member States.[3]

[3]An interesting first step towards understanding respective contemporaneous migration patterns is the paper by Sardadvar and Rocha-Akis (2016) who study the determinants of interregional net-migration flows in the enlarged European Union.

Given the vast amount of existing literature, in this chapter we do not intend to provide an exhaustive account of the studies on inter-regional migration in Europe. Instead, we will focus on some aspects that we consider of particular interest as they appear to be important and peculiar of the European context, compared to others and particularly to the USA. We will start, in the second section, by reporting some empirical results about mobility in Europe, with particular attention to the consequences and implications of the enlargement of the European Union to the New Member States in Eastern and Central Europe. Then, in the third section, we will discuss the change of commuting patterns as a form of spatial adjustment alternative to migrations. Indeed, a branch of the literature has indeed shown that the more densely crowded are sets of local labour markets and the more they are open to cross commuting, the more important are changes of those flows as a source of adjustment. Finally, in the fourth section we will get into the issue of forced migration, a phenomenon that has afflicted Europe especially since the 2010s and is still a severe emergency from both the migrants and refugees and the resident population perspectives.

5.2 Mobility in Europe: Consequences and Implications of the Enlargement of the European Union to the New State Members

Mobility is in the agenda of European Union (EU) from its foundation. Since the treaty of Rome in 1957, the principle of free movement within European Union (EU) has been a founding postulate of European integration. The Maastricht Treaty of 1992, establishing the concept of European citizenship, further consolidated the aim of pursuing a complete and effective freedom of movement within the European territory and this was subsequently enhanced by the Amsterdam Treaty of 1997, with the incorporation of the Schengen agreements into the EU law.[4]

A further stimulus to the inclusion of mobility among the crucial items of the EU agenda comes after the introduction of the euro—first as 'book money' in 1999 and later as physical notes and coins in 2002—that is one of the European Union's

[4]Here follows the description of the acronyms of the groups of State Members of the European Union:

EU-12 (1 November 1993–31 December 1994): Belgium (BE), Denmark (DK), France (FR), Germany (DE), Greece (EL), Ireland (IE), Italy (IT), Luxembourg (LU), Netherlands (NL), Portugal (PT), Spain (ES) and United Kingdom (UK)

EU-15 (1 January 1995–30 April 2004): EU-12 + Austria (AT), Finland (FI) and Sweden (SE)

EU-25 (1 May 2004–31 December 2006): EU-15 + Cyprus (CY), Czech Republic (CZ), Estonia (EE), Hungary (HU), Latvia (LV), Lithuania (LT), Malta (MT), Poland (PL), Slovakia (SK) and Slovenia (SI)

EU-27 (1 January 2007–30 June 2013): EU-25 + Bulgaria (BG) and Romania (RO)

EU-28 (from 1 July 2013): EU-27 + Croatia (HR).

crowning achievements. The decision to form an Economic and Monetary Union was taken by the European Council in the Dutch city of Maastricht in December 1991, and was later enshrined in the Treaty on European Union (the Maastricht Treaty). Economic and Monetary Union takes the EU one step further in its process of economic integration, which started in 1957 when it was founded. Economic integration brings the benefits of greater size, internal efficiency and robustness to the EU economy as a whole and to the economies of the individual Member States. On the other hand, within a common monetary area, the exchange rate is not available as a policy instrument and labour mobility is considered one of the most relevant adjustment mechanisms. Also, after the economic crisis that started in 2008 and the consequent rise in unemployment, European policy makers have maintained their focus on increasing geographical labour mobility as an essential tool for addressing the strong and increasing demand of skilled labour and for reducing discrepancies between supply and demand in European labour markets.

As a matter of fact, migration within and between EU Member States was (and still is) rather low. The Eurofound (2014) report documented that in 2010, the annual cross-border migration rate for the European working age population (15–64 years) was just 0.3% of the EU population; if we consider interregional migration, this percentage rises to 1% only. By comparison, the migration rate across the four main regions of the USA is 1.2%, while the rate across USA states is 2.4%. Table 5.1 reports data on migration flows within Europe in 2015, in which the movements are classified by country of citizenship of the migrant or previous country of residence. Given the limited inclination expressed by Europeans to move to another country, as evidenced in this table, or even to move to another region within their own country, it does not surprise that the European Commission stresses the benefits of interregional migration in its Europe 2020 strategy.

Mobility is both an opportunity and a challenge for European regions and Member States. The benefits the economy and the functioning of EU labour markets would have from a higher level of geographic mobility are evident by simply looking, as said above, at the differences in unemployment levels within different EU countries, showing, at the same time, shortages of skilled labour in some areas and excesses in others. However, there are risks as well. For both receiving and sending regions, social cohesion and economic performance can be threatened by higher level of mobility. On the one hand, the receiving region is in charge of the integration of new workers and their families; on the other hand, the sending region often loses the most valuable labour resources (brain drain versus brain gain). In our view, benefits from an integrated single labour market will be fully perceived by Europe only by trying to find solutions to these trade-offs.

Since 2004, after the accession of the New Member States (NMS) to the EU, European law guarantees free movements of capital, goods, services and people from Central and Eastern Europe. These enlargements were unprecedented as they took place under exceptional conditions: income differentials between the Central and Eastern European (CEEC) countries and EU-15 were large, unemployment rate differentials were also high, migration from these countries was restricted and a process of transition from socialist to market economies was ongoing. Potentially, there were strong economic incentives in the CEEC states to migrate to the EU-15 states.

Table 5.1 Total immigrants in the European Union in 2015

	Total immigrants		By citizenship								By previous country of residence			
			Nationals		Other EU member states		Non-member country		Stateless		Other EU member states		Non-member country	
	thsd	%	thsd	%	thsd	%	thsd	%	thsd	%	thsd	%	thsd	%
Belgium	146.6	3.2	17.9	2.1	61.8	4.4	65.8	2.8	0.0	0.0	76.2	4.1	70.0	2.6
Bulgaria	25.2	0.5	10.7	1.2	1.4	0.1	12.9	0.5	0.1	0.6	7.1	0.4	18.1	0.7
Czech Republic	29.6	0.6	4.5	0.5	14.5	1.0	10.6	0.5	0.0	0.0	15.4	0.8	14.2	0.5
Denmark	78.5	1.7	19.8	2.3	24.9	1.8	32.3	1.4	1.5	7.9	33.0	1.8	44.9	1.6
Germany	1543.8	33.2	87.4	10.2	460.1	33.1	967.5	41.1	5.3	28.0	513.2	27.4	1015.6	37.1
Estonia	15.4	0.3	8.0	0.9	3.2	0.2	3.7	0.2	0.5	2.7	10.2	0.5	4.5	0.2
Ireland	76.9	1.7	18.8	2.2	26.4	1.9	31.7	1.3	0.0	0.0	38.7	2.1	38.2	1.4
Greece	64.4	1.4	30.5	3.5	16.5	1.2	17.5	0.7	0.0	0.0	43.0	2.3	21.5	0.8
Spain	342.1	7.4	52.1	6.1	106.2	7.6	183.7	7.8	0.2	0.8	119.4	6.4	222.7	8.1
France	363.9	7.8	131.2	15.2	84.2	6.1	148.5	6.3	0.0	0.0	133.4	7.1	230.5	8.4
Croatia	11.7	0.3	6.5	0.8	2.2	0.2	3.0	0.1	0.0	0.0	4.4	0.2	7.2	0.3
Italy	280.1	6.0	30.1	3.5	63.5	4.6	186.5	7.9	0.0	0.1	73.8	3.9	206.3	7.5
Cyprus	15.2	0.3	3.2	0.4	6.1	0.4	5.9	0.3	0.0	0.0	8.3	0.4	6.9	0.3
Latvia	9.5	0.2	5.0	0.6	0.7	0.0	3.8	0.2	0.0	0.1	4.9	0.3	4.6	0.2
Lithuania	22.1	0.5	18.4	2.1	0.8	0.1	2.9	0.1	0.0	0.1	15.4	0.8	6.7	0.2
Luxembourg	23.8	0.5	1.2	0.1	16.4	1.2	6.1	0.3	0.0	0.0	21.7	1.2	2.1	0.1
Hungary	58.3	1.3	32.6	3.8	10.5	0.8	15.2	0.6	0.0	0.0	30.5	1.6	27.7	1.0
Malta	12.8	0.3	1.6	0.2	5.6	0.4	5.6	0.2	0.0	0.0	6.3	0.3	6.5	0.2
Netherlands	166.9	3.6	39.2	4.6	60.1	4.3	61.4	2.6	4.6	23.9	78.0	4.2	87.6	3.2
Austria	166.3	3.6	9.4	1.1	68.8	4.9	86.5	3.7	1.3	6.7	71.1	3.8	90.1	3.3
Poland	218.1	4.7	84.8	9.9	29.4	2.1	103.9	4.4	0.0	0.2	102.9	5.5	115.2	4.2
Portugal	29.9	0.6	14.9	1.7	6.4	0.5	8.6	0.4	0.0	0.0	16.5	0.9	13.3	0.5
Romania	132.8	2.9	115.5	13.4	8.2	0.6	9.0	0.4	0.0	0.0	93.7	5.0	28.6	1.0

Slovenia	15.4	0.3	2.8	0.3	2.8	0.2	9.9	0.4	0.0	0.0	4.4	0.2	11.0	0.4
Slovakia	7.0	0.2	3.2	0.4	3.1	0.2	0.7	0.0	0.0	0.0	5.6	0.3	1.4	0.1
Finland	28.7	0.6	7.3	0.9	7.6	0.5	13.1	0.6	0.1	0.3	13.1	0.7	15.1	0.6
Sweden	134.2	2.9	20.4	2.4	29.8	2.1	78.2	3.3	5.4	28.5	38.1	2.0	92.7	3.4
United Kingdom	631.5	13.6	83.6	9.7	269.2	19.4	278.6	11.8	0.0	0.0	295.3	15.8	336.2	12.3
Total	4651.0		860.4		1390.4		2353.0		19.1		1873.6		2739.5	

Source: Eurostat

Note: The individual values do not add up to the total due to rounding and the exclusion of the "unknown" category

However, given the very wide differences in, for example, wages, most of EU-15 states feared the potentially negative impacts on their labour markets and welfare systems brought in by a massive workers inflow from the NMS. Consequently, with the exception of the United Kingdom, Ireland and Sweden, in 2004 the EU states resorted to the so-called transitional measures that restricted—to varying degrees—the right to work in EU-15 countries for NMS citizens over a period of up to 7 years.

Alongside these measures, there has been a fairly controversial and heated debate in Europe in the last few years on the effects of the enlargement on the degree of workers' mobility from the New Member States and several studies have attempted not only to evaluate the actual size of migration flows stimulated by the enlargement, but their likely impact on sending and receiving countries as well.

According to the EU Commission's Report (2006), the overall increase in immigration after 2004 was rather limited and was attributable mainly to flows directed to Austria, Ireland and United Kingdom. In addition, the report stresses the lack of conclusive evidence of a direct link between the scale of migration and the transitional arrangements. Zaiceva and Zimmermann (2008) analyse migration intentions before and after the 2004 enlargement using different waves of Eurobarometer data and find no actual differences in the determinants of migration intentions between EU-15 and New Members States. In particular, in line with human capital theory, they find that potential migrants from both NMS and EU-15 continue to be young and better educated.

More recent studies found somewhat different results. Fic et al. (2011) provide an assessment of the macro-economic impact on both host and home countries of the increased labour mobility that has resulted from the two recent EU enlargements. More specifically, they evaluate the macro-economic impact of the total population flows from the EU-8[5] and EU-2[6] to the EU-15 economies between 2004 and 2009, they also try to estimate which share of these flows can be directly attributed to the enlargement process itself and which share is instead likely to have occurred even in the absence of the EU expansion. The estimates suggest that, since the 2004 enlargement, about 1.8% of the population of EU-8 has moved to the EU-15, raising the host country population by 0.4%. Of this flow, approximately 75% can be attributed to the enlargement process itself, while the remaining 25% of the population shifts are likely to have occurred even in the absence of enlargement. In addition, since 2007, about 4.1% of the EU-2 population has moved to the EU-15, raising the host country population by a further 0.3%. Of these flows, just over 50% can be directly attributed to the enlargement process itself.[7] In other terms, according to the results by Fic et al. (2011), the EU enlargement has resulted in a substantial

[5]EU-8: Czech Republic (CZ), Estonia (EE), Hungary (HU), Latvia (LV), Lithuania (LT), Poland (PL), Slovakia (SK), Slovenia (SI).

[6]EU-2: Romania (RO) and Bulgaria (BG).

[7]These flows, that are not homogeneously distributed across Europe, insist on a context where there are profound cultural differences and the system is not ready to accommodate them so their weight is more relevant than what the figure itself would suggest.

increase in labour mobility. More than 99% of migration flows between newer and older member states have been East-West migration flows from EU-8 and EU-2 to EU-15 countries. Although many EU-15 members have applied transitional restrictions on access to their labour markets by EU-8 and EU-2 migrants, the stock of EU-8 and EU-2 nationals residing in EU-15 countries tripled over the period 2003–2009, increasing from about 1.6 million in 2003 to about 4.8 million in 2009. On the other hand, the share of West-East migration has remained marginal, much below 1%, and has not shown any trend over time.[8]

The difference in the results portrayed in these more recent studies and, specifically, the fact that the enlargement appears to have been much more effective in stimulating migration flows, should not come as a complete surprise: with the exceptions of UK, Ireland and Sweden, the majority of the EU-15 members did not effectively open their labour markets until more recent years as an effect of the long transitional agreements (up to 7 years) adopted. This is illustrated in Leschke and Galgóczi (2015). The authors thoroughly analyse the complexity of the interrelation between the transitional agreements put into place and the push and pull factors behind international migration flows between old and new state members. Within this analysis, flows from the largest EU-8 country, Poland, to UK and Ireland exemplify the modification to historical migration patterns brought in by the differential system of movement controls emerging from transitional agreements. Among EU-15 countries, UK and Ireland were in fact among the very few that opened up their labour markets immediately after enlargement; in contrast, Germany that used to be major destination country for labour migration from Poland during the 1999–2003 period, adopted a restrictive transitional measures. At the same time, the very favourable conditions in terms of labour market demand existing in UK and Ireland constituted a quite strong pull factor. As a result of the complex interaction between different inclinations to accommodate migrations and push and pull factors, after the enlargement the UK became the principal destination country for Polish migrants (Fihel and Okolski 2009).

5.3 Alternative Forms of Spatial Labour Market Adjustment: Commuting

As it has already been pointed out, interregional migration in the EU appears to be rather restricted. However, given the specific conditions that characterize the continent, alternative forms of spatial labour market adjustment have gained importance: change in commuting patterns, that can also include cross-border commuting, and "circular" migration.

[8]To our knowledge, there is no research evidence on the impact of these flows (EU-8 and EU-2 to EU-15) on the existing intra EU-15 flows.

During the late 1970s and 1980s, the literature on the functioning of local labour markets has considered the possibility that commuting pattern adjust to even out differences in labour market opportunities between neighbourhoods belonging to the same metropolitan area. Central to this idea was the difference between what Cheshire (1979) called discontinuous and continuous mobility: while the former requires a change in both place of work and residence, the later simply implies a change in work place. Several empirical studies thus demonstrated that local labour markets which are integrated into wider urban regions tend to interact with each other primarily through adjustment of commuting patterns (Cheshire 1979; Burridge and Gordon 1981; Evans and Richardson 1981; Gordon and Lamont 1982; Gordon 1985; and, more recently, Morrison 2005). Indeed, this thread of research has shown that the more densely crowded are sets of local labour markets and the more they are open to cross commuting, the more important are changes in commuting flows as a source of adjustment.

The question is then the extent to which, in highly urbanized regions, changes in commuting patterns may similarly adjust to changes in the spatial distribution of opportunities across different urban regions. Some portions of Europe are in fact characterized by a very elevated density of urbanization: in areas such as the Ruhr region of Germany, much of the Benelux, the M4 corridor in England, the Padana plain in Italy, there are swathes of densely urbanized territory where urban regions are not just tightly clustered, but the boundaries of their commuting hinterlands touch and, at the commuter shed, still there is substantial cross-border commuting. In such conditions, it is indeed possible that changes in commuting patterns might act as a spatial adjustment mechanism alternative to migrations: if the degree of economic attractiveness of one urban region increases relative to its neighbours, it will attract additional commuters. Since changes in commuting patterns are cheap—particularly if there are good transport links—such adjustments between adjacent urban regions should be expected to respond to small changes in the spatial distribution of opportunities. As time passes, the effects of the initial localised shock are therefore transmitted to areas further apart mainly by 'chain interdependence' of local labour markets.

The necessary condition for the 'chain interdependence' of local labour markets to occur is a sufficiently high connectivity via commuting patterns and this appears to be certainly fulfilled in Europe. Also thanks to the substantial reduction of transport costs and time, the continent is characterised by a high percentage of commuting flows that cross regional borders. The OECD (2005) reports that in countries like Austria, France, the Netherlands, UK, Italy and Germany the share of employed workers crossing NUTS1 borders to get from their place of residence to their place of work ranges between 9% and 16%; in addition, according to Bonin et al. (2008), the average commuting rate across EU-15 NUTS2 regions was 7.3% in 2006.

A number of papers have then studied the interrelations that exist between European urban regions arising from the existence of intense cross-region commuting. Eliasson et al. (2003) analyze how individual labour market status and spatial variations in employment opportunities influence interregional job search behaviour and mobility decisions in Sweden. Not surprisingly, results show that the larger the number of job positions that open in surrounding regions, the higher the propensity of workers to commute. Cheshire and Magrini (2000, 2006) and, more directly, Cheshire et al. (2004) conclude that commuting between urban regions behaves exactly as would be predicted by the inter-regional migration literature: commuting flows appear in fact to respond both to push factors and pull factors as well as, negatively, to the extent of commuting time. Similarly, Marvakov and Mathä (2007) find that regional commuting flows in the EU-15 respond to differentials in both wage and unemployment and provide an equilibrating mechanism to labour market disequilibria. In particular, their results suggest that educational attainment, labour force participation of women and the size of the service sector affect positively commuting behaviour, while distance exerts a negative role.

The paper by Overman and Puga (2002) not only reports that regions have unemployment outcomes that are more homogenous to those of their neighbours compared to the outcomes of other, more distant, regions in the same country, but it also shows that the neighbourhood effect does not stop at national borders. The latter result is of particular interest as it provides the opportunity to introduce an issue, cross-border commuting, that has recently gained some importance in the literature. Mathä and Wintr (2009) analyse the determinants of commuting for a set of bordering regions belonging to four EU countries—Belgium, France, Germany and Luxembourg—and find that commuting flows respond to wage and unemployment differences between regions in the expected way; moreover distance, as well as language differences, appear to impede cross-border commuting. Nerb et al. (2009) analyse the issue of cross-border commuting in relation to the enlargement process. In particular, the authors characterise the trends emerging in EU-27 both from a quantitative point of view (e.g., the number of commuting workers, the shifts in mobility flows) and a qualitative one (e.g., the relative importance of the involved sectors, the changes that have derived, the analysis of the motivations and expectations). According to this analysis, the main countries of destination are Switzerland, Luxembourg, Germany, the Netherlands, Austria and Belgium which, combined together, receive about 75% of all EU-commuters. The main countries of origin are France, Germany and Belgium, providing about 60% of all out-commuters in the EU.[9] A further interesting aspect that arises from this study is the profound difference between EU-15 and EU-12 with respect to the level of qualification of cross-border commuters and type of job: on the one hand, high skilled cross-border commuters originate mainly from EU-15 and are mainly employed on a permanent basis in economic core areas; on the other hand, flows of low skilled workers originate predominantly from EU-12 countries, and mostly in connection with temporary jobs in peripheral business areas. Finally, in most cross-border regions, in-commuters are mainly conceived as complementary working resources to the

[9]To better understand the meaning of such percentages, consider that Switzerland, Luxembourg, Germany, the Netherlands, Austria and Belgium represent about 25% of the E-27 (plus Switzerland) population, whereas France, Germany and Belgium represent about 31%.

local labour force, building on the idea that they predominantly occupy secondary activities of little interest to domestic workers. Switzerland is an exception since generally in-commuters occupy well remunerated, attractive job positions, e.g., high-skilled Germans in the branch "health and social work" (Müller-Jentsch 2008).

Increasingly, migration analysts in Europe are becoming aware of the existence of a further form of cross-country mobility, namely "circular migration", which can be seen as a sort of intermediate category of mobility between migration and commuting. More precisely, circular migration is a repeated migration experience between an origin and a destination, involving more than one migration and return; it is usually differentiated from "return migration" which entails one single emigration and return after an extended absence. Empirical analysis of intra-EU movements in fact shows that the traditional concept of migration, where individuals leave their country permanently has become far less relevant while an increasing number of people go abroad (particularly, from Central European Region to Western Europe) for short periods of time to find temporary and seasonal employment (Mau and Büttner 2010).

Finally, two relevant implications that arise from these results are worth mentioning. First, given the importance of cross-regional commuting in densely urbanized regions of Europe, analysts and policy makers should become aware of the fact that differences in the mean values of indicators such as unemployment rates or income per capita should be interpreted with caution: for such indicators to provide a reasonable measure of welfare, one should relate them to individuals of constant characteristics. A further relevant consequence of these results stems from the fact that migration and change in commuting patterns have quite different impacts on regional (night) population and, hence, different implications for regional policy and planning. For example, a significant decrease in local labour demand may induce mobility to other regions. The effects of this mobility on, say, the region's tax base and housing market will depend on the individual's choice between migration and commuting. Take the case of a negative shock to the local labour demand, if there is relevant out-migration, this shock determines a reduction in the housing demand (with consequent downward pressure of rents) and a reduction of the tax base. Both these effects can be, however, limited in case workers, instead of migrating, decide to maintain the existing residence and commute to a nearby region.

5.4 New Challenges of the European Union: Forced Migration and Its Impact

According to the International Association for the Study of Forced Migration (IASFM), forced migration is defined as the "flow of people who are forced to flee their homes for one or more of the following reasons and where the state authorities are unable or unwilling to protect them: armed conflict including civil war, generalized violence and persecution on the grounds of nationality, race, religion, political opinion or social group".[10]

Clearly, at the moment of their first entrance in the continent, the reason why these people move is essentially to escape from a condition of oppression. It is only afterwards that their movements in the continent may be guided by drivers that resemble those of the other forms of migration, i.e., changes of residence in search of better economic conditions.

After 2015, the migrant crisis has become particularly severe in Europe because of the increase of the number of people who make the journey to the European Union to seek asylum or better economic prospects, travelling across the Mediterranean Sea or through Southeast Europe. Data from the United Nations High Commissioner for Refugees reveal that these people mostly come from Western and South Asia, Africa, Western Balkans. More in details, over one million of Mediterranean Sea arrivals between January 2015 and March 2016, the top three nationalities were Syrian (46.7%), Afghan (20.9%) and Iraqi (9.4%); of the refugees and migrants arriving in Europe by sea in 2015, 58% were men, 17% women and 25% children. The number of deaths at sea rose to record levels in April 2015, when five boats carrying almost 2000 migrants to Europe sank in the Mediterranean Sea, with a combined death toll estimated at more than 1200 people.

According to the latest Eurobarometer survey data (Eurobarometer 2015), immigration is now top of the most important concerns facing the EU, with 38% of respondents citing this response up from 24% in the previous year. One of the themes by which the European immigration policy debate is fuelled, is the rise of the levels of anti-foreign sentiment connected to the population growth in the European Union due to immigration. Often, this form of hostility derives from the widespread idea that immigrants take jobs away from natives (Bauer et al. 2000).

Some literature has directly investigated the issue of whether immigrants do take jobs away from natives in Europe. Angrist and Kugler (2003) study, in particular, the institutional aspects of the immigration issue in Western Europe. They move from the position that persistently high unemployment in Europe is due to institutions that increase turn-over and employment costs (OECD 1994); consequently, they try to figure out whether institutional characteristics, such as employment protection, high replacement rates, rigid wages and high business entry costs, affect the employment consequences of immigration on the work force. The main findings are that in case natives and immigrants are somewhat substitutable in production, immigration may reduce native employment. Although not entirely clear cut, the empirical results seem to be consistent with the view that the lower is the degree of flexibility in the labour market, the more painful could be the immigrant absorption, at least from the perspective of native employment.

[10]To be precise, according to the IASFM definition, forced migration also includes "people displaced by natural or environmental disasters, chemical or nuclear disasters, famine, or development projects".

Another interesting contribute is in the paper by Carrasco et al. (2008) who tried to evaluate the labour market effects of immigrants in Spain. By using alternative data sets, the authors estimate the impact of both legal and total immigration flows on the employment rates and wages of native workers. Using different samples and estimation procedures, they did not find any significant negative effect of immigration on either the employment rates or wages of native workers. According to the authors, two main conclusions can be drawn from the literature on the effects of immigration on the host country. First, it is very difficult to prove that an increase in the supply due to immigration should reduce the wages of native workers in flexible labour markets or reduce their employment rates in rigid ones. Moreover, empirical results seem to be time- and country-dependent, with a variety of studies finding different estimates of the labour market impact of immigration depending on the episode under consideration.

D'Amuri et al. (2010) contribute to the literature by analyzing the impact of immigration in Western Germany within a labour market equilibrium framework that fully accounts for the interactions between production factors. Within Europe, Germany hosts the largest number of immigrants; in actual facts, more than 10% of the total German labour force since the late 1990s is represented by workers with a foreign origin. The socio-economic worries due to the rise of immigration led the German government to introduce selective immigration measures and stimulated a heat debate. To study the interactions between immigration, employment and wages, the approach adopted by D'Amuri et al. (2010) is based on Borjas's (2003) structural labour market equilibrium. By modelling the aggregate production function through a multi-level constant elasticity of substitution (CES), they aim at obtaining a complete picture of the adjustment process that takes place in the labour market in response to immigration under the assumption that migrants and natives are imperfect substitutes because of different observable characteristics. In this way, competition and complementary effects of immigrants on natives can be detected. Differently from similar analyses such as those by Ottaviano and Peri (2008) for the USA and Manacorda et al. (2006) for the UK, a relevant feature introduced by D'Amuri et al. (2010) is the distinction between new and old immigrants; in addition, they focus on the effects of immigration on wages as well as employment levels.[11] The reason for this is that, unlike the labour markets in the USA and in the UK that can be reasonably considered as fully flexible with wages adjusting to their market clearing level, in Germany, where labour market institutions are characterized by generous unemployment benefits and other sources of wage rigidities, the employment effect of immigration are stronger. On the basis of this framework, D'Amuri et al find that the inflow of immigrant workers that took place in the 1990s had no adverse effects on native wages and employment levels; in contrast, adverse employment and wage effects were felt by workers that entered the country during previous waves of immigration.

[11]The original framework proposed by Borjas (2003) focusses only on wage adjustment.

As a final consideration, it is clear that Europe is facing an enormous challenge in its attempt to deal with the recent dramatic flow of migrants that are trying to reach its territory. This displacement of people is in fact "traumatic" for refugees and migrants as well as for the receiving population, and the European economic systems must be adequately prepared to provide aid to refugees and migrants while, at the same time, protecting the resident population. In our view, this requires cooperation among the countries of origin, transit and destination and a more coherent migration policy based on solidarity between Member States. A good response to the challenges of people on the move requires health system preparedness and capacity, including robust epidemiological data and migration intelligence, careful planning, training and, above all, adherence to the principles of equity and solidarity and to human rights and dignity.

5.5 Concluding Remarks

Europe has become a "continent of integration" over the past 50 years, with increasing ethnic and cultural diversity evident in the majority of the countries. In some countries the process has started a long time ago (France, UK, the Netherlands), in some others it is a recent phenomenon (Italy, Spain, Portugal), yet in others it has barely started (Eastern Europe, in particular). Integration into the labour market of the receiving country often represents the foundation of the wider integration process that means finding housing, making social contacts, learning the language and so on. However, the Single European Labour Market, which has been a European objective for so long, remains a vision. The core challenge in this context is to enhance labour mobility as in present years cross-country movements within Europe are still very restricted. For instance, a recent study by Dao et al. (2014) shows that, although the role of migration as a labour demand shock absorber has increased in Europe since 2004, its absolute importance is significantly larger in the US: about 60% of the shock tends to be absorbed via migration in the latter country compared to only 30% in Europe.

The literature is very rich of studies on inter-regional migrations in Europe and, in the present chapter, we focussed on some topics that appear to be peculiar aspects of the migration phenomenon within this continent. In particular, we started from the review of the studies about the consequences and the implications of the enlargement of the EU to the New State Members. Then, we concentrated on the thread of literature on the adjustment of commuting pattern as an alternative mechanism to even out differences in labour market opportunities. Finally, we devoted our attention to forced migration, a theme that nowadays is possibly one of the most important concerns facing the EU.

Some themes are still open in the literature. First of all, a global EU perspective is lacking: often studies on inter-regional migration within the EU only focus on the EU-15, disregarding the NMS or confining their role as purely sending countries (towards the EU-15).

Recently, the literature has also shown some interest on the European students' migration process. In Europe, thanks to the process of harmonization of university education and student exchange programs, students' migration flows have increased, although in a still geographically uneven fashion (Tremblay 2002). Parey and Waldinger (2011) analyse data on the European ERASMUS student exchange program and find that, in case individuals study abroad, their probability of subsequently working in a foreign country significantly increases. As a way to encourage and reinforce the flow of young Europeans across Member States, the European Commission has recently launched the initiative "Move2Learn, Learn2Move" that endows a minimum of 5000 European students between 16 and 19 years old with a sum to purchase travel tickets to visit at least one other EU country.

In general, it must be emphasized that studying mobility in Europe is a rather difficult task fundamentally because of severe data availability limitations (Sardadvar and Rocha-Akis 2016). Transnational surveys are missing and country surveys, which only capture individuals before or after migration, do not provide exhaustive measures of international migration. Moreover, migrants are not followed across countries; consequently, it is not possible, for instance, to study forms of circular migration. Hopefully, future empirical studies will benefit from improved data quality, such as migration data between pair of regions or covering longer time spans.

References

Angrist J, Kugler A (2003) Protective or counter-productive? Labor market institutions and the effect of immigration on EU natives. Econ J 113:302–331

Bauer T, Lofstrom M, Zimmermann KF (2000) Immigration policyassimilation of immigrants and native's sentiment towards immigrants: evidence from 12 OECD countries. IZA discussion paper no. 187, August

Bentivogli C, Pagano P (1999) Regional disparities and labour mobility: the Euro-11 versus the USA. Labour 13:737–760

Biagi B, Faggian A, McCann P (2011) Long and short distance migration in Italy: the role of economis, social and environmental characteristics. Spat Econ Anal 6:111–131

Bonin H, Eichhorst W, Florman C, Hansen MO, Skiöld L, Sturhler J, Tatsiramos K, Tomasen H, Zimmermann KF (2008) Geographic mobility in the European Union: optimising its economic and social benefits. IZA research report no. 19

Borjas G (2003) The labour demand curve is downward sloping: reexaming the impact of immigration on the labour market. Q J Econ 118:1335–1374

Burridge P, Gordon I (1981) Unemployment in the British metropolitan labour areas. Oxf Econ Pap 33:274–297

Carrasco R, Jimeno JF, Ortega AC (2008) The effect of immigration on the labour market performance of native-born workers: some evidence from Spain. J Popul Econ 21:627–648

Cheshire PC (1979) Inner areas as spatial labour markets: a critique of the inner area studies. Urban Stud 16:29–43

Cheshire PC, Magrini S (2000) Endogenous processes in European regional growth: convergence and policy. Growth Change 31:455–479

Cheshire PC, Magrini S (2006) Population growth in European cities: weather matters but only nationally. Reg Stud 40:23–37

Cheshire PC, Magrini S, Medda F, Monastiriotis V (2004) Cities are not isolated states. In: Boddy M, Parkinson M (eds) City matters. The Policy Press, Bristol
D'Amuri F, Ottaviano GIP, Peri G (2010) The labor market impact of immigration in Western Germany in the 1990s. Eur Econ Rev 54:550–570
Dao M, Furceri D, Loungani P (2014) Regional labor market adjustments in the United States and Europe. IMF working paper WP/14/26
Decressin J, Fatas A (1995) Regional labour market dynamics in Europe. Eur Econ Rev 39:1627–1655
Eliasson K, Lindgren U, Westerlund O (2003) Geographical labour mobility: migration or commuting? Reg Stud 37:827–837
Eurobarometer (2015) Public opinion on the European Union. Standard Eurobarometer Spring 2015. http://europa.eu.int/comm/public_opinion/archives/eb/eb62/eb62_en.hmt
Eurofound (2014) Labour mobility in the EU: recent trends and policies. Publications Office of the European Union, Luxemburg
European Commission (2006) Report on the functioning of the transitional arrangements set out in the 2003 Accession Treaty. Communication from the Commission, COM(2006) 48 final, Brussels
European Commission (2010a) Fifth report on economic, social and territorial cohesion. Office for Official Publications of the European Communities, Luxembourg
European Commission (2010b) Europe 2020: a strategy for smart, sustainable and inclusive growth. Communication from the Commission, COM(2010) 2020 final, Brussels
Evans AW, Richardson R (1981) Urban employment: interpretation and additional evidence. Scott J Polit Econ 282:107–124
Faini R, Galli G, Gennari P, Rossi F (1997) An empirical puzzle: falling migration and growing unemployment differentials among Italian regions. Eur Econ Rev 41:571–579
Fic A, Holland D, Rincon-Aznar T, Stokes L, Paluchowski P (2011) Labour mobility within the EU: the impact of enlargement and the functioning of the transitional arrangements. National Institute of Economic and Social Research, London
Fidrmuc J (2004) Migration and regional adjustment to asymmetric shocks in transition economies. J Comput Econ 32:230–247
Fihel A, Okolski M (2009) Case study on the dimensions and effects of EU labour migration – Poland. In: Galgoczi B, Leschke J, Watt A (eds) EU labour migration since enlargement: trends, impacts and policies. Ashgate, Aldershot, pp 185–210
Florida R (2002) The economic geography of talent. Ann Assoc Am Geogr 92:743–775
Gordon I (1985) The cyclical sensitivity of regional employment and unemployment differentials. Reg Stud 19:95–109
Gordon I, Lamont D (1982) A model of labour-market interdependencies in the London region. Environ Plan A 14:238–264
Graves P (1976) A re-examination of migration, economic opportunity, and the quality of life. J Reg Sci 12:107–112
Graves P (1980) Migration and climate. J Reg Sci 20:227–237
Graves P (1983) Migration with a composite amenity: the role of rents. J Reg Sci 23:541–546
Greenwood MJ (1975) Research on internal migration in the United States: a survey. J Econ Lit 13:397–433
Greenwood MJ (1985) Human migration: theory, models and empirical studies. J Reg Sci 25:521–544
Greenwood MJ (1997) Internal migration in developed countries. In: Rosenzweig MR, Stark O (eds) Handbook of population and family economics, vol 1B. Elsevier, Amsterdam, pp 647–720
Hicks JR (1932) Theory of wages. Macmillan, New York
Huber P (2004) Intra-national labour market adjustment in the candidate countries. J Comput Econ 32:248–264
Leschke J, Galgóczi B (2015) Arbeitskräftemobilität in der EU im Angesicht der Krise: Gewinner und Verlierer. WSI Mitt 68:327–337

Manacorda M, Manning A, Wadsworth J (2006) The impact of immigration on the structure of male wages: theory and evidence from Britain. CEP discussion paper no. 754. London School of Economics

Marvakov J, Mathä T (2007) An analysis of regional commuting flows in the European Union. Working paper no. 28. Banque Central du Luxembourg

Mathä T, Wintr L (2009) Commuting flows across bordering regions: a note. Appl Econ Lett 16:735–738

Mau S, Büttner S (2010) Transnationality. In: Immerfall S, Therborn G (eds) Handbook of European societies: social transformations in the 21st century. Springer, London, pp 537–570

Morrison PS (2005) Unemployment and urban labour markets. Urban Stud 42:2261–2288

Müller-Jentsch D (2008) Die Neue Zuwanderung: die Schweiz zwischen Brain Gain und Überfremdungsangst. Avenir Suisse, Verlag neue Zürcher Zeitung

Nerb G, Hitzelsberger F, Woidich A, Pommer S, Hemmer S, Heczko P (2009) Scientific report on the mobility of cross-border workers within the EU-27/EEA/EFTA countries. Final report. European Commission DG Employment and Social Affairs Brussels

OECD (1994) The OECD jobs study: facts, analysis, strategies. OECD, Paris

OECD (2005) OECD employment outlook. OECD, Paris

Ottaviano GIP, Peri G (2008) Immigration and the national wages: clarifying the theory and the empirics. NBER working paper no. 14188

Overman HG, Puga D (2002) Unemployment clusters across Europe's regions and countries. Econ Policy 17:115–148

Parey M, Waldinger F (2011) Studying abroad and the effect on international labour market mobility: evidence from the introduction of Erasmus. Econ J 121:194–222

Partridge MD (2010) The dueling models: NEG vs. amenity migration in explaining US engines of growth. Pap Reg Sci 89:513–536

Partridge MD, Rickman DS (2003) The waxing and waning of US regional economies: the chicken-egg of jobs versus people. J Urban Econ 53:76–97

Partridge MD, Rickman DS (2006) Fluctuations in aggregate US migration flows and regional labor market flexibility. South Econ J 72:958–980

Puga D (2002) European regional policies in light of recent location theories. J Econ Geogr 2:373–406

Rodríguez-Pose A, Ketterer T (2012) Do local amenities affect the appeal of regions in Europe for migrants? J Reg Sci 52:535–561

Rodríguez-Pose A, Ketterer T, Castells-Quintana D (2015) Do we follow the money? The drivers of migration across regions in the EU. Region 2:27–46

Sardadvar S, Rocha-Akis S (2016) Interregional migration within the European Union in the aftermath of the eastern enlargements: a spatial approach. Rev Reg Res 36:51–79

Sjaastad LA (1962) The costs and returns of human migration. J Polit Econ 70:80–93

Stark O, Micevska M, Mycielski J (2009) Relative poverty as a determinant of migration: evidence from Poland. Econ Lett 103:119–122

Tremblay K (2002) Student mobility between and towards OECD countries: a comparative analysis. In: OECD (ed) International mobility of the highly skilled. OECD, Paris

Zaiceva A, Zimmermann K (2008) Scale, diversity, and determinants of labour migration in Europe. Oxf Rev Econ Policy 24:428–452

Chapter 6
The Geography of Asylum Seekers and Refugees in Europe

Marco Percoco and Ugo Fratesi

Abstract Recent waves of immigration flows and asylum seekers are posing serious social and political problems in European countries. Between 2009 and 2015, it has been estimated a total of 3–3.5 millions of asylum applications to national governments. This chapter discusses the geography of asylum seekers in the European Union and proposes some descriptive statistics concerning the behavioral reaction of residents. In particular, it is shown a strong correlation between the size of the population of asylum seekers and the fear of terrorism and crime, whereas no economic concern was found. This evidence is interpreted as need to provide also correct information to residents when implementing immigration policies.

Keywords Refugees · Asylum seekers · Migration · European Union · Attitudes

6.1 Introduction

Europe has experienced many waves of refugees in the twentieth century with different directions of flows. Notably, before 1939 thousands of Jews from Germany sought for asylum in other European countries or even in the Americas. This wave of refugees is particularly interesting from a social perspective for its content of human capital. Waldinger (2010) and Moser et al. (2014) have in fact estimated the (negative) impact of the expulsion of thousands of Jewish professors from German universities and the (positive) effect on U.S. economy which eventually received them. In those years, US public opinion was divided on the issue of Jewish refugees from Europe. The Gallup Institute has recently assembled an interesting set of pools

Paola Proietti provided assistance in collecting some of the data used in the paper. Percoco gratefully acknowledges financial support from FIRB-MIUR.

M. Percoco (✉)
Università Bocconi, Milano, Italy
e-mail: marco.percoco@unibocconi.it

U. Fratesi
Politecnico di Milano, Milano, Italy
e-mail: ugo.fratesi@polimi.it

B. Biagi et al. (eds.), *New Frontiers in Interregional Migration Research*,
Advances in Spatial Science, https://doi.org/10.1007/978-3-319-75886-2_6

regarding refugees in the opinion of Americans and found a 61% opposition against Jewish refugees.[1]

The most recent refugees wave, before that generated by turbulence in the Middle East, has been in correspondence of the breakup of war in Kosovo, where thousands of Muslim refugees sought asylum in Western Europe and in the US. Those flows were welcomed in receiving countries without manifestation of opposition, possibly because of the involvement of Western countries in the war against Serbia.

Despite these events, Europe or the European Union was almost unprepared to manage current refugee crisis, both in institutional and socio-economic terms. Dustmann et al. (2016) have calculated that between 2009 and 2015 3–3.5 millions of asylum applications have been received by national governments. This situation is exacerbating centripetal tensions with discussions of the fair versus balanced distribution of refugees and asylum seekers lasting for years, further deteriorating the political and institutional landscape of the continent.

Several geographical dimensions form the institutional and economic background of current situation, especially in Europe. Asylum seekers embark in dangerous trips, primarily through the Mediterranean Sea, to escape from wars and political and religious persecutions. Economic motives of these forced migration flows are very likely to be marginal. Nevertheless, their economic impacts, or at least as they are perceived by European residents and decision makers might be substantial in destination countries in terms of both public finances and local labour markets. Moreover, Europe is the destination of asylum seekers from different geographical areas, and while those coming from the middle east are in most cases escaping from wars (e.g. the Syrians), there is a large number of asylum demands which come from people coming from different places which are not at war and, as such, generally end up being classified as migrants rather than refugees. The European governments, and the public opinion, are not able to distinguish between these until the end of the process by which asylum demands are accepted or rejected, which may last many months and even a few years. For this reason, perceptions are as important as facts at the heart of the aforementioned discussion among European governments on whether and how to relocate asylum seekers. Interestingly, this process is eminently political and allows us to shed some light on the underlying political economic mechanism at work.

The aim of this paper is to review the main institutional and political factors influencing the debate over the spatial distribution of refugees and asylum seekers in Europe. In particular, we will review the main literature regarding the causes and consequences of refugee flows and provide an updated picture of the spatial distribution of refugees and asylum seekers among European countries. Furthermore, we will present some data concerning the perceptions of Europeans and how this is shaping the debate over migration policies.

---

[1]http://www.gallup.com/opinion/polling-matters/186716/historical-review-americans-views-refugees-coming.aspx

6.2 The Issue of Refugees and Asylum Seekers in the Recent Literature

International migration is a global phenomenon which has expanded in recent years. The international migration report (UN 2013) estimates that the number of international migrants has been constantly growing over the period 1990–2013. Europe is the main destination for migrants, being the residence of about one third of the total, and is closely followed by Asia. Even more interesting is the fact that international migration flows have specific characteristics in terms of origin-destination. North-south flows have remained stable and very low, while north-north flows have grown slowly and steadily. The most remarkable trend, however, is the very sizeable growth of south-south and south-north flows, which now account for the very large majority of migrants (UN 2013).

Global migration flows have been significantly studied in the literature, at both the national the regional level. Particular focuses of academic research have been the reasons behind choices to migrate, the determinants of the location of migrants (e.g. Pedersen et al. 2008; Wang et al. 2016) and the impact of migration on the places of origin and of destination of migrants (e.g. Kanbur and Rapoport 2005; De Haas 2010; Di Maria and Stryszowski 2009; Dustmann et al. 2011; Borjas 2015; The World Bank 2006).

Refugees constitute a relatively small part of global migration, since they are defined by the 1951 Refugee Convention as a person who "owing to a well-founded fear of being persecuted for reasons of race, religion, nationality, membership of a particular social group or political opinion, is outside the country of his nationality, and is unable to, or owing to such fear, is unwilling to avail himself of the protection of that country".

However, refugees and asylum seekers also constitute a rapidly growing and highly visible part of international migration. The UNHCR (2015) estimates that more than two million asylum applications were received in 38 European countries in 2015. This is a substantial increase from the slightly more than 700,000 lodged in 2014.

A large (and now growing) body of literature has long considered the effect of mass migration or refugees on local economies. An early study was conducted by Card (1990) on the effect of the Miami boatlift in the early 1980s on the Florida labour market, finding limited evidence of an effect on wages and employment.

Hunt (1992) and Carrington and De Lima (1996) have considered the case of repatriates from the African colonies of France and Portugal, reporting a negative effect on employment and wages in locations where repatriates settled.

These early papers on the impact of "return" migrants are interesting, as they consider a shock occurring in other countries as an influence on the decision to migrate, although it was sometimes not a properly free decision. However, they are not immune from critique of their identification strategy, given the highly-aggregated data they made use of and the endogeneity of the location decision. To circumvent the issue of self-selection, Glitz (2012) exploits an exogenous variation in German migration law which occurred in 1989. This made the migration of family members of immigrated workers easier. In this case, non-significant effects on wages and internal migration were found.

In general, however, the main effect of large migration inflows, if any, could be found in the re-distribution of income. If migrants are on average less skilled than residents, then unskilled workers will face tougher competition for jobs and a consequent reduction in wages, which may be not apparent if only average wages are considered.

The case of refugees and asylum seekers is different from the general case of migrants, as in most cases they are not allowed to work in hosting countries, at least in the short term. Subsequently, in the medium-term they have lower employment rates than other immigrants and finally have higher benefit use rates (European Parliament 2016; Martìn et al. 2016; Ruist 2015). These features imply that their impact on local economies is usually worse than that of economic migrants.

Besides Europe in these last few years, Africa is certainly the continent that has witnessed the largest displacements of people because of wars, political unrest and natural disasters. Therefore, such cases have attracted some scholars aiming to shed new light on the relationship between forced migration and development in receiving countries. The most interesting case in recent years has certainly been the refugee crisis in Tanzania, due to masses of individuals fleeing from Burundi (1993) and Rwanda (1994).

In a first attempt to evaluate the effect of such phenomena, Baez (2011) has argued in favour of a negative effect, since the socio-economic stress imposed by refugee influence is too strong to be absorbed by weak local labour markets. Interestingly, Maystadt and Duranton (2014) consider the same case and reach opposite conclusions. In a rigorous econometric analysis, they consider a panel of Tanzanian households over the period 1991–2010 and find that the presence of refugees from Burundi and Rwanda has had a positive effect on welfare. They also argue that such positive change was due to public investment in infrastructure, decreasing transportation costs and leading to a higher mobility of individuals. This result is interesting and important, since it implies that a temporary population shock may have permanent positive effects thanks to efficient and appropriate public policies.

The Syrian conflict is currently generating large refugee inflows in neighbouring countries, especially Lebanon and Turkey, deeply affecting local economies. Akgunduz et al. (2015) exploit the geographical distribution of refugee camps in Turkey to analyse the impact of the inflows of Syrians in terms of housing and food prices, as well as market outcomes. They find a slight increase in the level of prices and no significant changes in the employment rate of natives.

As it is also clear from the work of Maystadt and Duranton (2014), considering a long period of time is of paramount importance to disentangling the effect of massive population shock. An interesting case is the Great Migration to the USA from Europe, which occurred between the second half of the nineteenth century and the beginning of the twentieth. Those migration flows were driven by both economic reasons and persecutions, especially in the case of Jews in Eastern Europe facing the worrying diffusion of pogroms. Rodriguez-Pose and von Berlepsch (2012) find that countries that had attracted more migrants between 1880 and 1910 had better economic indicators in 2005, even after controlling for self-selection of migrants into locations.

Finally, it should be noted that one of the most important drivers of development in modern economies is innovation capacity. Moser et al. (2014) find that high-skilled refugees may boost innovation in destination countries through scientific spillovers. In particular, they consider the impact on the number of patents in the USA of Jewish scientists who were expelled from German universities and who fled to the USA.

As should be evident at this point of the review, the economic literature on refugees and asylum seekers has primarily focused on the impact of displaced individuals while comparatively less attention has been devoted to the analysis of the location of refugees and asylum seekers. This is affected by a variety of factors, some of which are eminently political and cultural.

In particular, there is little evidence on the factors that, at a sub-national level, influence the attitude towards hosting refugees and asylum seekers. The International Organization for Migration (IOM) (2015) provided a survey of public attitudes towards immigration worldwide, finding that in most of the world the attitude towards immigrants is rather positive. Europe is an important exception in which the majority of the population believes immigration levels should be decreased. This is the outcome of two different models, one prevailing in northern Europe in which migration is welcome, and another prevailing in southern Europe in which migration is considered to be excessive (IOM 2015, p. 7). This might also be related to the fact that southern Europe is not only the front-door of migration into Europe and the hub of the refugee crisis, but is also the part of the continent which has been affected most by the economic crisis. Therefore, the economies of these countries are structurally weaker and have important issues in terms of public finances (Moro and Beker 2016; Fonseca and Fratesi 2016).

This is consistent with the fact, also found in IOM (2015), that the attitude towards migrants is more negative among those people who are more likely to compete with migrants for job opportunities (i.e. the lower educated and unemployed).

6.3 Refugees and Asylum Seekers in Europe

6.3.1 The Spatial Distribution of Asylum Seekers

According to recent estimates of the International Migration Outlook (2016), OECD countries received about 1.5 million of new asylum seekers in 2015, with an expected further increase in 2016. However, because of fragmented regulation, only a limited share of this flow is actually granted asylum. In the European Union, in particular, because of a lack of common and harmonized regulation and of a substantial overlapping between political refugees and economic migrants in terms of origin countries and especially points of entry (mainly in Mediterranean countries), the probability to obtain a refugee status is relatively low.

Data, in fact, show that the majority of those who applied for asylum in Europe were denied it, in many cases because they are considered by the tribunals as economic migrants. Figure 6.1 shows that the number of asylum seekers in the European Union having a first instance decision has been constantly increasing, especially after 2014, and that rejections have been attributed in the majority of cases, until 2015 and 2016, when the number of those who received a positive outcome was larger than those who were in the first instance rejected, most likely due to the Syrian crisis.

There exist significant differences between countries in the percentage of asylum seekers who are given a positive reply to their application (Table 6.1). In particular, these are higher in Denmark, Sweden and Austria, and are above the EU average also in Germany, which is the country which receives most of them. They are lower than the average, though, in other large countries, such as Italy, France and, especially, the UK. The sources of these differences in terms of percentage of applications are likely to depend on two different aspects: on one side the source of asylum seekers, which can come from different routes and different countries, so that some of them, like Syrians, are normally allowed the status of refugee, while others are often classified as economic migrants. The second aspect is the different legal system in the different countries, which rely on different types of courts with different outcomes.

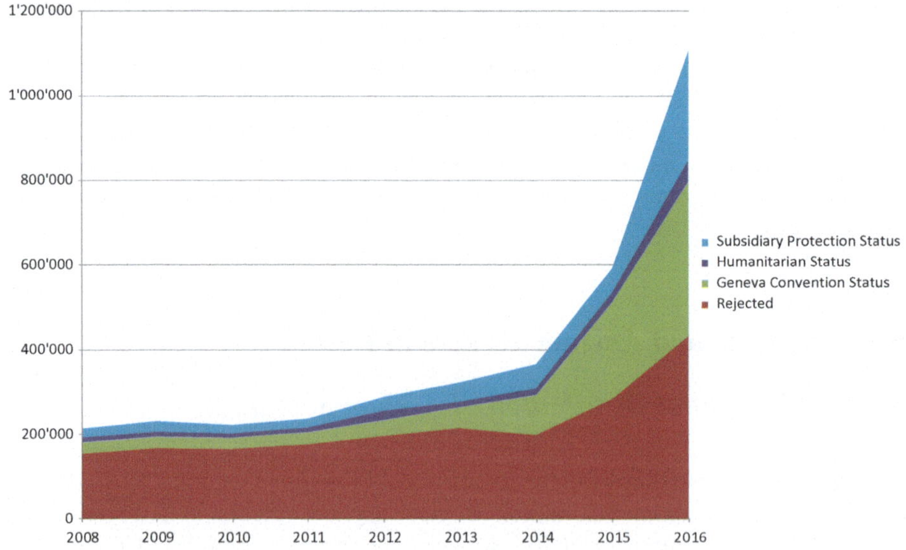

Fig. 6.1 First instance decisions on asylum applications by type of decision—annual aggregated data. Source of data: Eurostat

Table 6.1 Number of first instance decisions on asylum applications by type of decision and by country in 2015

Country	Percentage with positive first instance decision	Rejected	Total positive	Geneva convention status	Humanitarian status	Subsidiary protection status	Total
EU28	51.9	285,165	307,510	229,460	22,080	55,970	592,680
DE	56.5	108,370	140,910	137,135	2070	1705	249,280
FR	26.5	57,280	20,630	16,790	0	3845	77,910
IT	41.5	41,730	29,615	3575	15,770	10,270	71,345
SE	72.2	12,375	32,215	12,740	1350	18,125	44,590
UK	36.6	24,115	13,950	12,175	1650	125	38,070
CH	64.1	7840	14,000	6285	5080	2630	21,840
AT	71.3	6050	15,045	12,590	355	2100	21,095
NL	80.4	4015	16,450	6660	390	9400	20,465
BE	53.9	8945	10,475	8825	0	1650	19,420
DK	81.1	2305	9920	7605	70	2245	12,225
EL	41.8	5610	4030	3665	10	355	9640
NO	66.0	3225	6250	5410	165	675	9475
BG	90.6	580	5595	4705	0	890	6175
PL	18.2	2870	640	350	120	165	3510
HU	14.8	2915	505	145	5	355	3420
ES	31.5	2220	1020	220	0	800	3240
FI	56.8	1280	1680	1060	160	460	2960
CY	76.8	480	1585	195	0	1390	2065
MT	83.9	240	1250	265	75	915	1490
CZ	34.5	875	460	55	15	390	1335
RO	36.4	840	480	240	0	235	1320
IE	33.0	665	330	150	0	180	1000
LU	23.9	590	185	170	0	15	775
PT	52.7	180	195	35	0	160	370
HR	21.6	145	40	35	0	5	185
EE	44.4	100	80	20	0	55	180
IS	27.8	130	50	30	5	15	180
LT	47.2	95	85	15	0	65	180
LV	11.8	145	20	5	0	15	170
SI	34.6	85	45	35	0	10	130
SK	61.5	50	80	5	35	40	130
LI	16.7	25	5	0	0	0	30

Source of data: Eurostat

According to the Eurostat definitions (Decisions on applications and resettlement (migr_asydec) Reference Metadata in Euro SDMX Metadata Structure (ESMS)):

> Refugee status means a person covered by a decision granting refugee status, taken by administrative or judicial bodies during the reference period. Refugee status means status as defined in Art.2(e) of Directive 2011/95/EU within the meaning of Art.1 of the Geneva

(continued)

Convention relating to the Status of Refugees of 28 July 1951, as amended by the New York Protocol of 31 January 1967
Subsidiary protection status: means a person covered by a decision granting subsidiary protection status as defined in Art.2(g) of Directive 2011/95/EC i.e. 'the recognition by a Member State of a third country national or a stateless person as a person eligible for subsidiary protection'
Authorisation to stay for humanitarian reasons: means a person covered by a decision granting authorisation to stay for humanitarian reasons under national law concerning international protection by administrative or judicial bodies. It includes persons who are not eligible for international protection as currently defined in the Qualifications Directive (Directive 2011/95/EU) but are nonetheless protected against removal under the obligations that are imposed on all Member States by international refugee or human rights instruments or on the basis of principles flowing from such instruments. Examples of such categories include persons who are not removable on ill health grounds and unaccompanied minors. This concept refers only to persons who have been previously reported as asylum applicants in the Asylum data collection. As a consequence, persons granted a permission to stay for humanitarian reasons but who have not previously applied for international protection are not included under this concept

6.3.2 *The Routes*

One of the interesting spatial aspects of the recent surge in the arrival of refugees and asylum seekers in Europe concerns the routes through which they arrive. The main routes to Europe according to FRONTEX are: the Western One, between Senegal, Mauritania and Morocco and the Spanish Canary Islands, the routes of Western, Central and Eastern Mediterranean, which respectively are those connecting Africa to Spain, Africa to Italy and Malta and finally Turkey with Cyprus, Greece and Bulgaria. In addition there are the Eastern Balkan route which it is also called the circular route from Albania to Greece, the Western Balkan route connecting the countries from the Western Balkan region to Greece, Bulgaria, Romania, Hungary and Croatia and last but not least the Eastern Route mainly used by Moldova, Ukraine, Belarus and Russia to enter Romania, Hungary, Slovakia, Poland, Lithuania, Latvia, Estonia, Finland and Norway.

The flows relative importance in quantitative terms changes in relation to shocks in country of departure but it might also change according to destinations' countries answers to fluxes e.g. the construction of border fences and walls or the implementation of restrictive hosting policies. For example, in 2015, Syria (23%), Afghanistan (16%) and Iraq (11%) represented half of the asylum demands in OECD countries. Looking at more recent data, they show that immigrants from Syria, Afghanistan and Iraq diminished and the number of migrants from Nigeria and Eritrea, increased. The change in nationalities, reflects the changing routes and port of arrival; while Greece received more migrants from Syria (46.6%), Afghanistan (24.2%) and Iraq (15.2%), Italy received a much greater variety of nationalities, and in particular Nigerians (21.0%), Eritreans (11.7%), Guineans (7.2%). Indeed, the central Mediterranean Route was the preferred one in 2016 and Italy saw a 115% increase in cumulative arrivals (177,729 in 2016 vs. 153,842 in 2015), while the Eastern Balkan route became less practiced and Greece saw in 2016 a 83% decrease in cumulative arrivals (175,666 arrivals in 2016 vs. 1,033,029 in 2015) (IOM 2016).

Refugees coming from different routes and different countries had different locations in Europe. As it can be observed in the maps of Fig. 6.2. In particular, it is clear the higher presence of refugees from Afghanistan in the Balkans, and especially in Serbia. Refugees from Albania are predominantly present in Germany. Those from Syria are either in the Balkans, especially in Serbia, or in Germany and Sweden. Refugees from African countries, who follow the southern Mediterranean route have as a consequence a different distribution. In particular, those from Eritrea are in central and Northern European countries, Switzerland, Germany, The Netherlands, Sweden and Norway. Those from Somalia follow a similar path but even more concentrated in Germany and Sweden.

The hype in the flows in the Central Mediterranean Sea has been accompanied by a significant increase in the death toll because of the joint cause of adverse meteorological conditions and precarious ships used by human trafficker. It is difficult to estimate the death toll of the refugee crisis because of the substantial informality. However, an attempt was made by the project "Human costs of border control". The period covered by the Deaths at the Borders Database is 1/1/1990 to 31/12/2013, reflecting the period under study by the broader research project. As a consequence, a few cases from the late 1980s—in Cadiz region, Spain, for instance—are missing. Nonetheless, the period covered captures the years in which 'border deaths' became a phenomenon in the southern EU border regions precarious ships, although we do not observe recent dramatic events. Given these data and data on refugees from the UN, it is possible to highlight the dramatic increase in the mortality risk in the Central Mediterranean route, as depicted in Fig. 6.3.

6.4 Attitudes of Europeans Towards Refugees

One of the major issues with the recent wave of refugees is certainly the issue of attitudes and opinions of Europeans towards asylum seekers, refugees and in general towards migrants, with the average citizen usually little informed on the differences between the three concepts, also because the political debate is too often (deliberately?) confusing in this sense.

The wave has been accompanied by a severe economic crisis and several terrorist attacks. Although causality among those phenomena is far from being established, individuals form their opinions even by means of superficial perceptions and spurious correlations.

In the previous sections, while reviewing the major literature, we have made also an attempt to clarify the uncertainty over the effect of refugees in destination countries. This uncertainty, along with some more general conditions, influences negative opinions of Europeans with respect to refugees. However, it should be noted that the fear of terrorism accompanied by a severe economic crisis should be thought to be as a major force behind the growing diffidence of residents.

People form their attitudes and opinions in several ways; it may take the form of an information network, which can be effectively used by politicians in order to

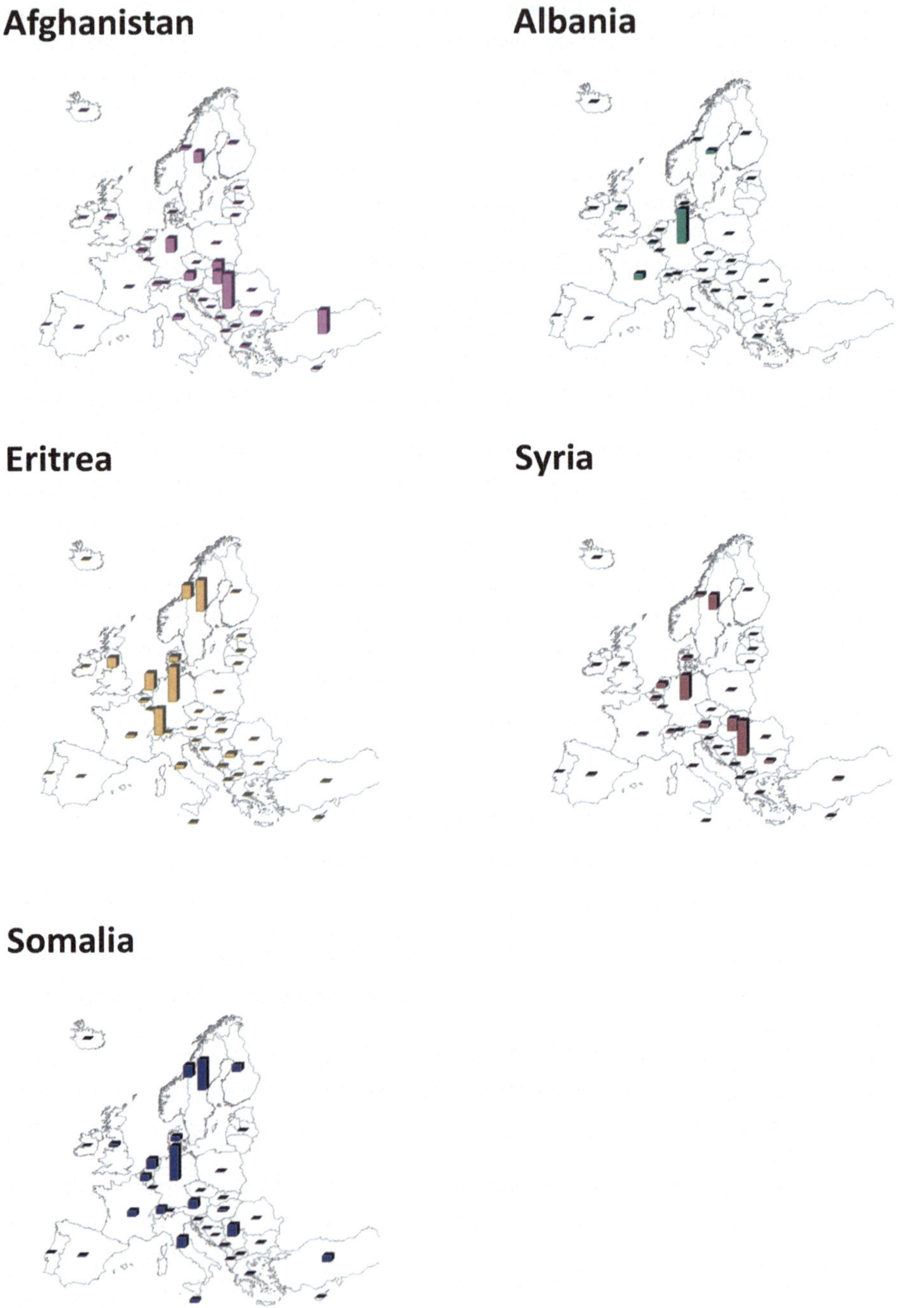

Fig. 6.2 The spatial distribution of refugees by source and destination country in 2015 (selected countries only). Source: UNHCR

Fig. 6.3 Mortality risk of major routes

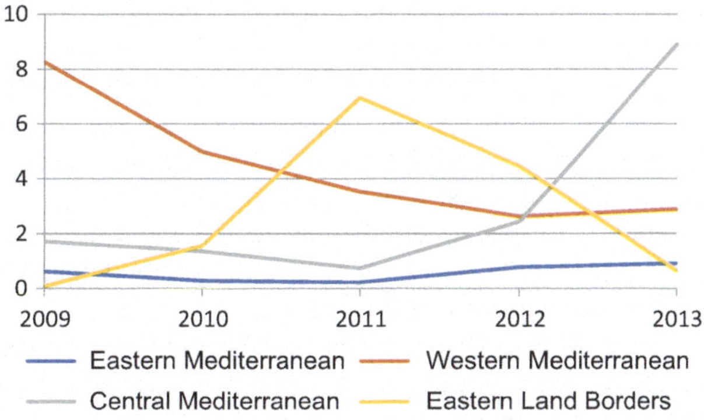

persuade voters and then to gain political consensus or simply votes (Murphy and Shleifer 2004). Several sources of persuasion have been analyzed; people are often persuaded by those they personally interact with (Granovetter 1973); in the political debate, since voter awareness of specific issues is quite low, vulnerability to persuasion is high (Zaller 1992); Mullainathan and Shleifer (2005) develop a theoretical paper on the formation of social networks and on their use by politicians to obtain support; assuming that people are influenced by those inside their network, the model shows how entrepreneurs create networks using core issues that are centrally important to members. These networks can then be rented out to politicians who seek votes as well as support for other initiatives.

In the last two decades there has been an increase in the body of literature regarding public opinion towards migrants and immigration in general with particular attention to USA and UK (see, for instance, Bauer et al. 2000; Card et al. 2009; Citrin et al. 1997; Dustmann and Preston 2007; Espenshade and Hempstead 1996; Hanson et al. 2007; Kessler 2001; Scheve and Slaughter 2001). More recently, Facchini and Mayda have considered the opinions of Europeans over migration policies and found that only a small portion of voters tend to support policies more open with respect to migrants.

The economic crisis is also a major driver of negative attitudes on refugees. Colloca (2016) has in fact argued that during bad times for the economy, people tend to focus on themselves and to reduce the extent of social networks. Under these circumstances, the spatial reach of trust is limited and sentiments of aversion, rivalry and revenge against who is perceived as an outsider may prevail. This argument is consistent with the theory of social capital as proposed by Banfield (1954) who postulated that uncertainty, inequality and an excessive reliance on short social ties are the main determinants of weak cooperative behavior and low generalized trust, that is trust in strangers. The framework proposed by Colloca (2016) introduces second order effects in this view as it states that economic downturns may change individuals' attitudes and behavior, especially in terms of their spirits of trust, cooperation and empathy for those out of their social networks. Fratesi et al. (2016), in studying the spatial allocation of refugees among Italian provinces have in fact found that strong and established communities are less prone to accept larger numbers of asylum seekers.

Recently, the Pew Research Center (2016) has reported results of a survey among Europeans regarding their opinions on refugees. About 59% perceive them as a threat to their security (Fig. 6.4), as respondents think that refugees will increase the likelihood of terrorist attacks in their countries.

Half of European are also concerned about the impact of labour markets since 50% think that refugees will be a burden for their country because they will take their jobs and social benefits (Fig. 6.5).

Interestingly, there is a considerable variation among countries with Hungarians and Poles as the most concerned and Italian and Greeks also raining their concern on the economic dimension. Considerably less "fear" is perceived with respect to crime as only 30% of Europeans think that refugees are a major cause of crime (Fig. 6.6).

Figures 6.7, 6.8 and 6.9 report simple and admittedly weak scatterplots in which the results of the survey are correlated with the effective presence of refugees in the countries, all variables being in a logarithmic scale. Despite the weak statistical power, let us consider the regression line as a reliable conditional expected value of the attitudes. Interestingly, respondents in all countries tend to overestimate the link between refugees and terrorism, whereas respondents to the question regarding the

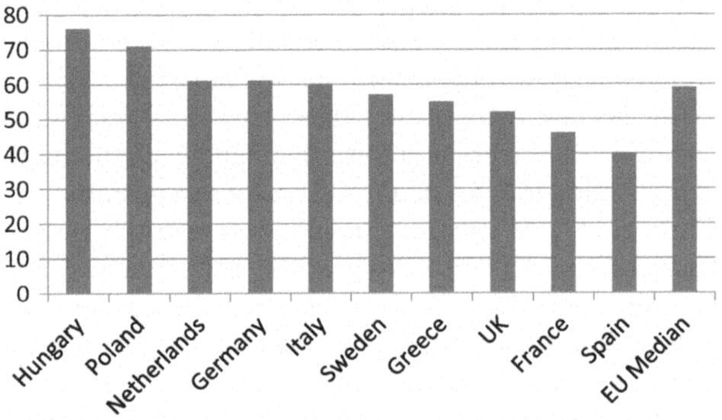

Fig. 6.4 "Refugees will increase the likelihood of terrorism in our country" (top choice; %). Source: Pew Research Center (2016)

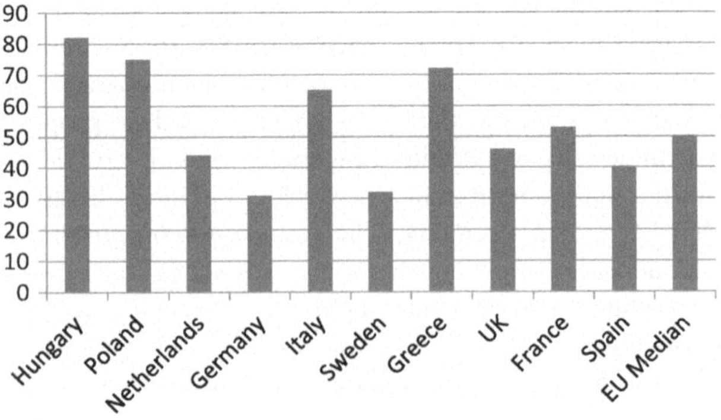

Fig. 6.5 "Refugees are a burden on our country because they take our jobs and social benefits" (top choice; %). Source: Pew Research Center (2016)

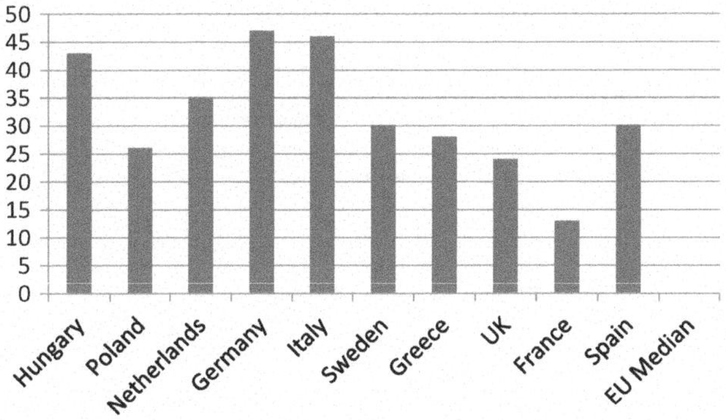

Fig. 6.6 "Refugees in our country are more to blame for crime than other groups" (top choice; %). Source: Pew Research Center (2016)

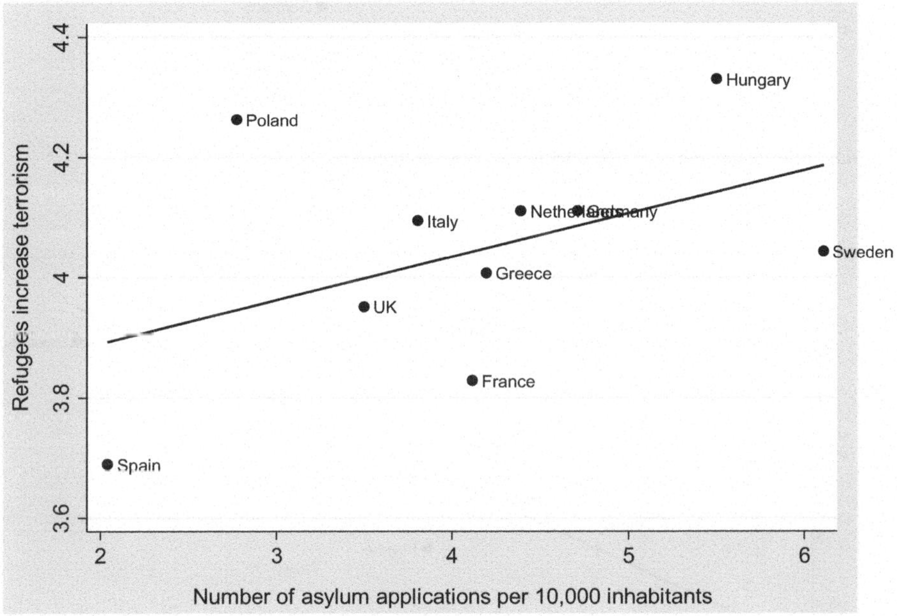

Fig. 6.7 Presence of refugees and perceived terrorist threats

impact of refugees on labor markets seem to be relatively "rational", as there seems to be no correlation between the presence of refugees and the perceived economic risk.

Overall, our analysis points at a positive association between the presence of refugees and the negative attitudes of Europeans, although in some cases an overreaction has been detected. This behavioral response is a policy ground that is

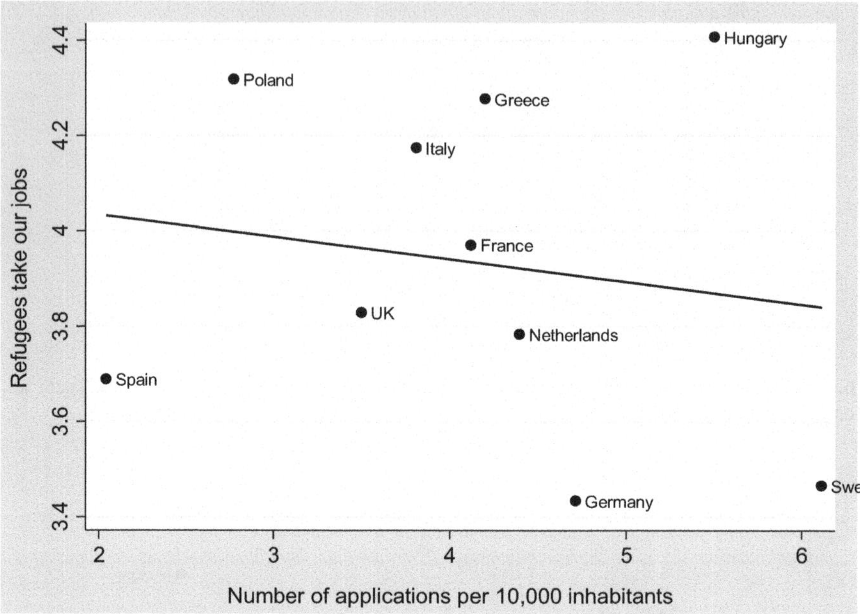

Fig. 6.8 Presence of refugees and perceived economic threats

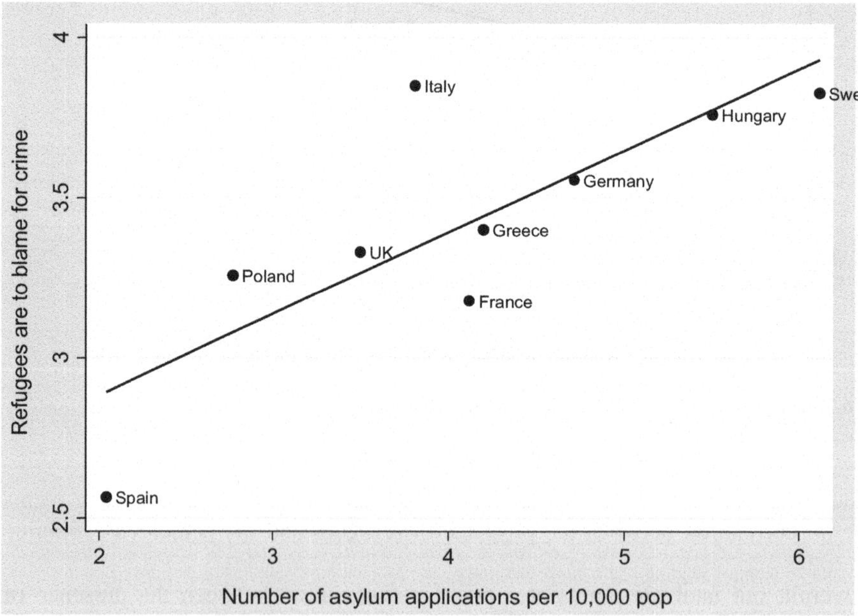

Fig. 6.9 Presence of refugees and perceived crime threats

neglected by most of the EU policy makers and provides fertile soil for the upcoming wave of nationalisms.

6.5 The Distribution of Refugees at Sub-national Level: Hints from the Italian Case

All the analysis so far has been almost exclusively at national level. However, there are very significant differences between regions within countries.

One rare example for which it has been possible to collect the data is the Italian one, a case which is especially interesting because the country is, due to geographical reasons, the southern door of Europe towards the Mediterranean, so that it attracts very important flows of asylum seekers mostly coming from African countries through Libya. These flows have increased and reached new peaks every year since 2014, so that Ismu (2017) estimates that more than 500,000 asylum seekers have reached the country in the 3 years 2014–2016, more than in the 17 previous years.

To deal with these large flows, the distribution of asylum seekers mechanism in Italy has three phases. The first phase is a phase, centralized by the national government, in which asylum seekers are first assisted in nationally managed structures. The second phase is a phase in which, during the process of appraisal of the asylum request, the refugee stays in structures which are manages in public-private partnership. In the third phase an asylum seeker who is granted refugee status is free to move where he/she wants, while if the status is not granted there is a repatriation.

The second phase is the most interesting because in this phase it is the local communities who "bid" for having asylum seekers in their communities, with economic advantages but also, sometimes, negative reactions from the local public opinion.

As it can be seen in Fig. 6.10, not all regions (at Nuts3 level) host asylum seekers, but some regions are more willing to host them. It is evident a pre-dominance of poorer provinces and of provinces closer to the places where asylum seekers land (mostly by sea). Interestingly, it also appears that in the Italian case those regions where the levels of social capital are higher are also less willing to host asylum seekers (Fratesi et al. 2016), possibly also because of the confusion in the national politics between refugees and economic migrants.

This is an interesting result, which it is not yet possible to compare with other European countries, in which the attitudes towards asylum seekers are not detected by polls but by actual behaviours and the political and economic variables are not the only determinants but the social situation of places is also important and, apparently, the most internally cohesive places are also more closed towards the external (Fratesi et al. 2016).

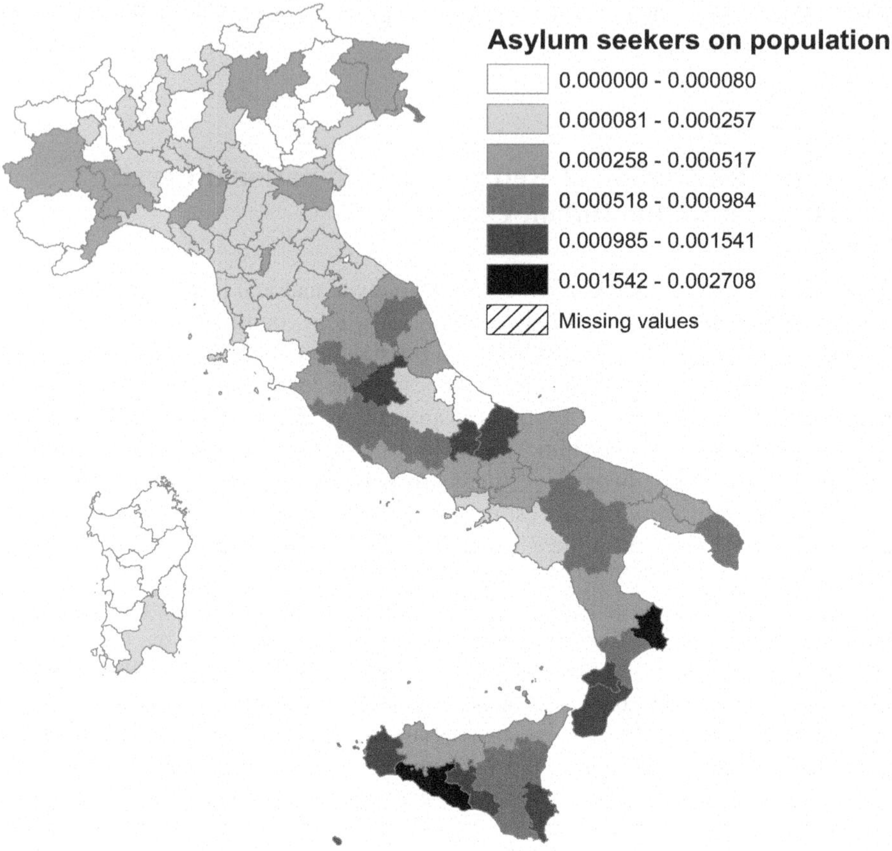

Fig. 6.10 The spatial distribution of asylum seekers in Italy in 2015 (asylum seekers per capita). Source: ISTAT

6.6 Conclusions

Political turmoil, civil conflicts and wars are driving the displacement of large mass of civilians in Africa and in the Middle East. A significant portion of those refugees decide to start a long and dangerous trip to Europe to seek asylum.

From 2009 to 2015 European countries received 3–3.5 millions of applications to obtain asylum and this is causing significant issues in the EU. On one hand, this fosters nationalism and populism in most countries, with centrifugal effects between the EU and its members. On the other, the arrival and the distribution of refugees among EU members is a source of main concern for the cohesion of the Union because the large numbers make it more difficult the integration process.

In this chapter, we have reviewed the main issues and the state of the art of the literature. In particular, we have pointed at a fragmentation of the research as no consensus has been reached with respect to the effects and burden of refugees in destination countries. In particular, we believe that the analysis of the impacts and distribution of refugees would need to be upgraded to a finer spatial scale with respect to the national one which is currently the only possible one. The impacts are in fact localized, and there is need to know where they pass through and where they end-up to really understand the phenomenon.

Looking forward, we see in particular the following research avenues as especially fruitful and helpful from a socio-economic point of view:

- The analysis of the economic impact of refugees on places, which might depend on the human capital possessed by the refugees and on the economic structure or the places where they end up.
- The analysis of the social impact of refugees on places, which depends on the personal characteristics of the refugees and on the social characteristics of places.
- The analysis of the impact of places on the well-being of refugees, since different places could provide different integration opportunities.
- An analysis of the impact of refugees on the local innovation systems. In fact, refugees could provide new knowledge or new ideas which could spark, in some cases, the economic and social innovativeness of places, especially where innovation is not so diffused.

Finally, and in a positive perspective, migration policies should be informed by rational and consistent data and analyses. We have in fact documented, although in a rudimentary way, that individuals tend to overreact to the presence of asylum seekers and refugees and this is fertile soil for public discontent with respect to the European Union. Efforts should be made to provide not only correct information, including a clearer distinction between asylum seekers, refugees and migrants, but also to understand in depth the sources of fear and shape policies and their communication campaigns accordingly. Although a harmonized regulation is needed for granting asylum, policies meant to integrate migrants should be conceived at a more local level, where refugees and asylum seekers in fact locate or are located.

References

Akgunduz YE, van den Berg M, Hassink W (2015) The impact of refugee crises on host labor markets: the case of the Syrian refugee crisis in Turkey. IZA discussion paper no 8841

Baez JE (2011) Civil wars beyond their borders: the human capital and health consequences of hosting refugees. J Dev Econ 96(2):391–408

Banfield E (1954) The moral basis of a backward society. Free Press, New York

Bauer TK, Lofstrom M, Zimmermann KF (2000) Immigration policy, assimilation of immigrants and natives' sentiments towards immigrants: evidence from OECD countries. IZA discussion paper no. 187

Borjas GJ (2015) Immigration and globalization: a review essay. J Econ Lit 53:961–974

Card D (1990) The impact of the Mariel Boatlift on the Miami labor market. Ind Labor Relat Rev 43(2):245–257

Card D, Dustmann C, Preston I (2009) Immigration, wages and compositional amenities. NBER WP 15521

Carrington WJ, De Lima PJ (1996) The impact of 1970s repatriates from Africa on the Portuguese labor market. Ind Labor Relat Rev 49(2):330–347

Citrin J, Green D, Muste C, Wong C (1997) Public opinion toward immigration reform: the role of economic motivation. J Polit 59(3):858–881

Colloca P (2016) La "recessione" civica. Crisi economica e deterioramento sociale, Bologna: il Mulino

De Haas H (2010) Migration and development: a theoretical perspective. Int Migr Rev 44 (1):227–264

Di Maria C, Stryszowski P (2009) Migration, human capital accumulation and economic development. J Dev Econ 90(2):306–313

Dustmann C, Preston I (2007) Racial and economic factors in attitudes to immigration. B E J Econ Anal Policy 7:Article 62

Dustmann C, Fadlon I, Weiss Y (2011) Return migration, human capital accumulation and the brain drain. J Dev Econ 95(1):58–67

Dustmann C, Fasani F, Minale L, Frattini T, Schoenberg U (2016) On the economics and politics of refugee migration. CReAM DP No 16/16

Espenshade TJ, Hempstead K (1996) Contemporary American attitudes toward U.S. immigration. Int Migr Rev 30:535–570

European Parliament (2016) Directorate general for internal policies. Policy department A: economic and scientific policy. Labour market integration of refugees: strategies and good practices. European Parliament

Fonseca M, Fratesi U (eds) (2016) Regional upgrading in Southern Europe – spatial disparities and human capital. Springer, Berlin

Fratesi U, Percoco M, Proietti P (2016) Who welcomes them? Determinants of the spatial distribution of asylum seekers in Italy. Mimeo

Glitz A (2012) The labor market impact of immigration: a quasi-experiment exploiting immigrant location rules in Germany. J Labor Econ 30(1):175–213

Granovetter M (1973) The strength of weak ties. Am J Sociol 78(6):1360–1380

Hanson GH, Scheve K, Slaughter M (2007) Public finance and individual preferences over globalization strategies. Econ Polit 19:1–33

Hunt J (1992) The impact of the 1962 repatriates from Algeria on the French labor market. Ind Labor Relat Rev 45(3):556–572

International Organization for Migration (IOM) (2015) How the world views migration. International Organization for Migration, Geneva

IOM (2016) Migration flows to Europe. The Mediterranean digest. Report N.3

Ismu (2017) Richiedenti asilo e protezione internazionale: il 2016 è l'anno dei record, Comunicato Stampa. http://www.ismu.org/wp-content/uploads/2017/02/Comunicato-Ismu-richiedenti-asilo_febbraio-2017_pdf. Accessed 15 July 2017

Kanbur R, Rapoport H (2005) Migration selectivity and the evolution of spatial inequality. J Econ Geogr 5(1):43–57

Kessler (2001) Immigration, economic insecurity, and the "ambivalent" American public. The Center for Comparative Immigration Studies. Working paper no. 41

Martìn I et al (2016) From refugees to workers mapping labour-market integration support measures for asylum seekers and refugees in EU member states. Bertelsmann Stiftung, Gütersloh

Maystadt J-F, Duranton G (2014) The development push of refugees: evidence from Tanzania, University of Pennsylvania, Mimeo

Moro B, Beker VA (2016) Modern financial crises: Argentina, United States and Europe. Springer, Berlin

Moser P, Voena A, Waldinger F (2014) German-Jewish Émigrés and U.S. Invention. Am Econ Rev 104(10):3222–3255

Mullainathan S, Shleifer A (2005) The market for news. Am Econ Rev 95(4):1031–1053

Murphy K, Shleifer A (2004) Persuasion in politics. Am Econ Rev 94(2):435–439
OECD (2016) International migration outlook 2016. OECD Publishing, Paris
Pedersen PJ, Pytlikova M, Smith N (2008) Selection and network effects-migration flows into OECD countries 1990–2000. Eur Econ Rev 52(7):1160–1186
Pew Research Center (2016) Europeans fear wave of refugees will mean more terrorism, fewer jobs. Pew Research Center, Washington, DC
Rodriguez-Pose A, von Berlepsch V (2012) When migrants rule: the legacy of mass migration on economic development in the United States. Ann Assoc Am Geogr 103(3):628–651
Ruist J (2015) The fiscal cost of refugee immigration: the example of Sweden. Popul Dev Rev 41 (4):567–581
Scheve KF, Slaughter MJ (2001) Labor market competition and individual preferences over immigration policy. Rev Econ Stat 83:133–145
United Nations, Department of Economic and Social Affairs, Population Division (2013) International Migration Report 2013, New York
United Nations High Commissioner for Refugees (UNHCR) (2015) Global report, Geneva
Waldinger F (2010) Quality matters: the expulsion of professors and the consequences for PhD student outcomes in Nazi Germany. J Polit Econ 118(4):787–831
Wang Z, De Graaff T, Nijkamp P (2016) Cultural diversity and cultural distance as choice determinants of migration destination. Spat Econ Anal 11(2):176–200
World Bank (2006) Global economic prospects 2006 economic implications of remittances and migration. The International Bank for Reconstruction and Development/The World Bank, Washington, DC
Zaller J (1992) The nature and origins of mass opinion. Cambridge University Press, Cambridge

Chapter 7
State of the Art and Future Challenges of Interregional Migration Empirical Research in Oceania

Kathryn Benier and Jonathan Corcoran

Abstract With an estimated eight million international immigrants, Oceania is a region with the highest proportion of immigrants worldwide. The flow of migrants between Australia and New Zealand is especially large given their geographic proximity, cultural similarities, and a shared history as part of the British Commonwealth. This chapter places a particular focus on the interregional flows in Australia and New Zealand given that they represent the two most popular immigration destinations in Oceania. We discuss how immigration policy in both nations are likely to continue to focus on attracting and retaining immigrants that are selected based on their skills in an attempt to address persistent skill shortages and to ameliorate the effects of ageing populations. The challenge for regional scientists, population geographers and labour economists will be to identify sources of data through which we can better understand the migratory pathways through which both domestic and new international arrivals pass. Understanding these complex pathways will be the first step to unveiling the factors that underpin interregional migrations and how these shape outcomes for both individuals and local labour markets.

Keywords Oceania · Immigration history · Australia · New Zealand · Temporary migration · Migration pathway

K. Benier (✉)
School of Social Sciences, Monash University, Clayton, VIC, Australia
e-mail: kathryn.benier@monash.edu

J. Corcoran
Queensland Centre for Population Research, School of Earth and Environmental Sciences, The University of Queensland, Brisbane, QLD, Australia
e-mail: jj.corcoran@uq.edu.au

B. Biagi et al. (eds.), *New Frontiers in Interregional Migration Research*, Advances in Spatial Science, https://doi.org/10.1007/978-3-319-75886-2_7

7.1 Introduction

Oceania refers to the agglomeration of Australia, New Zealand and proximate Pacific island nations. With a population of around 40 million, Australia and New Zealand constitute around 70% of the total (Worldometers 2016). The region is estimated to currently host approximately eight million international immigrants (International Organisation of Migration 2015), placing Oceania with the highest proportion of immigrants worldwide (Mohanty 2006). This migration balance is consistently positive, with more people entering the region than leaving. Oceania's immigrant population is almost exclusively located in Australia and New Zealand—countries which offer attractive destination economies and opportunities for a certain lifestyle. This immigrant population includes interregional immigrants from Fiji and the other Pacific Island countries, as well as skilled immigrants from other global regions. The channel of migration between Australia and New Zealand is particularly large as a result of the geographic proximity, cultural similarities, and a shared history as part of the British Commonwealth. At the 2011 census, 483,398 New Zealand-born people, or 15% of the New Zealand population, were living in Australia (Australian Government: Department of Immigration and Border Protection 2013) and 62,712 Australia-born people were living in New Zealand in the 2013 census (Statistics New Zealand 2014a). According to the International Organisation of Migration (2015), the immigrant population of Australia was 28.22% of the total resident population—a total of 6,763,000 people. This proportion is higher than in other immigrant-receiving countries such as New Zealand (23.0%), Canada (21.8%), the United States (14.5%) and the United Kingdom (13.2%; International Organisation of Migration 2015). With the highest proportion of immigration in this region, it is vital to study the consequences of such trends and migration dynamics on the social and economic growth of Australia and New Zealand.

There are several parallels to be drawn between Australia and New Zealand. Both are settler societies with initial British populations who relied upon primary products for economic growth. Both had shared values, with heavy restrictions on immigration, whether embedded in law (Australia) or simply a preference (New Zealand), until World War II threatened the security of the nation and immigration was required to build population growth and accommodate an expanding labour market. In both countries, strict policies were abandoned in favour of non-discriminatory selection of potential immigrants based on the traits that they may contribute to their host country or their humanitarian considerations instead of selecting people based on their national origin or language spoken (Ongley and Pearson 1995). Differences include New Zealand's limited relative proportion of refugee intake as part of both the total population and the immigration flows, and New Zealand supporting temporary migrants whereas Australia's population building objectives favour permanent settlers (Ongley and Pearson 1995) although there is also a sizeable population of temporary migrants in the country. There are also differences in the treatment of the indigenous population, with New Zealand arguably recently providing more recognition of their indigenous heritage despite their initial treatment of the Maori population at the time of settlement.

In this chapter, we place a particular focus on interregional migration in Australia and New Zealand as these are the two most popular immigration destinations in the Oceanic region, and have been argued to share a labour market due to the similarities between the nations (Hugo et al. 2013). The chapter commences with an overview of the immigration history of Australia and New Zealand, before outlining more recent developments in migration policies and how this has been picked up in migration research that has examined the various drivers and consequences of these movements. We conclude with a discussion of the future challenges of interregional migration research in Oceania.

7.2 Australia's Immigration History

Since white settlement in Australia in 1788, Australia's population and economic growth has largely been driven by immigration. From 2006, immigration arrivals in Australia have contributed more to population growth each year than the rate of natural increase (ABS 2014). Australia's population of 24 million people comes from over 200 countries, and almost half of the population have one or both parents that were born outside of Australia (Australian Bureau of Statistics 2016). Immigration in the early history of the country was designed to build the colony and to provide labour, while maintaining the perceived ideal of a white Australia policy that restricted immigration to those from Western Europe—primarily from the United Kingdom. More recently, although immigration still continues to constitute the majority of population growth, policies have targeted skill shortages, meaning that immigration is used as a tool to redress the imbalance between labour supply and demand. As such, changing patterns of migration have important consequences for the labour market and for the education and training sector as a major source of the skilled labour supply.

Early migration was to build the growth of the nation: both in terms of an increase in the population numbers, as well as an increase in labour to build infrastructure and the economic growth of the country. During the period of convict settlement in Australia between 1788 and 1850, European migration and population growth in Australia were low, with about 400,000 people of European descent recorded in 1850; 150,000 of whom were convicts (Burnley 2001). In the 1850s, the gold rushes in Victoria brought another 730,000 immigrants from the United Kingdom and Ireland, Germany, America and China (Burnley 2001). Between 1851 and 1890, a further 1.4 million immigrants from the United Kingdom and Ireland settled in Australia (Burnley 2001). The motivating factor for many was the premise of creating a better life for themselves and their children, as well as potential economic opportunities (Hitchcock 1990). By 1901, 98% of the population of Australia were white (Migration Heritage Centre 2010).

On 1 January 1901, the six British colonies united as the Commonwealth of Australia. Until this point, early immigration was almost entirely a white population from Western Europe, meaning that there was limited diversity of residents in Australia. Maintaining this idea was of upmost importance to the new government, and a series of legislation passed shortly after federation sought to guarantee the continuity of a homogenous white population. The first legislation passed by the new parliament was the *Immigration Restriction Act 1901*, which deemed the preservation of a racially homogenous society as essential to the success of the country (Lack and Templeton 1988). This 'White Australia policy' restricted Asian and other non-European migration through the implementation of a dictation test in any selected European language as selected by the interviewer on the day of the test (DIMA 2001; Lack and Templeton 1988; Louis et al. 2010). This policy was designed to restrict immigration to those who shared the same cultural identity as the population, predominantly those from the United Kingdom.

While immigrants arriving in Australia in these early years were almost exclusively from the United Kingdom, only a fraction of the British leaving the United Kingdom were migrating to Australia. Many others chose the United States and Canada over Australia (Ferenczi and Willcox 1929), although there is limited migration research that discusses the factors associated with these decisions. It is believed that Australia became more preferable as a destination country with the rising demand for primary products as land in the United States and Canada became harder to obtain (Kelley 1965). Further, heavy subsidisation of travel expenses and the provision of land upon arrival for some categories of immigrants constituted a strong pull factor, as did high demand for workers (Kelley 1965). While over 70% of the population in Australia today live in the capital cities, less than 40% lived in the cities in 1910 (Australian Bureau of Statistics 2014). This illustrates the importance of primary produce as an industry in Australia's early development and growth.

Between 1919 and 1940, almost 600,000 immigrants settled in Australia, of which 63% were from the United Kingdom and a further 10% from Ireland (Burnley 2001). The remaining migrants were predominantly from Greece and Italy, as well as a number of Jewish settlers who arrived in the 1930s, seeking refuge from Hitler's Europe (DIMA 2001; Migration Heritage Centre 2010). World War II and the near-invasion by Japanese forces demonstrated that Australia required population growth to defend itself from potential incoming threats, particularly from Asia (Burnley 2001). Politicians emphasised Australia's vulnerability by highlighting that its small population could not adequately defend its large land area, leading to the mantra of 'populate or perish' (Burnley 2001; DIMA 2001; Migration Heritage Centre 2010). The natural rate of population increase was 1%, so with aims of further increasing population by an additional 1% per year, or 70,000 people, immigration was expanded and a Department of Immigration established (Burnley 2001; DIMA 2001). Although immigration restrictions were partially relaxed, immigration was still heavily targeted towards those from Europe. The Government also accepted a minimum of 12,000 displaced persons per year during this time—many of whom were from Eastern Europe, including the Ukraine, Estonia, Latvia, Lithuania and Turkey (Burnley 2001; DIMA 2001). These refugees received assistance with passage and settlement in exchange for 2 years of government work, usually in manual labour such as the building of the Snowy River Hydro-Electric Scheme, on the railways, in mines or in iron and steel industries (DIMA 2001; Migration Heritage Centre 2010).

In 1969, the migrant program peaked with 185,000 people immigrating in that year (Burnley 2001). At this point the population of Australia was 12 million people, and there was public concern about Australia's capacity to integrate this large number of migrants (Lahmeyer 2003). As a result, the migrant program numbers were lowered (DIMA 2001). Although the intake was limited to 110,000 in 1972, the government disbanded the White Australia policy and immigrants were selected by personal attributes and occupational groups, meaning that priority for immigration permission was given to close relatives and workers in professions that had unmet demands (DIMA 2001; Migration Heritage Centre 2010). This means that even into the late twentieth century, Australia still favoured immigrants who brought a culture similar to their own.

Since 1975, Australia's policies have placed less importance on mass immigration to enhance population growth and more emphasis on attracting skilled workers who would economically contribute to Australian society, with the migration program fluctuating between 15,000 and 120,000 immigrants per year (DIMA 2001; Markus et al. 2009). Despite the relaxation of immigration policies, many immigrants still arrived from the United Kingdom, New Zealand and Europe (Makkai and Taylor 2009), as well as many immigrants from Cambodia, Fiji, Malaysia and the Philippines in the 1980s (Mukherjee 1999). From 1988, Australia has also allocated places for immigration opportunities under the Humanitarian program for refugees and asylum seekers from countries experiencing unsettled situations (DIMA 2001). This has included refugees from Vietnam, East Timor, Cyprus, El Salvador, Sri Lanka, Yugoslavia, Lebanon, Sudan, Afghanistan and Iraq. In recent years, places for immigration for refugees and asylum seekers have been allocated to displaced persons from the Syrian conflict ('Australia to Accept 12,000 Syrian Refugees' 2015; Hasham 2015).

7.3 New Zealand's Immigration History

New Zealand has had similar transition periods in its immigration history to that of Australia. Early populations of Maori were severely affected by the diseases brought to New Zealand by the British settlers, and the Gold Rush of the nineteenth century brought a number of Asian immigrants (Phillips 2015). Although New Zealand did not have the official policy to ensure a culturally homogenous society as in Australia, preference and additional assistance was offered to immigrants from Western Europe, particularly the United Kingdom. In more recent years, New Zealand has accepted a number of immigrants on humanitarian visas, and many skilled workers from India and China (Statistics New Zealand 2014a). In the 2013 census, 1,001,787 people were born overseas, with 31.6% of the total population of New Zealand born in Asia, with a majority of this category born in China (Statistics New Zealand 2014a). A further 26.5% of the population were born in the United Kingdom and Ireland (Statistics New Zealand 2014a). The proportion of overseas-born population was highest in Auckland and Wellington, which suggests that like Australia, immigrants in New Zealand favour the capital cities over rural areas.

From 1800 to 1950, the majority of people who immigrated to New Zealand were British, who were offered free travel or other benefits upon arrival, such as free land (Phillips 2015). In many instances, these immigrants came via Australia where they had previously been convicts or free settlers. They travelled to New Zealand for employment in the whaling and sealing industry or to work in the goldfields in Otago and on the West Coast. In the early twentieth Century many labourers left Australia in search of employment in New Zealand in response Australia's economic depression that stagnated the growth of the economy along with high unemployment rates (Bedford et al. 2000). New Zealand's population was slow to grow, with less than 200 white settlers in 1819, 50 years after its discovery by James Cook in 1769 (Phillips 2015). In 1839, the non-Maori population was approximately 2000 people, 90% of whom were British. In 1840, the Treaty of Waitangi—a written agreement between the Maori chiefs and the British monarchy that labelled New Zealand a colony of Britain and the Maoris as British subjects—brought drastic change to the numbers of immigrants in New Zealand, with 28,000 immigrants in 1852 (Phillips 2015; Walker 1995). The immigrant population continued to increase to over 250,000 in 1870, as conditions in Britain deteriorated and many sought a better life, coupled with the offer of free land and subsidised travel, providing that they were 'sober, industrious, of good moral character, of sound mind and in good health' (Borrie 1991, p. 52). Many of these immigrants were under 35 years of age. This assistance stopped in 1890, with immigrants paying their own expenses from this time. This brought a different group of immigrants, who were wealthier, older, and more likely to be male, coming from the industrial areas of northern England.

Similarly to Australia, a law was introduced in 1899 to ensure all immigrants not of British or Irish birthplace spoke fluent English. The laws were to limit the number of Chinese and Eastern European, Indian and Lebanese immigrants who were working in the goldfields and gumfields. In the early twentieth Century, a substantial number of migrants from Australia travelled to New Zealand to avoid the depression and droughts that were limiting their prosperity in Australia.

World War II brought the same calls to 'Populate or Perish' as were heard in Australia. Levels of out-migration and a declining birth rate created concerns about an inability to defend the nation. At this time, the government favoured population increase through childbirth, and a family benefit allowance was implemented to encourage this growth. Preference for immigration was given to those with industrial skills rather than farming skills, and immigrants were selected through an interview process at the New Zealand High Commission in London. In 1950, an assisted passage scheme was extended to the Netherlands as the Dutch were perceived to be the mostly easily assimilated. Pacific Islanders, from the Cook Islands, Samoa, and Tonga, further increased the population of New Zealand in the mid-1960s as work opportunities in these islands declined.

As a result of growing concern about racist attitudes in the immigration policy in New Zealand, it was deemed in 1974 that all prospective migrants, British or not, were required to obtain an entry permit which was based on skills and qualifications rather than national origin or race. While this opened immigration to people from many different origins, the years following this change were marked by poor economic performance in New Zealand and the migration flows reversed, with few people arriving and many people moving to Australia between 1977 and 1990 to increase their opportunities for employment (Ongley and Pearson 1995). While this recession was associated with the international oil crisis and therefore out of New Zealand's control, New Zealand's relatively small economy was unable to support large-scale immigration and also lost many native-born residents to Australia (Bedford 2003). The Immigration Act 1987 further emphasised non-discriminatory policies, with the need for an individual to possess certain skills rather than a certain national background. A points system was introduced to rank participants on their age, skills, education and social capital and therefore, their potential to positively contribute to the New Zealand economy and society (Ongley and Pearson 1995). Eight hundred places per year were also allocated for humanitarian visas society (Ongley and Pearson 1995; Phillips 2015). In 2001, the proportion of foreign born residents was the highest since 1936 at almost 700,000 people. In most cases, the new immigrants are educated people who are comparatively wealthy. While immigrants in recent years have faced some public and political response to the establishment of cultural groups' churches, schools, restaurants and social rituals, New Zealand does not appear to have the rhetoric around immigration and the prejudicial attitudes to the extent that Australia does.

7.4 The Role of Temporary Migration

In both Australia and New Zealand, recent immigration policies (post-2000) have transitioned from a focus on national growth to those that target the attraction of skilled workers with the potential to economically contribute to society and build national human capital (Hugo 2004; Phillips 2015). These trends still encourage a large proportion of immigrants from European countries, but also open immigration up to those from Eastern Asia, Africa and India. Both Australia and New Zealand use a points-based system, where applicants are allocated a fixed number of points for their characteristics and ability to enrich the fabric of society and the future well-being of their new country (Bedford et al. 2000; Collins 2013). Those who reach a minimum point threshold are eligible for a visa. This means that both countries are increasingly focused on temporary migration as an important source of growth, rather than the class 'settler' migration of the previous centuries (Bedford et al. 2000).

Australia continues to be a major destination country for humanitarian and other permanent immigrants, as well as short-term visitors such as skilled and professional workers on the *457* visa (Collins 2013). In addition to the sizeable number of people who come to Australia each year via legal and regular pathways, Australia manages the small proportion of people who arrive at its borders in an irregular manner via air and sea routes. This population is the subject of media and public debate. The New Zealand government has also focused on immigration from countries in the Asia-Pacific rim, such as Hong Kong, Taiwan, Malaysia, and Korea as sources of migrants with business skills and investment capital (Lidgard et al. 1998). Recent policy initiatives are designed to rejuvenate flows of entrepreneurs and investment capital from Asia (Bedford et al. 2000). The spatial concentration of this human capital is primarily focused on metropolitan areas, with a large majority of immigrants electing to live in the capital cities in both Australia and New Zealand.

International migration has been and remains a crucial part of economic, social and cultural development in Australia (Hugo 2004). An ageing population due to increasing longevity and decreasing birth rates means that Australia must turn to immigration to sustain population growth and the availability of social and human capital (Karuppannan 2011). While Australia has previously focused on immigration as a permanent move for individuals, international immigration in Australia today is more complex, especially with temporary visa categories introduced in the last two decades to attract different types of immigrants. An increasing number of people enter Australia on temporary visas, although some of these immigrants obtain residency at the expiration of these temporary visas. The selection process for immigration to Australia is highly selective, and usually favours those who are young and highly skilled, with a high income and high level of education. Such a population brings 'brain gain', with immigrants increasing the level of human capital by contributing the skills which have been identified to be in a shortage by the Australian government. There is also a large student population who migrate to Australia for the duration of their education, particularly from Asian countries. These students bring further human capital, and many transition to working visas at the completion of their studies.

7.5 The Current State of Migration Research in Oceania

This is not to say that once immigrants arrive in Australia or New Zealand, they remain in one location indefinitely. Similarly, many Australian and New Zealand-born residents migrate within their country, seeking a change from a rural to urban environment, an interstate migration, or a trans-Tasman migration. Evidence shows that in Australia and New Zealand, the population changes their usual place of residence more often than those in other countries (Hugo 2002). This means that Australia and New Zealand have a dynamic population stock who are prone to multiple migrations. According to the Australian Bureau of Statistics, in the 2014–2015 period, Melbourne had the highest net internal migration gains of all Greater Capital Cities in Australia, followed by Brisbane (Australian Bureau of Statistics 2016). The majority of arrivals into Melbourne came from other towns in Victoria, and from Sydney (Australian Bureau of Statistics 2016). In contrast,

Sydney had the highest net losses of all Great Capital Cities, followed by Adelaide and Darwin. Sydney lost many residents to regional New South Wales and Melbourne (Australian Bureau of Statistics 2016). Looking at smaller spatial units of analysis, the highest net migration in Australia in 2014–2015 was Melbourne West, which includes some of the fastest growing suburbs in Victoria (Australian Bureau of Statistics 2016). Queensland's Sunshine and Gold Coasts also recorded significant gains, suggesting that many people are seeking a certain relaxed lifestyle (Australian Bureau of Statistics 2016). In this section, we expand on the previous focus on international immigration to unpack the state of the migration research that has examined rural-to-urban, interstate, and trans-Tasman migration patterns. Figure 7.1 provides the context and settlement patterns of Australia and New Zealand to provide an overview of the geography of the nations.

Data collated by Australia's Department of Immigration and Border Protection and New Zealand's Customs Service records the intended length of stay and an initial intended address for each immigrant. Given that both Australia and New Zealand are island nations, we have a high degree of accuracy in measuring who is arriving into the country as Marr (2011, p. 89) states that "border control in Australia remains the most effective of any country in the world". Both Australia and New Zealand have a census held every 5 years, which measures people's location of

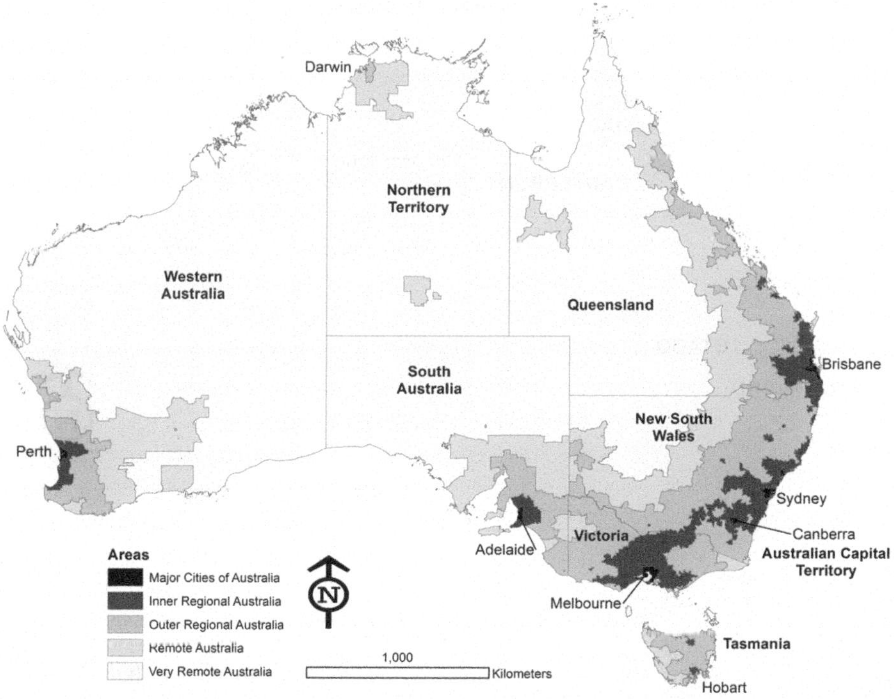

Fig. 7.1 (**a**) The settlement geography of Australia. (**b**) The settlement geography of New Zealand

Fig. 7.1 (continued)

usual residence, 1 year and 5 years before the census. While this is a rich data source in its ability to capture both international and interregional movements, this is a broad time frame and census data may not capture a series of different forms of migration such as temporary, circular and seasonal each of which play an important role in understanding migration patterns in Oceania. Seasonal and temporary migration programs are widely used around the world as a way of overcoming job shortages without the costs of assimilating workers and their families. Despite their wide usage, and a body of literature that highlights the benefits and limitations of these schemes and discusses their implementation, there is little empirical evidence towards their developmental impacts (Gibson et al. 2014). According to Constant et al. (2013, p. 2), "empirical evidence about circular migration is scarce and empirical analyses are limited due to missing or problematic data". There is no published research of this nature in Australia or New Zealand. As census data in Australia and New Zealand measure annual movement, it is probable that such data does not encapsulate these short-term movements of several months and are thus missing an important type of migration pattern.

7.5.1 Rural-Urban Migration

Australia is one of the world's most urbanised but least densely populated countries (Pretty et al. 2006). While over 70% of the population in Australia today live in the capital cities, less than 40% lived in the cities in 1910 (Australian Bureau of Statistics 2014). This illustrates the importance of primary produce as an industry in Australia's early development and growth. Yet in recent years, the role of primary industries has become less important as other capital (such as the finance, manufacturing or construction industries) becomes increasingly vital to Australia's growth and the number of residents who live in the major cities has increased dramatically.

Most studies that examine the movement of rural to urban migration draw on census data, which provides important information such as aggregated demographic and labour market details. However, these data do not include specific information for international immigrants such as their visa, job and employer details or their family composition. This means that while the literature has made some attempt to evaluate the efficacy of programs such as State-Specific Regional Migration and the Regional Sponsored Migration Scheme, the studies are limited in their ability to speak to these initiatives (Taylor and Gerritsen 2014). In contrast, the Department of Immigration and Border Protection holds data on visa issue and compliance, but have limited data on an individual's movements within Australia once they have arrived (Taylor and Gerritsen 2014). There is some attempt to measure migrant outcomes, although such studies aim to create a national picture and often do not have the reliability at the smaller geographical level.

The Remoteness Structure of the Australian Standard Geographical Classification considers the distribution of Australia's population into five remoteness area categories: major cities, inner regional, outer regional, remote and very remote. These categories are used to classify data obtained from the census conducted every 5 years in Australia. Census questions record every individual's address 1 year and 5 years prior to the night of the census and are used to measure migration. As at June 2011, 69% of the population resided in Australia's major cities, compared to only 2.3% in remote or very remote Australia (Australian Bureau of Statistics 2012). While the proportion of the population who live in the major cities is increasing at the fastest growing rate (17%) over the last decade, remote areas are growing at the slowest rate of 3.8% (Australian Bureau of Statistics 2012). Between 2001 and 2011, the population of many inland, rural areas declined including those in Western and South-Western Queensland, Western and North-Western New South Wales, Western Victoria, and many areas of South Australia (Australian Bureau of Statistics 2012). According to Burnley et al. (2007) 56% of people who had recently migrated believed that they were better off after the move. In particular, 64% of migrants said that they were more satisfied with their work opportunities (Burnley et al. 2007). In the migration literature, there are a number of push and pull factors that have been identified as encouraging migration from rural to urban areas.

In Australia, the level of socioeconomic disadvantage, that is, the availability of education, social, health, recreation, and employment services and opportunities, is related to the size of the rural community (Pretty et al. 2006). Rural areas have usually been overrepresented in the distribution of Australian socioeconomic disadvantage (Ciurej et al. 2006). Out-migration occurs because of the socioeconomic disadvantage present in smaller rural towns, but the disadvantage is also a result of the out-migration and the loss of social and human capital. Many individuals are motivated by economic considerations when considering a rural to urban migration, which invariably involves a change of employment and housing (Karuppannan 2011). The major cities often offer better employment outcomes (Tang et al. 2014). In recent years, Australia has seen several extreme weather conditions including severe bush fires, flooding and droughts. In regional Australia, farmers and graziers have been struggling for steady incomes off the land as they are vulnerable to such natural disasters (Karuppannan 2011). Rural areas have less opportunities for employment and occupation growth and progression, meaning that individuals' dissatisfaction with their careers may constitute an important push factor.

The outflow of young, skilled, educated people is associated with a loss of significant social and human capital. Young people, in particular, are likely to move from a rural to an urban environment for more opportunities (Pretty et al. 2006). Smaller, rural communities have a lack of structural or functional factors (Eversole 2001). For example, some towns have a lack of educational facilities, with youths having to board in nearby towns for high school education, or move to the major towns to attend university. Given that youth are the future of the community, their relocation takes away energy, ideas, and part of the identity of the town. This has created a sustainability crisis with many small towns in Australia, with rural areas having an increasingly older age profile (Kettlewell 2010). The loss of young people represents a significant barrier to the development of a rural towns—yet there are a limited number of immigrants who would prefer to live in a rural town than a major city, and therefore fill a vacuum (Hugo et al. 2013).

Immigrants are needed in rural areas because they bring crucial skills and knowledge, growth of rural economies, and are a major component of local labour supply, particularly in the industries of health and education. Their presence expands communities and helps justify infrastructure and social services. Research into the settlement of immigrant patterns shows that those who are likely to settle in rural settings are predominantly male, and come from an English-speaking background such as Europe, North America, or Africa, and have qualifications in a health or education related field (Tang et al. 2014). Immigrants in non-metropolitan areas are more likely to hold a full-time job, with a higher income than the locals (Tang et al. 2014). However, retention levels of immigrants who initially settle in regional and remote locations appears to be low, as these areas are unable to compete with urban areas for housing, education, health, culture and social needs (Griffiths et al. 2010). Although immigrants may nominate a rural environment as their preference to increase their likelihood of being allocated a visa, there is no legislation that enforces that residents stay for an extended period of time (Birrell 2003). Thus there is a consistent outflow of skills workers and their families from regional and remote areas to urban areas (Taylor and Gerritsen 2014).

With a majority of the population living in the capital cities, skill shortages in regional Australia are acute (Gerritsen 2010). This shortage, coupled with a strong growth in the mining industry, has led to the growth of a Fly-In, Fly-Out (FIFO) industry where workers in a town are non-residents, but travel to work in different locations. Here, workers forgo opportunities for long-lasting employment in favour of very high wages, and rapid career advancement in some cases. However, the use of temporary, non-resident workers restricts the opportunities for local infrastructure and services, meaning that these destinations are less attractive for new residents and new businesses, which further effect existing employment shortages and local town growth (Carson 2011; Rolfe and Kinnear 2013; Taylor and Gerritsen 2014).

Many studies consider the impact of the temporary FIFO industry on local communities, particularly in Queensland, South Australia and Western Australia (McKenzie 2010; Petkova et al. 2009; Tonts 2010). However, one of the common characteristics of these studies is a discussion or analysis of a single town or small region rather than broader analyses that incorporate multiple locations and sectors (Hajkowicz et al. 2011). Thus there are several place-based effects that cannot be considered, and little information details how these migration effects might vary across different towns, areas or even states. Petkova et al. (2009) argue that there are important patterns of the social and economic impacts of this type of migration that varies depending on the community's size, structure, history, and the proportion of non-resident workforce.

To counteract the effect of people migrating to urban centres, there are several state-specific and rural regional migration schemes that seek to reduce the proportion of immigrants settling in capital cities, particularly Sydney (Hugo 2004). State and federal governments are being proactive in their attempts to redirect overseas graduates to rural areas. Bonus points are offered on visa for relocation to non-metro area, and overseas graduates who studied in a designated area get five bonus points when they apply for permanent residency (Hugo 2008). Thus this is a step towards getting the 65 points required to obtain residency. Several occupations also get bonuses—for example, teachers, lawyers, and health practitioners get cash bonuses, housing assistance, travel allowances, professional development opportunities, and non-cash bonuses such as computers (Tang et al. 2014). However, as Tang et al. (2014) states, "Despite the marked increase in overseas student numbers remaining in the country, little is still known about their inter-regional migration flows and settlement choices in the country."

7.5.2 Interstate Migration

A number of studies have examined interregional flows at the level of the state or territory. In Australia this equates to movement across 8 states and territories and in New Zealand across its 16 regions (see Fig. 7.1). Studies of interstate migration primarily draw on census data to measure changes in population. However, these only capture movement at 1 year and 5 year intervals prior to the census. Further, given that the release of census data is some time after its initial collection this can often make the information several years old (McCracken 1987). While there are many studies that describe the net migration between the states, there are fewer that consider the drivers for such movements. These drivers outline a range of social, economic, cultural, political, institutional, psychological and physical consideration which influence migration decisions, yet there is no single model that explains these decisions (Stimson and Minnery 1998). Despite suggestions that we need to look beyond the standard push-pull factors to study interstate migration in Australia (Stimson and Minnery 1998), it is unlikely that one single model may be used to explain migration within Australia due to the sheer size of the country and unique differences that exist between its constituent states and regions.

During 2013–2014, it was estimated that 349,000 people in Australia moved interstate, an increase of 2.5% from the previous year (Australian Bureau of Statistics 2015). New South Wales, South Australia, Tasmania, the Northern Territory and Australian Capital Territory recorded migration losses, while Victoria, Queensland and Western Australia reported increases (Australian Bureau of Statistics 2015). People may migrate for a number of reasons, including location-specific capital, the presence of family and friends, and known employment opportunities. Given that each state holds responsibility for a large proportion of its own economy, the provision of services, and that employment opportunities, particularly in the primary industries, vary by state, states can have significant differences in their pull factors that may encourage migration. For example, evidence shows that in Queensland, interstate migrants are usually younger than the average resident population. This younger age profile adds to the state's labour force participation rate, as well as moderating the effects of population ageing (Queensland Government Statistician's Office 2008). Studies also show that lifestyle factors are predominant in decisions to migrate to Queensland (Stimson and Minnery 1998). In contrast, other states may have other pull factors that encourage migration.

In remote areas, population growth, and therefore economic growth, are core ambitions of governments such as in the Northern Territory (Carson 2011; Martel et al. 2013). An increasing number of residents moving from the Northern Territory to areas with more amenities has been found to have left a deficit in the population of the Territory (Golebiowska and Carson 2009). Escalator theory describes the in-migration, usually by young and male migrants, to regions that reward new arrivals with high wages and job promotion prospects. Savage and Fielding (1989) draw on this theory to explain that workers can often progress their careers quickly due to less competition for jobs and promotions by relocating to areas with skills shortages in areas like construction, mining or defence force personnel. In areas such as the Northern Territory, workers are often content to work in low amenity areas for short-term periods to increase their long-term career and well-being. While these areas are attractive to the young, it is becoming increasingly difficult to retain this population in these areas on a long-term basis as this migration is not seen as a permanent move (Martel et al. 2013).

The majority of inter-state migration studies use an aggregate approach that focuses on the spatial effects, concentrating on the employment circumstances, wage levels, housing costs, weather and amenities of the area (Karuppannan 2011; Stimson and Minnery 1998). Studies primarily use census data to measure migration, meaning that more individual reasons such as status, lifestyle, family circumstances, and the role of human agency are discounted. The different states and territories have characteristics that may be more likely to encourage someone with a certain lifestyle choice or culture. These nuances are not picked up in aggregated data from the Australian Bureau of Statistics, meaning that it is difficult to fully understand inter-state migration in the Australian context.

Similar patterns have also been noted with studies of migration in New Zealand. With an on-going interest in the dynamics of migration, several studies examine the socioeconomic status of communities that have high migration rates. For example, Clark and Morrison (2012) employ data from The Survey of Dynamics and Motivation for Migration in New Zealand to detail movement at 2-year intervals. The authors argue that the migration patterns differ according to income level, with both groups moving in response to economic opportunity, but find different places and situations to be attractive. The study employs a smaller time interval than many Australian studies at 2 years, and while using aggregated data, determines that individual differences are important in migration decisions. Limited studies examine in inter-region migration within New Zealand.

7.5.3 Trans-Tasman Migration

There is a wealth of literature that examines Trans-Tasman migration, that is, migration that exclusively takes place between Australia and New Zealand. Under the Trans-Tasman Agreement, citizens of New Zealand and Australia have no restrictions on migration between the two countries, and in Australia, citizens of

Fig. 7.2 The Trans-Tasman born population (1881–2006): Source: Poot (2010, p. 321)

New Zealand are permitted to live and work indefinitely (Bedford et al. 2000; Markus et al. 2009). See Fig. 7.2 for a historical perspective on migration flows between the two nations. In 2013, there was an estimated 640,770 New Zealand citizens living in Australia, with New Zealand citizens the second largest foreign-born group in Australia behind England at approximately 2.6% of the population (Department of Home Affairs 2014). Trans-Tasman migration is a larger component of New Zealand migration than of Australian migration. While New Zealanders are most likely to migrate to Australia, Australians are more likely to emigrate to the United Kingdom. However, according to the 2013 census, there is still a sizeable population of some 62,712 Australians who have emigrated to New Zealand (Statistics New Zealand 2014b).

Studies of migration flows between Australia and New Zealand predominantly employ spatially aggregated data, such as statistics from immigration controls that detail the number of travellers completing arrival and departure cards in the two countries and capture their next intended country of permanent residence (Bedford et al. 2003; Brosnan and Poot 1987). Drawing on these data, studies document broad trends in migration patterns (see, for example, Poot 2010), and consider historic trends and some generate forecasts of future migration patterns (see, for example, Gorbey et al. 1999). A number of studies focus on the economic push-pull factors associated with trans-Tasman migration and demonstrate the importance of employment and economic conditions in the decision to immigrate, given that both Australia and New Zealand share a similar culture and lifestyle. However, there are also empirical studies that consider immigration on a more individual level, and evaluate the push-pull factors that underpin such migration decisions. In one such analysis, Green et al. (2008) study migrants in Australia through interviews and surveys recording reasons for the move, maintenance of ties with New Zealand, current national identification, responses to migration and the probability of return migration to New Zealand. Their findings demonstrate that pull factors included better climate, better future for their family, more job opportunities and a better standard of living. Meanwhile, push factors included problematic personal circumstances in New Zealand, social problems in New Zealand society and dissatisfaction with life in Australia.

Economic considerations are crucial in migration decisions, particularly in when examining the pull factors that attract immigrants. One of the most often-cited factors is earning capacity. In New Zealand there has been, at times, a lack of economic growth (Bedford et al. 2003; Poot et al. 1988), and high rates of inflation and unemployment (Brosnan and Poot 1987). In such times, Australia may have better long-term employment prospects. Migration flows are sensitive to employment, and are responsive to changes in the demand for labour across the two countries (Brosnan and Poot 1987; Gorbey et al. 1999). Further, when the value of the exchange rate between the New Zealand dollar and the Australian dollar is poor, the emigration rate is higher (Poot 2010). While there has been concern about the numbers of New Zealanders migrating to Australia and the associated loss of human capital, Hugo (2004) identifies that New Zealanders in Australia are representative of those in New Zealand, and that the highly skilled and educated are not over-represented in those who migrate. In Australia, New Zealand citizens have a higher labour force participation rate compared to native-born Australians (78.2% and 68% respectively) (Queensland Government Statistician's Office 2008). They are also amongst the most highly paid in Australia (Pope 1985). This suggests that migrants from New Zealand are likely to be working and may have moved seeking this employment. Green et al. (2008) highlights that economic factors were more important than lifestyle factors in decisions to migrate.

Alongside economic considerations which are the focus of many studies of trans-Tasman migration, there are also cultural, environmental, life cycle, quality of life and social reasons that feature in a migration decision (Green et al. 2008). These are often parallel those in other countries who select Australia, such a greater opportunities for their family, and a better climate (Green et al. 2008). Yet these factors are rarely discussed in the literature, with most studies exclusively focusing on economic factors. Given that Australia and New Zealand share a similar history, culture and society, it is not surprising that these factors receive limited attention.

One unique feature of Trans-Tasman migration is the relatively large proportion of return migration, and it is noted that these patterns of return migration contrast typical global patterns of one way migration (Markus et al. 2009). Brosnan and Poot (1987) highlight the prevalence of citizens of New Zealand moving to Australia for a working holiday in a different and attractive environment, but where it is still convenient and relatively cheap to travel home to visit family and friends. Cheap airfares and increased technology encourage people to migrate and experience life in a different environment, yet one that still has close physical, historical and cultural connections to their own country. In some cases, travel between Australia and New Zealand is cheaper than travel within the one country, and with no restrictions on the period of time someone lives or works in the opposite country, travel is open. To this end, several schemes are designed to provide placements for temporary workers for seasonal work in the horticultural sector in both Australia and New Zealand.

Under the Recognised Seasonal Employer Scheme in New Zealand and the Pacific Seasonal Worker Pilot Scheme in Australia, low-skilled workers are employed to work for registered and certified employers in the horticulture and viticulture sections (New Zealand Department of Labour 2010). In Australia and New Zealand, lower birth rates, the ageing demographic profile, increased personal wealth, the provision of social welfare, sustained economic growth, low unemployment and higher levels of education have combined to reduce the supply of workers who are available (or willing) to undertake physically demanding labour for relatively low pay (Maclellan and Mares 2006). Much of the work completed in Australia is unattractive to Australian citizens as it is largely based in rural and remote locations, is considered low social status and often poorly paid for manually-intensive work (The Australian Worker's Union 2006). In Australia, facilitating labour mobility is a key issue for the region, and the Scheme developed in 2008 is important to relations with the Pacific with citizens from NZ, Tonga, and Vanuatu participating (Gibson and McKenzie 2011). The programs reduce unmet demand for seasonal work, particularly in the food producing industries and offer 4–6 month contracts (Department of Education 2010). In NZ, a number of Pacific Islanders participate in these schemes developed in 2007 which require employers to meet certain labour conditions and be registered on a database (Ball et al. 2011). This seasonal supply of experience labour is sustainable as arrangements allow workers to return to their country when the demand for workers is low, thus obtaining other work or spending time with their families (Ball et al. 2011). Measuring the participation statistics on the Schemes is difficult and Ball et al. (2011) state that although records of the number of workers are a new implementation, the seasonal workforce appears to be increasing. This population of temporary workers is becoming vital to horticulture in the two countries.

7.6 Future Work and Challenges

There exists a rich literature that has examined the characteristics and dynamics of migration in Australia and New Zealand. In this chapter we have sought to offer a broad overview of this body of work commencing with a look at the history of immigration before examining the current state of migration research in Oceania.

The current trend in the literature of examining the non-economic determinants of migration is likely set to continue. The challenge is now to understand how the relative roles of the economic and non-economic factors interact to drive migration dynamics. To this end the increasing availability of individual-level data will be important to enable researchers to explore how these roles vary based on the individual and household characteristics along with their implications at the regional level.

Demographic analyses points to a decline in interregional migration in Australia and the broader region (Bell et al. 2018). Set against this emerging demographic phenomenon, a number of interesting questions remain unanswered, including: *what is the likely role of place-based policies in terms of their effectiveness in regional development given the reduction in people moving*? And; *what are the economic consequences for this slow-down in internal migratory flows and how do these impacts varying across the urban hierarchy?* The challenge to research wishing to explore these questions will concern the capture and assembly of suitable data.

Future immigration policy in Australia and New Zealand is likely to continue in the same vein whereby immigrants are selected based on their skills to address persistent skill shortages and attempt to ameliorate the effects of ageing populations. More work in the area of the educational, labour market and migratory pathways of newly arrived immigrants that are essential in terms of long-term nation building is needed. In particular immigrant pathways to regional and rural Australia and New Zealand require more attention. A survey of new immigrants who settled in regional and rural Australia showed that most got jobs in the areas for their skills; most were happy in their new regional and rural homes, most intended to stay there and most reported a warm welcome from their new neighbours (Jordan et al. 2009). These new immigrants relieve some of the labour shortages in regional and rural Australia and reduce the trend to population decline in many non-coastal regional and rural cities and towns, helping to regenerate non-metropolitan Australia. The challenge will be in assembling the necessary data to reconstruct these pathways on a scale that will permit analyses both at the country-level as well as across Oceania.

There is no doubt that the global hunt for talent continues to intensify. OECD nations persist in their search to attract and retain highly skilled human capital to integrate with domestic labour supplies to bolster their economic fabric ameliorating the negative consequences of their ageing societies. The challenge for regional scientists, population geographers and labour economists will be to identify new sources of data through which we can better understand the migratory pathways through which both domestic and new international arrivals pass. Understanding these complex pathways will be the first step to unveiling the factors that underpin interregional migrations and how these shape outcomes for both individuals and local labour markets.

References

Australian Bureau of Statistics (2012) Regional population growth, Australia, 2011. Report number 3218.0

Australian Bureau of Statistics (2014) Australian historical population statistics, 2014. Report number 3105.0.65.001

Australian Bureau of Statistics (2015) Migration, Australia, 2013–14. Report number 3412.0

Australian Bureau of Statistics (2016) Migration, Australia, 2014–15. Report number 3412.0

Australian Government: Department of Immigration and Border Protection (2013) The New Zealand-born community: historical background. https://wayback.archive.org/web/20140212131237/http:/www.immi.gov.au/media/publications/statistics/comm-summ/textversion/newzealand.htm

Ball R, Beacroft L, Lindley J (2011) Australia's pacific seasonal worker pilot scheme: managing vulnerabilities to exploitation. Trends Issues Crime Crim Justice 432:1

Bedford R (2003) New Zealand: the politicization of immigration. http://www.migrationpolicy.org/article/new-zealand-politicization-immigration

Bedford R, Ho E, Lidgard J (2000) International migration in New Zealand: context, components and policy issues. University of Waikato, Population Studies Centre, Hamilton

Bedford R, Ho E, Hugo G (2003) Trans-Tasman migration in context: recent flows of New Zealanders revisited. People Place 11(4):53

Bell M, Wilson T, Charles-Edwards E, Ueffing P (2018) The long-run decline in Australian internal migration intensities. In: Champion T, Cooke T, Shuttleworth I (eds) Internal migration in the developed world: are we becoming less mobile? Ashgate, Farnham

Birrell B (2003) Redistributing migrants: the Labor agenda. People Place 11(4):15

Borrie WD (1991) Immigration to New Zealand, 1854–1938. Australian National University, Canberra

Brosnan P, Poot J (1987) Modelling the determinants of Trans-Tasman migration after World War II. Econ Rec 63(4):313–329

Burnley I (2001) The impact of immigration on Australia: a demographic approach. Oxford University Press, Oxford

Burnley IH, Marshall N, Murphy PA, Hugo GJ (2007) Housing factors in welfare migration to and from metropolitan cities in Australia. Urban Policy Res 25(3):287–304

Carson D (2011) Political economy, demography and development in Australia's Northern Territory. Can Geogr 55(2):226–242

Ciurej M, Tanton R, Sutcliffe A (2006) Analysis of the regional distribution of relatively disadvantaged areas using 2001 SEIFA. 1351(55.013). Australian Bureau of Statistics, Canberra

Clark WA, Morrison PS (2012) Socio-spatial mobility and residential sorting: evidence from a large-scale survey. Urban Stud 49(15):3253–3270

Collins J (2013) Rethinking Australian immigration and immigrant settlement policy. J Intercult Stud 34(2):160–177. https://doi.org/10.1080/07256868.2013.781981

Constant AF, Nottmeyer O, Zimmermann KF (2013) The economics of circular migration. In: Constant AF, Zimmermann KF (eds) International handbook on the economics of migration. Edward Elgar, Cheltenham, p 55

Department of Education EaWR (2010) Important changes to the pilot provide more flexibility

Department of Home Affairs, Australian Government (2014) Fact sheet—New Zealanders in Australia. https://www.homeaffairs.gov.au/about/corporate/information/fact-sheets/17nz

Department of Immigration and Multicultural Affairs (DIMA) (2001) Immigration: federation to century's end. 1901–2000. Department of Immigration and Multicultural Affairs, Canberra, ACT

Eversole R (2001) Keeping youth in communities: education and out-migration in the south west. Rural Soc 11(2):85–98

Ferenczi I, Willcox W (1929) International migration statistics. Bureau of Economic Research. http://www.nber.org/chapters/c5126.pdf
Gerritsen R (2010) A post-colonial model for North Australian political economy: the case of the Northern Territory. In: Gerritsen R (ed) North Australian political economy: issues and agendas. Charles Darwin University Press, Darwin
Gibson J, McKenzie D (2011) Australia's PSWPS: development impacts in the first two years. Asia Pac Viewp 52(3):361–370
Gibson J, McKenzie D, Rohorua H (2014) Development impacts of seasonal and temporary migration: a review of evidence from the Pacific and Southeast Asia. Asia Pac Policy Stud 1(1):18–32
Golebiowska K, Carson D (2009) What is the role of net overseas migration in population growth and interstate migration patterns in the Northern Territory? People Place 17(3):40
Gorbey S, James D, Poot J (1999) Population forecasting with endogenous migration: an application to Trans-Tasman migration. Int Reg Sci Rev 22(1):69–101
Green AE, Power MR, Jang DM (2008) Trans-Tasman migration: New Zealanders' explanations for their move. N Z Geogr 64(1):34–45
Griffiths J, Laffan W, Jones A (2010) Factors that influence skilled migrants locating in regional areas. Institute for Social Science Research, Brisbane
Hajkowicz SA, Heyenga S, Moffat K (2011) The relationship between mining and socio-economic well being in Australia's regions. Resour Policy 36(1):30–38
Hasham N (2015) Syrian refugees in Australia—where will they go? http://www.smh.com.au/federal-politics/political-news/syrian-refugees-in-australia--where-will-they-go-20150909-gjiek1.html
Hitchcock NE (1990) Migration to Australia: an authoritative guide to seeking migrant and other visas for Australia. Neil E. Hitchcock and Associates Pty Ltd, Sydney, NSW
Hugo G (2002) Changing patterns of population distribution in Australia. J Popul Res (Special ed. 2002), 1
Hugo G (2004) A new paradigm of international migration: implications for migration policy and planning in Australia. http://www.rssfeeds.aph.gov.au/binaries/library/pubs/rp/2003-04/04rp10.pdf
Hugo G (2008) Immigrant settlement outside of Australia's capital cities. Popul Space Place 14 (6):553–571
Hugo G, Feist H, Tan G (2013) Internal migration and regional Australia, 2006–2011. Australian population and migration research centre – policy brief. https://www.adelaide.edu.au/apmrc/pubs/policy-briefs/APMRC_Policy_Brief_Vol_1_6_2013.pdf
International Organisation of Migration (2015) Global migration flows
Jordan K, Krivokapic-Skoko B, Collins J (2009) The ethnic landscape of rural Australia: Non-Anglo-Celtic immigrant communities and the built environment. J Rural Stud 25(4):376–385. https://doi.org/10.1016/j.jrurstud.2009.05.004
Karuppannan S (2011) Population change and internal migration in Australia. http://soac.fbe.unsw.edu.au/2011/papers/SOAC2011_0116_final.pdf
Kelley AC (1965) International migration and economic growth: Australia, 1865–1935. J Econ Hist 25(03):333–354
Kettlewell N (2010) The impact of rural to urban migration on wellbeing in Australia. Australas J Reg Stud 16(3):187–213
Lack J, Templeton J (1988) Preserving British Australia: introduction. In: Templeton JLJ (ed) Sources of Australian immigration history. University of Melbourne, Melbourne, VIC, pp 7–10
Lahmeyer J (2003) Australia: historical demographical data. http://www.populstat.info/Oceania/australc.htm

Lidgard J, Bedford R, Goodwin J (1998) International migration from Northeast Asia and population change in New Zealand, 1986 to 1996. Population Studies Centre, University of Waikato, Hamilton

Louis WR, Duck JM, Terry DJ, Lalonde RN (2010) Speaking out on immigration policy in Australia: identity threat and the interplay of own opinion and public opinion. J Soc Issues 66 (4):653–672. https://doi.org/10.1111/j.1540-4560.2010.01669.x

Maclellan N, Mares P (2006) Labour mobility in the Pacific: creating seasonal work programs in Australia. Global Gov Pac Islands:137–171

Makkai T, Taylor N (2009) Immigrants as victims of crime: the Australian experience. In: McDonald WF (ed) Immigration, crime and justice. Emerald Group Publishing Ltd., Bingley, pp 95–105

Markus A, Jupp J, McDonald P (2009) Australia's immigration revolution. Allen & Unwin, Sydney

Marr D (2011) Panic. Black Books, Melbourne

Martel C, Carson D, Taylor A (2013) Changing patterns of migration to Australia's Northern Territory: evidence of new forms of escalator migration to frontier regions? Migrat Lett 10 (1):101

McCracken K (1987) How many going where? Postcensal estimates of interstate migration in Australia, 1981–1986. Aust Geogr 18(2):176–179

McKenzie FH (2010) Fly-in fly-out: the challenges of transient populations in rural landscapes. In: Luck GW, Race D, Black R (eds) Demographic change in Australia's rural landscapes. Springer, Dordrecht, pp 353–374

Migration Heritage Centre (2010) Australia's migration history. http://www.migrationheritage.nsw.gov.au/belongings-home/about-belongings/australias-migration-history/

Mohanty M (2006) Globalisation, new labour migration and development in Fiji. In: Firth S (ed) Globalisation and governance in the Pacific Islands. ANU Press, Canberra, pp 107–120

Mukherjee S (1999) Ethnicity and crime: an Australian research study. Australian Institute of Criminology, Canberra, ACT

New Zealand Department of Labour (2010) Final evaluation report of the recognised seasonal employer policy (2007–2009). NZDoL, Wellington. http://dol.govt.nz/publications/research/rse-evaluation-final-report/rse-final-evaluation.pdf

Ongley P, Pearson D (1995) Post-1945 international migration: New Zealand, Australia and Canada compared. Int Migr Rev 29:765–793

Petkova V, Lockie S, Rolfe J, Ivanova G (2009) Mining developments and social impacts on communities: Bowen Basin case studies. Rural Soc 19(3):211–228

Phillips J (2015) History of immigration – the end of a 'white New Zealand' policy. http://www.TeAra.govt.nz/en/history-of-immigration/page-15

Poot J (2010) Trans-Tasman migration, transnationalism and economic development in Australasia. Asian Pac Migr 19(3):319–342

Poot J, Nana G, Philpott B (1988) International migration and the New Zealand economy: a long-run perspective. Victoria University Press for the Institute of Policy Studies, Wellington

Pope D (1985) The trans-Tasman connection: facts and implications of Australia-New Zealand migration. J Popul Res 2(1):55–67

Pretty G, Bramston P, Patrick J, Pannach W (2006) The relevance of community sentiments to Australian rural youths' intention to stay in their home communities. Am Behav Sci 50(2):226–240. https://doi.org/10.1177/0002764206290636

Queensland Government Statistician's Office (2008) Queensland economic review June 2008. http://www.qgso.qld.gov.au/subjects/economy/economy-general/reports/qld-econ-review/qld-econ-review-200806.php

Rolfe J, Kinnear S (2013) Populating regional Australia: what are the impacts of non-resident labour force practices on demographic growth in resource regions? Rural Soc 22(2):125–137

Savage M, Fielding T (1989) Class formation and regional development: the 'service class' in South East England. Geoforum 20(2):203–218

Statistics New Zealand (2014a) 2013 Census QuickStats about culture and identity. http://www.stats.govt.nz/Census/2013-census/profile-and-summary-reports/quickstats-culture-identity/birthplace.aspx
Statistics New Zealand (2014b) Census QuickStats about culture and identity. Statistics New Zealand, Wellington
Stimson RJ, Minnery J (1998) Why people move to the 'Sun-belt': a case study of long-distance migration to the gold coast, Australia. Urban Stud 35(2):193–214. https://doi.org/10.1080/0042098984943
Tang AZR, Rowe F, Corcoran J, Sigler T (2014) Where are the overseas graduates staying on? Overseas graduate migration and rural attachment in Australia. Appl Geogr 53:66–76. https://doi.org/10.1016/j.apgeog.2014.06.004
Taylor AJ, Gerritsen R (2014) Benefits of skilled migration programs for regional Australia: perspectives from the Northern Territory. J Econ Soc Policy 16(1):0_1
The Australian Worker's Union (2006) Submission to the senate employment, workplace relations and education reference committee inquiry into Pacific region seasonal contract labour. http://www.aph.gov.au/Senate/committee/eet_ctte/completed_inquiries/2004-07/contract_labour/submissions/sub034.pdf
Tonts M (2010) Labour market dynamics in resource dependent regions: an examination of the Western Australian goldfields. Geogr Res 48(2):148–165
Walker R (1995) Immigration policy and the political economy of New Zealand. In: Greif SW (ed) One people, two peoples, many peoples? Dunmore Press, Palmerston North, pp 282–302
Worldometers (2016) Oceania population. http://www.worldometers.info/world-population/oceania-population/

Part III
Shifting the Research Frontiers: The Interaction of Migrants, Their Backgrounds, Contexts and Impacts

Chapter 8
Inter-regional and Inter-sectoral Labour Mobility and the Industry Life Cycle: A Panel Data Analysis of Finnish High Technology Sector

Jaakko Simonen, Rauli Svento, Santtu Karhinen, and Philip McCann

Abstract Much of the literature on agglomeration emphasises labour mobility between firms as a potential source of externalities. However, while there is a large literature on interregional migration, the empirical literature on the employment-mobility of workers within the local arena is surprisingly thin. Furthermore, there is almost no empirical evidence on the relationship between local and non-local employment movements, especially across industries. In this paper we analyse how agglomeration of the high technology industry as well as regional amenities affects labour mobility. In order to do this we employ panel data on the regional and industrial labour mobility of the Finnish high technology firms and regional economies on a period of 1991–2007. Analysing this dataset allows us to identify the roles which the structure of the high technology sector, regional economic and amenity variables have played both in the inter-regional and inter-sectoral labour mobility of high technology workers over the industry life-cycle. Our findings confirm that the structure of the high technology sector as well as regional economic and amenity variables have an influence on the migration decisions of the high technology workers, and their roles vary in within-region and across-region mobility. In addition, the effects of the variables seem to vary at different stages of the industry life cycle.

Keywords Labour mobility · Agglomeration · Industry life-cycle · High technology

J. Simonen (✉) · R. Svento
Department of Economics, Oulu Business School, University of Oulu, Oulu, Finland
e-mail: jaakko.simonen@oulu.fi; rauli.svento@oulu.fi

S. Karhinen
Department of Economics, Oulu Business School, University of Oulu, Oulu, Finland

Finnish Environment Institute, Oulu, Finland
e-mail: santtu.karhinen@oulu.fi

P. McCann
Sheffield University Management School, Sheffield, UK
e-mail: p.mccann@sheffield.ac.uk

B. Biagi et al. (eds.), *New Frontiers in Interregional Migration Research*,
Advances in Spatial Science, https://doi.org/10.1007/978-3-319-75886-2_8

8.1 Introduction

A large sub-set of papers on agglomeration and clustering concerns high technology industries. High technology industry has received special interest in this field of research because it involves the deployment of advanced scientific and engineering skills and knowledge more than any other sector. Knowledge of high technology firms is to a large extent embodied in their workers and the output of innovative activity is the result of firms to appropriate this knowledge. Furthermore, the success of places such as Silicon Valley and other similar high technology agglomerations in other countries have increased interest in research relating to agglomeration processes especially within the high technology industries. Empirical evidence has shown that workers in the high technology industries are also highly mobile compared to the workers in many other industries. Power and Lundmark (2004), for instance, show that in the mid-1990s labour market mobility was significantly higher in the high technology clusters than in the rest of the urban economy in Sweden. Given the important contribution that the high technology sectors make to overall economic growth, understanding the mechanisms by which these sectors generate and transmit knowledge is seen as very important. The mobility of human capital is one such potential mechanism, and a variety of evidence suggests that the rapid growth of these high technology sectors and clusters was accompanied by very high rates of labour turnover and mobility among the professional and production workers (Angel 1991; Carnoy et al. 1997; Fallick et al. 2006; Power and Lundmark 2004; Saxenian 1994).

For these high technology sectors there is a small number of papers which indirectly deal with various aspects of inter-firm, inter-sector and inter-regional labour mobility (Audretsch and Stephan 1996; Almeida and Kogut 1999; Arita and McCann 2000; Mukkala 2008; McCann and Simonen 2005; Simonen and McCann 2008, 2010). Yet, apart from Simonen et al. (2016) modelling the explicit links between these high technology labour mobility flows and the specific features of the region or industry has not as yet been comprehensively attempted. From labour economic theory, there are strong grounds for assuming that the labour mobility and matching processes may be rather different between inter-firm, intra-sector, inter-sector, intra-regional, or inter-regional movements. Yet, our knowledge of exactly which processes dominate in which particular contexts is still very limited. This chapter therefore aims to move this research forward by examining a detailed Finnish dataset covering some approximately 117,000 workers per year in 1991–2007.[1] We investigate the patterns of high technology employment change

[1]In Finland high technology firms and their success in international markets has been an engine of economic growth over the past two decades. The strong growth of information and communication technology cluster in the 1990s (led by Nokia Corporation) made Finland internationally known as a small technology intensive economy where economic growth is mainly based on technology know-how. The strong high technology sector had an extremely important role especially in early 1990s when the Finnish economy was recovering from deep recession. For instance in 2008, the

in different parts of Finland, and examine the key underlying features driving these inter-firm intra-industry, intra-region and inter-region flows over the industry life-cycle.

The rest of the chapter is organised as follows. In the next section we provide a brief review of the current literature by focusing on the question of how agglomeration externalities and other regional features affect labour mobility. In Sect. 8.3 we discuss the data and variables used in our empirical analysis, and Sect. 8.4 reports our empirical results based on a series of panel data models. Section 8.5 provides some brief conclusions.

8.2 Agglomeration, Industry Life-Cycles and Labour Mobility

In general, workers change jobs and locations according to the existing geography of jobs. The balance between the advantages and costs associated with agglomeration heavily shape the spatial patterns of labour flows and these flows are also likely to depend heavily on the prevailing macroeconomic conditions.

One of the most important reasons for the emergence of industrial agglomeration are the benefits which local (skilled) labour pool provides for firms (Hanson 2000). The geographical proximity of many firms generally assumed to facilitate job-matching and employment switching (Di Addario 2011; de Blasio and Di Addario 2005; Scott and Storper 1990). Labour mobility between firms is argued to be an important means of transferring knowledge and fostering innovation (Almeida and Kogut 1999) by reducing the costs of job search (Di Addario 2011; Angel 1991). A large local labour pool typically gives firms flexibility regarding the number of workers hired and functional flexibility in the kinds of labour skills employed (Kim 1987) while the mobility of labour provides great flexibility also for both start-up firms and existing producers in putting together requisite teams of skilled professional and production workers. Rather than hiring workers at the entry level and generating skills in-house, firms are able to respond swiftly to changing labour demands by hiring experienced workers from the local labour market (Carnoy et al. 1997; Angel 1991). Proximity also provides benefits for people with high-level human capital, who tend have relatively greater employment opportunities and wage premia and who also tend to change jobs relatively frequently. These general arguments would tend to point to migration flows being primarily towards agglomeration centres, especially for high skilled workers such as those in high technology fields, we would expect these effects to be clearly evident (De La Roca and Puga 2016).

share of high technology sector was about 6% (in 1989, 3.6%) of the total labour force and almost 18% of the total export (in 1991, 6%) (Simonen et al. 2015).

At the same time, however, agglomeration and labour mobility can also have negative effects for high technology firms and workers. Intensive intra-regional and inter-firm worker mobility may break up existing research teams and lead to the dissipation of knowledge and resources to competing firms (Angel 1991; Traore and Rose 2003), while a tendency to use short-term and subcontracted employment creates worker instability and (Carnoy et al. 1997). Similarly, in the case of the industry-specific shock, high levels of localisation may cause difficulties for workers to find a job if most of the employers in the region are in the same negatively shocked industry. Thus living and working in a specialized city or region may expose a worker to greater of risk losing a job. These arguments also suggest that migration flows will also be heavily dependent on aggregate fluctuations in the fortunes of particular sectors.

In the case of advanced and high technologies, labour mobility is also likely to be heavily dependent on the industry life-cycle, because the life-cycles of these types of technologies tend to be rather short, displaying as new generations of technologies rapidly emerge from different sub-sectors or places. Indeed, following the analyses of Potter and Watts (2011), by looking at the development of employment of the Finnish high technology sector we see in Fig. 8.1 that both national and regional employment trajectories follow a patterns which is something like a logistic curve (the s-shape dotted line curve in top-left in Fig. 8.1), exactly as the industry life cycle theory would suggest. In Fig. 8.1 we see that while the national patterns corresponds closely to the logistic curve type of shape, the specific trajectories are slightly different for each of the different high technology city-regions of Finland; Tampere, Oulu, Jyväskylä, with some also facing downturns.

Similar types of development paths have also been found in number of empirical studies which have analysed the evolution of regional agglomerations (Potter and Watts 2011). Importantly for our purposes, however, is the fact that in addition to the agglomeration and clustering types of influences on labour mobility flows and behaviour, there are also likely to be aggregate life cycle types of effects on these flows. In Sect. 8.3 we provide some figures which show how labour flows are linked to industry life cycles.

Mukkala (2008) and Mukkala and Tohmo (2013) have studied mobility of highly educated workers within the high technology sector in Finland using the individual level data. However, in their research the scope of regional and industrial analysis as well as length of the observation period are much more limited compared to our research. In this study we move beyond existing analyses (Simonen et al. 2016; Mukkala 2008; Mukkala and Tohmo 2013) to identify the major characteristics and drivers of these flows over time at a detailed firm, sub-industry and regional levels. In order to investigate the nature of these flows in the context of the Finnish high technology industries we develop a panel data analysis of different types of labour mobility behaviour between firms, sub-sectors and regions.

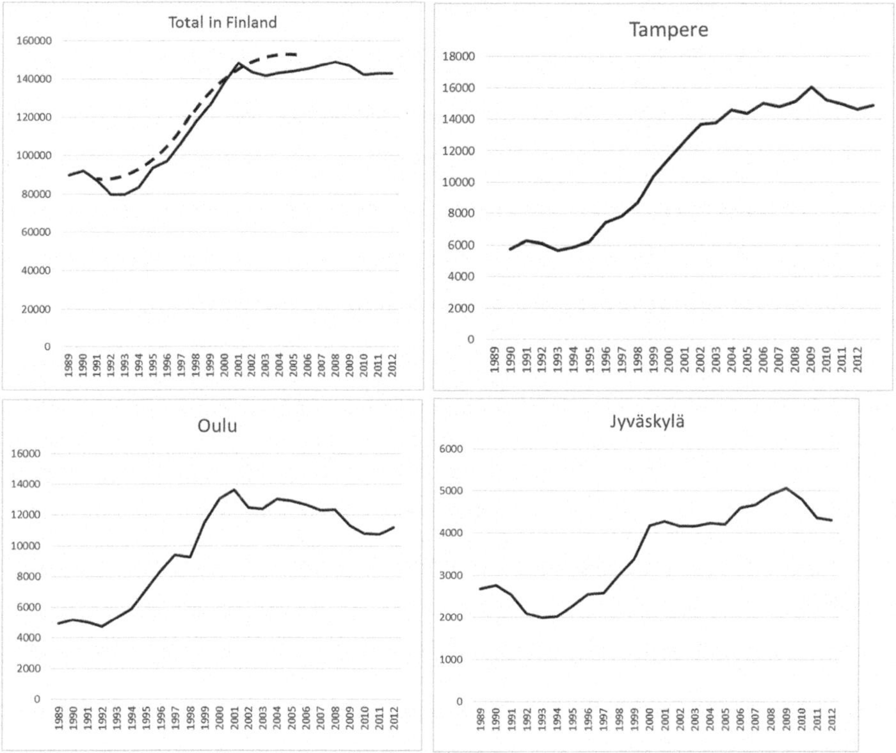

Fig. 8.1 The development of the high technology employment in Finland and some selected regions in 1989–2012

8.3 Data and Variables

The regional labour mobility data that we employ is derived from the Finnish Longitudinal Employer–Employee Database (FLEED) maintained by the national statistical authority, Statistics Finland. The data covers all of the workers employed in high technology industries in Finland in 1991–2007, approximately 117,000 workers per year. Our dataset is also comprised of all the Finnish high-technology establishments, as defined according to the standard industrial classification 2002 (SIC 2002) and listed in Table 8.1.

The regional-level used for this research is NUTS4 area level, and this is the most frequently used unit of analysis in these types of regional growth studies in Finland. NUTS4 is a somewhat smaller area classification than is often used in other research

Table 8.1 High technology industries (SIC 2002)

Manufacture of pharmaceuticals, medicinal chemicals and botanical products (244)
Manufacture of office machines and computers (30)
Manufacture radio, television, communications equipment and apparatus (32)
Manufacture of aircraft and spacecraft (353)
Manufacture of medical, precision and optical instruments (33)
Telecommunications (642)
Computers and related activities (72)
Research and Development (73)
Architectural and engineering activities and related technical consultancy (742, 743)

in European states. However, it is appropriate in the Finnish case because it is the smallest administrative area where the required data is extensively available, thereby providing the requisite level of micro-detail, and also because this is the geographic area (a total of 71 regional units) which best describes the commuting areas of Finland, given Finland's particular spatial population distribution.[2]

For the workers in these industries we classify the labour mobility behaviour of these high technology workers into five different and mutually exclusive categories defined as:

- Category 1: Remain in the same high-tech firm within the same industry and region
- Category 2: Change the firm within the region and stay within the same high-tech industry
- Category 3: Change the region but stay within the same high-tech industry
- Category 4: Change the high-tech industry within the same region
- Category 5: Change the high-tech industry and the region

For consistency in categories 3–5 we only use outflow numbers of employees across industries and regions rather than inflow numbers. We focus on only the labour mobility within high technology sector, not mobility between the high technology sector and other sectors in Finland. Workers may or may not change their residential location. Labour flows from high technology sector to other sectors are not considered as dependent variables. We analyse labour flows by looking at those employees who switch their job in particular year. For instance, in year 2000, the labour flow values show the number of employees who worked in different job in 2001. The last year pair in our panel data is 2006–2007.

We shall estimate various panel models in order to test the relationship between the different types of high technology labour mobility and the importance of various regional variables related to the region of origin. In order to begin this we first reclassify the five mobility categories into three data sets as follows.

[2]Due to the availability of the data, the number of regions in our study is 70 for the period of 1991–2007.

In the first case (Model 1) the dependent variable is defined as the *share of movers (i.e. those persons which exhibit any of the above mentioned mobility categories 2–5) of the total high technology labour in a region.*

In the second case (Model 2) the dependent variable is the *share of those movers that change the region (i.e. those persons which exhibit categories 3 and 5) of the total high technology movers in a region.* The person may or may not have changed the high technology industry. The estimations exclude workers who remain in a same high-tech firm in a region (i.e. category 1).

In the third case (Model 3) the dependent variable is the *share of those movers that change the industry (i.e. those persons which exhibit categories 4 and 5) of the total high technology movers in a region.* The person may or may not have changed the region. Also these estimations exclude workers who remain in a same high-tech firm in a region.

In models 4–7 the dependent variables are the *shares of workers which exhibit in different categories of the total movers in a region.*

Table 8.2 provides of descriptive statistics of these variables in a period of 1991–2007 across the regions. As is clearly evident, when people change job they often also change region. This may well be a function of the relatively sparse and dispersed spatial structure of the Finnish economy.

Figures 8.2–8.4 show how the high technology employment and the mobility in total, between regions and high technology industries, and in different categories have developed in absolute values in 1990–2006. The value in particular year shows how many employees left their current job at that year. We see that during the first years of ICT life-cycle growth, 1993–1996, labour mobility was quite modest, slightly below 7000 on average (Fig. 8.2). However, after that from 1997 to 2000 mobility increased significantly. In 2001, there was a dramatic turnaround in mobility. Just after the IT-bubble was collapsed, number of employees who switched their job dropped almost 3000 employees compared to year 2000. After 2004 labour mobility started to increase again. Similar kind of pattern can be seen both in inter-regional and inter-industry mobility (Fig. 8.3). In a same way we see that all type of mobility increased during the growth period, and also decreased after the crash of IT-bubble (Fig. 8.4). However, it seems that only Category 2 type of mobility, and to some extent Category 3 type of mobility increased after 2004. Other type of mobility increased only slightly.

Figure 8.5 shows how the *labour mobility developed as a share of total high technology employment.* We see that during the first years of growth the share of movers, as a percentage of total employment, first increased but then dropped for couple of years. After that the share increased in a similar way as the absolute mobility until 2000. After 2000 mobility dropped almost 4% points by the end of 2003. In 2006 it finally reached the level of 1999. When we are looking at *the inter-regional (i.e. Categories 3 and 5 together) and inter-industry mobility (Categories 4 and 5 together) as a share of movers* (Fig. 8.6), we see that during the first years of growth the share of inter-regional mobility actually decreased. Inter-industry mobility in turn increased. After 1995 the development was the opposite.

Table 8.2 Values measured across regions

	Total mobility[a]	Inter-regional mobility[b]	Inter-industry mobility[b]	Category 2 mobility[b]	Category 3 mobility[b]	Category 4 mobility[b]	Category 5 mobility[b]
Average	0.06	0.64	0.15	0.30	0.56	0.07	0.08
Std. Dev.	0.06	0.26	0.17	0.24	0.27	0.10	0.13
Min	0	0	0	0	0	0	0
Max	0.72	1	1	1	1	1	1

[a]Labour mobility of the total high technology employment
[b]Between regions and high-tech industries and in different categories of the total movers

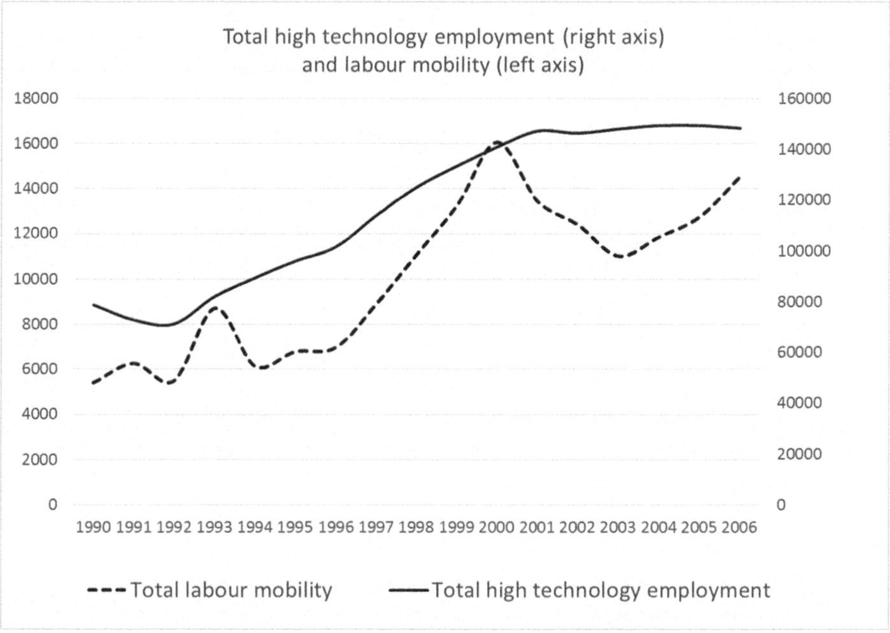

Fig. 8.2 Total high technology employment and labour mobility in absolute values in 1990–2006

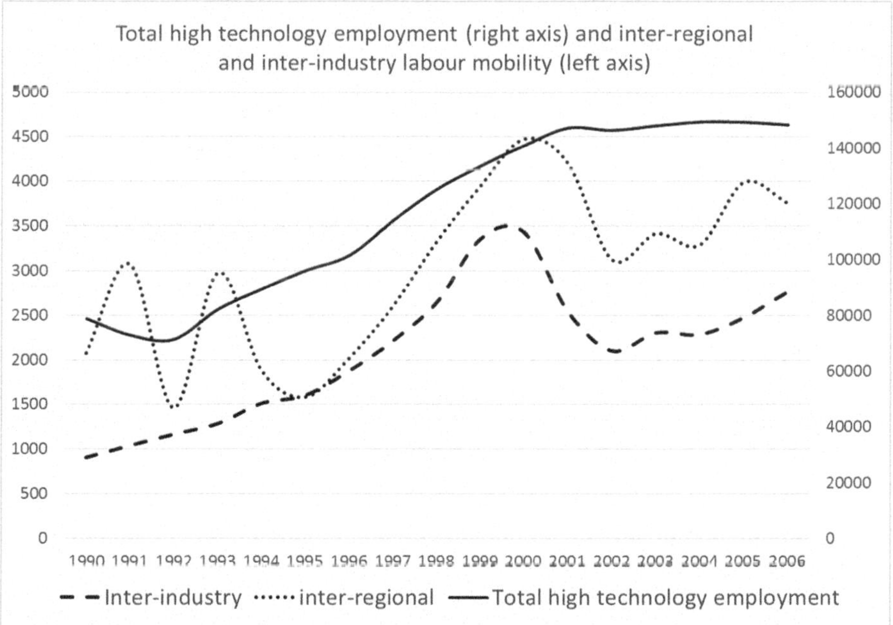

Fig. 8.3 Total high technology employment and inter-regional and inter-industry mobility in absolute values in 1990–2006

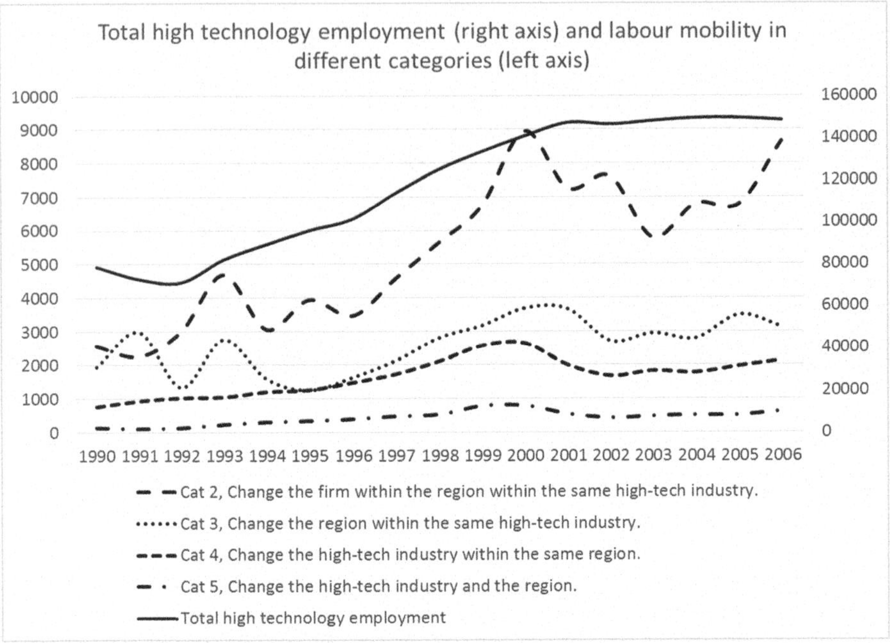

Fig. 8.4 Total high technology employment and mobility in absolute values in different categories in 1990–2006

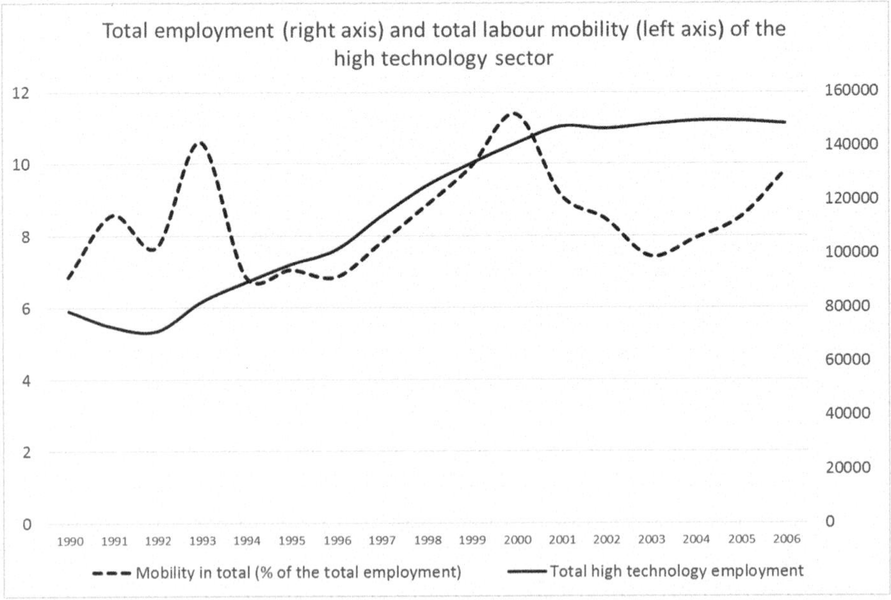

Fig. 8.5 Total high technology employment (right axis) and the labour mobility of the total high technology employment (left axis)

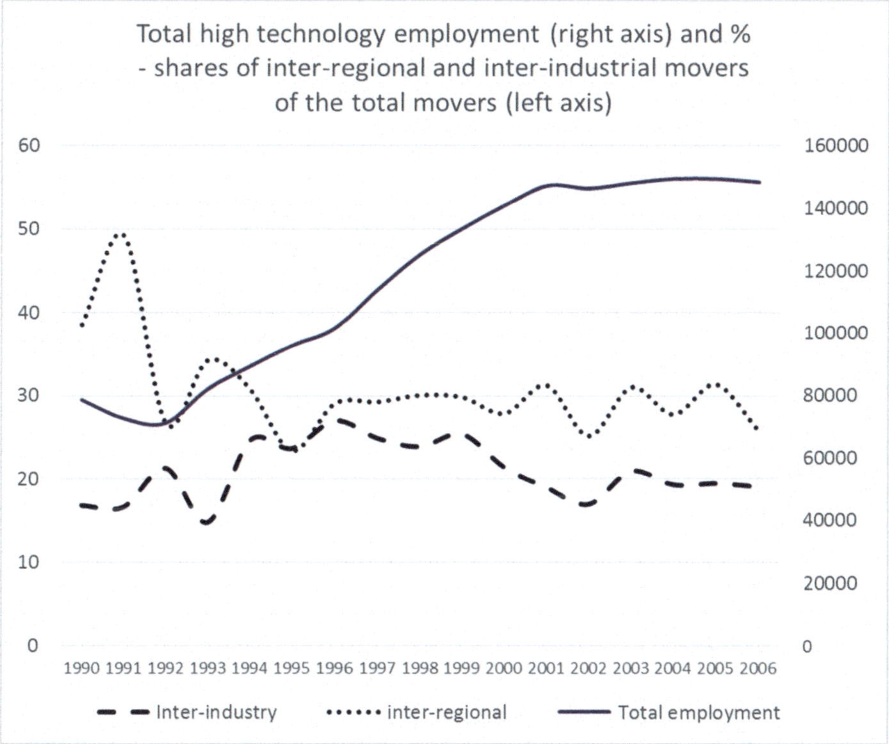

Fig. 8.6 Total high technology employment and the shares of inter-regional and inter-industry movers

When we are looking at Fig. 8.7, i.e. the how *mobility has developed in different categories, as a share of total movers,* we see that in the early years of growth, it became more and more common to switch the job especially within the same high technology industry in same region (Category 2 type of mobility). But this same happened also in categories 4 and 5 even if not that clearly. At the same time Category 3 type of mobility, i.e. people switch their job without switching the industry but moving to another region, became less common. Actually in 1995 it was equally common that employees switch region within the same industry (Cat. 3) or they switch industry within the same region (Cat. 4) However, after 1995 Category 3 type of mobility remained more common type of mobility compared to Category 4 and 5. The decrease in inter-industrial mobility, that we saw in Fig. 8.6, is realised in both type of mobilities (Cat. 4 and 5).

What happened was that during the early period of growth inter-industrial and intra-regional mobility increased, inter-regional mobility generally decreased. However, during the last years of growth also inter-regional labour mobility started to increase, although very slightly. Interestingly, at the same time when inter-regional

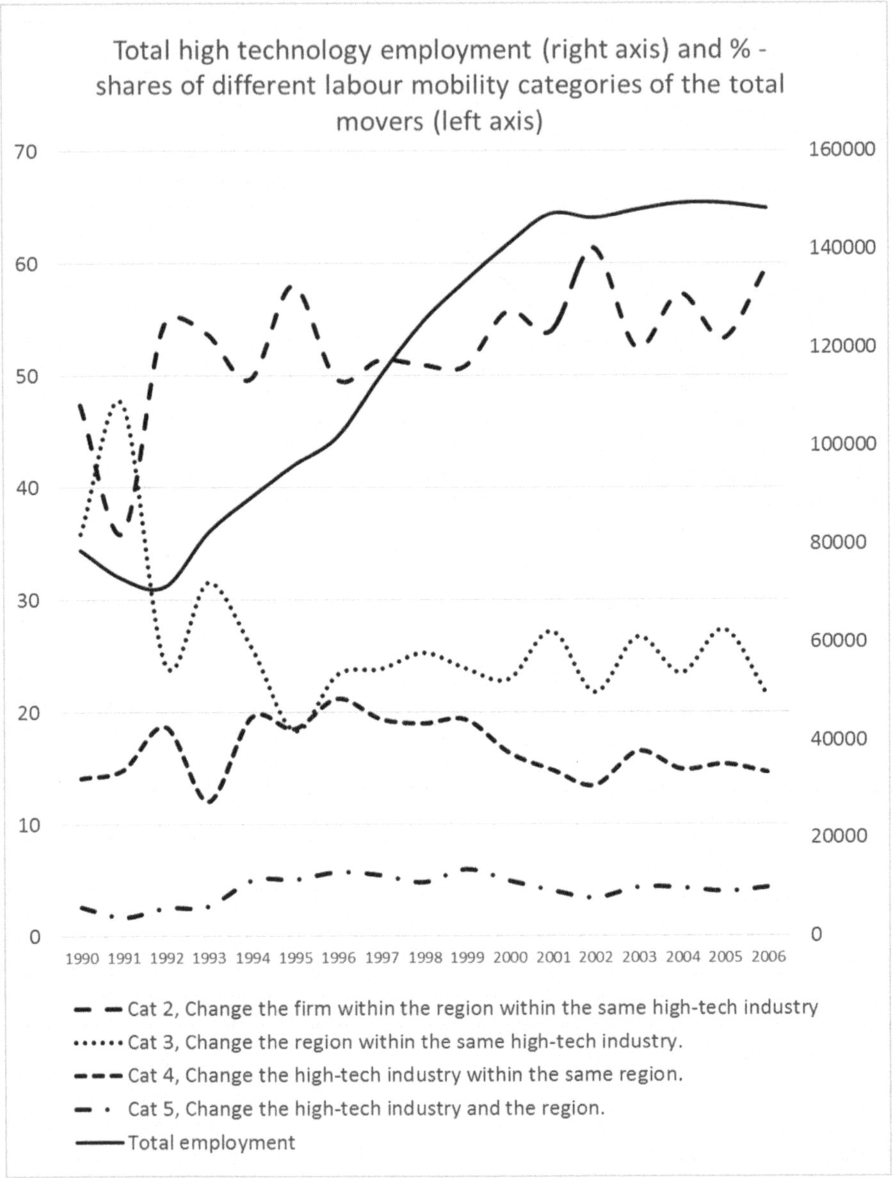

Fig. 8.7 Total high technology employment and the shares of different categories of the total movers

mobility started to increase especially in Category 3 (inter-regional intra-industry mobility), Category 4 type of mobility (intra-regional inter-industry mobility) started to decrease.

If we are to analyse labour mobility over time we must control for the different trends and fluctuations which are evident between the different categories of migration. Of course, it is likely that the crash of IT-bubble caused a nationwide structural change in Finnish labour mobility, in that the mobility of employees, in absolute terms, decreased significantly in all its forms. At the same time the share of total high technology as a percentage of total employment also dropped for couple of years (Fig. 8.5). Yet, the share of the intra-industry type of mobility (Categories 2 and 3) did not drop. The same happened in the case of Category 5 type of mobility. Indeed, the only form of labour mobility which became significantly less common was inter-industry mobility inside the region (Category 4). As such the picture is rather more nuanced than might at first appear.

In order to model these different types of high technology worker mobility, we employ various independent explanatory variables some of which are specific to the regional high technology sector and some of which reflect general state of the regional economy. The large literature on labour mobility suggests that each of these variables ought to influence worker mobility patterns. The following sections which provide the definitions of our variables draw largely from Simonen et al. (2016).

Our first independent explanatory variable is the *Location Quotient of the high technology sector*, which captures the region's relative specialisation in high technology activities.

Our second variable reflects the *Diversity of the high technology secto*r, and for this we use the well-known Shannon index. The Shannon index is an entropy measure which was originally developed in the field of information sciences and this index captures two features of diversity, namely richness and evenness. For this particular research the index has been calculated using the number of establishments in each of the nine different high-technology industry sub-sectors, and is calculated as follows:

$$SI_i = -\sum_{j=1}^{9} s_{ij} ln s_{ij},$$

where s_{ij} is the share of industry j of the total high technology sector in region i. The larger is the number of industries and the more evenly distributed are the high-tech establishments across these industries, the higher is the value of this measure in a particular region.[3]

[3]The difference between commonly used Herfindahl-Hirschmann index (HHI) and Shannon index is that the HHI assigns higher weights to the largest branches than does the Shannon Index. Therefore the value of HHI is largely driven by the share of the dominant branch, whereas the value of the Shannon Index depends more strongly on shares of several industries. Therefore, it reflects more accurately the variety of the high technology sector in terms of how many industries, including even small ones, are present in a region (Aiginger and Davies 2004; Simonen et al. 2015).

Our third high technology variable is the *Number of the high technology establishments* in the region (defined on a natural logarithmic scale). This gives a measure of the likely density of different employment roles and opportunities available in a locality. Taken together these first three variables capture the regional and sectoral specialisation, diversity and density of Finnish high technology employment patterns.

Our fourth high technology variable is *the share of the high technology service establishments* of the total high technology establishments in the region. According to the Simonen et al. (2015), high technology services have played an important role in regional development in Finland in the period of 1994–2008 because the share of employment in high technology services has increased significantly since 2000 while that of high technology manufacturing employment has fallen. A greater share for high technology service employment might be expected to increase job-mobility because the necessary skills required to fulfil the employment tasks in these service sectors, tend to be more generic in nature than in science-based or manufacturing sectors.

In addition to these four variables specific to the high technology sectors we have also used two additional variables to control for regional aggregate trends affecting these sectors. These variables are firstly the *Proportion of the high technology sector workers who leave the high technology sector but stay employed (either within the region or in another region)*, and secondly, the *Proportion of the workers who leave high technology sectors and become unemployed (either within the region or in another region)*. As with Simonen et al. (2016), these variables are both calculated as a percentage of the total high technology labour force within the region, and are calculated to control for any possible increased employment-termination rates in one or more of the local high technology industries.

We also include four independent explanatory variables which reflect the broad economic characteristics of each region but which are independent of high technology issues. Our first region-specific variable is the *Population density*, and the second region-specific variable that we control for is the *Proportion of the service establishments in the private sector*. This second variable is expressed in terms of the difference between the regional value and the average value across all of the regions, and is intended to measures the relative service intensity of the region. The third region-specific variable is the *Growth rate of the establishments in private sector*, and this is used as a proxy for the general economic conditions in a region, and our fourth regional control variable which is the *Proportion of the total population who are unemployed*.

The correlation matrix and the summary statistics regarding all of the explanatory variables over the whole period of 1990–2006 are presented in Appendix Tables 8.8 and 8.9.

Our modelling approach is the following. We start with the panel model which is aimed at identifying which factors affect the mobility of high technology workers in general. After that we analyse whether there are similarities or differences between inter-regional and inter-sectoral employment mobility patterns. As we see below our results demonstrate that the influences on these distinct types of employment-mobility patterns are quite different. For this reason we then move on to a discussion of the results of panel models which examine the influences on the four different individual categories of employment-mobility behaviour; inter-firm within the same high tech industry and region, inter-regional within the same high tech industry, inter-industry within the same region, and finally combination of inter-industry and inter-regional employment movement. In other words, we analyse the movement of workers, who have made the decision to change jobs. Again, we see that the differences are very marked. We also employ panel models for two different time periods; 1990–2000 and 2001–2006. The idea is to provide a picture how different factors effect labour mobility in different stages of industry life-cycle. These results produce a consistent picture which is quite different to many of the assumptions implicit in much of the existing literature. In all forms of models the dependent variables are based on the outflows of employees across high technology industries and regions, who stay employed after switching the firm, industry or region, or combination of these.

8.4 Results and Discussion

We begin with our three panel models (Random effects models[4]) examining the major influences on high technology labour mobility in general, inter-regional mobility, and inter-industry mobility.

Column 1 in Table 8.3 presents the results of the first panel model for a period 1990–2006 which estimates how different regional general economic and high technology sector specific factors affect the extent of the labour mobility, independently of the destination. Our dependent variable is the *share of movers (i.e. those persons who exhibit any of the above mentioned mobility Categories 2–5) of the total high technology labour in a region.* As we may expect, greater levels of Location quotient of the high technology sector, which reflects the region's relative specialisation in high technology activities in comparison to the national average, have a positive and significant effect on inter-firm mobility. High levels of labour flows from high technology sector to unemployment are also associated with greater employment-mobility. In contrast, unemployment, regional economic growth and high number of high technology establishments tend to reduce mobility as does high local levels of high technology industrial diversity. Although these results are in line with expectations they do, however, raise the question to what extent they are related to only inter-regional or inter-industrial movement, or whether they are actually related to both types of labour mobility.

Column 2 in Table 8.3 presents the results of the second panel model where we look at the *shares of workers who change regions relative to the total movers,*

[4]We decided to use Random effect models based on the Hausman test. Only in a case of model 1, column 2 in Table 8.4 have we used a Fixed effect model.

Table 8.3 Models 1–3. Random effects model

Variable (regional variables)	The coefficients of Model 1 (p-value in parenthesis)	The coefficients of Model 2 (p-value in parenthesis)	The coefficients of Model 3 (p-value in parenthesis)
Intercept/Constant	0.1687 (<0.0001)***	1.3302 (<0.0001)***	0.1611 (0.2338)
Population density	−0.0001 (0.1680)	−0.0003 (0.0022)***	−0.0000005 (0.9949)
Proportion of the service establishments (private sector) (*difference to the average across regions*)	0.0008 (0.1200)	0.0029 (0.2448)	−0.0041 (0.0140)**
Unemployment rate	−0.0020 (<0.0001)***	−0.0053 (<0.0001)***	0.0020 (0.0247)**
Growth rate of the establishments (total in private sector)	−0.0010 (0.0002)***	−0.0043 (0.0026)***	0.0030 (0.0023)***
Location quotient of the high technology sector (employment)	0.0154 (0.0117)**	−0.0164 (0.4864)	0.0644 (<0.0001)***
Diversity of the high technology sector, (Shannon index, nine industries)	−0.0249 (0.0122)**	−0.0919 (0.0723)*	0.0323 (0.3741)
Number of the high technology establishments (in logarithmic (ln) scale)	−0.0156 (<0.0001)***	−0.0664 (<0.0001)***	0.0221 (0.0558)*
Share of the high technology service establishments of the total high technology establishments	0.0003 (0.4130)	−0.2452 (0.1739)	−0.2000 (0.1155)
Labour flow from high technology sector to unemployment (%-share of the total H-T employment)	0.0009 (0.0021)***	0.0040 (0.0067)***	−0.0006 (0.5630)
Labour flow from high technology sector to other sectors (%-share of the total H-T employment)	−0.0001 (0.4974)	−0.0027 (0.0203)**	−0.0005 (0.5700)
Number of obs	*1094 (average group size 15.63)*	*1094 (average group size 15.63)*	*1094 (average group size 15.63)*
R-square	0.33	0.38	0.27

Notes: Model 1: High-tech mobility, Model 2: Inter-regional mobility, Model 3: Inter-industry mobility

White/Hetero. corrected covariance matrix used. Variances assumed equal within groups

*,** and *** indicate significance at the level of 10%, 5% and 1% level, respectively

i.e. inter-regional mobility. We exclude those workers who do not change their job. The dependent variable is then the share of persons who exhibit Categories 3 and 5 in comparison to the total high technology movers in a region. There are many factors which decrease the mobility of workers. The lower levels of inter-regional mobility shares are associated with population density, unemployment rate, regional economic growth and number of high technology establishments, but also high technology industrial diversity as well labour flows from high technology sector to other sectors. Only high labour flows from high technology sector to unemployment increases the regional outflows. At the same time, interestingly, features such as high levels of service activities as well as region's relative specialisation in high technology activities and high share of high technology services play no statistically significant role in determining inter-regional employment-mobility.

Column 3 in Table 8.3 presents the results of the third panel model where we examine the employment-mobility between high technology sectors. The dependent variable is the *share of those movers that change the industry relative to the total high technology movers in a region* (i.e. the share of people who exhibit Categories 4 and 5). The person may or may not have changed the region. These estimations also exclude workers who remain in a same high-tech firm in a region. The results show that economic growth and region's relative specialisation in high technology activities (measured with the location quotient) are associated with greater shares of inter-sectoral mobility as are the unemployment level and the high number of regional high technology establishments. High levels of service activities are in turn negatively associated with employment-mobility between high technology industries.

The widely differing results of the three models suggest that there are very different influences on inter-firm, inter-regional and inter-industrial employment-mobility. As such, discussions regarding the 'mobility' of high technology workers between jobs are far too general to be meaningful, because it depends on what type of mobility we are actually considering.

In order to deepen our analysis of labour mobility while explicitly allowing for the heterogeneity of employment-mobility patterns, we therefore now utilise the data in a way that we use individual Categories 2–5 described above, and measure their shares of the total regional high technology movers.

Table 8.4 reports the results of models 4–7. As we see, especially urbanisation, the degree of unemployment and the high number of high technology establishments, but also economic growth, industrial diversity, share of high technology services and labour flows outside high technology sectors are positively associated with inter-firm, intra-region mobility (model 4). As one would expect, the flow from high technology sector to unemployment is negatively associated with Category 2 type of mobility.

In contrast to inter-firm, intra-regional mobility, population density i.e. urbanisation, the degree of unemployment, economic growth and the high number of high technology establishments as well as industrial diversity are negatively associated with, inter-regional intra-industry, i.e. Category 3 type of mobility (model 5). Now only the share of high technology services and labour flows from

Table 8.4 Models 4–7. Random effects model

Variable (regional variables)	The coefficients of Model 4 (Cat. 2 mobility) (p-value in parenthesis)	The coefficients of Model 5 (Cat. 3 mobility) (p-value in parenthesis)	The coefficients of Model 6 (Cat. 4 mobility) (p-value in parenthesis)	The coefficients of Model 7 (Cat. 5 mobility) (p-value in parenthesis)
Intercept/Constant	−0.3379 (0.0712)*	1.2639 (<0.0001)***	0.0813 (0.3490)	0.1061 (0.3200)
Population density	0.0003 (0.0036)***	−0.0003 (0.0029)***	−0.000005 (0.9200)	−0.00001 (0.8837)
Proportion of the service establishments (private sector) (*difference to the average across regions*)	−0.0018 (0.4507)	0.0054 (0.0354)**	−0.0012 (0.2866)	−0.0032 (0.0112)**
Unemployment rate	0.0051 (<0.0001)***	−0.0072 (<0.0001)***	−0.00008 (0.8896)	0.0020 (0.0045)***
Growth rate of the establishments (total in private sector)	0.0034 (0.0002)**	−0.0064 (0.0026)***	0.0008 (0.1555)	0.0023 (0.0048)***
Location quotient of the high technology sector (employment)	−0.0264 (0.3157)	−0.0368 (0.1366)	0.0557 (<0.0001)***	0.0223 (0.0900)*
Diversity of the high technology sector, (Shannon index, nine industries)	0.0928 (0.0588)*	−0.1234 (0.0194)**	−0.0027 (0.9042)	0.0333 (0.2484)
Number of the high technology establishments (in logarithmic (ln) scale)	0.0487 (0.0009)***	−0.0685 (<0.0001)***	0.0168 (0.0201)**	0.0023 (0.8015)
Share of the high technology service establishments of the total high technology establishments	0.0030 (0.0870)*	−0.0016 (0.3789)	−0.0009 (0.2499)	−0.0010 (0.3046)
Labour flow from high technology sector to unemployment (%-share of the total H-T employment)	−0.0043 (0.0025)***	0.0050 (0.0011)***	0.0003 (0.5525)	−0.0010 (0.2531)
Labour flow from high technology sector to other sectors (%-share of the total H-T employment)	0.0026 (0.0214)**	−0.0023 (0.0568)*	0.00003 (0.9520)	−0.0005 (0.4051)
Number of obs	*1094 (average group size 15.63)*	*1094 (average group size 15.63)*	*1094 (average group size 15.63)*	*1094 (average group size 15.63)*
R-square	0.30	0.36	0.37	0.16

Notes: White/Hetero. corrected covariance matrix used. Variances assumed equal within groups
*,** and *** indicate significance at the level of 10%, 5% and 1% level, respectively

high technology sector to unemployment are positively associated with Category 3 type of mobility. The effect of high technology unemployment to the labour mobility this is exactly we could expect.

In contrast to previous models, only region's relative specialisation in high technology activities and the number of high technology establishments are positively associated with inter-industrial, intra-regional mobility, Category 4 type of mobility (model 6). At the same time, quite surprisingly, features such as high technology industrial diversity as well as labour flows form high technology sector to other sector or unemployment play no statistically significant role in determining inter-industrial intra-regional employment-mobility.

Finally, Category 5 mobility (changing both region and high technology industry), which in many ways is the most radical and challenging form of behaviour, is positively associated with the unemployment rate, regional economic growth and a region's relative specialisation in high technology activities (model 7). Only high levels of service activities seem to decrease the Category 5 type of mobility. No other explanatory variables offer any explanatory power regarding this particular form of labour mobility.

As we see, the impacts of different variables on labour mobility are both strongly and differently felt by the different categories of mobility. As already mentioned, there is no simple picture of high technology worker 'mobility', because it depends on which specific type of labour mobility we are interested in. Our results broadly explain inter-regional mobility rather well but not inter-industry mobility, and especially the Category 4 type of intra-regional inter-industry mobility. In particular, the effect of regional unemployment on labour mobility is not at all straightforward, as already found in previous studies (Pissarides and Wadsworth 1989; Hughes and McCormick 1981).

Tables 8.5–8.7 reports the results of panel models for two different time periods, 1990–2000 and 2001–2006. The idea is to provide information whether different factors effect labour mobility differently in early and later stages of industry lifecycle. As we see, mobility is positively and negatively associated with the number of different variables on a period of 1990–2000 (Table 8.5). Instead in the period of 2001–2006, there are only three variables which are significantly associated with the mobility in general over the period of 2000–2006. In both periods, specialisation in high technology activities (measured with the location quotient) as well as the number of high technology establishments are associated positively with employment-mobility. When we are looking at the inter-regional mobility, we see that effects of the variables are highly similar (their signs remain same) in a period of 1990–2000 and over the whole period. However, again none of the variables is significantly associated with this type of mobility in a period of 2000–2006. On the other hand, when we look at the inter-industry mobility, results for both sub-periods are in the line with the results of the whole period. Economic growth, region's relative specialisation in high technology activities as well as the unemployment level are associated positively and the levels of service activities negatively with employment-mobility between high technology sectors. Table 8.10 summaries the effect of different variables in different sub-periods.

Table 8.5 Models 1–3. Random effects model

Variable (regional variables)	The coefficients of Model 1 (p-value in parenthesis)		The coefficients of Model 2 (p-value in parenthesis)		The coefficients of Model 3 (p-value in parenthesis)	
Periods	1990–2000	2001–2006	1990–2000	2001–2006	1990–2000	2001–2006
Intercept/Constant	0.1900 (0.0001)***		1.3594 (<0.0001)***	0.8966 (0.0269)**	0.0504 (0.7740)	0.1078 (0.6921)
Population density	−0.0001 (0.1054)	−0.0019 (0.1956)	−0.0007 (<0.0001)***	0.0003 (0.2662)	0.00002 (0.8423)	0.00006 (0.7809)
Proportion of the service establishments (private sector) (*difference to the average across regions*)	0.0013 (0.0927)*	0.0056 (0.0771)*	0.0077 (0.0132)**	−0.0047 (0.2904)	−0.0038 (0.0997)*	−0.0065 (0.0389)**
Unemployment rate	−0.0027 (<0.0001)***	0.0017 (0.1809)	−0.0110 (<0.0001)***	0.0069 (0.1672)	0.0017 (0.1113)	0.0079 (0.0149)**
Growth rate of the establishments (total in private sector)	−0.0010 (0.0010)***	−0.0010 (0.2810)	−0.0043 (0.0018)***	0.0012 (0.8225)	0.0024 (0.0280)**	0.0109 (0.0007)***
Location quotient of the high technology sector (employment)	0.0136 (0.0627)*	0.1105 (0.0126)**	−0.0264 (0.3942)	0.0406 (0.4671)	0.0576 (0.0028)***	0.1110 (0.0001)***
Diversity of the high technology sector, (Shannon index, nine industries)	−0.0286 (0.0329)**	0.0275 (0.3340)	−0.0264 (0.6594)	−0.1454 (0.1534)	0.0287 (0.5599)	−0.0363 (0.6084)
Number of the high technology establishments (in logarithmic (ln) scale)	−0.0216 (<0.0001)***	0.0420 (0.0384)**	−0.0766 (<0.0001)***	−0.0386 (0.1294)	0.0262 (0.0812)*	−0.0065 (0.7481)
Share of the high technology service establishments of the total high technology establishments (%)	0.0007 (0.1618)	−0.0001 (0.8759)	−0.0010 (0.6331)	−0.0013 (0.7095)	−0.0006 (0.6910)	−0.0003 (0.8889)

Labour flow from high technology sector to unemployment (%-share of the total H-T employment)	0.0003 (0.43253)	−0.0010 (0.4107)	−0.00006 (0.9692)	−0.0036 0.4695)	−0.0007 (0.5583)	−0.0010 (0.7338)
Labour flow from high technology sector to other sectors (%-share of the total H-T employment)	−0.0001 (0.6134)	−0.0003 (0.4378)	−0.0026 (0.0441)**	−0.0004 (0.8539)	−0.0002 (0.8491)	−0.0020 (0.1567)
Number of obs	*676 (average group size 9.66)*	*418 (average group size 5.97)*	*676 (average group size 9.66)*	*418 (average group size 5.97)*	*676 (average group size 9.66)*	*418 (average group size 5.97)*
R-square	0.39	0.44	0.49	0.44	0.33	0.47

Notes: Model 1: High tech mobility, Model 2: Inter-regional mobility, Model 3: Inter-industry mobility for both sub-periods, except in column 2 we have used FE model

White/Hetero. corrected covariance matrix used. Variances assumed equal within groups

*,** and *** indicate significance at the level of 10%, 5% and 1% level, respectively

Table 8.6 Models 4–5. Random effects model

Variable (regional variables)	The coefficients of Model 4 (p-value in parenthesis) Category 2		The coefficients of Model 5 (p-value in parenthesis) Category 3	
Periods	1990–2000	2001–2006	1990–2000	2001–2006
Intercept/Constant	−0.3477 (0.1023)	0.2264 (0.5654)	1.3704 (<0.0001)***	0.9117 (0.0190)**
Population density	0.0007 (<0.0001)***	−0.0003 (0.1689)	−0.0007 (<0.0001)***	0.0002 (0.2404)
Proportion of the service establishments (private sector) (*difference to the average across regions*)	−0.0072 (0.0122)**	0.0074 (0.0863)*	0.0100 (0.0030)***	−0.0019 (0.6373)
Unemployment rate	0.0111 (<0.0001)***	−0.0102 (0.0354)**	−0.0127 (<0.0001)***	0.0029 (0.5525)
Growth rate of the establishments (total in private sector)	0.0038 (0.0042)***	−0.0084 (0.1135)	−0.0061 (<0.0001)***	−0.0013 (0.8126)
Location quotient of the high technology sector (employment)	0.0079 (0.7714)	−0.0908 (0.0665)*	−0.0386 (0.3398)	−0.0041 (0.9212)
Diversity of the high technology sector, (Shannon index, nine industries)	0.0103 (0.8550)	0.1534 (0.1205)	−0.455 (0.4828)	−0.1896 (0.0519)*
Number of the high technology establishments (in logarithmic (ln) scale)	0.0598 (0.0003)***	0.0258 (0.2841)	−0.0799 (0.0001)***	−0.0395 (0.0818)*
Share of the high technology service establishments of the total high technology establishments (%)	0.0012 (0.5395)	0.0005 (0.8690)	−0.0012 (0.5775)	−0.0008 (0.8008)
Labour flow from high technology sector to unemployment (%-share of the total H-T employment)	0.00009 (0.9517)	−0.0043 (0.3794)	0.0010 (0.5277)	0.0052 (0.2768)
Labour flow from high technology sector to other sectors (%-share of the total H-T employment)	0.0024 (0.0525)*	0.0019 (0.4173)	−0.0024 (0.0806)*	−0.0003 (0.8813)
Number of obs	*676 (average group size 9.66)*	*418 (average group size 5.97)*	*676 (average group size 9.66)*	*418 (average group size 5.97)*
R-square	0.41	0.39	0.48	0.39

Model 4: Cat 2, Model 5: Cat 3, for both sub-periods

Table 8.7 Models 6–7. Random effects model

Variable (regional variables)	The coefficients of Model 6 (p-value in parenthesis) Category 4		The coefficients of Model 7 (p-value in parenthesis) Category 5	
Periods	1990–2000	2001–2006	1990–2000	2001–2006
Intercept/Constant	0.1504 (0.1958)	0.0142 (0.9369)	0.1969 (0.8854)	0.1236 (0.5773)
Population density	−0.0000001 (0.9982)	0.00008 (0.7792)	0.000004 (0.9707)	−0.000007 (0.9603)
Proportion of the service establishments (private sector) (*difference to the average across regions*)	−0.0002 (0.9012)	−0.0043 (0.0368)**	−0.0041 (0.0172)**	−0.0038 (0.1319)
Unemployment rate	−0.0003 (0.6343)	0.0036 (0.0824)*	0.0021 (0.0135)**	0.0033 (0.2081)
Growth rate of the establishments (total in private sector)	0.0005 (0.4418)	0.0072 (0.0002)***	0.0020 (0.0222)**	0.0039 (0.1525)
Location quotient of the high technology sector (employment)	0.0542 (<0.0001)***	0.0474 (0.0042)***	0.0101 (0.5104)	0.0838 (0.0019)***
Diversity of the high technology sector, (Shannon index, nine industries)	0.0026 (0.9362)	−0.0896 (0.0436)**	0.0200 (0.6022)	0.0552 (0.3560)
Number of the high technology establishments (in logarithmic (ln) scale)	0.0159 (0.0888)*	0.0144 (0.2734)	0.0093 (0.4212)	−0.0348 (0.0374)**
Share of the high technology service establishments of the total high technology establishments (%)	−0.0015 (0.1686)	0.0004 (0.7970)	−0.0001 (0.9058)	−0.00005 (0.9795)
Labour flow from high technology sector to unemployment (%-share of the total H-T employment)	−0.00003 (0.9741)	0.0026 (0.1668)	−0.0005 (0.5964)	−0.0037 (0.1361)
Labour flow from high technology sector to other sectors (%-share of the total H-T employment)	0.0002 (0.8082)	−0.0016 (0.0586)*	−0.0005 (0.5317)	−0.0007 (0.5394)
Number of obs	*676 (average group size 9.66)*	*418 (average group size 5.97)*	*676 (average group size 9.66)*	*418 (average group size 5.97)*
R-square	0.44	0.49	0.19	0.37

Notes: Model 6: Cat 4, Model 7: Cat 5, for both sub-periods
White/Hetero. corrected covariance matrix used. Variances assumed equal within groups
*,** and *** indicate significance at the level of 10%, 5% and 1% level, respectively

All in all we may say that by comparing inter-regional and inter-industrial labour mobility, it is the inter-regional labour mobility (Categories 3 and 5) which is more clearly linked to the industry life-cycles (Tables 8.6 and 8.7). In the early stages of life-cycle, there is a number of variables which appear to decrease labour mobility out of the region and increase people's willingness to remain in the region. Only the levels of service activities are positively associated to the inter-regional labour mobility, and our regional variables do appear to broadly capture the decreasing trend of inter-regional mobility during in the growth period. However, in the later stages of life-cycle, none of our variables seem to play a role in inter-regional mobility. We know that mobility is a largely pro-cyclical phenomenon and this may also be the case in terms of industry life-cycles, suggesting that the drivers of labour mobility as typically understood tend to be rather more associated with the earlier stages of the industry life-cycle than the later stages.

8.5 Conclusions

The major finding from this analysis is that we cannot talk simply of high technology worker 'mobility', because there are different forms of high technology worker mobility, each which is influences in different ways by different factors and at different time periods. Of all of the different types of labour mobility behaviour it is the intra-industry mobility, of both intra-regional and inter-regional forms, which is the most significantly linked to the industry life-cycles and textbook types of arguments. Interestingly, neither the share of the high technology services and nor the labour flows to unemployment from high technology sectors have any role in any specific type of labour mobility nor at any stage in the life-cycle of the industry.

Appendix

Table 8.8 Correlation matrix of the explanatory variables: the whole period of 1990–2006

Variable	Population density	Proportion of the service establishments (private sector) (*difference to the average across regions*)	Unemployment rate	Growth rate of the establishments (total in private sector)	Location quotient of the high technology sector (employment)	Diversity of the high technology sector, (Shannon index, nine industries)	Number of the high technology establishments (in logarithmic (ln) scale)	Share of the high technology service establishments of the total high technology establishments (%)	Labour flow from high technology sector to unemployment (%-share of the total H-T employment	Labour flow from high technology sector to other sectors (%-share of the total H-T employment)
Population density	1.00									
Proportion of the service establishments (private sector) (*difference to the average across regions*)	0.36	1.00								
Unemployment rate	−0.29	0.20	1.00							
Growth rate of the establishments (total in private sector)	0.00	−0.01	−0.22	1.00						
Location quotient of the high technology sector (employment)	0.08	0.30	−0.10	0.03	1.00					
Diversity of the high technology sector, (Shannon index, nine industries)	0.12	0.13	−0.06	−0.09	0.29	1.00				

(continued)

Table 8.8 (continued)

Variable	Population density	Proportion of the service establishments (private sector) *(difference to the average across regions)*	Unemployment rate	Growth rate of the establishments (total in private sector)	Location quotient of the high technology sector (employment)	Diversity of the high technology sector, (Shannon index, nine industries)	Number of the high technology establishments (in logarithmic (ln) scale)	Share of the high technology service establishments of the total high technology establishments (%)	Labour flow from high technology sector to unemployment (%-share of the total H-T employment	Labour flow from high technology sector to other sectors (%-share of the total H-T employment)
Number of the high technology establishments (in logarithmic (ln) scale)	0.20	0.52	−0.23	0.11	0.51	0.23	1.00			
Share of the high technology service establishments of the total H-T establishments (%)	0.11	0.07	−0.27	0.13	−0.24	−0.50	0.21	1.00		
Labour flow from high technology sector to unemployment (%-share of the total H-T employment)	−0.16	0.02	0.38	−0.22	−0.17	0.07	−0.32	−0.23	1.00	
Labour flow from high technology sector to other sectors (%-share of the total H-T employment)	0.01	−0.07	−0.05	0.18	−0.15	−0.08	−0.12	0.11	0.04	1.00

Table 8.9 Values of the explanatory variables over the whole period of 1990–2006

Variable	N	Mean	Std Dev	Minimum	Maximum
Population density	1094	35.36	106.79	0.55	918.07
Proportion of the service establishments (private sector) (*difference to the average across regions*)	1094	0.25	5.87	−16.71	14.64
Unemployment rate	1094	18.53	7.96	1.04	47.60
Growth rate of the establishments (total in private sector)	1094	0.36	4.92	−36.77	47.82
Location quotient of the high technology sector (employment)	1094	0.49	0.60	0.03	5.18
Diversity of the high technology sector, (Shannon index, nine industries)	1094	1.14	0.20	0.23	1.61
Number of the high technology establishments (in logarithmic (ln) scale)	1094	4.09	1.24	1.10	8.72
Share of the high technology service establishments of the total high technology establishments (%)	1094	86.95	6.28	61.11	100.00
Labour flow from high technology sector to unemployment (%-share of the total H-T employment)	1094	5.90	5.43	0.00	38.46
Labour flow from high technology sector to other sectors (%-share of the total H-T employment)	1094	8.86	5.98	0.00	62.20

Table 8.10 Summary table: Statistically significant variables in different models in Table 8.5

	Models and sub-periods					
	High technology mobility (model 1 in Table 8.5)		Inter-regional high technology mobility (model 2 in Table 8.5)		Inter-industry high technology mobility (model 3 in Table 8.5)	
Variables	1990–2000	2001–2000	1999–2000	2001–2006	1990–2000	2001–2006
Intercept/Constant	+ + +		+ + +	+ +		
Population density			– – –			
Proportion of the service establishments (private sector) (*difference to the average across regions*)	+	+	+ +		–	– –
Unemployment rate	– – –		– – –			+ +

(continued)

Table 8.10 (continued)

Variables	Models and sub-periods					
	High technology mobility (model 1 in Table 8.5)		Inter-regional high technology mobility (model 2 in Table 8.5)		Inter-industry high technology mobility (model 3 in Table 8.5)	
	1990–2000	2001–2000	1999–2000	2001–2006	1990–2000	2001–2006
Growth rate of the establishments (total in private sector)	− − −		− − −		+ +	+ + +
Location quotient of the high technology sector (employment)	+	+ +			+ + +	+ + +
Diversity of the high technology sector, (Shannon index, nine industries)	− −					
Number of the high technology establish-ments (in logarithmic (ln) scale)	− − −	+ +	− − −		+	
Share of the high technology service establish-ments of the total high technol-ogy establishments						
Labour flow from high technology sector to unem-ployment (%-share of the total H-T employment)						
Labour flow from high technology sector to other sectors (%-share of the total H-T employment)			− −			

Note: +/−, + +/− − and + + +/− − − indicate significance at the level of 10%, 5% and 1% level as well as sign of the variable, respectively

References

Aiginger K, Davies SW (2004) Industrial specialization and geographic concentration: two sides of the same coin? Not for the European Union. J Appl Econ 7:231–248

Almeida P, Kogut B (1999) Localisation of knowledge and the mobility of engineers in regional networks. Manag Sci 45:905–917

Angel DP (1991) High-technology agglomeration and the labor market: the case of Silicon Valley. Environ Plan A 23:1501–1516

Arita T, McCann P (2000) The spatial and hierarchical organization of Japanese and US multinational semiconductor firms. J Int Manag 8:121–139

Audretsch DB, Stephan PE (1996) Company-scientist locational links: the case of biotechnology. Am Econ Rev 86:641–652

Carnoy M, Castels M, Benner C (1997) Labour market and employment practises in the age of flexibility: a case of Silicon Valley. Int Labour Rev 136:27–48

de Blasio G, Di Addario S (2005) Do workers benefit from industrial agglomeration? J Reg Sci 45:797–827

De la Roca J, Puga D (2016) Learning by working in big cities. Rev Econ Stud 84(1):106–142

Di Addario S (2011) Job search in thick markets. J Urban Econ 69:303–318

Fallick B, Fleischman CA, Rebitzer JB (2006) Job hopping in Silicon Valley: some evidence concerning the micro-foundations of a high technology cluster. Rev Econ Stat 88(3):472–481

Hanson GH (2000) Firms, workers, and the geographic concentration of economic geography. In: Clark G, Gertler M, Feldmann M (eds) The Oxford handbook of economic geography. Oxford University Press, Oxford, pp 477–494

Hughes G, McCormick B (1981) Do council housing policies reduce migration between regions? Econ J 91:917–937

Kim S (1987) Diversity in urban labor markets and agglomeration economics. Pap Reg Sci Assoc 62:57–70

McCann P, Simonen J (2005) Innovation, knowledge spillovers and local labour markets. Pap Reg Sci 84:465–485

Mukkala K (2008) Knowledge spillovers: mobility of highly educated workers within the high technology sector in Finland. In: Poot J, Waldorf B, van Wissen L (eds) Migration and human capital. Edward Elgar, Cheltenham, pp 131–149

Mukkala K, Tohmo T (2013) Inter-industry job mobility in the knowledge economy in Finland. Int J Manpow 34:918–938

Pissarides C, Wadsworth J (1989) Unemployment and the inter-regional mobility of labour. Econ J 99(397):739–755

Potter A, Watts HD (2011) Evolutionary agglomeration theory: increasing returns, diminishing returns, and the industry life-cycle. J Econ Geogr 11:417–455

Power D, Lundmark M (2004) Working through knowledge pools: labour market dynamics, the transfer of knowledge and ideas, and industrial clusters. Urban Stud 41:1025–1044

Saxenian A (1994) Regional advantage: culture and competition in Silicon Valley and Route 128. Harvard University Press, Cambridge

Scott A, Storper M (1990) Work organization and local labour markets in an era of flexible production. Int Labour Rev 129:573–591

Simonen J, McCann P (2008) Firm innovation: the influence of R&D cooperation and the geography of human capital inputs. J Urban Econ 64(1):146–154

Simonen J, McCann P (2010) Knowledge transfers and innovation: the role of labour markets and R&D cooperation between agents and institutions. Pap Reg Sci 89:295–309

Simonen J, Svento R, Juutinen A (2015) Specialization and diversity as drivers of economic growth: evidence from high-tech industries. Pap Reg Sci 94:229–247

Simonen J, Svento R, McCann P (2016) The regional and sectoral mobility of high technology workers: insights from Finland. Ann Reg Sci 56(2):341–368

Traore N, Rose A (2003) Determinants of biotechnology utilization by the Canadian industry. Res Policy 32:1719–1735

Chapter 9
Ethnic and Economic Determinants of Migrant Location Choice

Cindy Smart, Arthur Grimes, and Wilbur Townsend

Abstract This chapter addresses the determinants of migrant location choice within the migrant's adopted country. We focus on two sets of location determinants: economic determinants and ethnic (country of origin) determinants. Ethnic determinants are found to be important across a wide range of studies. By contrast, prior literature indicates that impacts of economic factors differ according to the characteristics both of locations and of migrants. The first part of the chapter summarises key findings of prior studies into migrant location choice, focusing on economic and ethnic determinants. Much of the literature in this field relates to migrants to the United States of America. The second part of the chapter extends knowledge of migrant location choice by considering another country that hosts a high proportion of international migrants, New Zealand. We draw on unit record New Zealand census data from 2013 for this analysis. The importance of ethnic (country of origin) networks is confirmed in this analysis but so too is the importance of economic factors. The latter finding is in contrast to much of the US based literature. It plausibly reflects the greater emphasis that New Zealand places on skills-based migration relative to the United States. At a technical level, this study uses the average regional wage of the industry in which the migrant is employed, together with region fixed effects, which may contribute to more precise estimates of wage effects than does the more standard use of average regional wages.

Keywords Migrant location · Ethnicity · Country of origin · Economic determinants

C. Smart
Boston Consulting Group, Sydney, NSW, Australia

A. Grimes (✉)
Motu Economic and Public Policy Research, Wellington, New Zealand

Victoria University of Wellington, Wellington, New Zealand
e-mail: arthur.grimes@vuw.ac.nz

W. Townsend
Motu Economic and Public Policy Research, Wellington, New Zealand

B. Biagi et al. (eds.), *New Frontiers in Interregional Migration Research*,
Advances in Spatial Science, https://doi.org/10.1007/978-3-319-75886-2_9

9.1 Introduction

Migration is observed at several scales, including international migration (across countries) and inter-regional migration (within countries). An intersection of these two scales occurs when we consider the location choice within a country of international migrants to that country. The determinants of international migrants' location choice in their adopted country is the topic of this chapter.

Following two key strands of the literature, the study focuses on two sets of location determinants: economic determinants versus ethnic (defined here as country of origin) determinants. Ethnic determinants are found to be important across a wide range of studies, but prior literature indicates that the impacts of economic factors differ according to the characteristics of locations and characteristics of the migrants themselves.

The chapter comprises two main parts. First, we summarise key findings of prior studies into migrant location choice, focusing on both economic and ethnic determinants.[1] Much of the literature in this field relates to migrants to the United States of America. These studies have the advantage of relating to a high number of international migrants, with a wealth of available data. However, the danger of restricting attention mainly to the US is that findings may be country-specific reflecting, for instance, migration policies of the host country.

For this reason, the second part of this study examines determinants of international migrants' location choice within another country that hosts a high proportion of international migrants, New Zealand. We draw on unit record New Zealand census data for this analysis. Approximately a quarter of New Zealand's population is born overseas. New Zealand's nearest neighbours (New Caledonia, Tonga, Fiji and Australia) are each at least 1800 km distant from the country's major city (Auckland) so proximity to an international border does not directly affect location choices. Nevertheless, immigrants do not locate uniformly throughout the country, tending to cluster in the larger cities. In particular, Auckland (which comprises approximately one third of the country's population) has nearly 40% of its residents born outside New Zealand. These aspects make New Zealand an ideal counterpart with which to compare results derived from countries such as the US. Both the US and New Zealand are relatively open developed countries, so the contrasts and similarities in findings across these countries may still be specific to open developed countries. This observation should be borne in mind in interpreting the findings.

9.2 Key Prior Findings

Standard theories of migration have long hypothesised that economic factors such as unemployment rates, wage levels and costs of living will influence where immigrants choose to settle (Harris and Todaro 1970). Separately, the social capital

[1]This part highlights key findings rather than covering all relevant papers in the field.

literature indicates that culturally-related factors are likely to impact on location choice. Bonding social capital is likely to be high where an immigrant chooses to settle in an area with a high proportion of immigrants from the migrant's home country whereas bridging social capital will be enhanced by locating in an area with diverse population characteristics (Lancee 2012; Battisti et al. 2016).

We summarise key empirical findings on migrant location choice from the social capital related literature in Sect. 9.2.1 followed by findings on economic determinants of migrant location in Sect. 9.2.2. Across these two sets of studies, empirical work has found that culturally-related factors have significant impacts on immigrant location whereas less importance is attached to economic factors when considered by themselves. The interaction of individuals' and location characteristics, however, gives a more nuanced picture relative to the aggregate findings. We review some of these interactive effects in Sects. 9.2.3 and 9.2.4 where we examine the roles of language and education on migrant location choice. Section 9.2.5 examines the importance of migrant relocation within the host country as part of the settlement process. In Sect. 9.2.6, as a precursor to the empirical part of the paper, we review prior findings related to migrant clustering in New Zealand.

9.2.1 The Importance of Migrant Networks

A pioneering study into migrant settlement location choices (Bartel 1989) examined patterns of settlement for new immigrants to the United States after the 1965 amendments to the Immigration Act. Her research indicated that economic factors, such as wage and unemployment rates of the region, were unimportant in settlement decisions. By contrast, the percentage of the same ethnic group as the immigrants living in that area was the most important factor across every migrant group examined. This correlation between location choice and the proportion of migrants from the same home country has been found in many subsequent studies. A number of potential reasons have been suggested for the phenomenon.

The first reason relates to network effects. Benefits (positive network externalities) are gained from co-locating with previous migrants through the presence of bonding social capital. There are a number of ways in which these externalities can play out. For instance, Mexican immigrants to the United States are found to be more likely to find jobs and be higher paid when they moved to an area with a large Mexican migrant population (Munshi 2003). This is attributed to the migrants obtaining job referrals from their local migrant network. Similarly, Carrington et al. (1996) argue that the costs of migration decrease when migrants move to an area with a high stock of previous migrants through help with securing work. Additionally, migrant networks can reduce migration costs by helping with living arrangements, such as through temporary lodging, or financial assistance. Culturally, there are costs associated with adapting to a new environment, such as learning a new language (Church and King 1983) or fitting into the new culture (Carrington et al. 1996). By locating in an area with a well-established network of migrants from the same home country, new migrants can reduce both the monetary and mental costs of this adaptive process.

However, these network externalities are not necessarily all positive, and there may be some disadvantages to locating in areas with high migrant populations. One example is increased competition for jobs, which lowers wages and reduces the chance of immigrants finding work (Bauer et al. 2007, 2009; Epstein 2008). Initially, positive externalities from having an ethnic network outweigh the negative externalities, but as the stock of immigrants in a given location increases, competition for work accelerates. There is, therefore, a tipping point where there are no longer net positive externalities to be gained from these migrant networks (Bauer et al. 2007). Bauer et al. (2009) suggest further negative impacts of networks, such as adverse selection leading to low-productivity workers immigrating, which may negatively impact the high-productivity workers. The increased density of migrants also reduces incentives to assimilate with the host country's culture and language, potentially trapping immigrants into ethnic enclaves and potential poverty. So while migrant communities provide benefits to immigrants, these effects may be mitigated by other negative externalities. These findings suggest that other theories of migrant clustering need to be examined.

One additional explanation for the clustering phenomenon is herd effects. Herd effects arise from migrants observing choices of previous migrants and following the migrant flow, even if this choice does not appear to be optimal to an outsider (Bauer et al. 2007). This explanation rests on the existence of imperfect information. A migrant choosing to move to a new country will explore multiple options and search for information about each location in order to make a decision about where to locate (Epstein 2008). However, the information each migrant receives will not be complete, and will not be the same for each individual migrant. Migrants are aware of this uncertainty (Epstein 2008). A migrant, seeing other migrants moving to a given location, may assume that those migrants are privy to valuable additional information, and will discount her own private information (Bauer et al. 2002; Epstein 2008). Migrants may then choose to move to a location which they would not choose based on full information, simply because they see others moving there (Epstein 2008). Bauer et al. (2002) set up this decision process as a game, where individuals receive a signal, and can observe behaviour of others, but not the signals that the previous migrants received. Based on this process, individuals follow the herd and migrate to where others go in preference to where their private information may indicate is best (Bauer et al. 2002).

This herd effect may also help to understand why economic factors seem unimportant in migrants' settlement location decisions. As they are discounting their private information, migrants may choose a location with less attractive economic opportunities, even though they would prefer somewhere with better work and pay prospects, because they assume that the herd knows best (Bauer et al. 2002).

A third potential explanation for the clustering of migrants is the presence of gateway cities, being the first place of contact for a transport network within a country. Chiswick and Miller (2004) identify the "Big 6" immigrant states in the United States, which are the main states through which immigrants enter the US. The gateway phenomenon is seen in other countries where particular cities are the main entry points for immigrants coming to the country, based on the quality of their international transport connections. These cities may also offer amenities, education and employment opportunities suited to migrants. The international linkages prevalent in gateway cities allow for greater connection back to the home country and even for potential return migration (Friesen 2012). Gateway cities may not be the initial target settlement point, but since migrants typically have to pass through these cities, their circumstances (such as career and education opportunities, family reasons, or new relationships) may change and cause them to stay. Migrants may therefore be observed to cluster in these areas, but this may not necessarily be due to any particular ethnic networks from previous migrants. This kind of clustering is likely in larger cities, even if they are not specifically gateway cities, as these cities will also have many of the attractors of gateway cities. These factors help to explain why clustering occurs mainly in large urban areas (Chiswick and Miller 2004; Jaeger 2000).

9.2.2 Where Economic Factors Start to Matter

While most literature subsequent to Bartel's (1989) study supports her finding of the importance of ethnic communities for migrant location, a number of studies dispute the finding that economic factors are not significant (Borjas 2001; Jaeger 2000, 2006). Borjas (2001) for example, identified clustering of immigrants in the US in states with high wages, arguing that immigrants play an important role in labour efficiency. Wage differentials are observed between US cities and states, and these differentials have persevered due to the high cost of relocation for natives. However, migrants can act as an equilibrating force since their cost of moving is relatively stable regardless of where they chose to settle. They are therefore expected to move to areas of high wages so decreasing the wage differential.

Following Borjas, economic factors affecting location choice have been examined in the context of immigration categories. Jaeger (2006) found that economic factors such as wages and unemployment were important for certain categories of immigrants to the US, specifically those entering on employment based (as opposed to family reunification) visas. These findings highlight the individual nature of the location decision, so that outcomes may reflect the personal characteristics of the individual.

Economic factors may matter more to poorer immigrants. Unlike some wealthy migrants, poorer immigrants will seek low costs of living and a high probability of gaining employment. Bauer et al. (2005) postulate that the costs of migration are more heavily considered by poorer immigrants and therefore factors such as travel costs matter more for these migrants in their location choice. White (1998) examines the flow of immigrants into London. He hypothesises that those coming from the developing world are more constrained in their location choices owing to lower resources and potential regulatory controls. By contrast, those coming from the developed world face fewer constraints and can choose where to settle more freely and should therefore be less impacted by economic factors. Despite this freedom, developed world migrants still tend to cluster with migrants from similar regions. He suggests that this may occur because highly skilled workers tend to move frequently during their careers and are therefore less concerned about integrating into the local culture. Allen and Turner (1996) also find clustering of high-income migrants, reinforcing the importance of cultural factors and maintenance of social ties for these immigrants.

Jaeger (2000) challenges the idea that the causality relating to clustering of migrants for economic reasons necessarily starts with the immigrant's own preferences and circumstances. He postulates that the causality could start with firms which actively seek employees from overseas. In particular, firms in an area with low unemployment and high wages may face a shortage of appropriately skilled workers, and so seek workers from abroad. This is in accordance with Borjas's (2001) argument that immigrants act as an equilibrating force in the labour market due to their lower costs of settling in different places relative to natives.

9.2.3 How Language Affects Location Choice

The importance of these economic and cultural factors may differ across different migrant groups. For example, Bartel (1989) found that Hispanics in the US were more geographically concentrated than Asians or Europeans. This outcome may reflect a number of factors including the role of language. In the US context, there has been a particular focus on the difference between those coming from English and non-English speaking backgrounds. Chiswick and Miller (2004), for instance, found high geographic concentration of immigrants compared to natives, but found that concentration was less pronounced for English speakers. Furthermore, they found that speakers of different non-English languages cluster in particular areas and states.

English fluency appears to be correlated with settlement choice, with those who are fluent in English being less likely to locate in areas with migrants from their home country (Lazear 1999 cited in Bauer et al. 2005). It is unclear, however, whether this is a cause or effect relationship; those who have better English language skills may have them because they are located with people who speak English, rather than choosing to locate there because their English is better.

In terms of economic factors, Bauer et al. (2005) find that for Mexican immigrants to the US, those with worse English skills are more likely to locate in places with high levels of unemployment. The economic reasoning here is that there is a trade-off reflecting the costs and benefits of learning a language in order to gain employment. For those who have low ability to learn language the cost is not worth the benefit of work, so they care less about unemployment rates and locate in areas with high levels of unemployment. However, care must be taken in interpreting results based on language differences since other features of migrants (such as motivations for migration, personal circumstances and educational background) may be correlated with language skills (Maré et al. 2007).

9.2.4 How Education Affects Location Choice

The education level of immigrants has been identified as impacting on settlement patterns. Higher skilled migrants tend to be less ethnically clustered than those with lower levels of education (Bartel 1989; Allen and Turner 1996; Alba and Logan 1993). One reason for this outcome is that different amenities and characteristics of cities may appeal to a greater or lesser extent to highly educated individuals in comparison to those with minimal education. Another explanation is that more educated individuals may be able to access better information about alternative locations resulting in these migrants placing less weight on the existence of ethnic networks (and herd effects) when selecting a location in which to settle (Bartel 1989). In Germany, Gang and Zimmermann (2000) find that migrants who are well-educated are less clustered with other immigrants as they both have more information about locations and have more opportunities to integrate.

Zhou and Kim (2006) offer a related explanation to the greater clustering of the less educated. They note that children of Asian immigrants typically fare well in the US school system and that this may, in part, reflect the institutional context within ethnic communities that help children to learn and to integrate. Those who are less educated, with poor English language skills, locate within their ethnic network in order to access education as they may be excluded from the mainstream system. For those who are better educated, these networks and institutions are not as necessary, so they can locate in other, less clustered, areas. This example illustrates the multi-faceted nature of the migrant location choice, which may vary both with life cycle circumstances and length of residence within the host country.

9.2.5 The Role of Relocation in Migrant Clustering

The initial settlement location of immigrants may not reflect their underlying preferences and instead may reflect temporary constraints that are part of the settlement process. Bartel's (1989) study found that internal movement is more common amongst immigrants than natives within the United States. Migrants may stay in gateway cities for a time, even if these cities are not their intended settlement point. Lichter and Johnson (2006) found evidence of an outward dispersion of migrants from US gateway cities, supporting the idea that relocation may be considered as part of the settlement process.

A second possible reason for relocation is related to herd effects in which migrants with imperfect information initially locate in cities with like people. As their information set enlarges, they learn about the relative merits of alternative locations and so become less reliant on information sourced from the herd's behaviour. This can result in relocation to places that better reflect their own circumstances and preferences.

One methodological issue with examining relocation is that immigrants may assimilate and their values or circumstances may start to change. If this is the case, the better established migrant may no longer value the same things they did at the time of their initial move (Friesen 2012). In these circumstances, their initial settlement decision may be a more accurate reflection of immigrant preferences than is reflected through their subsequent location choice.

9.2.6 Prior New Zealand Evidence

Given its high proportion of migrants, New Zealand has been the subject of a number of studies of migrant location behaviour (see, especially, Maré et al. 2007, 2012, 2016; Friesen 2012).[2] Auckland (with one-third of the country's population and its largest international airport) is New Zealand's main gateway city (Friesen 2012). Immigrants typically pass through Auckland when locating to New Zealand, and may stay in the city for some time as their initial settlement point. Asian and Pacific Island immigrants, in particular, are clustered in Auckland (Friesen 2012). More generally, Maré et al. (2007) found differences in concentrations based on migrants' country of birth, with immigrants from Eastern Europe, Asia and the Pacific Islands very concentrated compared to immigrants from other regions.

Unlike the United States, which has a skew towards immigration for family reunification reasons, New Zealand's immigration is principally skills-based. Given the US evidence, this suggests that economic factors such as wages and employment rates may be of importance for many migrants. However, Maré et al. (2007) study of settlement patterns of New Zealand immigrants from 1996–2001 found no evidence that immigrants choose to settle initially in areas with better labour market conditions. This finding may reflect how New Zealand is viewed as a migrant destination. The country may be seen less as a place for work opportunities (even for those with the requisite skills), and more as a place to improve quality of life. This idea is supported in the official longitudinal study of immigrants (LisNZ) in which the primary reasons given for relocating to New Zealand were the relaxed lifestyle and the appealing climate (Department of Labour 2009 cited in Friesen 2012). Thus, despite the focus of New Zealand's immigration policy on attracting skilled workers, employment opportunities may not be the main reason for migrants choosing to move to the country. While immigrants did not appear initially to choose settlement locations based on economic factors, there was some evidence that location choice for earlier migrants was affected by the employment rate for the

[2]Maré et al. 2012, 2016 focus on residential location decisions within a single city, Auckland, rather than across the country. These studies find that both self-identified ethnicity and country of birth are correlated with location choice within the city.

general population, but notably not by the employment rate for the migrant group or by any income variable (Maré et al. 2007).

Another finding by Maré et al. (2007) that contrasts with the US literature is that migrant networks have a greater association with location choice for immigrants from English-speaking backgrounds. Economic factors of house prices and employment rates were found to impact decisions of immigrants for whom English was not their first language, but were not significant in the decision of those coming from English speaking nations. Again, one possible reason for these observations is that those moving to New Zealand from English speaking backgrounds typically move for a change in quality of life, rather than primarily for work reasons, and so may come from an already affluent background. They may therefore be less affected by economic factors than less affluent (non-English speaking) migrants. Conversely, those coming from a non-English speaking background may be more likely to move for work reasons, and come from a less wealthy background, so place more emphasis on economic factors. Maré et al. (2007) find that better educated migrants are less geographically concentrated than less educated migrants. This is the opposite pattern to those born in New Zealand, in which greater clustering amongst people with university degrees is observed.

The contrasts in findings across countries suggest that results derived from one country may not necessarily be generalisable to other countries' circumstances. It is also possible that patterns may change across different cohorts of migrants, as established in the Maré et al. (2016) study of residential assimilation of migrants within Auckland. In the following section, we use more recent data than that used by the cited New Zealand-wide studies and refine key variables, to provide additional tests of the ethnic and economic determinants of migrant location choice.

9.3 Empirical Analysis

For the empirical analysis within New Zealand, we first present descriptive statistics to help understand clustering patterns of migrant groups, and then present econometric estimates explaining migrant location choice. We have data on both region of birth and self-identified ethnicity; however these two variables are highly correlated. For example, one region of birth is defined as 'Asia' and one ethnicity is defined as 'Asian'; similarly, we have 'Pacific Islands' as a birth region and 'Pacific Island' as an ethnicity. Given this correlation, we focus on region of birth (which we refer to also as ethnicity) as our indicator of migrant networks, and exclude the self-identified ethnicity variable from our analysis.

9.3.1 Data

Our primary data are sourced from the 2013 New Zealand Census confidentialised unit record file (CURF). This is a subset of 217,000 individual records from the 2013

Census which has been confidentialised; Statistics New Zealand (2014) provides a full explanation of the confidentialising process. The dataset provides information for each individual on their location within New Zealand across 16 regions, and provides information on their birthplace (New Zealand plus seven broad international groups), making it possible to determine whether the individual is a migrant and, if so, their birth region. As these classifications are necessary for this study, any individual with missing region data for either of these variables has been excluded from the analysis. This results in around 50,000 migrants considered in the study. A map of the 16 regions is shown as Fig. 9.1.

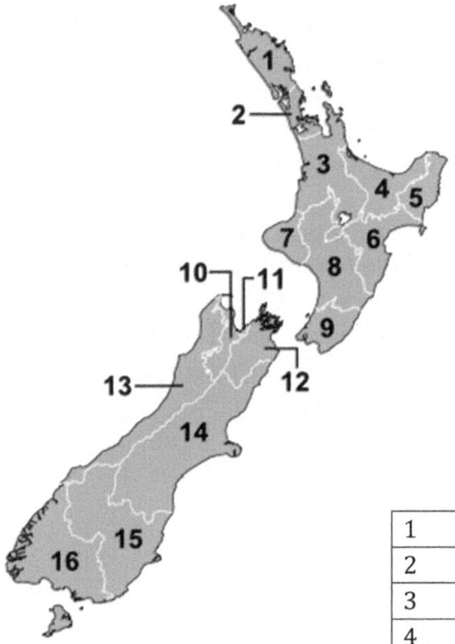

1	Northland
2	Auckland
3	Waikato
4	Bay of Plenty
5	Gisborne
6	Hawke's Bay
7	Taranaki
8	Manawatu-Wanganui
9	Wellington
10	Tasman
11	Nelson
12	Marlborough
13	West Coast
14	Canterbury
15	Otago
16	Southland

Fig. 9.1 New Zealand regions

9.3.2 Descriptive Statistics

Exploratory analysis uses the Herfindahl index and location quotient. The Herfindahl index is calculated for the different groups to see to what degree they cluster. This is examined for groups from different regions of birth and different education levels. For each group i, the Herfindahl index is given by

$$H_i = \sum_{j=1}^{16} \theta_{ij}^2$$

where θ_{ij} is the share of group i located in region j. Higher values of H_i indicate higher levels of clustering.

The location quotient for different birthplace groups is calculated to understand the pattern of different groups across different locations. The location quotient is calculated by[3]:

$$LQ_{ij} = \frac{Proportion\ of\ group\ i\ living\ in\ region\ j}{Proportion\ of\ total\ population\ in\ region\ j} = \frac{Pop_{ij}/Pop_i}{Pop_j/Pop}$$

where: Pop_{ij} is the population of group i in region j, Pop_i is the population of group i in New Zealand, Pop_j is the population of region j, and Pop is the population of New Zealand. A value greater than 1 indicates over-representation and a value less than 1 indicates under-representation of a group in a given region.

In Fig. 9.2, the Herfindahl index for the different region of birth groups shows more clustering for the migrant groups than for the New Zealand born population. Clustering is highest amongst the Pacific Island group, with the Asian and the Middle-East and Africa (MEA) groups also having high levels of concentration. Migrants from Australia (and to a lesser extent the UK and Ireland, Europe and the Americas) have similar levels of concentration to the New Zealand born population, suggesting these groups are better integrated, likely indicative of shared cultural background and language.

The education levels of migrants was classified into two groups, degree or no degree, with the Herfindahl index for each migrant group shown in Fig. 9.3. Here we see higher concentration for migrants with a degree for each birth group. This outcome is in contrast to the US-based studies which find that the better educated are typically more dispersed. The New Zealand pattern may be due to concentration of people with degrees in cities with universities, or as a result of agricultural work in rural areas being predominantly low-skilled.

Table 9.1 presents the location quotients for country of birth groups. The Asian, Pacific Island and MEA groups have high levels of over-representation in Auckland, and are under-represented in all other regions. This is consistent with the gateway city hypothesis, that migrants cluster in the largest city and entry point into the

[3]Note that LQ_{ij} can be expressed equivalently as: $\frac{Pop_{ij}/Pop_j}{Pop_i/Pop}$.

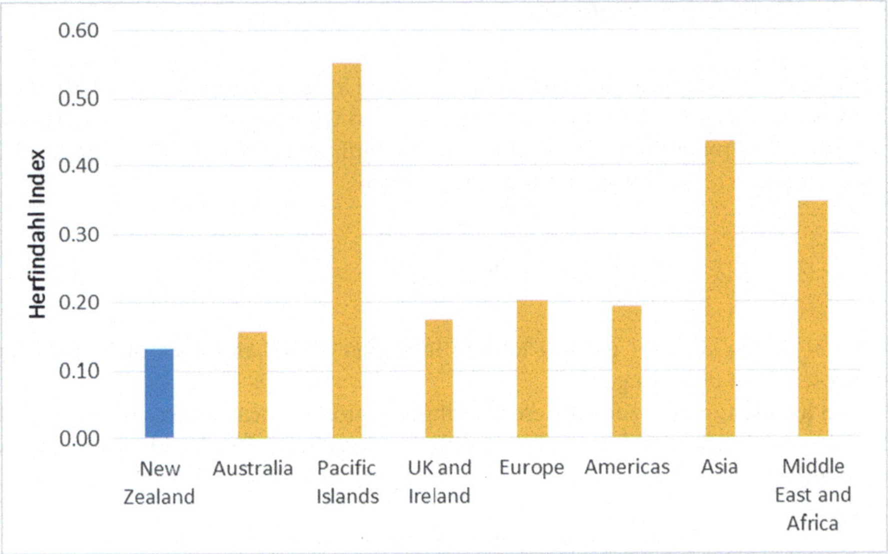

Fig. 9.2 Herfindahl index by region of birth

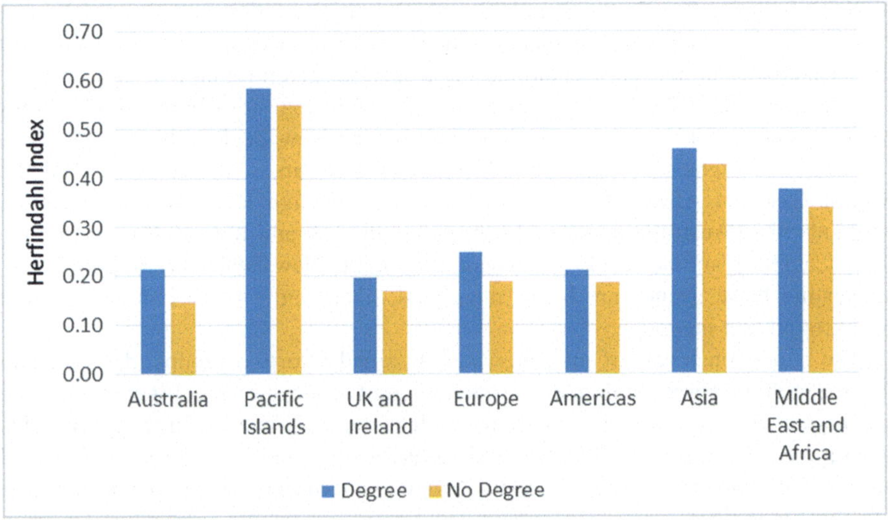

Fig. 9.3 Herfindahl index for region of birth by qualification for migrants

country. "Western" migrants (UK and Ireland, Australia, Americas and Europe) are over-represented in regions such as Tasman and Nelson which prior econometric work has shown to have high amenity value (Donovan 2011). This pattern may reflect different motivations for this group of migrants, suggesting that they may migrate to New Zealand more for lifestyle than for economic reasons.

Table 9.1 Location quotients for New Zealand regions

	Region of origin							
	New Zealand	Australia	Pacific Islands	UK and Ireland	Europe	Americas	Asia	Middle East and Africa
Northland	1.1	1.1	0.2	1.1	1.0	0.9	0.2	0.7
Auckland	0.8	1.0	2.2	1.0	1.2	1.1	1.9	1.7
Waikato	1.1	1.0	0.4	0.8	0.9	0.7	0.6	0.9
Bay of Plenty	1.1	1.2	0.3	1.1	0.9	1.0	0.5	0.6
Gisborne	1.2	0.9	0.3	0.5	0.1	0.6	0.2	0.1
Hawke's Bay	1.1	0.9	0.4	0.9	0.6	0.6	0.3	0.5
Taranaki	1.2	1.0	0.2	0.7	0.7	0.7	0.3	0.6
Manawatu-Wanganui	1.2	0.8	0.3	0.7	0.5	0.5	0.4	0.5
Wellington	1.0	1.0	0.9	1.2	1.2	1.2	0.8	0.9
West Coast	1.2	1.4	0.1	0.5	0.6	0.5	0.2	0.5
Canterbury	1.1	1.1	0.3	1.1	1.0	1.0	0.7	0.6
Otago	1.1	1.3	0.3	1.0	1.0	1.6	0.5	0.5
Southland	1.2	0.7	0.2	0.5	0.7	0.5	0.3	0.4
Tasman	1.1	1.3	0.1	1.3	1.6	1.0	0.1	0.2
Nelson	1.1	1.2	0.2	1.5	1.4	1.3	0.4	0.2
Marlborough	1.1	1.1	0.4	1.0	0.8	1.0	0.3	0.4

Note: A value >1 indicates over-representation of the group in the region, a value <1 indicates under-representation

Australians are over-represented in the West Coast region which is a major mining area (consistent with Australia's comparative advantage in the mining industry) while Americans are over-represented in Otago. The latter region has both a substantial number of workers in the tourism industry and a large number of students and faculty associated with the University of Otago, a major institution in the region. Thus industry-related effects appear to have an influence, over and above gateway city effects, for the location choices of certain migrant groups.

9.3.3 Econometric Methodology

Consistent with many prior studies, the McFadden conditional choice logit model is used initially to model migrants' location choices (McFadden 1973). The model is based on the assumption that each immigrant achieves a certain level of utility based on where they choose to locate. The (random) utility function for individual i in a location j is given by:

$$U_{ij} = \alpha L_{ij} + \beta X_{ij} + e_{ij} \tag{9.1}$$

Utility is a function of a vector of location characteristics (L_{ij}) multiplied by a coefficient vector α, a vector of individual characteristics (X_{ij}) multiplied by a coefficient vector β, and an error term. Each individual has N locations to choose from, in this case 16 different regions, and they choose the location which maximises their utility. The probability that individual *i* will choose location *j* is given by:

$$P_{ij} = \frac{exp(\alpha L_{ij} + \beta X_{ij})}{\sum_{n=1}^{N} exp(\alpha L_{ij} + \beta X_{ij})} \tag{9.2}$$

where α and β are chosen through estimation so that the probability of a migrant choosing their actual location is the highest across all possible alternatives.

As our focus is to determine whether location choice of migrants is impacted by cultural factors, economic factors, or both, a measure of each is included in the model. First, we include the variable *origin* which is the proportion of each region's population from the same birth region as the migrant.

Second, we include a wage variable. Our preferred wage variable, *ind_reg_wage*, is the natural log of the average wage for the industry in which the migrant is employed for each region. We test the robustness of our results by alternatively including the variable, *region_wage*, which is the natural log of the average wage for the migrant's chosen region. We present results for the equations that include *ind_reg_wage* both with and without the inclusion of region fixed effects. The inclusion of fixed effects enables us to control for unobserved region-specific factors that may influence migration patterns. Given the potential importance of differences in climatic, natural and built features across regions for migration decisions, the inclusion of regional fixed effects is an important component of our modelling. (The fixed effects cannot be included when we include the *region_wage* variable given that this is a cross-sectional regression and *region_wage* does not differ across individuals within regions.)

Initially we present results using the values from the 2013 census dataset for *origin*, *ind_reg_wage* and *region_wage*. However use of these contemporaneous variables may result in endogeneity bias. To mitigate the potential for this bias, we also present results using values from the 2006 census for *origin*, and using 2006 wage data drawn from the Linked Employer Employee Database (LEED) for each of the *wage* variables.[4]

For the individual characteristics vector, consistent with prior literature, we include variables for language, education and age group, plus a variable for the number of years since arrival to control for assimilation and dispersal over time. To test whether location factors matter more or less for different groups, interaction terms between *origin* and the *wage* variables with each of education, language and years since arrival are included. Definitions for all variables are provided in Table 9.2. Table 9.3 details the number of migrants from each birth region together

Table 9.2 Variable definitions

Variable name	Description
origin	Proportion of regional population born in same region as the migrant
ind_reg_wage	Log of average industry-region wage in which the migrant is employed
region_wage	Log of average wage in the region
longterm	Dummy variable =1 if migrant has been in NZ for ≥10 years
noqual	Dummy variable =1 if migrant has no qualification
degree	Dummy variable =1 if migrant has a degree qualification
missingqual	Dummy variable =1 if education information is missing for the migrant
twoyrsNZ	Dummy variable =1 if migrant has been in NZ for 0–2 years
fouryrsNZ	Dummy variable =1 if migrant has been in NZ for 3–4 years
nineyrsNZ	Dummy variable =1 if migrant has been in NZ for 5–9 years
nineteenyrsNZ	Dummy variable =1 if migrant has been in NZ for 10–19 years
missingyrsNZ	Dummy variable =1 if information on migrant's time in NZ missing
bilang	Dummy variable =1 if migrant is bilingual
langmissing	Dummy variable =1 if information on migrant language status missing
age_grp_20	Dummy variable =1 if migrant is 0–19 years old
age_grp_40	Dummy variable =1 if migrant is 20–39 years old
age_grp_80	Dummy variable =1 if migrant is 60–79 years old
age_grp_>80	Dummy variable =1 if migrant is >80 years old

Source: All 2013 variables sourced from Statistics NZ 2013 NZ Census CURF. 2006 *origin* sourced from 2006 census; 2006 *ind_reg_wage* and *region_wage* sourced from Linked Employer Employee Database (both from Statistics NZ Infoshare database)

Notes: For all dummy variables, value =0 otherwise

Base (omitted) categories are: sub-degree qualification; ≥20 years in NZ; 40–59 years old

[4]The 2006 data are sourced from the Statistics New Zealand Infoshare database. LEED industry wages were aggregated for the small contiguous Marlborough, Nelson, Tasman and West Coast regions; Latin American and Other birth regions have been grouped since Latin America was not separately available.

Table 9.3 Personal characteristics by birth region (as proportion of birth region sample)

	New Zealand	Australia	Pacific Islands	UK and Ireland	Europe	Americas	Asia	Middle East and Africa
Speaks at least two languages	0.097	0.075	0.656	0.074	0.753	0.302	0.638	0.490
No qualification	0.168	0.105	0.230	0.126	0.082	0.041	0.101	0.053
Bachelor or higher degree	0.118	0.183	0.090	0.230	0.269	0.353	0.309	0.259
Migrant in NZ for $\geq$10 years	0.000	n.a.	0.585	0.661	0.615	0.417	0.452	0.466
Observations	149,188	3168	7489	13,335	3489	2076	15,674	4467

Note: Length of stay in New Zealand not available for migrants born in Australia

with proportions of that migrant group having each of the four individual characteristics that we interact with the *origin* and *wage* variables.

Validity of the conditional logit model requires independence of the unobserved components of utility across individuals and locations. This independence of irrelevant alternatives (IIA) assumption implies that the cross-elasticities of the probability of choosing between two locations, given a change in the characteristics of a third location, must be equal. The implied substitution patterns may be unrealistic in the context of location choice because they do not account for similarities and dissimilarities of unobserved location features. We can address this issue by using mixed logit estimation which allows individual-specific coefficients on the location attributes. This involves choosing a distribution for which the coefficients on each variable vary across individuals, so relaxing the IIA property; thus α is replaced by α_i in the expression above. We assume a multivariate normal distribution such that the distribution parameters to be estimated are the means and standard deviations of each random coefficient. Because of the computational burden involved in estimating the mixed logit model (which requires simulation) we limit the random coefficients to just the *origin* and *wage* variables. Furthermore, to reduce the computational burden, we do not include interaction terms when estimating the mixed logit model.

9.3.4 Results

Table 9.4 presents our conditional logit results (as odds ratios[5]) for the key variables of interest. The first three columns use 2013 data for the *origin* and *wage* variables while the final three columns use 2006 data for these variables. Within each group of three equations, the first column uses the *region_wage* variable while the second and third columns use *ind_reg_wage*. The first two columns in each case do not include region fixed effects while the third column does so. The use of *ind_reg_wage* plus region fixed effects is the most complete specification, while the use of 2006 data is less susceptible to endogeneity bias, so column (6) is our preferred set of estimates and our discussion focuses on this set of results.

Prior to discussing findings for key variables of interest, we discuss results for the regional fixed effects.[6] (Each of these is expressed relative to the omitted region, Northland, which is ranked eighth of the 16 regions, so can be considered the median region for this purpose.) The regions with the largest international airport (Auckland) and second largest international airport (Canterbury) are ranked first and second for their regional fixed effects (with odds ratios of 6.0 and 2.7 respectively), consistent with their gateway city status. The capital city (Wellington) is ranked third. Other regions near Auckland (Waikato and Bay of Plenty) are ranked fourth and fifth. At

[5]An odds ratio greater than (less than) unity denotes a positive (negative) impact of that variable on location choice; statistical significance (relative to unity) at $p < 0.05$ is indicated through a coefficient shown in bold.

[6]These fixed effects are estimated but are not reported explicitly in Table 9.4.

Table 9.4 Conditional logit estimates of migrant regional location choice

	(1)	(2)	(3)	(4)	(5)	(6)
Origin and wage data	2013	2013	2013	2006	2006	2006
Region fixed effects	No	No	Yes	No	No	Yes
Wage variable	region	ind_reg	ind_reg	region	ind_reg	ind_reg
origin	**1.46**	**1.48**	**1.40**	**1.49**	**1.52**	**1.42**
	(0.02)	(0.02)	(0.02)	(0.02)	(0.02)	(0.02)
wage	**2.28**	**2.14**	**1.56**	**2.21**	**2.10**	**1.56**
	(0.08)	(0.09)	(0.07)	(0.08)	(0.09)	(0.07)
origin × *bilang*	**0.87**	**0.85**	**0.91**	**0.86**	**0.83**	**0.91**
	(0.01)	(0.01)	(0.01)	(0.01)	(0.01)	(0.01)
wage × *bilang*	**1.63**	**0.66**	1.00	**1.61**	**0.67**	1.00
	(0.04)	(0.03)	(0.05)	(0.04)	(0.03)	(0.05)
origin × *no qual*	**0.92**	**0.90**	1.00	**0.92**	**0.90**	1.01
	(0.02)	(0.02)	(0.02)	(0.02)	(0.02)	(0.02)
wage × *no qual*	**0.92**	**0.90**	1.00	**0.92**	**0.90**	1.01
	(0.04)	(0.04)	(0.06)	(0.04)	(0.04)	(0.07)
origin × *degree*	**0.88**	**0.86**	**0.95**	**0.87**	**0.85**	**0.94**
	(0.01)	(0.01)	(0.01)	(0.01)	(0.01)	(0.01)
wage × *degree*	**1.30**	**0.82**	**1.23**	**1.30**	**0.84**	**1.24**
	(0.03)	(0.04)	(0.07)	(0.03)	(0.04)	(0.07)
origin × *longterm*	**1.22**	**1.25**	**1.11**	**1.24**	**1.29**	**1.12**
	(0.02)	(0.02)	(0.01)	(0.02)	(0.02)	(0.02)
wage × *longterm*	**0.87**	**1.74**	1.05	**0.87**	**1.70**	1.05
	(0.03)	(0.08)	(0.05)	(0.03)	(0.07)	(0.05)
# Individuals	49,698	49,698	49,698	49,698	49,698	49,698
Log likelihood	−85,420	−83,989	−83,519	−85,286	−83,983	−85,498

Notes: Odds ratios from conditional logit models shown; standard errors within parentheses. Bold indicates significantly different from unity at $p < 0.05$. All estimates control for person-specific variables (see Table 9.2). 2013 independent variables are from the Census, 2006 independent variables are from the census (*origin*) and LEED (*wage*). NB: An odds ratio >1 [<1] indicates that the likelihood of choosing a given region based on this variable increases [decreases] with the variable

the other end of the spectrum, the small isolated regions of Gisborne and West Coast are ranked 15th and 16th respectively. All results that follow in Table 9.4 are obtained after controlling for these regional location patterns which reflect the underlying attractiveness of regions for international migrants.

The first result to note in Table 9.4 is that the odds ratios for both *origin* and *ind_reg_wage* are greater than unity and (highly) significant. This suggests firstly that migrants are more likely to locate in a region with a higher proportion of other migrants from the same birth region as themselves (supporting the findings of other studies), and secondly that they are more likely to locate in a region where they can earn a higher wage for their particular industry. Thus economic factors also matter for their location choice. While this latter finding is in contrast to many other studies, particularly for the United States, its robustness is shown when we use *region_wage* as the wage variable (albeit without inclusion of region fixed effects). One potential reason for the discrepancy in findings here from those of the US-based literature is that New Zealand has a greater emphasis on skills-based immigration than does the United States. It may therefore be expected that economic factors have an impact on the decision-making processes of migrants coming to New Zealand, as Jaeger (2000, 2006) found with skills-based immigrants to the United States.

Our wage result also stands in contrast to the findings of a previous study in New Zealand (Maré et al. 2007) that did not find this effect. We use more recent data and our preferred specification uses the average wage in each region for the migrant's industry, rather than the average across all industries. Different industries have differences in average wages across regions depending on their significance for that region. For example, agriculture is an important part of the New Zealand economy, but is understandably focused in rural areas. While large cities have higher average wages, a migrant looking to work in the agricultural sector may choose a predominantly rural region where they are likely to receive the highest agricultural wages. Thus even after the inclusion of region fixed effects, we still find the *ind_reg_wage* variable to be a highly significant predictor of migrants' location choice.

Several interaction terms are significant in our preferred specification (each of these results is robust across all specifications). First, for migrants who are bilingual, *origin* is found to be significantly less important than for monolingual migrants. Migrants to New Zealand who are bilingual are likely to speak English (plus at least one other language) so are more able to communicate and be less reliant on migrant networks than migrants who speak only one (non-English) language.

A degree level qualification has a significant impact relative to other migrants for the effect of each of the *origin* and *wage* variables. Those who have a degree are more likely to choose a location where they can obtain a higher wage than those without a degree and are less likely to choose a location based on migrant networks. This result is consistent with those who have invested in a degree wishing to obtain a higher wage to leverage their investment. There may also be some correlation based on industry. People with a degree may be more likely to locate in a region where that industry is important, implying that that industry would have a higher wage in the chosen area. This is consistent with the agglomeration literature and, in particular, with the importance of worker matching (Duranton and Puga 2004). The better educated are likely to have more specialised skills, and therefore have a higher risk of facing a mismatch cost. Educated workers will look for regions with a focus on their industry to help to avoid mismatch costs, and so choose a location with higher own-industry wages.

The final significant interaction term relates to whether the individual is a long-term migrant interacted with *origin*. A migrant is treated here as being long-term if they have been in New Zealand for 10 or more years. Contrary to prior literature, longer term migrants are estimated to be more likely to be in a given location where there is a higher concentration of migrants from the same region of birth. The current study is not a cohort study and so cannot differentiate between migrant relocation behaviour and changing patterns of immigration across different cohorts. Immigration policy prior to 1987 took a preferred country approach, while later migration was opened up to people from a greater range of countries, with notably increased flows from Asia (Collins and

Friesen 2011; Friesen 2012). This interaction term may therefore relate to changes in source country migration patterns rather than to length of stay.[7]

Each of the individual characteristics is entered as a separate term for each region.[8] Notable migrant clustering is observed according to qualification level, language and age. Those with degrees are more likely to locate in university cities, particularly Auckland, Palmerston North (Manawatu-Wanganui), Wellington and Dunedin (Otago). Bilingual migrants are most likely to locate in the three major North Island cities (Auckland, Hamilton (Waikato) and Wellington) plus Nelson. The latter region attracts migrants from Northern Europe, particularly Germany (Börnisch-Brednich 2002). University locations have a comparatively high preponderance of younger adults (<40 years old) as do Southland and Taranaki. The former has a 'free-fees' scheme for its polytechnic which may attract younger migrants, while the latter region has had strong economic growth over the past decade which may also have attracted young migrants.

The association of each region with years since arrival in New Zealand sheds light on the potential effects of relocation. The estimates indicate the importance of temporary workers in certain regions. Those with less than 2 years residence in New Zealand are over-represented in areas associated with seasonal agricultural work (Hawke's Bay, Bay of Plenty, Nelson and Marlborough), tourism (Otago) and mining (West Coast). The over-representation of short-term residents in agricultural regions reflects temporary workers who come to these regions through the recognised seasonal employment (RSE) scheme, which employs temporary migrants from the Pacific Islands in seasonal jobs in the agriculture and viticulture industries (New Zealand Government n.d.). Recent migrants also have a higher likelihood of residing in Canterbury, which is likely to be a result of the inward migration for reconstruction following the massive Christchurch earthquakes of 2010 and 2011 (Chang-Richards et al. 2012). Nelson is notable for having a preponderance of migrants with up to 4 years and up to 9 years residence in New Zealand suggesting that migrants either tend to stay in Nelson after their initial experience in the area or that migrants relocate to Nelson after first residing elsewhere. The West Coast (which has a mining oriented economy) also appears to retain or attract migrants who have up to 4 years residence in New Zealand. None of the other regions which attracts short-term migrants has an over-representation of longer term migrants implying that their shorter residence migrants either leave the country or relocate to other regions beyond their initial stay in the region.

Table 9.5 presents results using mixed logit estimation for the (preferred) specification that includes regional fixed effects with the *ind_reg_wage* variable, and using 2006 data for the *origin* and *wage* variables. Unlike Table 9.4, we do not

[7]One other explanation for this result is a simple arithmetic one in that a migrant will inflate the proportion of own-group migrants in their own area. This explanation may be particularly relevant for the estimates using 2013 explanatory variable data. The finding that the size of the interaction term is almost equivalent across columns (3) and (6) suggests that this is not the (sole) reason for the significant positive result.

[8]One region (Northland) is omitted as the base region. We do not present all 225 coefficients (15 regions × 15 terms per region), instead summarising the key results in the text.

Table 9.5 Conditional and mixed logit estimates without interaction terms

	(1)	(2)
Origin and wage data	2006	2006
Region fixed effects	Yes	Yes
Estimation technique	Conditional logit	Mixed logit
origin: mean	**0.341**	**0.416**
	(0.0070)	(0.0140)
origin: standard deviation	–	**0.331**
		(0.0306)
ind_reg_wage: mean	**0.505**	**0.520**
	(0.0237)	(0.0248)
ind_reg_wage: standard deviation	–	**0.384**
		(0.1055)
# Individuals	49,698	49,698
Log likelihood	−84,138	−84,113

Notes: Estimated parameters shown; standard errors within parentheses. Bold indicates significantly different from unity at $p < 0.05$. All estimates control for person-specific variables (see Table 9.2). 2006 independent variables are from the census (*origin*) and LEED (*ind_reg_wage*). 20 replications used for mixed logit estimates

include interaction terms, in part owing to the time taken to obtain convergence for the mixed logit routine and in part because heterogeneity in response to the *origin* and *wage* variables is reflected in the estimated standard deviation terms. For comparison purposes, the first column of Table 9.5 presents a conditional logit estimate of the model without interaction terms. The second column presents the mixed logit estimates including the estimated standard deviations for both *origin* and *ind_reg_wage*. Because of the non-linearities involved, we present the estimated parameters rather than the odds ratios. (Hence a positive coefficient now represents a positive effect of the variable on the location choice.)

Column (1) of Table 9.5 shows the same positive influences of *origin* and *ind_reg_wage* as found in Table 9.4 using conditional logit estimation. The mixed logit estimates in column (2) produce similar estimates for the mean effect of these two variables on location choice, but also find significant estimates for each of the standard deviation variables. Thus, we find significant heterogeneity in response to these two variables, consistent with the estimated significant interaction terms in the conditional logit estimates of Table 9.4.

9.4 Discussion and Conclusions

Prior literature on immigrants' location choice has consistently established the importance of migrant networks for the initial settlement choice of migrants in their new country. The role of gateway cities, in particular, has been established whereby migrants tend to settle together with established migrants from their own background in cities that are relatively open and connected to the world. These choices are mediated by the role of education and language, but the over-riding importance of ethnic networks is apparent even after accounting for such factors.

What has hitherto been less apparent from the prior literature is the importance attached to economic factors such as wages and employment prospects in influencing migrant location choice. Much of the literature which has been conducted with United States data has found little influence of these economic factors on the initial location choice of migrants. To the extent that economic factors have been found important, their role has tended to be limited to influencing the location choice of migrants with work-related visas rather than of those with entry for family reunification purposes.

Against this background, the second part of this chapter (Sect. 9.3) has analysed the determinants of migrant location choice in a country, New Zealand, in which immigration is predominantly determined according to a skills-based system. New Zealand has a quarter of its population born outside the country and its largest (gateway) city, Auckland, has 40% of its population born overseas.

We use 2013 unit record census data together with 2006 census and labour market data to test the roles, *inter alia*, of ethnic and economic factors in determining the location choice of migrants to the country. Our results, using both conditional logit and mixed logit specifications, indicate that both the stock of previous migrants and the wage in a given region are related to the location choice of incoming migrants to New Zealand. The former aspect supports the findings of previous literature, that migrants tend to co-locate with previous migrants from the same source region. Thus even though New Zealand is distant from any source country, the same ethnic clustering phenomenon is observed as is observed elsewhere.

The second aspect extends understanding of migrant settlement patterns through the finding that wages are important for location choice. We find this result using two different wage variables: the average wage of the region and the average wage in each region for the migrant's chosen industry. The latter approach captures the idea that individuals are likely to be concerned with the wages that they can earn in their chosen industry, rather than the average wage, and accounts for the fact that wages by industry will vary according to the economic characteristics of regions. Technically, inclusion of the latter term also enables us to include regional fixed effects in our estimates (hence controlling for unobserved region-specific factors), so this is our preferred approach.

One potential limitation to the inclusion of the industry-region wage is that industry can be seen as a choice by individuals, rather than as an inherent individual characteristic. If industry is a choice, it means that migrants are choosing not only between different wages across regions for their industry, but are also considering multiple industries. Nevertheless, this still means that migrants are locating in places where those industries need workers (as signalled by the higher relative wages for that industry) and, as such, are acting as an economic equilibrating force as postulated by Borjas (2001). The importance of economic factors is further emphasised through the chosen regions in which certain types of migrants settle. Both short-term and long-term location choices appear to reflect industry concentrations most suited to migrants with particular educational and language attributes.

Overall, therefore, one of the two key findings of this study, relating to the importance of ethnic (country of origin) clustering effects, is in keeping with the prior international literature, while the second has a different emphasis. Here we find (contrary to much prior literature) that the wage rate is a significant determinant of migrants' location choices. Our result likely reflects the skills-based nature of most immigration to New Zealand. Our findings may help guide related work for other countries. It will be particularly instructive to see, through future research, whether inclusion of the industry-region wage is more relevant than the average regional wage for other countries, particularly for countries with predominantly skills-based migration as in New Zealand.

Acknowledgements An earlier version of this chapter was submitted as a dissertation for the degree of BCom(Hons) at University of Auckland by the first author. We thank an anonymous referee for comments on an earlier version of this chapter. Access to the data used in this study was provided by Statistics New Zealand under conditions designed to keep individual information secure in accordance with requirements of the Statistics Act 1975. The opinions presented are those of the authors and do not necessarily represent an official view of Statistics New Zealand, or of the authors' institutions.

References

Alba RD, Logan JR (1993) Minority proximity to whites in suburbs: an individual-level analysis of segregation. Am J Sociol 98(6):1388–1427

Allen J, Turner E (1996) Spatial patterns of immigrant assimilation. Prof Geogr 48(2):140–155

Bartel AP (1989) Where do the new U.S. immigrants live? J Labor Econ 7(4):371–391

Battisti M, Peri G, Romiti A (2016) Dynamic effects of co-ethnic networks on immigrants' economic success. NBER working paper 22389, National Bureau of Economic Research, Cambridge

Bauer TK, Epstein GS, Gang IN (2002) Herd effects or migration networks? The location choice of Mexican immigrants in the US. Discussion paper. http://papers.ssrn.com/sol3/papers.cfm?abstract_id=327560

Bauer T, Epstein GS, Gang IN (2005) Enclaves, language, and the location choice of migrants. J Popul Econ 18(4):649–662

Bauer T, Epstein G, Gang IN (2007) The influence of stocks and flows on migrants' location choices. Res Labor Econ 26(6):199–229

Bauer T, Epstein GS, Gang IN (2009) Measuring ethnic linkages among migrants. Int J Manpow 30(1/2):56–69

Borjas GJ (2001) Does immigration grease the wheels of the labor market. Brook Pap Econ Act 1:1–51

Börnisch-Brednich B (2002) Keeping a low profile: an oral history of german immigration to New Zealand. Victoria University Press, Wellington

Carrington WJ, Detragiache E, Vishwanath T (1996) Migration with endogenous moving costs. Am Econ Rev 86(4):909–930

Chang-Richards A, Wilkinson S, Seville E, Brunsdon D (2012) Resourcing the canterbury rebuild: changes and emerging themes. Research paper. http://www.resorgs.org.nz/images/stories/pdfs/Reconstructionfollowingdisaster/case_study_report_resourcing.pdf

Chiswick B, Miller P (2004) Where immigrants settle in the United States. IZA discussion paper No. 1231. Bonn
Church J, King I (1983) Bilingualism and network externalities. Can J Econ 26(2):337–345
Collins F, Friesen W (2011) Making the most of diversity? The intercultural city project and a rescaled version of diversity in Auckland, New Zealand. Urban Stud 48(14):3067–3085
Donovan S (2011) Space matters: agglomeration economies and spatial competition in New Zealand. Unpublished Master's Thesis, VU University Amsterdam, Amsterdam
Duranton G, Puga D (2004) Micro-foundations of urban agglomeration economies. In: Henderson VJ, Thisse JF (eds) Handbook of regional and urban economics, vol 4. Elsevier, Amsterdam, pp 2063–2117
Epstein GS (2008) Herd and network effects in migration decision-making. J Ethn Migr Stud 34(4):567–583
Friesen W (2012) International and internal migration dynamics in a pacific gateway city: Asian migrants into and out of Auckland. N Z Popul Rev 38:1–22
Gang IN, Zimmermann KF (2000) Is child like parent? Educational attainment and ethnic origin. J Hum Resour 35(3):550–569
Harris JR, Todaro MP (1970) Migration, unemployment and development: a two-sector analysis. Am Econ Rev 60(1):126–142
Jaeger DA (2000) Local labor markets, admission categories, and immigrant location choice. College of William and Mary. http://www.iza.org/conference_files/amm_2004/jaeger_d138.pdf
Jaeger DA (2006) Green cards and the location choices of immigrants in the United States, 1971–2000. Discussion paper. http://papers.ssrn.com/sol3/papers.cfm?abstract_id=905545
Lancee B (2012) Immigrant performance in the labour market: bonding and bridging social capital. Amsterdam University Press, Amsterdam
Lichter DT, Johnson KM (2006) Emerging rural settlement patterns and the geographic redistribution of America's new immigrants. Rural Sociol 71(1):109–131
Maré DC, Morten M, Stillman S (2007) Settlement patterns and the geographic mobility of recent migrants to New Zealand. N Z Econ Pap 41:163–195
Maré DC, Pinkerton RM, Poot J, Coleman A (2012) Residential sorting across Auckland neighbourhoods. N Z Popul Rev 38:23–54
Maré DC, Pinkerton RM, Poot J (2016) Residential assimilation of immigrants: a cohort approach. Migr Stud 4(3):373–401
McFadden D (1973) Conditional logit analysis of qualitative choice behavior. In: Zarembka P (ed) Frontiers in economics. Academic, New York
Munshi K (2003) Networks in the modern economy: Mexican migrants in the U.S. labor market. Q J Econ 118(2):549–599
New Zealand Government (n.d.) Recognised Seasonal Employer (RSE) policy. http://employment.govt.nz/initiatives/strategy/rse/index.asp. Accessed 2 Nov 2015
Statistics New Zealand (2014) 2013 census CURF: user guide. Statistics New Zealand, Wellington
White P (1998) The settlement patterns of developed world migrants in London. Urban Stud 35(10):1725–1744
Zhou M, Kim SS (2006) Community forces, social capital, and educational achievement: the case of supplementary education in the Chinese and Korean immigrant communities. Harv Educ Rev 76(1):1–29

Chapter 10
'Young, Talented and Highly Mobile': Exploring Creative Human Capital and Graduates Mobility in the UK

Roberta Comunian and Sarah Jewell

Abstract The human capital and regional economic development literature has become increasingly interested in the role of the 'creative occupations' on economic growth. Attracting quality human capital and cultivating creative industry/class have been given an unprecedented level of significance in regional policies. As a result of this, understanding the factors determining the migration behaviour of graduates—and especially graduates in creative disciplines—is becoming increasingly important. In addressing these issues, building on previous literature that looked at migration dynamics of creative graduates in the short-term (6 months after graduation) the chapter advances our understanding of the relationship between creativity and mobility in human capital, with the first longitudinal (3 years and half after graduation) empirical analysis of the migration patterns of creative graduates in the UK. By using UK higher education student micro-data, the characteristics and location determinants of creative graduates are investigated. It is found that disciplines and their different level of mobility influence the ability of graduates to enter creative occupations and to be successful in the labour market.

Keywords Graduate migration · Creative graduates · Human capital

10.1 Introduction

Much of literature and policy interventions of the last decade have focused on the importance of attracting and retaining human capital in order to favour economic growth and local development (Faggian and McCann 2009b; Mathur 1999). The argument presented is that regions and cities need to attract individuals with high

R. Comunian (✉)
Culture, Media and Creative Industries, King's College London, London, UK
e-mail: Roberta.Comunian@kcl.ac.uk

S. Jewell
Department of Economics, University of Reading, Reading, UK
e-mail: s.l.jewell@reading.ac.uk

B. Biagi et al. (eds.), *New Frontiers in Interregional Migration Research*, Advances in Spatial Science, https://doi.org/10.1007/978-3-319-75886-2_10

level human capital (Williams et al. 2004)—who are seen as highly mobile (Madsen et al. 2002)—not only through good job opportunities but also via the development of local amenities (Scott 2010; Storper and Scott 2009). Within this broader literature—the work of Florida (2002a, b) and the development of the 'creative class theory' has put particular emphasis on the role played by the quality of place and local amenities (Florida 1999) as an element of place attractiveness. In particular, he considers the role played by a local creative scene and the presence of 'bohemian' (core cultural workers) in increasing the attractiveness and diversity of cities and regions (Florida 2002a). As a result, the human capital and regional economic development literature has become increasingly interested in the role of the 'creative occupations' on economic growth (Lee and Drever 2013). However, while the attention has been placed on attracting the 'creative class' and mobile knowledge workers, less attention has been given to the mobility patterns of young creative and cultural workers, also originally identified by others as 'bohemian graduates' (Comunian et al. 2010). Furthermore, understanding the factors determining the migration behaviour of graduates—and especially graduates in creative disciplines—has clear implications for policy makers, which will be explored in the conclusions.

Following the work of Comunian et al. (2010) the chapter investigates further the career opportunities and mobility patterns experienced by individuals with higher human capital (graduates) who have specialised in disciplines within the creative and cultural arts. In this chapter we adopt the term 'creative human capital' to push further the development of research within this field. We specifically consider 'creative graduates' a sub-group of the highly educated individual who have specific specialised with artistic, creative and cultural disciplines and who (following Comunian et al. 2010, 2011; Faggian et al. 2012) are most likely to enter creative jobs both within and beyond the creative industries. From previous studies, we know that the geography of where students gain a degree is very different from the geography of the labour markets in the creative sub-field (Comunian and Faggian 2011; Faggian et al. 2012). Therefore, this chapter takes a closer look at the migration patterns and movement of recent creative graduates in the UK, considering pattern of interregional migration used to either enter a creative career or seek support towards establishing one. We build on Faggian et al. (2014), who consider the migration patterns of 'bohemian' graduates compared with the mobility of other non-creative disciplines at 6 months after graduation, by examining the medium term (3.5 years after graduation). Using micro-data from the Higher Education Statistical Agency (HESA) in UK, graduates are classified into five migration categories (going from the most migratory group, i.e. repeat migrants, to the least migratory, i.e. non migrants) based on their migration choices from domicile to university and then onto workplace. Using the data we explore the distribution of graduate jobs, creative jobs and salary levels in relation to the creative graduates' migration. However, taking further the work of Faggian et al. 2014, we consider how migration patterns influence the possibility of creative graduates to find a creative job and to achieve higher economic rewards (salary) for their talent in the medium term perspective (LDLHE: Longitudinal Destinations of Leavers from Higher Education). It is important to consider a longer term perspective than 6 months, as 6 month is a very short period for which individuals to assimilate fully into the labour market.

The chapter is articulated in three sections. Firstly, we review the literature particularly questioning whether creative graduates are more mobile than other graduates in the UK. Secondly, through descriptive statistics we consider the level of mobility of creative graduates and their relation to migration patterns (as in Faggian 2005 and Faggian et al. 2014). Finally, using four models we explore how mobility and migration patterns affects their working patterns and salaries and overall what factors help them, 3 years and half after graduation to secure a creative job and higher economic rewards as well as career satisfaction. The conclusions highlight the key findings and their implications to our understanding of mobility for creative human capital.

10.2 Human Capital, Mobility and Creative Talent

The role of human capital and mobility (Faggian and McCann 2009b) on the development of regions and knowledge economies has been the subject of increasing research. It is easy to acknowledge that the broader literature on human capital is mainly interested in the impact of graduates (Coniglio and Prota 2008; Faggian and McCann 2009a; Madsen et al. 2002; Mathur 1999)—independently from their subject background—on local development. Originally, Lucas (1988) formally explored the link between human capital and local economic growth. Nonetheless, it is recognised that many theoretical models often overlook the role of mobility of highly skilled workers, despite the increased attention to the importance of international and national migration patterns and their impact on regions (Beine et al. 2008; DaVanzo 1976; DaVanzo and Morrison 1981; Sjaastad 1962). Within this broader framework—as pointed out by Sjaastad (1962) in the so-called "human capital migration theory"—highly skilled (and knowledgeable) individuals are more likely to benefit from migration and hence tend to be more mobile, so there is a level of personal gain and interest which overlaps with the contribution that this can make at the regional level.

Recent contributions (Comunian and Faggian 2014; Comunian et al. 2011, 2014a; Faggian et al. 2014) have placed new attention towards a 'specialised' kind of human capital and its role in local development, this is what has been defined as 'creative human capital' (Comunian et al. 2015b)—the human capital which is specifically develop via education and advanced training in creative and artistic subjects.

The emphasis on this specific type of human capital derives from two set of contributions: on one side the 'creative class' theory and consequential research (Florida 2002b; Florida et al. 2008) on the role of talent in local development and the importance of openness and diversity in cities and regions, identified alongside other indicators with the presence and concentration of 'bohemians' (core creative and cultural workers); on the other, a growing interest from policy makers in demonstrating and quantifying the value and growth and of the creative economy (NESTA 2013) and its significance as sector of employment and contributors to the UK economy (DCMS 2015). Furthermore, there has recently been a shift towards trying to gain a better understanding of differences within the broader creative industries analysis—as often the heterogeneity of professions included can hide striking differences in careers patterns and economic dynamics (Comunian et al. 2014a, b; Cruz and Teixeira 2013, 2015).

Despite the stated importance and role of these individuals and professions in qualifying the local environment as well as contributing to its economic and employment growth, very little research has been conducted on the migration patterns, mobility and geography of this sub-sector of human capital.

As Faggian et al. (2014, p. 33) point out both in the traditional human capital theory and the creative class theory there is "the assumption that highly talented people are more mobile than the rest of the population and that retaining and attracting them is pivotal for economic growth". There is general recognition that "artists, musicians and writers have always been great travellers" (Addison 2008, p. 1). Similarly, some historical research shows the tendency for important visual artists and composers to cluster (O'Hagan and Hellmanzik 2008; O'Hagan and Borowiecki 2010) so migration patterns in relation to cultural work is not only determined by the amenities argument but also by the power of certain location (mainly cities) through history to provide the creative milieu and a creative knowledge pool (Hall 1998). However, apart from some recent studies, there are only a few contributions (Bennett 2010; Faggian et al. 2014; Hansen and Niedomysl 2009) that specifically investigate the mobility of creative workers and how it relates or differs from the mobility of other workers. Hansen and Niedomysl (2009), studying the case of Sweden, find that highly educated people are as mobile as the rest of the population. Martin-Brelot et al. (2010) also question the mobility of the 'creative class' in the European context as they argue that soft location factors play only a marginal role in attracting the creative class to a city. However, they find that these play an important role in retaining them in the locality. Similarly, Borén and Young (2013), studying specifically the case of artists in Sweden, also question the assumption of high mobility of creative workers. They point out that networks are vital for artists and that once artists are "embedded in their networks…it (is) more difficult for them to migrate" (p. 207). They also caution about reducing the migration histories of artists to a "simplistic set of assumptions" (p. 207) as the migration dynamics of creative occupations are very heterogeneous Bennett (2010).

These first reflections stemming from the literature highlight our limited knowledge of migration patterns for creative graduates. The most relevant and valuable contribution in pleading for a more solid and specific understand of the difference across type of human capital in migration (and economic rewards) across subjects is presented by Faggian et al. (2014). Their work specifically singles out 'bohemian' (also creative graduates) from other disciplines and demonstrate their different and limited level of mobility in comparison with the UK graduates overall. They, for example, suggest that "initial low salary level and cost of living considerations might push these graduates to return home (at least initially) to afford pursuing a career in their chosen field of study" (p. 41). They also highlight as a limitation to their work that "mobility and migration could be also read as strategies for resilience for Bohemian graduates trying to enter a creative career and more research is needed on the difference between short-term and long-term mobility" (p. 41). Therefore, this chapter builds on this existing knowledge but tries to specifically understand whether the consideration of a longer time frame after graduation (3.5 years instead of 6 months in Faggian et al. 2014) could provide a better picture and understanding of the migration patterns and career development of creative human capital.

In particular, the chapter addresses the following questions:

1. What are the characteristics of creative human capital migration and job patterns at 3.5 years after graduation, in comparison with other subject groups?
2. What influences the migration patterns of graduates in the medium-term?
3. How do migration patterns change the opportunities for creative employment, salary and career satisfaction for creative graduates?

10.3 Data and Methodology

Our analysis is based on data from the Longitudinal Destinations of Leavers from Higher Education (LDHLE) survey using the cohort of students who graduated in 2006/2007, conducted 3.5 years after graduation, collected by the UK Higher Education Statistical Agency (HESA). We match this data with the individual's responses to the 'Students in Higher Education' and the 'Destinations of Leaves from Higher Education' (DLHE) survey, both also collected by (on behalf of) HESA.

In total 49,065 responses were received for the 2006/2007 cohort LDLHE survey, with some groups deliberately oversampled (in particular: ethnic minorities, those with disabilities, those living in Wales, Scotland and Northern Ireland and those who reported being unemployed or self-employed at the DLHE stage), representing about 15% of those responding to the original 2006/2007 cohort DLHE survey. Weights are provided to allow for the over-sampling of some groups and hence reported results are weighted using these weights. Our sample focuses on British domiciled students, since the DLHE and hence the LDHE are predominately aimed at British domiciled students,[1] first degree graduates who studied full time and following Chevalier (2011, 2012) focus on individuals 25 and under at graduation, leading

[1]For example, HESA has a target response rate of 80% for full time home domiciled graduates, 70% for part time home domiciled graduates and 50% for EU graduates for the DLHE survey.

to a sample size of 23,066 students.[2] Older students (above 25) were excluded to reduce the likelihood that students had extensive work experience prior to graduation and students having responsibilities making them less likely to migrate. Part time students (10% of the sample) were removed from the sample because 48% had been in their job before graduation—suggesting a high proportion were undertaking their degree as part of their employment so less likely to migrate for work.[3] Our sample size reduces when we focus on only those in the labour market and those who have full information.

The Students in Higher Education data contains individual student record data, for all students enrolled in higher education, with information on: personal characteristics (such as gender, age and ethnicity), subject of study (Joint Academic Coding System (JACS) code), degree results and institution attended. The LDLHE survey contains information on employment activity 3.5 years after graduation and in particular includes information on employment activity and job characteristics: occupation, industry, location of employment and salary 3.5 years after graduation.

Our main interest is in creative subjects which are defined, on the basis of JACS codes,[4] as creative Arts and Design (JACS: W (not W6, W8)), creative media (JACS: P, W6, W8) and creative other (JACS: K1 and K3). We then grouped other subjects into three other groups, for aid of comparison:

- STEM—science technology, engineering and Maths (JACS: A, B, C, D, F, G, H, I, J, K2)
- Social sciences, Law, Business and education (JACS: K4, K9, L, M, N, X)
- Humanities (JACS: Q, R, T, V).

In total, 15% of our (weighted) sample are creative graduates, with the biggest group STEM (41%) followed by social studies, law, business and education (30%) and humanities (14%).

Creative job definitions were created following Comunian et al. (2014a, b). Using a creative job approach à la Cunningham et al. (2004) we consider both creative careers within the creative industries but also creative occupations in other non-creative industries (for more details refer to the extensive explanation in Comunian et al. (2014a, b) including endnotes). We also identified graduate level jobs, using the typology of Elias and Purcell (2004).

---

[2]We excluded individuals who graduated in combined subjects (90 observations) since it is not possible to code these subjects.

[3]Secondly part time students are typically older (and female—with 63% of part time students female) and potentially more likely to have other responsibilities which may have influenced the decision to study part time—the average (median) age on graduation of part time students is 40 (40), compared to 24 (22) for full time students. Only 16% of part time students are 25 and under, compared with 87% of full time students.

[4]JACS codes is HESA's subject coding system and more information can be found at https://www.hesa.ac.uk/content/view/158/233/.

Furthermore, we classified the students according to their sequential migration: migration to study and migration to work. Using Faggian (2005) we classify students according to five different migration paths or categories: repeat migrants, return migrants, university stayers, late migrants, and non-migrants. To classify migration behaviour, we require information (post code) on student's pre-university domicile, university and employment location, for those in employment.[5] A student is considered to have migrated between locations if they moved more than 15 km.[6]

The first three migration categories include students who all migrated to study, but they differ in regards to the second migration, following graduation. Repeat migrants are those who move to work in an area different from both their original pre-university domicile and the university area; whilst university stayers remain in their university area. Return migrants also move out of their university area to work, but only to go back to their original domicile. Late migrants remained in their original domicile to study but migrated for employment, whilst non-migrants lived, studied and work in the same area.

In particular in this chapter we are interested in testing whether creative graduates exhibit different migration behaviour compared to other graduates, in particular whether creative graduates are more mobile as some studies suggests, than other graduates, but also if they are more likely to exhibit other patterns such as remaining in their university area. We then explore what factors influences migration decisions and the impact migration behaviour has on entering the creative sector and rewards: both in terms of salary and career satisfaction, with a focus on creative graduates.

After having defined creative graduates, jobs and the categories of sequential migration, our methodology followed three main steps:

1. Firstly, we use some simple descriptive statistics to profile the migration patterns of graduates and their relation to jobs obtained;
2. Secondly, we are interested in modelling the sequential migration behaviour of students and the job type for those in the labour market with full information.

$$P_{\mathrm{im}} = f(X_{1i}, X_{2i}) \tag{10.1}$$

Equation 10.1 models the probability that an individual (i) choose a sequential migration decision m (non-migrant, late migrant, university stayer, return migrant and repeat migrant), as a function of personal characteristics (X_{1i}) and course characteristics (X_{2i}). Personal characteristics include: gender, age, ethnicity, socio-economic background, A-level points (a proxy for underlying ability) and whether

[5]Ninety six percent have information on location for both their original domicile and the institution of study. and 88% of those employed at 3.5 years have full information (location of domicile, work and study).

[6]The choice of threshold distance is based on Faggian (2005) and Faggian et al. (2006), who find that a radius of 15 km is appropriate to capture most urban areas in the UK.

they lived in London prior to university.[7] Course characteristics include subject group, type of institution attended,[8] and degree classification.[9]

We use a multinomial logit[10] to estimate Eq. 10.1; this allows us to simultaneously evaluate which factors affect the sequential migration of graduates. For a multinomial logit (MNL) the probability of an individual choosing option k from a choice set ($j = 1 \ldots J$ and $k \neq j$) as a function of a series of explanatory variables (vector **x**) is:

$$P_{\text{ik}} = \frac{\exp\left(x_i'\beta_k\right)}{\sum_{j=1}^{J} \exp\left(x_i'\beta_j\right)} \tag{10.2}$$

β_j are the estimated parameters and hence there are J-1 sets of coefficients each relative to a base category. As multinomial logit coefficients are not directly interpretable, we estimate average marginal effects (which takes an average across the marginal effects for each individual), the impact of each explanatory variable on the probability of being in a given category.

We then model the probability of obtaining a creative job, in Eq. 10.3, as a function of personal and course characteristics (excluding whether they lived in London prior to university), and the addition of migration category (X_{3i}), using a probit (and again reporting average marginal effects)

$$\text{CreatJob} = \beta_1 X_1 + \beta_2 X_2 + \beta_3 X_3 + \varepsilon \tag{10.3}$$

[7]A-level points only apply to those students who entered with A-levels (92%) and not all have information on socio-economic background (82% do). Socio-economic background was measured using the National Statistics Socio-economic Classification (NS-SEC), for more information see http://www.ons.gov.uk/ons/guide-method/classifications/current-standard-classifications/soc2010/soc2010-volume-3-ns-sec--rebased-on-soc2010--user-manual/index.html, and we created three groups (managerial and professional (categories 1 and 2); intermediate and small employers and own accounts (categories 3 and 4) and categories 5 to 8 comprised the "other" group.

[8]UK HEIs can be classified into at least four different groups: (1) Russell Group universities (20 research intensive universities who receive the majority of research grant and contract income); (2) Other 'old' universities; (3) New universities (established as part of the abolition of the binary divide in 1992); (4) Higher Education/Further education colleges. The Russell group universities, followed by the other old universities are generally considered to be more prestigious.

[9]We excluded those who reported an unclassified degree as this is hard to interpret with around 5% of the sample reporting this.

[10]One important assumption of the multinomial logit is that of the independence of irrelevant alternatives (IIA). Our multinomial logit fails the IIA tests, however Cheng and Long (2007) conclude that the standard IIA tests are not useful (since different tests often giving conflicting conclusions) and recommend following McFadden's (1974) advice that the multinomial logit should only be used when the alternatives in the model "can plausibly be assumed to be distinct and weighted independently in the eyes of each decision maker". We ran a multinomial probit which gave identical results so keep the multinomial logit results since a multinomial logit is utilised in the selection models in Table 10.6.

3. Finally we are interested in graduate's success and focus on earnings and career satisfaction (a indicator variable of very/fairly satisfied versus not very/not at all satisfied) using ordinary least squares and a probit for career satisfaction:

$$\ln(\text{Salary}) = \beta_1 X_1 + \beta_2 X_2 + \beta_3 X_3 + \beta_4 X_4 + \varepsilon \tag{10.4}$$

$$\text{Careersat} = \beta_1 X_1 + \beta_2 X_2 + \beta_3 X_3 + \beta_4 X_4 + \varepsilon \tag{10.5}$$

Equation 10.4 models the log of salary as a function of personal, course, location and job characteristics. The factors included in the personal (except socio-economic background), course, location characteristics (with an indicator of whether they worked in London) are the same as in Eq. 10.2. Job characteristics (X4) include job type i.e. whether they had a creative job, non-creative graduate job or non-creative non-graduate job. Following HESA's approach only full time employed individuals are included when examining salary.[11] Salaries were only included if they were greater or equal than the amount that would be earned at the minimum wage rate and less than £100,000 (with high values potentially as a result of an extra 0 added or extreme outliers). Equation 10.5 models career satisfaction with the same variables used as in Eq. 10.4, with the addition of the log of salary to job characteristics (X4) .

Since we are particularly interested in the impact of migration on the likelihood of getting a creative job, on salary and career satisfaction we adjust for potential selection of migrating. For example, although we control for socio-economic background and A-level results, those who may be more likely to earn higher salaries and get a creative job, and hence have a higher career satisfaction, may also be more mobile. We therefore make use of a doubly robust method estimator for multivalued treatments: the inverse probability weighted regression adjustment (IPWRA) estimator. The IPWRA is a regression adjustment (RA) estimator which uses an inverse probability weighted (IPW) method to correct the estimator in the case the outcome model is mis-specified. If the outcome model is correct then these weights do not affect the consistency of the estimates. The IPWRA estimator has three stages:

1. Estimate a treatment probability model (we use a multinomial logit) and use the estimates of the parameters to calculate the inverse probability weights (propensity scores) of each category
2. Using these inverse probability weights estimated in part 1, fit a weighted regression model of the outcome for each treatment group and obtain a predicted value of the outcome for each individual and each treatment level.
3. Then compute the mean of the differences between the treatment specific outcomes; by restricting the sample to the just those in the treatment group we get the average treatment effect on the treated (ATET).

[11] Firstly, part time and self-employed individual's salaries are less reliable (part time students salary reports are not necessarily pro-rata) and secondly the salary response rate (for salaries that are sensible) is higher for full time employed individuals).

We estimate the ATET relative to a base category of non-migration so estimate the ATET of being in each category relative to non-migrating. We therefore use the multinomial logit we estimate in Eq. 10.1 and use socio-economic background and whether they lived in London prior to university as selection variables that do not appear in the outcome model (salary, obtaining a creative job and career satisfaction), with the variables otherwise the same as used in Eq. 10.3 (for a creative job), Eq. 10.4 (for salary) and Eq. 10.5 (career satisfaction).

10.4 Findings and Discussion

10.4.1 The Mobility of Creative Human Capital: Some Descriptive Statistics

We firstly explore through some descriptive statistics. We look at the employment and migration patterns of our cohort, in Table 10.1. If we examine employment patterns at 3.5 years we see the familiar patterns for creative graduates (Comunian et al. 2011), they are more likely to be self-employed and in part-time/unpaid work, and more likely to be unemployed (compared to other subjects), confirming once again that their career difficulties remain when considered even in a longer timeframe (Abreu et al. 2012).

We now explore the migration patterns during the 3.5 years period. We use the five categories of migration behaviour identified by Faggian (2005) and explained in the methodology. As Table 10.1 highlights creative graduates by 3.5 years are the least likely to be repeat migrants—behaviour commonly associated in the literature with higher economic rewards (Faggian 2005; Faggian and McCann 2009b) and the

Table 10.1 Employment status and migration category (for those in the labour market) by subject

	Creative	STEM	Soc, Law, Bus and Educ	Hum	All
Employment status					
Full-time employment	64.6	74.73	82	72.09	74.97
Self-employed/freelance	9.85	3.07	2.07	3.05	3.81
Part-time/unpaid employment	10.24	4.33	5.28	7.07	5.9
Further study	7.29	13.35	5.42	11.85	9.86
Unemployed	5.18	2.96	3.49	4.07	3.61
Other	2.84	1.56	1.73	1.88	1.85
Migration status					
Non-migrant	10.85	10.47	13.65	8.34	11.24
Late migrant	6.31	6.82	5.87	3.26	5.96
University stayer	16.05	14.35	12.34	12.19	13.69
Return migrant	26.08	21.3	24.24	27.03	23.74
Repeat migrant	40.71	47.05	43.9	49.18	45.36

Table 10.2 Creative job and graduate job by migration for creative and non-creative

	All graduates		Creative graduates	
	Creative job	Graduate job	Creative job	Graduate job
Non-migrant	16.47	69.13	39.64	67.27
Late migrant	22.79	78.32	56.81	69.54
University stayer	22.38	78.11	51.6	71.64
Return migrant	16.94	70.49	33.46	63.96
Repeat migrant	24.55	83.01	56.75	80.28
All	21.45	77.56	48.03	72.57

most likely to be university stayers and are more likely to be return migrants than STEM and social sciences, law, business and education and have a similar propensity to be return migrants to humanities. This seems to confirm qualitative data collected by Borén and Young (2013) that highlight the importance of local networks and embeddedness of creative workers and artists.

If we examine the relationship between migration patterns and creative and graduate level jobs (which include both creative and non-creative graduate level jobs) in Table 10.2, we see that the highest proportion of both graduate and creative jobs are among repeat migrants—confirming previous research on human capital in general (DaVanzo 1976; DaVanzo and Morrison 1981)—with the lowest proportion among return migrants, also confirmed in the short-term (6 months after graduation) analysis of Faggian et al. (2014). University stayers also have a higher proportion with a graduate job.

10.4.2 *Modelling Migration, Jobs Salary and Career Satisfaction*

10.4.2.1 Understanding Migration Patterns

We estimate the likelihood of being in each migration category at 3.5 years. We start by briefly discussing our control variables. Contradicting the results of Faggian et al. (2007) looking at pre-2000 cohorts, our results suggest that at 3.5 years females have a higher probability than men of being return migrants and are less likely to be repeat migrants. As shown in Table 10.3, older students have a higher probability than younger students of being a repeat migrant and less likely to be return migrants and at also have a lower probability of being a non-migrant. There are some ethnic differences with whites more migratory, and they have a lower probability of being a non or late migrant.

As would be expected Russell Group and other old graduates are more migratory with Russell Group graduates also having a greater probability for being a university stayer compared to other graduates which may mean they have the pick of jobs in

Table 10.3 Multinomial logit of migration behaviour: average marginal effects

	Non-migrant	Late migrant	University stayer	Return migrant	Repeat migrant
Average probability	0.092	0.052	0.130	0.242	0.483
Female	0.014**	−0.001	0.002	0.023***	−0.037***
	[0.006]	[0.004]	[0.007]	[0.008]	[0.009]
Subject (Reference Soc, Law, Bus and Edu)					
Creative	−0.024***	−0.009	0.029**	0.008	−0.003
	[0.008]	[0.006]	[0.012]	[0.014]	[0.016]
STEM	−0.015**	0.011**	−0.003	−0.006	0.013
	[0.006]	[0.005]	[0.008]	[0.009]	[0.011]
Humanities	−0.010	−0.014**	−0.018*	0.047***	−0.006
	[0.009]	[0.006]	[0.009]	[0.013]	[0.014]
Age > 21	0.004	0.0001	0.021***	−0.042***	0.016*
	[0.005]	[0.004]	[0.006]	[0.008]	[0.009]
White	−0.069***	−0.030***	−0.015	0.015	0.098***
	[0.006]	[0.006]	[0.010]	[0.013]	[0.015]
Institution type (Ref: Post 1992)					
Russell Group	−0.020**	−0.030***	0.020**	−0.052***	0.081***
	[0.009]	[0.006]	[0.010]	[0.012]	[0.014]
Other old	−0.043***	−0.027***	−0.045***	−0.022**	0.137***
	[0.007]	[0.006]	[0.008]	[0.011]	[0.012]
FE/HE college	0.002	0.024	−0.015	−0.037	0.026
	[0.017]	[0.015]	[0.017]	[0.022]	[0.027]
Degree classification (Ref: upper second)					
First class	0.009	0.009	0.012	−0.059***	0.029**
	[0.008]	[0.007]	[0.009]	[0.010]	[0.013]
Lower second	0.005	−0.002	0.005	0.059***	−0.068***
	[0.006]	[0.005]	[0.008]	[0.010]	[0.011]
Third/pass	0.016	−0.019**	0.030	0.088***	−0.114***
	[0.015]	[0.009]	[0.021]	[0.026]	[0.028]
NS-SEC background (ref: NS-SEC 5–8)					
Managerial/professional background	−0.050***	−0.019***	0.000	−0.033***	0.101***
	[0.007]	[0.005]	[0.009]	[0.011]	[0.012]
Intermediate/small employers and own account	−0.023***	−0.008	−0.003	−0.017	0.051***
	[0.007]	[0.005]	[0.010]	[0.012]	[0.014]
A level points (<240)					
241–340	−0.014*	−0.006	0.014	0.003	0.003
	[0.008]	[0.006]	[0.009]	[0.012]	[0.014]
341–420	−0.035***	−0.003	0.031***	−0.018	0.026*
	[0.009]	[0.007]	[0.010]	[0.013]	[0.015]
>420	−0.045***	−0.016**	0.053***	−0.047***	0.055***
	[0.010]	[0.007]	[0.011]	[0.014]	[0.016]

(continued)

Table 10.3 (continued)

	Non-migrant	Late migrant	University stayer	Return migrant	Repeat migrant
London original domicile	0.060***	0.003	−0.022*	0.172***	−0.212***
	[0.007]	[0.006]	[0.012]	[0.012]	[0.016]
Observations	12,803	12,803	12,803	12,803	12,803
Log likelihood	−16,749	−16,749	−16,749	−16,749	−16,749
LR Chi^2	1465	1465	1465	1465	1465
Pseudo r-squared	0.0539	0.0539	0.0539	0.0539	0.0539

Standard errors in brackets
***$p < 0.01$, **$p < 0.05$, *$p < 0.1$

their university catchment area (this fits with the idea that employers recruit the best students from local universities). Those students of higher ability, as proxied by A-level points, have a greater probability of being repeat migrants and are less likely to be non-migrants. Similarly, having a first class degree also increases the chance of migrating, compared to other classifications, and lessens the chance of being a return migrant—we would expect higher ability students to gain more for migration and have less need to correct any previous migration move as predicted by human capital theory (Sjaastad 1962).

Social class also seems to be making a difference as we see those from a higher social class having a greater probability of repeat migration, possibly connected also to being able to afford to migrate or being able to risk moving before finding a job.

We now turn to the comparison of subject groups. In comparison with the reference subject of 'Social sciences, Law, Business and education', creative graduates are the least likely to be non-migrants and have a higher probability of being a university stayer while STEM graduates are more likely to be a late migrant and also less likely to be non-migrants at 3.5 years, and more likely to be repeat migrants at 3.5 years. Humanities are the most likely to be return migrants and at are less likely to be return migrants, and having a lower probability of being a late migrant.

While Faggian et al. (2014) find an important role played by 'return migration' for creative graduates soon after graduation; we find that at 3.5 years 'staying around the university' is the more likely for creative graduates compared to other students, despite 'repeat migration' being the most common migration choice for creative graduates and for other graduates. This of course can have positive and negative connotations: in general, university stayers do not benefit from the highest economic rewards (compared to repeat migrants) however, as will be shown in Table 10.4, can help creative graduates enter a creative job (Faggian et al. 2014).

Our findings seem to confirm some of the general theoretical discussion at the start of the chapter. It is true that creative graduates are less likely to be in the non-migration category; therefore mobility is a common aspect of this group of graduates. However, confirming other elements of the literature—specifically in relation to place attachment—we see that creative graduates are the most likely to be university stayers (although not the most common category), confirming the

Table 10.4 Probability of obtaining a creative job: average marginal effects (probit)

	Graduate job	Creative job	Creative job—creative graduates only
Average probability	0.776	0.211	0.467
Female	−0.023***	−0.091***	−0.104***
	[0.008]	[0.007]	[0.027]
Subject (Reference Soc, Law, Bus and Edu)			
Creative	−0.011	0.360***	
	[0.013]	[0.015]	
STEM	0.071***	0.048***	
	[0.009]	[0.007]	
Humanities	−0.058***	0.140***	
	[0.013]	[0.012]	
Age > 21	0.019**	0.028***	0.057**
	[0.008]	[0.007]	[0.026]
White	0.016	−0.018	−0.040
	[0.011]	[0.011]	[0.041]
Degree classification (Ref: upper second)			
First class	0.035***	0.055***	0.164***
	[0.010]	[0.011]	[0.037]
Lower second	−0.050***	−0.035***	−0.098***
	[0.010]	[0.009]	[0.032]
Third/pass	−0.161***	−0.061***	−0.183***
	[0.027]	[0.019]	[0.064]
Institution type (Ref: Post 1992)			
Russell Group	0.039***	0.003	−0.097**
	[0.011]	[0.011]	[0.045]
Other old	0.019*	−0.002	−0.071*
	[0.010]	[0.010]	[0.037]
FE/HE college	0.000	−0.026	0.014
	[0.022]	[0.019]	[0.043]
Migration category (ref: Non-migrant)			
Late migrant	0.062***	0.031*	0.104
	[0.021]	[0.019]	[0.073]
University stay	0.053***	0.037**	0.057
	[0.018]	[0.015]	[0.054]
Return migrant	0.006	−0.010	−0.089*
	[0.016]	[0.013]	[0.049]
Repeat migrant	0.096***	0.063***	0.108**
	[0.015]	[0.013]	[0.047]
A level points (<240)			
241–340	0.019	−0.005	−0.007
	[0.012]	[0.011]	[0.034]
341–420	0.057***	0.005	0.077**
	[0.013]	[0.012]	[0.039]
>420	0.065***	−0.022*	0.043
	[0.014]	[0.013]	[0.042]

(continued)

Table 10.4 (continued)

	Graduate job	Creative job	Creative job—creative graduates only
NS-SEC background (ref: NS-SEC 5–8)			
Managerial/professional background	0.031***	0.010	−0.028
	[0.010]	[0.010]	[0.034]
Intermediate/small employers and own account	0.023**	0.014	−0.006
	[0.012]	[0.011]	[0.040]
Observations	12,569	12,784	1543
Log likelihood	−6566	−6192	−1163
LR Chi^2	576.6	976.5	113.1
Pseudo r-squared	0.0510	0.0924	0.0621

Robust standard errors in brackets
***$p < 0.01$, **$p < 0.05$, *$p < 0.1$

findings of some previous works (Chapain and Comunian 2010) as well as the role played by higher education in this sector (Comunian and Gilmore 2015).

In the next section we consider specifically the probability of obtaining a creative job.

10.4.2.2 Creative Jobs and Their Relation to Migration

We now estimate a model (Table 10.4) to investigate the probability of getting a creative job to see if migration behaviour is related to obtaining a creative job. We also compare results with a probit of the probability of getting a graduate level job (which encompasses both creative and non-creative graduate level jobs).

As would be expected creative graduates are the most likely to get a creative job, followed by graduates from the humanities then STEM. If we use all subjects we find being a repeat migrant, university stayer (suggesting that there might be a value in developing local networks in a place of study towards the goal of a creative job) and late migrant increases the probability of getting a creative jobs. If we restrict the focus to creatives only we find that repeat migration is important and return migration decreases the probability. This seems to support Faggian et al. (2014) idea that return migration is used as a coping mechanism for graduates who were not successful in obtaining a job or developing local networks and need to revert to old networks and support mechanisms (family or friends). We can see those who are more mobile are more likely to get a creative job but of course it is not possible to determine if they moved to find the job or moved because they had the job. This seems to confirm the findings of Bennett (2010) that highlights how employment opportunities play a role in attracting artists but that migration remains financially risky considering the temporary and part-time nature of many jobs in the creative industries. Socio-economic background only impacts on the likelihood of getting a graduate job as opposed to the likelihood of getting a creative job. Overall we can see that women are less likely to get a creative job—this seems to confirm the gender and diversity unbalance in the creative industries (Conor et al. 2015) but more likely to get a non-creative graduate job than men, which seem to suggest an issue specific to the sector rather than overall gender disadvantage.

Degree class seems much more important for getting a creative job. Institution type play less of a role for creative graduates as we know from previous research that they are less present in more prestigious (Russell Group) institutions (Comunian et al. 2011). In reference to A level points we see creative graduates are less likely to be in the >420 category than other graduates. All of this seems to confirm that these factors might be more relevant for jobs outside the creative sector and that qualifications are considered less important within the creative industries and occupation (The Work Foundation 2008).

10.4.2.3 Migration and Salary Changes and Career Satisfaction Over Time

If we examine our salary model estimates in Table 10.5, creative graduates tend to earn less than other subject groups, followed by humanities. We can confirm earlier findings and arguments of human capital scholars (Chevalier 2011; Naylor et al. 2002) that a better degree class, attending a more prestigious university (this only at 10% level) and having greater ability (as proxied by A-level points) increases wages. Consistent with previous studies, females earn less, as do some ethnic minorities, with older students earning more. Geography of course plays a role and London provides greater nominal wages, similar to earlier studies (Faggian et al. 2013).

Overall we can see that late and repeat migrants earn the most followed by university stayers Overall if we look at the salary that jobs can offer a non-creative graduate job will earn the most however, if we interact job type (see the third column in Table 10.5) with subject we see that STEM graduates earn the most within creative jobs and humanities the least. This highlights the fact that there are well paid jobs within the creative industries but they are not specifically taken by students from creative subjects but by other students (Comunian et al. 2015a).

A non-creative graduate job brings the greatest rewards followed by a creative job compared to a non-graduate job—creative graduates do better getting a non-creative graduate job (see the second column of Table 10.5). There are no differences, on average, within the premium for a non-creative graduate job among subjects. Creative graduates (both from the interaction in column 3 and the second column) get a penalty from return migration which other students do not get. Creative graduates also get a smaller London premium than other graduates with Social sciences, Law, Business and education getting the greatest London premium.

Of course salary is not the only motivation so we can also look at career satisfaction asked at 3.5 years. For satisfaction we have undertaken a probit of very/fairly satisfied, as reported in Table 10.5; again estimating this for all, creative

Table 10.5 Salary and career satisfaction

	Salary			Career satisfaction—probit		
	All	Creative only	Interaction	All	Creative only	Interaction
Female	−0.093***	−0.031*	−0.088***	0.010	−0.002	0.010
	[0.011]	[0.014]	[0.010]	[0.007]	[0.022]	[0.007]
Age > 21	0.033***	0.017*	0.032***	−0.013***	−0.026***	−0.014***
	[0.004]	[0.009]	[0.004]	[0.003]	[0.007]	[0.004]
Subject (Reference Soc, Law, Bus and Edu)						
Creative	−0.116***	−0.062**		−0.012		−0.020*
	[0.010]	[0.024]		[0.010]		[0.011]
STEM	0.008	0.002		0.004		0.002
	[0.012]	[0.022]		[0.007]		[0.006]
Humanities	−0.084***	−0.051		0.008		0.011
	[0.011]	[0.032]		[0.013]		[0.011]
Degree classification (Ref: upper second)						
First class	0.063***	0.012	0.062***	0.006	0.036	0.006
	[0.009]	[0.028]	[0.010]	[0.008]	[0.031]	[0.009]
Lower second	−0.053***	−0.020	−0.053***	−0.013*	−0.018	−0.013*
	[0.003]	[0.024]	[0.003]	[0.008]	[0.034]	[0.007]
Third/pass	−0.097***	−0.085	−0.097***	−0.057***	−0.052	−0.058***
	[0.018]	[0.058]	[0.019]	[0.016]	[0.049]	[0.016]
White	0.019*	0.077***	0.019*	0.037***	0.028	0.040***
	[0.009]	[0.018]	[0.009]	[0.011]	[0.038]	[0.012]
Institution type (Ref: Post 1992)						
Russell Group	0.037*	0.031*	0.036*	−0.026***	−0.024	−0.025***
	[0.020]	[0.016]	[0.020]	[0.007]	[0.036]	[0.008]
Other old	0.019	0.055**	0.018	−0.033**	−0.041	−0.031**
	[0.016]	[0.029]	[0.016]	[0.013]	[0.036]	[0.013]
FE/HE college	−0.017	−0.013	−0.016	0.022*	0.011	0.023*
	[0.016]	[0.034]	[0.017]	[0.013]	[0.025]	[0.013]

(continued)

Table 10.5 (continued)

	Salary			Career satisfaction—probit		
	All	Creative only	Interaction	All	Creative only	Interaction
A level points (<240)						
241–340	0.036***	0.046**	0.037***	−0.019**	−0.039*	−0.019**
	[0.012]	[0.019]	[0.011]	[0.008]	[0.024]	[0.008]
341–420	0.053***	0.046**	0.055***	−0.018	−0.028	−0.018
	[0.013]	[0.015]	[0.013]	[0.011]	[0.038]	[0.011]
>420	0.097***	0.089***	0.100***	−0.037***	−0.029	−0.038***
	[0.015]	[0.021]	[0.015]	[0.007]	[0.039]	[0.007]
London	0.205***	0.172***	0.232***	−0.031***	−0.015	−0.029***
	[0.015]	[0.020]	[0.020]	[0.009]	[0.019]	[0.009]
Migration category (ref: Non-migrant)						
Late migrant	0.072***	0.046	0.052*	−0.018	−0.004	−0.010
	[0.016]	[0.048]	[0.026]	[0.022]	[0.104]	[0.022]
University stay	0.025**	0.004	0.025	−0.045***	−0.034	−0.039***
	[0.009]	[0.025]	[0.028]	[0.011]	[0.044]	[0.011]
Return migrant	0.007	−0.050**	0.016	−0.032**	−0.003	−0.027*
	[0.008]	[0.021]	[0.017]	[0.014]	[0.048]	[0.015]
Repeat migrant	0.072***	0.051***	0.081***	−0.023*	−0.024	−0.018
	[0.007]	[0.016]	[0.016]	[0.013]	[0.051]	[0.014]
Job type (ref: other non-graduate)						
Creative job	0.154***	0.143***	0.144***	0.095***	0.156***	0.095***
	[0.019]	[0.020]	[0.022]	[0.006]	[0.038]	[0.008]
Other graduate job	0.222***	0.218***	0.219***	0.076***	0.101***	0.078***
	[0.009]	[0.022]	[0.011]	[0.008]	[0.039]	[0.011]
Log (Salary)				0.298***	0.364***	0.298***
				[0.026]	[0.042]	[0.026]

Job type*subject						
Creative job*creative			−0.018			
			[0.024]			
Creative job*STEM			0.073***			
			[0.022]			
Creative job*humanities			−0.061***			
			[0.019]			
Other graduate*creative			−0.003			
			[0.023]			
Other graduate*STEM			0.011			
			[0.017]			
Other graduate*humanities			0.015			
			[0.017]			
Migration category*subject						
Late migrant*creative			0.006			
			[0.045]			
Late migrant*STEM			0.043			
			[0.034]			
Late migrant*humanities			−0.001			
			[0.039]			
University stayer*creative			−0.017			
			[0.043]			
University stayer*STEM			0.015			
			[0.030]			
University*humanities			−0.032			
			[0.049]			
Return migrant*creative			−0.053**			
			[0.022]			

(continued)

Table 10.5 (continued)

	Salary			Career satisfaction—probit		
	All	Creative only	Interaction	All	Creative only	Interaction
Return migrant*STEM			−0.003			
			[0.023]			
Return migrant*humanities			−0.015			
			[0.033]			
Repeat migrant*creative			−0.011			
			[0.019]			
Repeat migrant*STEM			−0.010			
			[0.025]			
Repeat migrant*humanities			−0.026			
			[0.042]			
London*subject						
London*creative			−0.069***			
			[0.017]			
London*STEM			−0.044***			
			[0.009]			
London*humanities			−0.020*			
			[0.010]			
Observations	10,678	1117	10,678	10,609	1108	10,609
(Pseudo) R-squared	0.320	0.275	0.326	0.1513	0.1553	0.155

Robust standard errors in brackets
Estimates from the probit model are average marginal effects; the full effects are reported for the interaction average marginal effects
The r-squared value for the probit models are pseudo r-squared
$^{***}p < 0.01$, $^{**}p < 0.05$, $^{*}p < 0.1$

graduates and including interaction terms with subject[12] Again, confirming other human capital theory research, a higher degree class and a stronger institution of study, increase the salary level of graduates, however, we notice these factors do not have strong correspondence in relation to career satisfaction.

If we focus on creative graduates they have a lower probability of reporting they are very/fairly satisfied with their career (column 6 of Table 10.5) which is stronger if we remove salary (not shown).

Being in a creative job increases satisfaction and creative graduates (from column 5) in particular are more satisfied if they get a creative job.. Therefore while being in a creative job does not specifically increase the economic reward for creative graduates, it certainly affects their career satisfaction. Interestingly, the impact (column 5) of salary seems higher for creative graduates than graduates in general which goes against what we may expect i.e. creative graduate are less motivated by economic rewards. Compared to being a non-migrant, university stayers, return migrants and repeat migrants tend to be less satisfied with their careers. However, we know that migration has positive salary impacts and increases the likelihood of finding a creative job, with both having a positive impact on career satisfaction which outweigh these negative effects. If we interact subject with the migration categories (column 6) the negative impact of migration on career satisfaction reduces which is driven by a positive impact of migration for STEM graduates.

Table 10.6 provides the results from the inverse probability weighted regression adjustment (IPWRA) estimators to estimate the impact of migration on salary and obtaining a creative job, whilst allowing for the potential self-selection of migration which could potentially bias results. The results reported are the average treatment effect on the treated.

After allowing for selection we see the effects of repeat migration, late migration and university stayer remains for salary but when we focus on creative graduates the impact is only significant for repeat migration. Part of the impact of salary seems to be driven by the ability to find a graduate (creative job) since the impact of migration strategy increases if we exclude job type. If we examine the probability of getting a creative job we see that repeat migration is important and for creative only that return migration statistically significantly reduces the probability.[13] It seems that repeat migration is important for salary for all and creative graduates, and for getting a creative job. However, it seems that return migration has a negative impact for creative graduates on the likelihood of getting a creative job. Being a university stayer does not seem to have any significant impact once we allow for selection—we know from Table 10.3 that university stayers are partly connected to underlying ability and achievement measures. In terms of career satisfaction Table 10.6 suggests that late and repeat migration has a positive impact on career satisfaction but these

[12]When average marginal effects are reported with interaction effects the overall effects are reported by Stata and the interaction effects are not separately reported.

[13]The sample size falls when we examine creative only since the size of the other migration categories are still quite large but there is not enough power to reach significance.

Table 10.6 Creative job, salary and career satisfaction models: adjusting for selection using inverse probability weighted regression adjustment (IPWRA) estimators

		Salary—all		Career satisfaction	
	Creative job	All	No job type	All	No job type/salary
All					
Migration category (ref: Non-migrant)					
Late migrant	0.023	0.077***	0.092***	0.009	0.037**
	[0.019]	[0.016]	[0.017]	[0.016]	[0.016]
University stay	0.029	0.035**	0.045***	−0.034**	−0.01
	[0.018]	[0.015]	[0.015]	[0.015]	[0.016]
Return migrant	−0.013	0.006	0.011	−0.016	−0.015
	[0.014]	[0.013]	[0.013]	[0.015]	[0.015]
Repeat migrant	0.053***	0.084***	0.098***	−0.019	0.033**
	[0.016]	[0.016]	[0.017]	[0.013]	[0.014]
Creative graduates					
Migration category (ref: Non-migrant)					
Late migrant	0.112	0.023	0.022	0.002	0.012
	[0.093]	[0.049]	[0.053]	[0.065]	[0.057]
University stay	0.082	0.046	0.054	−0.029	−0.076
	[0.073]	[0.035]	[0.038]	[0.056]	[0.049]
Return migrant	−0.158**	−0.001	0.004	−0.043	−0.091**
	[0.062]	[0.036]	[0.032]	[0.055]	[0.043]
Repeat migrant	0.111	0.078**	0.095***	−0.002	−0.004
	[0.068]	[0.034]	[0.035]	[0.042]	[0.043]

Standard errors in brackets
$^{***}p < 0.01$, $^{**}p < 0.05$, $^{*}p < 0.1$

effects disappear when we control for salary and job type, again reiterating that migration has an indirect impact on career satisfaction through increasing salary and increasing the likelihood of finding a creative or graduate job. For creative graduate return migration has a negative impact on career satisfaction but this disappears when salary and job type are included.

10.5 Conclusions

The chapter builds on previous work on the relationship between migration and human capital. It specifically explores the need to distinguish between different types of human capital—related to different forms of specialisation at the higher education level. Following Comunian et al. (2010) initial work, it focuses on 'creative human capital': higher education graduates with a specialisation on artistic and creative disciplines. Building on the recent contribution of Faggian et al. (2014) it analyses what role migration patterns play in enabling graduates to obtain a creative job and better economic rewards and career satisfaction. Taking the work of Faggian et al. (2014) further we present a medium -term (3.5 years after graduation) view to the migration patterns of graduates and compare changes between the short and long term. The key finding of the chapter can be articulated in two main points:

Creative Human Capital, Same and Different Many of the migration dynamics of creative human capital reflect the general trends found in the general human capital theory and research. Students with higher abilities, a higher class degree, older and from Russell Group universities are more likely to migrate and be repeat migrants (Sjaastad 1962). This reinforces and supports previous work and findings across a range of disciplinary analysis (Faggian and McCann 2009b; Jewell and Faggian 2014). However, compared to other subject groups, we confirm Faggian et al. (2014) findings that creative graduates are less likely to be non-migrants but have a higher probability of being a university stayer, therefore they are less likely overall to benefit from the economic rewards of repeat migration and seems to be more likely to build networks and stay in the context where they studied (Comunian 2012).

Economic and Non-Economic Rewards Confirming previous work in Abreu et al. (2012) on salary expectations for creative graduates in the medium-term period (3.5 years after graduation), our findings confirm that creative graduates tend to earn less than other subject groups (followed by humanities) and the wage penalty of being a creative graduate decreases only marginally by 3.5 years. We also confirm that this is not specifically related to entering 'creative jobs' as STEM graduates earn the most within creative jobs and humanities the least. Alongside the economic measure of salary we wanted to consider also the level of career satisfaction—as other forms of personal rewards are usually put forward as explanation by economists working on cultural and creative labour dynamics (Abbing 2002; Throsby and Zednik 2011). We find that even in the medium term creative graduates are in general less satisfied with their career, followed by humanities, which weakens considerably when salary is included (although their satisfaction is increased by obtaining a creative job) .

Overall, our data further than confirming previous work point towards the longer-term struggle of creative graduates and the lower (economic and satisfaction) rewards experienced by creative human capital in the medium-term. Migration patterns, mobility and geography might for some students improve their outcomes in the medium-term but these still under-perform the other subjects. We need to confirm that—even after 3 years and half of potential adjustment—paradoxically and contradicting some of the general assumption about the creative class (Mellander and Florida 2011) "following your passion into a so-called cool career may more likely lead to misery or at least poverty". The dichotomy seems to remain across time "Do what you love. . .and starve?" (Nemko 2014).

Since our data does not allow us to delve deeper into the motivations for moving, there is scope for future research to understand the reasons for moving and willingness to move, and whether this varies by degree subject, as well as exploring longer term outcomes beyond 3.5 years.

References

Abbing H (2002) Why are artists poor?: the exceptional economy of the arts. Amsterdam University Press, Amsterdam

Abreu M, Faggian A, Comunian R, McCann P (2012) "Life is short, art is long": the persistent wage gap between Bohemian and non-Bohemian graduates. Ann Reg Sci 49:305–321. https://doi.org/10.1007/s00168-010-0422-4

Addison T (2008) The international mobility of cultural talent. In: Solimano A (ed) The international mobility of talent: types, causes, and development impact. Oxford University Press, New York, p 236

Beine M, Docquier F, Rapoport H (2008) Brain drain and human capital formation in developing countries: winners and losers. Econ J 118:631–652

Bennett D (2010) Creative migration: a Western Australian case study of creative artists. Aust Geogr 41:117–128

Borén T, Young C (2013) The migration dynamics of the "creative class": evidence from a study of artists in Stockholm, Sweden. Ann Assoc Am Geogr 103:195–210

Chapain C, Comunian R (2010) Enabling and inhibiting the creative economy: the role of the local and regional dimensions in England. Reg Stud 44:717–734

Cheng S, Long JS (2007) Testing for IIA in the multinomial logit model. Sociol Methods Res 35 (4):583–600

Chevalier A (2011) Subject choice and earnings of UK graduates. Econ Educ Rev 30:1187–1201

Chevalier A (2012) To be or not to be... a scientist? IZA DP No 6353

Comunian R (2012) Exploring the role of networks in the creative economy of North East England: economic and cultural dynamics. In: Warf B (ed) Encounters and engagements between economic and cultural geography, vol 104. Springer, Dordrecht, pp 143–157. https://doi.org/10.1007/978-94-007-2975-9_9. GeoJournal Library

Comunian R, Faggian A (2011) Higher education and the creative city. In: Mellander C, Andersson A, Andersson D (eds) Handbook on cities and creativity. Edward Elgar, London, pp 187–207

Comunian R, Faggian A (2014) Creative graduates and creative cities: exploring the geography of creative education in the UK. Int J Cult Creat Ind 1:19–34

Comunian R, Gilmore A (2015) Beyond the creative campus: reflections on the evolving relationship between higher education and the creative economy. King's College London, London. www.creative-campus.org.uk

Comunian R, Faggian A, Li QC (2010) Unrewarded careers in the creative class: the strange case of bohemian graduates. Pap Reg Sci 89:389–410

Comunian R, Faggian A, Jewell S (2011) Winning and losing in the creative industries: an analysis of creative graduates' career opportunities across creative disciplines. Cult Trends 20:291–308

Comunian R, Faggian A, Jewell S (2014a) Embedding arts and humanities in the creative economy: the role of graduates in the UK. Eviron Plann C Gov Policy 32:426–450

Comunian R, Faggian A, Jewell S (2014b) Exploring music careers: music graduates and early career trajectories in the UK. In: Crossley N, McAndrew S, Widdop P (eds) Social networks and music worlds. Routledge, Abingdon, pp 165–188

Comunian R, Faggian A, Jewell S (2015a) Digital technology and creative arts career patterns in the UK creative economy. J Educ Work 28:346–368. https://doi.org/10.1080/13639080.2014.997683

Comunian R, Gilmore A, Jacobi S (2015b) Higher education and the creative economy: creative graduates, knowledge transfer and regional impact debates. Geogr Compass 9(7):371–383

Coniglio ND, Prota F (2008) Human capital accumulation and migration in a peripheral EU region: the case of Basilicata. Pap Reg Sci 87:77–95

Conor B, Gill R, Taylor S (2015) Gender and creative labour. Sociol Rev 63:1–22. https://doi.org/10.1111/1467-954X.12237

Cruz S, Teixeira AAC (2013) Assessing the magnitude of creative employment: a comprehensive mapping and estimation of existing methodologies. Eur Plan Stud 22:2172–2209. https://doi.org/10.1080/09654313.2013.822475

Cruz S, Teixeira AC (2015) The neglected heterogeneity of spatial agglomeration and co-location patterns of creative employment: evidence from Portugal. Ann Reg Sci 54:143–177. https://doi.org/10.1007/s00168-014-0649-6

Cunningham S, Cutler T, Hearn G, Ryan M, Keane M (2004) An innovation agenda for the creative industries: where is the R&D? Media Int Aust: Inc Cult Policy 112:174–185

DaVanzo J (1976) Differences between return and non-return migration: an econometric analysis. Int Migr Rev 10:13–27

DaVanzo J, Morrison P (1981) Return and other sequences of migration in the United States. Demography 18:85–101. https://doi.org/10.2307/2061051

DCMS (2015) Creative industries: focus on employment detailed tables by Creative Industries Group. DCMS, London

Elias P, Purcell K (2004) Is mass higher education working? Evidence from the labour market experiences of recent graduates. Natl Inst Econ Rev 190:60–74

Faggian A (2005) Human capital, migration and local labour markets: the role of the higher education system in Great Britain. University of Reading, Reading

Faggian A, McCann P (2009a) Human capital, graduate migration and innovation in British regions. Camb J Econ 33:317–333

Faggian A, McCann P (2009b) Universities, agglomerations and graduate human capital mobility. J Econ Soc Geogr (TESG) 100:210–223

Faggian A, McCann P, Sheppard S (2006) An analysis of ethnic differences in UK graduate migration behaviour. Ann Reg Sci 40:461–471

Faggian A, McCann P, Sheppard S (2007) Some evidence that women are more mobile than men: gender differences in UK graduate migration behavior. J Reg Sci 47:517–539

Faggian A, Comunian R, Jewell S, Kelly U (2012) Bohemian graduates in the UK: disciplines and location determinants of creative careers. Reg Stud:1–18. https://doi.org/10.1080/00343404.2012.665990

Faggian A, Comunian R, Jewell S, Kelly U (2013) Bohemian graduates in the UK: disciplines and location determinants of creative careers. Reg Stud 47:183–200

Faggian A, Comunian R, Li QC (2014) Interregional migration of human creative capital: the case of "Bohemian graduates". Geoforum 55:33–42. https://doi.org/10.1016/j.geoforum.2014.05.003

Florida R (1999) The role of the university: leveraging talent, not technology. Sci Technol 15:67–73

Florida R (2002a) Bohemia and economic geography. J Econ Geogr 2:55–71

Florida R (2002b) The rise of the creative class: and how it's transforming work, leisure, community and everyday life. Basic Books, New York

Florida R, Mellander C, Stolarick K (2008) Inside the black box of regional development–human capital, the creative class and tolerance. J Econ Geogr 8:615–649

Hall P (1998) Cities in civilization: culture, innovation and urban order. Weidenfeld & Wishart, London

Hansen HK, Niedomysl T (2009) Migration of the creative class: evidence from Sweden. J Econ Geogr 9:191–206

Jewell S, Faggian A (2014) Interregional migration wage premia: the case of creative and STEM graduates in the UK. In: Kourtit K, Nijkamp P, Stimson R (eds) Applied modeling of regional growth and innovation systems. Springer, Berlin, pp 197–216

Lee N, Drever E (2013) The creative industries, creative occupations and innovation in London. Eur Plan Stud 21:1977–1997

Lucas RE (1988) On the mechanics of economic development. J Monet Econ 22:3–42

Madsen TL, Mosakowski E, Zaheer S (2002) The dynamics of knowledge flows: human capital mobility, knowledge retention and change. J Knowl Manag 6:164–176

Martin-Brelot H, Grossetti M, Eckert D, Gritsai O, Kovacs Z (2010) The spatial mobility of the 'creative class': a European perspective. Int J Urban Reg Res 34:854–870

Mathur VK (1999) Human capital-based strategy for regional economic development. Econ Dev Q 13:203–216. https://doi.org/10.1177/089124249901300301

McFadden D (1974) Conditional logit analysis of qualitative choice behaviour. In: Zarembka P (ed) *Frontiers in Econometrics*. Academic Press, New York

Mellander C, Florida R (2011) Creativity, talent, and regional wages in Sweden. Ann Reg Sci 46:637–660. https://doi.org/10.1007/s00168-009-0354-z

Naylor R, Smith J, McKnight A (2002) Why is there a graduate earnings premium for students from independent schools? Bull Econ Res 54:315–339

Nemko M (2014) Why following your passion is the worst kind of career advice. http://time.com/3503383/career-advice-following-passion/. Accessed 10 July 2015, Online

NESTA (2013) A manifesto for the creative economy. NESTA, London

O'Hagan J, Borowiecki KJ (2010) Birth location, migration, and clustering of important composers: historical patterns. Hist Methods 43:81–90

O'Hagan J, Hellmanzik C (2008) Clustering and migration of important visual artists: broad historical evidence. Hist Methods: J Quant Interdiscip Hist 41:121–136

Scott AJ (2010) Jobs or amenities? Destination choices of migrant engineers in the USA. Pap Reg Sci 89:43–63

Sjaastad LA (1962) The costs and returns of human migration. J Polit Econ 70:80–93

Storper M, Scott AJ (2009) Rethinking human capital, creativity and urban growth. J Econ Geogr 9:147–167

Throsby D, Zednik A (2011) Multiple job-holding and artistic careers: some empirical evidence. Cult Trends 20:9–24. https://doi.org/10.1080/09548963.2011.540809

Williams AM, Baláž V, Wallace C (2004) International labour mobility and uneven regional development in Europe human capital, knowledge and entrepreneurship. Eur Urban Reg Stud 11:27–46

The Work Foundation (2008) Staying ahead: the economic performance of the UK's creative industries. The Work Foundation, London

Chapter 11
Interregional Migration and Implications for Regional Resilience

Daniel Crown, Timothy Jaquet, and Alessandra Faggian

Abstract Regional resilience is a growing topic that encompasses many ideas, including what factors reduce the impact of negative shocks, or enhance a region's ability to recover or adapt. In this chapter we examine the relationship between patterns of migration during periods of recession and the overall economic resilience of an area. Determining whether the characteristics that attract migrants also contribute to an area's resilience is an important question to policymakers who seek to improve their local area's resilience to economic shocks. Our principal finding is that during an economic downturn migrants are less likely to move to an area with a different industrial composition than that of their origin county. We interpret this finding as evidence that migrants face frictions which prevent them from moving to counties with relatively high performing industries and instead respond to economic shocks by moving to a county with the same industrial sectors, but that may have been less-affected by the recession. When we examine the factors which contribute to the economic resilience of an area, we find that the characteristics which contribute to resilience during a recession are different than those that are significant in other periods. Specifically, during a recession, the role of a county's industrial structure is the primary factor that contributes to the resilience of an area. Together, these findings imply that a county's industrial composition is a driving force behind both migration during a recession and the economic resilience of an area.

Keywords Internal migration · Regional resilience · Industrial composition

D. Crown (✉) · T. Jaquet
Department of Agricultural, Environmental, and Development Economics, The Ohio State University, Columbus, OH, USA
e-mail: crown.17@osu.edu; jaquet.5@osu.edu

A. Faggian
Social Sciences, Gran Sasso Science Institute, L'Aquila, Italy
e-mail: alessandra.faggian@gssi.it

B. Biagi et al. (eds.), *New Frontiers in Interregional Migration Research*, Advances in Spatial Science, https://doi.org/10.1007/978-3-319-75886-2_11

11.1 Introduction

Hurricane Katrina, the collapse of the U.S. housing market, the global food crisis, the ongoing war in Syria, all of these events represent massive shocks to regional and global socioeconomic systems. The increasing frequency and intensity of these negative events has contributed to a growing interest in a variety of topics grouped under the umbrella of "regional resilience". In the face of mounting concern over climate change and political and economic stability, policymakers at all levels of government are expressing a growing interest in understanding what factors make a community impervious to negative shocks and aid in recovery during the aftermath.

The majority of research in the field of regional economic resilience has focused on characteristics such as the presence of industry structure and diversity of industrial composition, regional characteristics, or workforce demographics such as the level of human capital (e.g. Reggiani et al. 2002; Martin 2012; Hill et al. 2012; Faggian et al. 2017). However, there has been virtually no consideration of the role of migration in resisting or recovering from negative shocks. While the factors driving migration associated with natural disasters or conflict may be obvious, changes in patterns of human behavior during a recession are less straightforward. These broader recessionary periods lack the clear spatial point of impact, like that of an earthquake or civil war, which increases the difficulty of identifying and evaluating their direct and spillover effects. If industry and workforce factors are proven to be relevant factors of resilience, then migration represents a potentially relevant insight into understanding regional changes during recession and recovery.

Internal migration rates in the United States have steadily fallen since the 1980s (Partridge et al. 2012), and the decrease becomes even larger during periods of recession (Molloy et al. 2014). Explanations for this observed decline include the contraction of the housing market leading to 'lock-in' effects and a decline in the net benefit to migration for all migrants attributable to declines in the overall business cycle (Saks and Wozniak 2011). Surprisingly, little research has been conducted to determine whether the location specific characteristics that attract or repel migrants are the same depending on the state of the overall economy of a country. Determining how the preferences of migrants change according to the business cycle has important policy implications for local governments who seek attract migrants with high levels of human capital.

This chapter seeks to answer the following questions at the crossroads of resilience and migration: How do the location specific characteristics that attract migrants change during a recession? What is the role of these factors in contributing to economic growth and resilience? Do the characteristics that attract migrants also help bolster the economic resilience of an area?

Using ACS county to county migration flow data and a fixed effects negative binomial regression, we confirm several prior findings of the positive role of county size and human capital on attracting new migrants. By comparing a pre-recession period with the period of recession and recovery during 2008–2012, we find that migrants are less likely to migrate to a county with a different industrial composition during periods of recession. We interpret this finding as evidence that during periods of economic downturns, workers are unable to freely adjust their human capital in order to move to areas with high-performing industries, and instead will seek out destinations with similar occupations as their origin county, but that may have been relatively unaffected by the recession. When looking at the impact of these factors on regional resilience, we find that the characteristics which contribute to the growth of an area change during the recessionary period. Specifically, during a recession the primary factor that contributes to regional resilience is the industrial composition of a county. Taking these two results together, we conclude that the factors that areas traditionally use to attract migrants may be less effective during a recession due to increased industry lock-in. For areas concerned with resilience of their local labor market, focusing on industry composition is likely a more effective approach than others which might be successful in a normal business climate.

11.2 Background

11.2.1 Migration and the Great Recession

Previous work on the role of migration during periods of recession has attempted to explain why internal-migration rates fall during a recession. As outlined in Molloy et al. (2014), net migration rates in the United States have fallen steadily since the 1980s. However, recent studies have documented that the decline in migration rates has accelerated during periods of recession (Saks and Wozniak 2011). Figure 11.1 displays the percent of the population that has moved to a new county from 1980–2015 calculated from the IPUMS Current Population Survey (CPS) microdata. The accelerated decline in migration is evident from 2005–2010, where the percent of the population who moved to a new county fell from 5.8% to 3.7%.

Researchers attempting to explain the decline in migration rates during periods of recession have proposed several hypotheses related to the housing market and a change in the overall net benefit to migration. Early studies have found that when house prices fall, or interest rates rise, that homeowners are ‘locked-in’ to their current home, reducing mobility (Quigley 1987; Henley 1998). More recent estimates suggest that the ‘lock-in’ effect during a housing downturn are substantial. Ferreira et al. (2010) find that homeowners who suffer from negative equity are one-third less mobile, and that an additional $1000 in real annual mortgage costs lowers mobility by 12%.

An alternative explanation for why migration rates fall during times of recession is that the overall net benefit to migration may fall due to diminished labor market opportunities in potential destinations. In their study, Saks and Wozniak (2011) find that the net benefit to migration rises during boom-periods and falls during recessionary periods. Additionally, they find that young adults and those who are in the

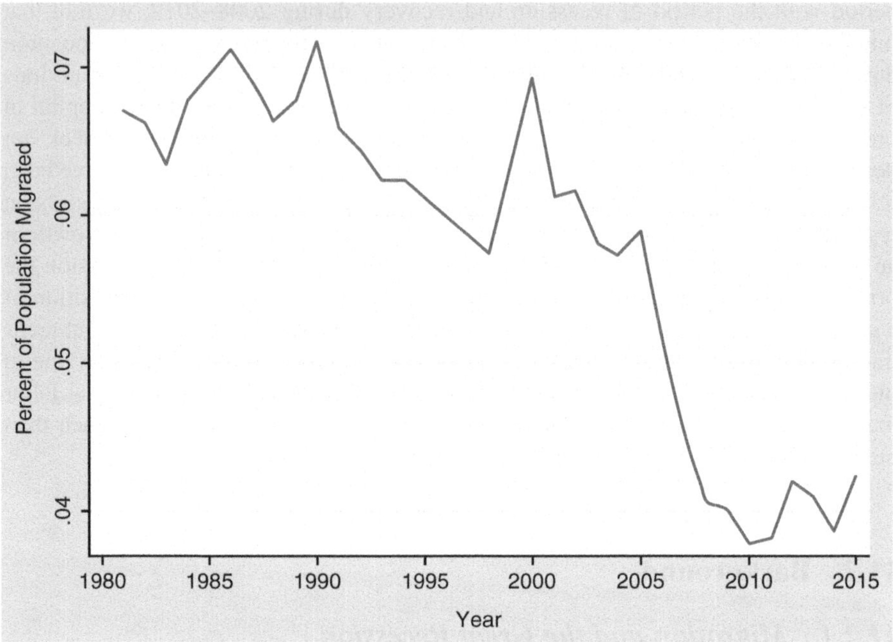

Fig. 11.1 Percent of population that migrated to a different county from 1980–2015. Source: IPUMS current population survey data

labor force exhibit the largest decline in migration during periods of recession, indicating that the primary mechanism could be more related to the labor market rather than the housing market.

In this chapter, our aim is to focus explicitly on how the factors that drive migration change when an economy is in a recession. This question has received considerably less attention in the literature. In a paper that is most similar to this chapter, Rupasingha et al. (2015) examines how the factors that drive non-metro to metro migration change over time, but does not consider the direct effects of the economic recession. To the best of our knowledge this chapter represents the first examination of this question.

11.2.2 Regional Resilience

Over the last 10 years, "resilience" has become a buzzword in the realm of regional science. It is not difficult to picture the concept of areas enduring and responding to negative shocks. However, formally defining resilience and measuring it represents a huge empirical challenge. Trying to adapt the various existing definitions from areas such as physics and ecology has proven difficult.

Martin and Sunley (2015) is often cited as the best comprehensive review of the various concepts, their history, and applications to economics. The two most intuitive definitions of resilience, originally articulated by the ecologist Holling (1973), are the ability to absorb or resist a negative shock (referred to in the literature as "ecological resilience"), and the ability to bounce back in the aftermath of one (referred to as "engineering resilience"). Originally considered separate definitions from different fields, Martin (2012) shows how varying definitions of resilience can be thought of as components of a larger framework.

While the components themselves seem intuitive, applying them to the analysis of a regional economy is not straightforward. And understanding the fundamental interactions between the pieces of the larger resilience concept is complicated. On the one hand, the less an area is impacted by a shock (resistance), the easier it will be to get back to where they were before (recovery). On the other hand, the traits that aid in resistance may actually inhibit recovery. Strengthening the rigidity of an area's systems may result in less flexibility and ability to adapt to a changing environment (Anderies 2015). There is also the question of what are you "locking in"? This focus on the status quo may lock in existing inequalities, injustices, or inefficiencies that prevent progress (MacKinnon and Derickson 2013). However, the idea of resistance as an approach to negative shocks has its own benefits. Avoiding or absorbing the shock eliminates the trauma and suffering that a community endures during the shock and recovery process. The concept of "bouncing back" necessarily contains an assumption that recovery is even an option. If a system possesses "tipping points" that can lead to a completely different equilibrium, then recovery may no longer be a viable alternative. As the formal concept of economic resilience moves forward, more work needs to be done identifying what traits best characterize these processes and their inherent synergies or trade-offs.

Regardless of which definition or component is of interest, there are many subjective decisions the researcher must make. What constitutes a "negative shock"? What time frame should be studied? What variable is best used as an indicator of resilience? What should be included in an index and how should the variables be weighted? Some of this may be guided by the research question, but many of these decisions vary with the researchers underlying beliefs about how regional economies work. As such, the bulk of the empirical work thus far has focused on identifying trends and applying different definitions to various settings.

Starting with Reggiani et al. (2002) much of the empirical work in resilience has focused primarily on employment as an indicator of regional resilience (e.g. Fingleton et al. 2012; Han and Goetz 2015; Lagravinese 2015). Other authors have used GDP (Cerra and Saxena 2008), GDP per capita (Cellini and Torrisi 2014), and patent generation (Balland et al. 2015). Just as there is a lack of consensus on which indicator of resilience to use, there has yet to be an agreement on the geographic unit of analysis. Past work has studied resilience at the level of local labor markets by using Metropolitan Statistical Areas (MSA) in the U.S. (Doran and Fingleton 2013) and Local Labor Systems (LLS) in Italy (Faggian et al. 2017), U.S. counties (Han and Goetz 2015), European regions (Martin 2012), or country level (Ormerod 2010).

For our analysis, we also use employment as our primary indicator of resilience. We measure this two different ways. First, we use a simple measure of growth in total employment. Alternatively, we construct a second measure of resilience, similar to the one used in Martin et al. (2016) that measures how well a county performs relative to if all industrial sectors had grown at their national rate. For our geographic unit, we chose the county level, in order to identify heterogeneity and patterns that might not be apparent at the state level.

11.3 Motivation and Empirical Approach

11.3.1 Empirical Migration Model

Starting from the migration side, in our model, individuals observe both economic and non-economic characteristics in a potential destination when deciding whether to move. We assume that individuals are rational, freely mobile, and seek to maximize their expected utility. Each individual i living in location j receives a level of utility that depends on the level of non-economic location specific amenities, a_j, and economic characteristics, e_j. The individual chooses to migrate if their expected utility in a new destination, k, is greater than that in their current location, j, minus the cost associated with moving from location j to k, c_{jk}.

$$NB = U_{ik}(a_k, e_k) - U_{ij}(a_j, e_j) - c_{ijk}, j \neq k \quad (11.1)$$

Thus, individuals will migrate if the net benefit of migration, NB, is greater than 0. This approach follows the random utility framework of McFadden (1974), and has been commonly used in the migration literature (Faggian and Franklin 2014; Biagi et al. 2011; Rupasingha et al. 2015).

Within the framework of the random utility model, we can express the utility for individual i facing the decision to move from location j to k as:

$$U_{ijk} = \beta X_{jk} + \varepsilon_{jk} \quad (11.2)$$

where X_{jk} is a vector of location specific characteristics and proxies for the costs of migration. By assuming that individuals move in order to maximize their expected utility, the probability of migrating from location j to k is:

$$P_{jk} = P(U_{ij} > U_{ik}) \quad (11.3)$$

which is equivalent to the probability that the net benefit to migration is greater than 0.

To link the migration behavior of individuals to the resilience of an area, we estimate whether the location specific characteristics which attract migrants change depending on the national business cycle. In order to do so, we use county-to-county migration flow data paired with a set of county-level characteristics.

Many applications of the random utility framework use the Conditional Logit Model (CLM) to estimate the effect of location specific characteristics on the decision to migrate. One well known drawback of such an approach is that the CLM relies on the Independence of Irrelevant Alternatives (IIA) assumption. This assumption states that the probability ratio of an individual choosing between two alternatives does not depend on the characteristics of another alternative. As shown in Cushing and Cushing (2007), this is not likely to hold in applications where the choice set is large, and will lead to incorrect estimates. The IIA assumption is unlikely to hold in the current application, as we will examine migration flows for 3144 counties in the United States. To relax the IIA assumption, many studies utilize the result of Guimaraes et al. (2003), who show that under certain conditions the likelihood function for the CLM and the Poisson regression model are equivalent.

However, one disadvantage of using the Poisson regression is the assumption of equidispersion, where the variance is assumed to be equal to the mean. In many empirical applications the data exhibits overdispersion, where the variance is larger than the mean. When the equidispersion assumption is violated, the parameter estimates from a Poisson regression will be biased (Cameron and Trivedi 2005). To accommodate our county-to-county migration flows which exhibit overdispersion, we will follow the recommendation of a number of previous studies and use the Negative Binomial model (Biagi et al. 2011; Faggian and Franklin 2014; Miguélez and Moreno 2014).

We use the gross county-to-county flow of migrants in the U.S., n_{jk}, as the dependent variable in the analysis. Thus, our dependent variable is the number of individuals who move from county j to county k. Assuming the n_{jk} follow a Poisson distribution, the equidispersion property requires that:

$$E\left[n_{jk}\right] = \mu_{jk} = e^{\alpha+\beta X_{jk}} = var\left[n_{jk}\right] \tag{11.4}$$

To relax this assumption that is unlikely to hold in most empirical applications, we add another parameter which is a function of an omitted variable, which can be interpreted as the unobserved heterogeneity of migrants. With this modification, the mean is given by:

$$E\left[n_{jk}\right] = e^{\alpha+\beta X_{jk}} * e^{\varepsilon_{jk}} \tag{11.5}$$

where $e^{\varepsilon_{jk}}$ is assumed to follow a gamma distribution with the following probability density:

$$Pr(n = X) = \frac{\Gamma(n+\alpha^{-1})}{n!\Gamma(\alpha^{-1})}\left(\frac{\alpha^{-1}}{\alpha^{-1}+\mu}\right)^{\alpha^{-1}}\left(\frac{\mu}{\alpha^{-1}+\mu}\right)^{n} \tag{11.6}$$

where Γ is the standard gamma function and α is the ancillary parameter which measures the degree of dispersion. Note that the Poisson model is a specific case of the Negative Binomial in which the degree of dispersion is exactly 0.

11.3.2 Empirical Resilience Model

Because we are interested in understanding how the factors that drive migration relate to the factors that affect resilience, we construct a simple model where we evaluate whether some of the variables that drive migration also have an impact on employment. We run the model with two specifications. The first uses change in total employment in county j, as the dependent variable:

$$\Delta E_j = \beta X_j + \gamma I_j + S + \varepsilon \tag{11.7}$$

where X_j is a vector of explanatory variables including county-level measures of human capital, amenities and baseline population. We also include a vector of industry shares, I_j, and state fixed effects.

In our second specification, we construct a measure of resilience similar to that of Martin et al. (2016) by calculating the difference between a county's actual future employment and its predicted employment if each sector in the county great at the national growth rate. Mathematically, we calculate this measure as:

$$R_j = \sum\nolimits_i \frac{E\left[e_{ij}\right] - e_{ij}}{E\left[e_{ij}\right]} \tag{11.8}$$

where $E[e_{ij}]$ is the predicted employment level that would occur if the industry grew according to the national growth rate for that industry during this time-frame. Our measure differs from that of Martin et al. (2016) because we use the difference in expected and actual industry employment levels rather than the difference in industry growth rates. In practice, if the expected growth rate of an industry is very small, the resilience measure of Martin et al. (2016) will approach infinity. It is for this reason that we choose to use the expected and actual levels of employment rather than growth rates in our measure of resilience.

This variable is interpreted as measuring a county's deviation from the path of an "average" county with the exact same industry structure. This deviation is the direct result of its unique traits that cause it to grow faster than average (or prevent it from keeping pace). By using this measure as a dependent variable in the resilience model, we not only control for growth that corresponds strictly to industry structure, but we are also able to estimate to what degree specific variables of interest correspond with these deviations.

The resulting model is:

$$R_j = \beta X_j + S + \varepsilon \tag{11.9}$$

Notice there is no term for the Industry Shares, because this is already being controlled by the Resilience measure. The resulting measure is a much cleaner expression of local economic processes.

11.4 Data and Methods

11.4.1 Migration Flow Data

To estimate the impact of location specific characteristics on the individual's migration decision, we utilize county-to-county migration flow data from the 2000 Decennial Census and the 2012 5-year American Community Survey (ACS). An ideal study would compare the county-level characteristics that attract migrants over three time periods. A pre-recession period, a recessionary period, and a post-recession period. Unfortunately, the migration flow data from the ACS is only available in 5-year estimates, which do not provide a temporal resolution to isolate the recession and recovery separately.[1] Thus the time periods chosen for this study are intended to represent a "normal" period (1995–2000) and a period of recession and recovery (2008–2012). While we leave studying the differences between periods of recession and recovery for future work, we can still examine changes in migration patterns compared to the baseline period of 1995–2000.

The county-to-county migration flows are generated from a survey question that asks respondents if they lived in the same residence 1 year ago for the 5-year ACS, and 5 years ago for the Census. If respondent answers that they did not live in the same residence, they are asked to provide the location of their previous residence. The individual answers to the survey question are aggregated into integer-numbers of migrants which can be thought of as a 3144 × 3144 origin to destination matrix, excluding the diagonal of non-migrants.

It is important to note that as a result of the difference in duration over which the migration question is asked between the Census and ACS, we have migration data for 687,845 county-to-county flows for the pre-recession time period, and 221,067 county-to-county flows for the 2008–2012 timeframe. While the literature suggests that migration declines during periods of recession, we believe that this effect is compounded by a change in data collection methods from the Census to ACS. Fortunately, as previously mentioned, our interest is not in levels of migration, but the patterns and determinants. Although the time period for migration in the survey questions differ across the ACS and Census, the resulting migration flows have been shown to be highly correlated across data sources and can be reliably used for comparing trends across samples (Benetsky and Koerber 2012).

11.4.2 County-Level Characteristics

Following the prior literature, we include a variety of economic and amenity based county-level characteristics, which are hypothesized to motivate migration. To mitigate concerns about endogeneity, we use county level variables that are

[1]The most recent release of the ACS county-to-county migration data covers the period of 2010–2014, which overlaps with the 2008–2012 used as our 'recessionary period'.

measured prior to the period of migration. Specifically, for the 1995–2000 migration period from the 2000 Census we use county characteristics from the 1990 Decennial Census. For the 2008–2012 5-year ACS migration flows we use county-level data from the 2006–2008 3-year ACS. Additionally, we include origin-county fixed effects in all specifications to control for unobservable time-invariant characteristics that may influence migration.

The distance between counties, calculated as the number of miles from centroid to centroid of the origin and destination county, is included as a proxy for the individual's cost of migration. This is motivated by the migration gravity model literature (for a review Sen and Smith 2012) and has been used in a variety of studies (e.g. Greenwood et al. 1991; Cushing and Poot 2003). This is hypothesized to have a negative effect on migration. To allow for a more flexible specification, we also include distance squared, which reflects the fact that there may be a diminishing negative effect of distance on the propensity to migrate.

The role of location specific amenities is emphasized in the equilibrium approach to migration modeling (Graves 1979; Knapp and Gravest 1989; Dotzel 2016). A large amount of recent evidence has shown that migrants are positively attracted to non-tradeable amenities such as weather, public services, and natural resources (Knapp and Gravest 1989; Rappaport 2007; Partridge 2010). To assess whether this relationship changes during periods of recession, we include the natural amenity index developed by McGranahan (1999). This index summarizes measures of natural resources including county-level measures of climate, topography, and amount of area covered by water. It has been shown in prior work that this variable is expected to have a positive effect on migration, as individuals typically seek areas with more favorable weather. Specific to this study, we expect that the magnitude of this effect should be reduced during periods of recession as individuals are primarily motivated by labor market conditions.

We include the percent of the population that is over the age of 65 to control for the migration patterns of retirees. Prior research has shown that retirees may be more likely to move from a metro to non-metro area for retirement (Jensen and Deller 2007). Migration of retirees may differ from that of younger adults as retirees are likely motivated by the presence of natural amenities rather than economic conditions. We also include the percent of the population that is married, and the percent of the county that has a bachelors degree or higher as sociodemographic control variables.

Median housing price is included to control for the fact that high housing prices in a county may discourage in-migration. While we expect median housing price to have negative sign due to higher housing prices reducing the incentive to migrate, it may be positive due to the presence of unmeasured amenities such as school quality or nearby natural attractions (Jeanty et al. 2010). In addition, we include the unemployment rate, percent below the poverty line, and median household income to control for county-level economic conditions. We expect prosperous counties with high income and low unemployment rates to attract migrants, and regions with less favorable economic characteristics to repel migrants.

Lastly, we control for local labor demand shocks by using the predicted growth of industry employment in a county if the county's industry sectors grew at the corresponding national rates (Bartik 1991; Partridge et al. 2012). As mentioned previously, the main advantage of this variable is that it does not suffer from the endogeneity bias that results from local labor demand shocks because it relies only on the initial industrial composition of the county and the national industry growth rates. This measure will only be biased to the extent that a region can influence the overall rate at the national level, which for a given county is almost none. To construct this variable we use industry employment data from the Quarterly Census of Employment and Wages collected by the Bureau of Labor Statistics. The predicted growth in employment is defined as:

$$L_j = \sum\nolimits_i \frac{e_{ij}}{E_j} * N_i \tag{11.10}$$

where e_{ij} is the level of employment in industry i and county j at the initial period and E_j is the total employment in county j. The fraction of employment in industry i in county j is then multiplied by the national growth rate measured over the time frame of interest. In our study, we use the national growth rate from 1990–2000 and 2008–2012, with 1990 and 2008 representing the baseline periods. Using this measure of predicted employment growth based only on the initial industrial composition of a county and the national growth rate of an industry allows us to control for local labor demand shocks and measure how employment in a county would be expected to grow if each industry grew according its corresponding the national growth rate. We expect this variable to have a positive effect on migration during both periods because areas with high predicted employment growth should be viewed as attractive for migrants, and even more attractive during periods of recession.

11.4.3 Cluster Analysis

To further understand the role of industry structure on migration, we cluster counties according to their industry composition at the start of our migration periods (1996 and 2008). Cluster analysis is a data-driven method of identifying the "natural" grouping of observations in a dataset. An advantage of cluster analysis over more straightforward methods of grouping, such as quantile analysis, is that cluster analysis allows for grouping on the values of multiple variables, by merging observations that are "close together". In the case of the industrial composition of a U.S. County, we grouped counties based on the share of employment in each industry.

There are several different ways to measure "distance" between observations in determining the similarity of groups. For our analysis we use Ward's Method, which forms groups by selecting the merger that results in the lowest within group variance.

Table 11.1 Description of cluster characteristics (1996 sample)

Cluster	Number of counties	Description
1	426	Dominated by manufacturing
2	321	Dominated by agriculture. Also strong in mining and wholesale trade. 77% rural
3	694	Largest shares in wholesale and retail trade, finance, and service industries. 86% urban
4	590	Rural with large shares in wholesale and retail trade, finance, and service industries. Slightly lower but balanced across the same groups, and higher in agriculture and mining. Most balanced group overall
5	87	Appear to be largely repressed areas with government jobs making up around 35% of their employment on average

Table 11.2 Description of cluster characteristics (2008 sample)

Cluster	Number of counties	Description
1	494	Dominated by manufacturing
2	149	Dominated by agriculture. 60% rural
3	384	Highest in professional and information services and FIRE industries. 92% urban
4	290	Highest in education and government sectors. Also strong in professional and information services and FIRE industries. 82% urban
5	494	Low house value and household income. 62% urban

By design, the members of any given cluster have a more similar industrial composition to each other, than they do to the members of any other cluster. Ward's Method is one of the most common clustering procedures and is considered the best method for producing homogenous groups. The resulting analysis revealed five clusters to be the optimal number across the two samples.[2]

Tables 11.1 and 11.2 provide a brief summary of the groups identified by the cluster analysis and Tables 11.6 and 11.7 in the appendix provide full summary statistics of county-level characteristics by cluster.

Due to the purely data-driven nature of the grouping process, it is striking how similar the interpretation of the groups are in the two different time periods. In both samples, Cluster 1 contained counties that were dominated by Manufacturing and contained an even split among rural and urban counties. Both samples also identified a largely rural group that was dominated by Agriculture. Lastly both samples identified a cluster of mostly urban counties that are relatively strong in Finance, Professional Services, and Trade. The remaining two clusters in each group did exhibit some differences depending on the sample. For 1996 the 4th cluster

[2]While clustering is a mathematical process, there are still subjective decisions that need to be made by the researchers. The 1996 group revealed principal modalities of 3 or 5, and the 2008 group leaned towards 4 or 5, so we selected 5 because it was well suited for both groups.

represents a group of counties that are largely rural, with a relatively high share of employment in the Mining and Construction sectors. The 5th cluster is greater than 50% urban counties and contains counties with the highest shares of Government employment. The 2008–2012 sample differs from 1996–2000 in that the 4th cluster is 82% urban counties and composed mostly of Education and Government industries. The 5th cluster is also mostly urban counties and composed of Retail Trade and Manufacturing firms.

We use the groups identified in the cluster analysis to estimate whether individuals choose to migrate to a destination with a similar industrial composition as the county they are leaving. To operationalize this procedure, we generate an indicator variable which equals 1 if the migrant moves from an origin in one cluster to a destination in a different cluster. We include the 'Migrated to Different Cluster' variable to estimate whether migrants respond to economic shocks by moving to a county with the same industrial composition, or to an area with a different industry structure. We perform this analysis for each sample separately to ensure that the differences in group composition across samples will not affect the results. A positive estimated coefficient indicates that people choose to migrate to a county that has a similar industrial makeup to their origin. A negative sign indicates that migrants are moving to a different type of area, where they may potentially switch industries. We expect that migrants are less likely to move to a county with a different industrial structure in both periods, however we anticipate that this effect will be smaller during the recessionary period, as migrants may switch occupations to industries that were less affected by the recession.

11.5 Results

11.5.1 Migration Model Results

We first examine whether the characteristics that attract or repel migrants have changed from 1995–2000 to 2008–2012. The results from the Negative Binomial county-to-county migration flow model are in Table 11.3.

Similar to past studies, we find that migrants are attracted to counties with larger populations (Biagi et al. 2011; Rupasingha et al. 2015). This finding is often attributed to the benefits of agglomeration, where migrants move to big cities in order to take advantage of thick labor markets and urban amenities. By comparing the estimate across samples, it appears that attractiveness of large counties remained relatively constant before and during the recession.

The role of distance also remained relatively constant across the two samples, with the estimate during the recession becoming slightly less negative. During the pre-recession period of 1995–2000, a one-mile increase in distance between an origin and destination county pair decreases the probability of migration by 3.4%, while during the recession a one mile increase in distance decreases the probability

Table 11.3 Results from negative binomial county-to-county migration model

	(1) 1995–2000	(2) 2008–2012
Baseline log population (1990, 2000)	0.341***	0.324***
	(0.00149)	(0.00266)
Percent with bachelors or higher (25 years and older)	0.00276***	0.00510***
	(0.000296)	(0.000440)
Unemployment rate	0.01000***	−0.00233
	(0.000873)	(0.00172)
Amenity index	0.0539***	0.0724***
	(0.000621)	(0.00129)
Percent married	0.000973*	0.00294***
	(0.000496)	(0.000627)
Percent over 65	−0.0102***	−0.0116***
	(0.000440)	(0.000719)
Median household income (in thousands)	−0.00446***	0.000787
	(0.000507)	(0.000519)
Median house value (in thousands)	0.000301***	−0.000520***
	(5.42e-05)	(4.04e-05)
Industry mix	0.0138***	0.00439*
	(0.000477)	(0.00255)
Percent below poverty line	−0.00123***	−0.000243
	(0.000453)	(0.00103)
Migrated to different cluster	−0.210***	−0.250***
	(0.00320)	(0.00584)
Distance between counties	−0.00340***	−0.00252***
	(6.63e-06)	(1.17e-05)
(Distance between counties)^2	1.04e-06***	7.33e-07***
	(3.23e-09)	(5.54e-09)
ln(alpha)	0.0889***	0.190***
	(0.00156)	(0.00270)
Constant	0.754***	0.750***
	(0.0801)	(0.146)
Observations	687,845	221,067
Origin county FE	Yes	Yes

Standard errors in parentheses
*** $p < 0.01$, ** $p < 0.05$, * $p < 0.1$

of migrating by 2.5%. Though the difference between these coefficients is small, the decreased negative effect of distance is consistent with the idea that migrants may be willing to move larger distances in search of jobs during periods of recession. Additionally we find a positive coefficient for the distance squared variable which indicates that there are diminishing marginal costs of moving larger distances.

When examining the economic factors that influence the migration decision, we find that migrants are more likely to move to counties with higher housing values in the pre-recession period, but prefer counties with lower housing values during the recession. This could reflect a change in migrant's preferences, as those who are affected by the recession could choose to move in order to find more affordable housing options.

When interpreting the estimated effect of industry structure on the decision to migrate, the results are somewhat surprising. We expected to find that during the period of recession and recovery migrants would be moving out of industries negatively affected by the recession and into industries performing relatively favorably. While we find this is weakly true, the magnitude is actually much lower than during the stable period. We also find that migrants are less likely to move to a county that is outside of their origin county's industrial cluster. It is interesting that this effect grows larger during the period of recession and recovery. If the people migrating during the recession are indeed individuals in the industries most affected, as indicated above, we would expect both estimates to move in the opposite direction relative to the initial estimate. These two signals together indicate that there may be frictions that prevent migrants from adjusting their skills in response to economic downturns. Another possibility is the decreased demand for labor drives increased competition in the labor market that makes applicants from outside fields less successful than they would normally be if they chose to switch industries. Either way, the results seem to indicate that workers are unable to quickly change industries, as might be the assumed response.

Together, our results suggest that migrants are not perfectly free to adjust their level of human capital and move to an area with relatively prosperous industries, but instead respond by becoming more geographically flexible within a group of counties with similar industrial structures.

11.5.2 Regional Resilience Results

Table 11.4 presents results from OLS regressions using both the county's employment growth and the resilience measure where we calculate as the difference in predicted employment growth and the actual employment level in the county. As discussed in Sect. 11.3, the resilience measure reflects how well a county performed relative to the national growth rate, weighted for its unique industrial composition.

When comparing the estimates across the two time periods we notice some striking differences. First, the two alternative specifications yield similar results for the first time period, but not for the second. While the employment growth model has controls for share of the various industry sectors, the Resilience Measure controls for industry structure much more thoroughly. We interpret the lower significance levels in the second time period as a signal that stable growth is much less correlated with

Table 11.4 Regressions of resilience measure and employment growth

	(1) Resilience measure	(2) Employment growth 1990–2000	(3) Resilience measure	(4) Employment growth 2008–2012
Baseline log population (1990, 2000)	−0.342***	−0.0937***	−0.0155	0.0352**
	(0.119)	(0.0139)	(0.0476)	(0.0140)
Amenity index	0.196**	0.0205***	−0.00667	0.0182**
	(0.0815)	(0.00778)	(0.0358)	(0.00794)
Median household income (in thousands)	0.000279***	2.98e-05***	2.25e-05*	1.43e-07
	(4.09e-05)	(4.17e-06)	(1.18e-05)	(2.89e-06)
Median house value	0.00205	−0.00155**	−0.00287*	−0.000397
	(0.00658)	(0.000642)	(0.00172)	(0.000389)
Percent married	0.103***	0.00733**	−0.00427	−0.00244
	(0.0290)	(0.00293)	(0.0114)	(0.00266)
Percent below poverty	0.172***	0.0179***	0.00563	0.00112
	(0.0293)	(0.00291)	(0.0137)	(0.00315)
Percent with bachelors or higher	−0.0298	0.00379	−0.00142	0.00830***
	(0.0241)	(0.00316)	(0.00981)	(0.00295)
Constant	−14.17***	−0.261	−0.874	−0.0124
	(3.735)	(0.462)	(1.032)	(0.403)
Observations	3089	3089	3103	3101
R-squared	0.081	0.140	0.061	0.097
State FE	Yes	Yes	Yes	Yes
Percent industry controls	N/A	Yes	N/A	Yes

Standard errors in parentheses
*** $p < 0.01$, ** $p < 0.05$, * $p < 0.1$

industry structure. Furthermore, the similarity between models (1) and (2) seems to indicate that much of the correlation is being captured by the industry controls.

However, in the second time period, variables such as population size, amenities, and education level are no longer significant, indicating that these effects are correlated with industry structure. The emergence of a negative estimate for Median House value and small positive value for household income are consistent with the results from our migration model, further suggesting there is a connection between migration and county employment growth.

We find that county-level demographics such as the percent married and percent below poverty are significantly positively correlated with employment growth for the 1990–2000 period, however they have no impact on employment growth from 2008–2012. This finding is consistent with the idea that the industrial structure of a county has the largest effect on the growth of a county during a recession. Again we find that after controlling for industry structure in specifications (3) and (4) these factors are no longer significant.

In Table 11.5, we estimate the resilience models with the inclusion of a variable representing the log inflow of migrants to the county. However, we caution that this variable is likely endogenous, as migrants are more likely to move into areas which are more resilient. However, we do find that in-migration is positively associated with the regional resilience of an area in all specifications. This provides some evidence that attracting new migrants to an area could be one strategy for increased growth during a recession.

Overall, our results from the resilience models are consistent with the conclusions from our migration model. While these findings do not prove a causal impact of migration on resilience, they indicate that both migration and resilience are responding to the same factors, namely a decreased significance of location specific characteristics and an increased dependence on industrial composition. Furthermore,

Table 11.5 Regressions of resilience measure and employment growth

	(1)	(2)	(3)	(4)
	Resilience measure	Employment growth 1990–2000	Resilience measure	Employment growth 2008–2012
Baseline log population (1990, 2000)	−3.449***	−0.266***	−0.264***	−0.0260***
	(0.556)	(0.0548)	(0.0750)	(0.00519)
Amenity index	0.339***	0.0310***	0.00799	0.00126**
	(0.0478)	(0.00476)	(0.00694)	(0.000508)
Median household income (in thousands)	0.190*	0.0239***	−0.0549**	−0.000850
	(0.0974)	(0.00913)	(0.0225)	(0.00143)
Median house value	−0.00266	−0.00183***	−0.000934	−1.21e-05
	(0.00730)	(0.000699)	(0.000944)	(6.15e-05)
Percent married	0.138***	0.00703**	0.0213***	0.000541
	(0.0362)	(0.00358)	(0.00740)	(0.000490)
Percent below poverty	0.247***	0.0202***	0.00788	0.000938
	(0.0359)	(0.00346)	(0.0101)	(0.000675)
Percent with bachelors or higher	−0.0811***	0.00366	0.00328	−0.000433
	(0.0305)	(0.00386)	(0.00580)	(0.000543)
Log inflow of migrants	3.157***	0.173***	0.230***	0.0324***
	(0.579)	(0.0586)	(0.0761)	(0.00497)
Constant	−12.93***	−0.176	−1.138*	−0.187**
	(4.632)	(0.554)	(0.661)	(0.0759)
Observations	2546	2546	1807	1807
R-squared	0.105	0.156	0.173	0.237
State FE	Yes	Yes	Yes	Yes
Percent industry controls	N/A	Yes	N/A	Yes

Standard errors in parentheses
*** $p < 0.01$, ** $p < 0.05$, * $p < 0.1$

we have shown there is a positive correlation between in-migration and regional resilience in both the pre-recession and post-recession periods.

11.6 Conclusion and Future Directions

This chapter has explored the relationship between migration and resilience during the Great Recession. Specifically, we examine whether the characteristics that attract migrants have changed with economic conditions, and if these characteristics also contribute to the resilience of a county. With regard to the first question of how the factors which attract migrants change during a recession we conclude that during periods of recession migrants are less likely to move to a county with a different industrial composition as their origin county. We speculate that this is attributable to the presence of frictions which prevent free adjustments to migrant's human capital. Rather than responding to a negative economic shock by changing industry, migrants appear to respond by moving to an area that has the same industrial structure, but may be relatively prosperous.

We examine the factors that contribute to a county's regional resilience and conclude that although demographic characteristics appear to contribute to growth before the recession, during an economic downturn the industrial composition of a county is the primary factor that drives resilience. Though we do not prove a causal relationship between migration and resilience, we interpret the results of this chapter as evidence that migration and regional resilience are connected through their relationship to the industrial structure of an area.

There is much yet to explore about the underlying dynamics of these migratory patterns. While we observe clear changes in migration patterns, future research needs to delve into the role of labor supply vs labor demand as driving forces. Is migration driving resilience or are people drawn to resilient areas? The first step in decoding this would be access to migration data with a much finer temporal resolution. This would allow more accurate exploration between migration rates an area's economic health. Plus, while we were able to compare a period of stability to a period of relative instability, better data would allow separation of changes in behavior during recession and the following time period. Insights into these specific effects, will contribute to the distinct components of resistance and recovery already being explored in the regional resilience framework.

While the goal of our resilience model was to look for significant drivers among the variables in our migration model, the opposite would be a worthwhile undertaking as well. By focusing specifically on the dynamics of the labor market, a better model can be established to identify the patterns of resilience in local labor markets. Seeing in turn, if these represent significant omitted variables from migration models could help bring some clarity to this picture. While there is much yet to be examined, our preliminary results support the idea that migration is an important variable in local economies that should not be neglected in future resilience research.

Appendix

Table 11.6 Summary statistics by cluster (1996 sample)

	Cluster 1		Cluster 2		Cluster 3		Cluster 4		Cluster 5	
Variable	Mean	Std. Dev.	Mean	Std. Dev.	Mean	Std. Dev.	Mean	Std. Dev.	Mean	Std. Dev.
Baseline log population (1990)	10.91	0.89	*9.70*	1.55	**12.38**	1.29	10.26	0.89	11.21	0.77
Percent with bachelors degree or higher	12.51	4.11	12.22	3.48	21.43	7.55	*12.08*	4.07	**21.69**	9.10
Unemployment rate	6.22	2.08	6.64	3.58	*6.20*	2.12	7.19	2.82	**7.55**	3.10
USDA natural amenity index	*−0.62*	1.63	0.94	2.89	**1.15**	2.97	0.35	2.32	0.82	1.92
Percent over 65 years old	13.60	2.56	**16.59**	5.07	12.59	4.16	14.64	3.79	*9.48*	2.57
Median household income	25.89	5.48	*21.74*	4.35	**30.55**	7.48	23.06	4.87	25.93	6.60
Median house value	53.64	16.21	*47.03*	31.47	**91.44**	56.91	48.59	18.02	66.40	21.99
Industry mix	*14.69*	2.82	18.78	3.30	21.35	2.36	17.15	2.81	**22.09**	2.32
Percent below poverty line	13.91	6.24	**19.27**	7.63	*12.53*	5.87	17.58	7.00	16.36	7.92
Metro	0.49	0.50	*0.32*	0.47	**0.86**	0.35	0.37	0.48	0.62	0.49
Agriculture	5.56	2.97	**23.87**	6.71	*2.56*	2.25	11.60	5.64	3.56	2.34
Mining	*0.38*	0.69	2.15	3.65	0.52	1.09	**2.95**	5.10	0.40	0.68
Construction	5.51	1.60	*4.78*	2.00	5.90	1.90	**5.94**	2.44	4.84	1.31
Manufacturing	**26.65**	6.22	*4.31*	2.52	10.99	4.80	12.61	6.04	5.70	3.02
Wholesale trade	3.16	1.30	3.60	1.81	**4.44**	1.74	3.42	1.71	*2.08*	1.16
Retail trade	16.59	2.60	*14.45*	2.75	**18.43**	3.11	16.47	2.97	17.24	2.70
Transportation	3.78	1.38	3.91	1.44	**4.66**	1.86	4.60	2.46	*3.17*	1.78
Financial services	*4.34*	1.14	4.58	1.16	**7.34**	2.41	4.68	1.24	5.14	1.71
Services	21.16	3.64	*19.85*	4.51	**30.80**	4.92	21.52	3.78	22.40	4.48
Government	*12.87*	3.84	18.50	5.78	14.35	4.84	16.20	4.31	**35.47**	8.93
Cluster size	426		321		694		590		87	

Bold indicates maximum value across all clusters. Italics denotes minimum value across all clusters

Table 11.7 Summary statistics by cluster (2008 sample)

	Cluster 1		Cluster 2		Cluster 3		Cluster 4		Cluster 5	
	Mean	SD	Mean	SD	Mean	SD	Mean	SD	Mean	SD
Baseline log population (2000)	11.12	0.87	*10.90*	0.94	**12.77**	1.31	12.03	1.04	11.31	0.92
Percent with bachelors or higher	17.30	5.34	*16.83*	4.82	30.21	9.42	**30.51**	10.54	20.21	6.84
Unemployment rate	**6.92**	2.14	6.76	2.75	6.07	1.62	*6.04*	1.88	6.63	2.19
USDA natural amenity index	*−1.01*	1.57	1.68	2.78	**1.90**	2.96	0.53	2.23	−0.14	1.86
Percent over 65 years old	**13.91**	2.34	13.10	4.44	12.31	5.13	*11.04*	3.32	13.40	2.89
Median household income	43.90	6.94	*43.61*	9.76	**57.29**	12.39	51.77	15.80	45.23	8.52
Median house value	*114.51*	30.19	149.37	105.68	**254.30**	140.21	209.74	131.81	135.11	62.00
Industry mix	*−3.89*	1.23	−2.47	0.86	−2.25	0.82	**−1.66**	0.76	−2.90	1.06
Percent below poverty line	10.72	3.88	**12.88**	5.28	*8.19*	3.20	9.98	5.06	10.95	4.39
Metro	0.48	0.50	*0.41*	0.49	**0.92**	0.27	0.82	0.39	0.62	0.49
Agriculture	2.86	2.25	**11.30**	5.34	*1.05*	1.23	1.52	1.54	2.98	2.55
Construction	*7.03*	1.76	8.44	2.82	**8.81**	2.89	7.07	1.83	7.98	2.34
Manufacturing	**22.53**	4.91	*7.05*	3.28	9.48	3.68	7.08	2.33	14.20	2.63
Wholesale trade	2.81	0.87	2.90	1.16	**3.28**	0.91	*2.46*	0.93	2.97	0.92
Retail trade	11.62	1.49	12.06	1.95	12.00	1.71	*11.50*	1.91	**12.26**	1.63
Transportation	5.04	1.27	**5.46**	1.58	5.14	1.86	*4.36*	1.41	5.38	1.82
Information	1.54	0.62	*1.50*	0.73	**2.60**	1.04	2.26	0.83	1.80	0.70
Financial services	*4.43*	1.30	4.44	1.27	**7.94**	2.17	6.46	2.45	5.07	1.41
Professional services	*5.85*	1.63	6.11	1.76	**11.36**	2.73	9.76	3.91	6.91	1.82
Education	20.87	2.97	22.21	3.91	*19.31*	2.62	**25.86**	6.12	23.04	3.93
Arts	*7.35*	1.75	8.09	2.08	**9.77**	3.52	9.32	2.18	7.85	1.87
Other	*4.51*	0.80	4.75	1.08	**4.85**	0.72	4.76	0.86	4.67	0.91
Government	*3.57*	1.32	5.70	2.33	4.41	1.72	**7.58**	4.43	4.89	2.46
	494		149		384		290		494	

Bold indicates maximum value across all clusters. Italics denotes minimum value across all clusters

Table 11.8 Source census and ACS migration flow data

Origin county	Destination county	Number of migrants
Panel A: 1995–2000		
Orange County, CA	Los Angeles County, CA	146,044
San Bernardino County, CA	Los Angeles County, CA	135,657
DuPage County, IL	Cook County, IL	80,286
Baltimore County, MD	Baltimore city, MD	77,991
Los Angeles County, CA	Orange County, CA	77,760
Panel B: 2008–2012		
Los Angeles County, CA	Orange County, CA	40,760
Los Angeles County, CA	San Bernardino County, CA	38,495
Orange County, CA	Los Angeles County, CA	31,676
Los Angeles County, CA	Riverside County, CA	25,575
Miami-Dade County, FL	Broward County, FL	23,952

References

Anderies JM (2015) Managing variance: key policy challenges for the Anthropocene. Proc Natl Acad Sci 112(47):14402–14403

Balland PA, Rigby D, Boschma R (2015) The technological resilience of US cities. Camb J Reg Econ Soc 8(2):167–184

Bartik TJ (1991) Boon or boondoggle? The debate over state and local economic development policies. W.E. Upjohn Institute for Employment Research, Kalamazoo

Benetsky M, Koerber K (2012) 2005–2009 American community survey county-to-county migration files. Working paper no. 2012-06

Biagi B, Faggian A, McCann P (2011) Long and short distance migration in Italy: the role of economic, social and environmental characteristics. Spat Econ Anal 6(1):111–131

Cameron AC, Trivedi PK (2005) Microeconometrics: methods and applications. Cambridge University Press, Cambridge

Cellini R, Torrisi G (2014) Regional resilience in Italy: a very long-run analysis. Reg Stud 48(11):1779–1796

Cerra V, Saxena SC (2008) Growth dynamics: the myth of economic recovery. Am Econ Rev 98(1):439–457

Cushing C, Cushing B (2007) Conditional Logit, IIA, and alternatives for estimating models of interstate migration. In: Annual meeting of the Southern Regional Science Association. Charleston

Cushing B, Poot J (2003) Crossing boundaries and borders: regional science advances in migration modelling. Pap Reg Sci 83(1):317–338

Doran J, Fingleton B (2013) US metropolitan area resilience: insights from dynamic spatial panel estimation. In: Annual conference of the Regional Science Association International (British and Irish section), vol 22, University of Cambridge. Aug 2013

Dotzel KR (2016) Do natural amenities influence undergraduate student migration decisions? Ann Reg Sci 59:677–705. https://doi.org/10.1007/s00168-016-0765-6

Faggian A, Franklin RS (2014) Human capital redistribution in the USA: the migration of the college-bound. Spat Econ Anal 9(4):376–395

Faggian A, Gemmiti R, Jaquet T, Santini I (2017) Regional economic resilience: the experience of the Italian local labor systems. Ann Reg Sci 58:1–18

Ferreira F, Gyourko J, Tracy J (2010) Housing busts and household mobility. J Urban Econ 68(1):34–45

Fingleton B, Garretsen H, Martin R (2012) Recessionary shocks and regional employment: evidence on the resilience of UK regions. J Reg Sci 52(1):109–133

Graves PE (1979) A life-cycle empirical analysis of migration and climate by race. J Urban Econ 6(2):135–147
Greenwood MJ, Hunt GL, Rickman DS, Treyz GI (1991) Migration, regional equilibrium, and the estimation of compensating differentials. Am Econ Rev 81(5):1382–1390
Guimaraes P, Figueirdo O, Woodward D (2003) A tractable approach to the firm location decision problem. Rev Econ Stat 85(1):201–204
Han Y, Goetz S (2015) The economic resilience of U.S. counties during the great recession. Rev Reg Stud 45(2):131–149
Henley A (1998) Residential mobility, housing equity and the labour market. Econ J 108 (447):414–427
Hill E, St. Clair T, Wial H, Wolman H, Atkins P, Blumenthal P, Ficenec S, Friedhoff A (2012) Economic shocks and regional economic resilience. Urban policy and its effects. Brookings Institution Press, Washington
Holling CS (1973) Resilience and stability of ecological systems. Annu Rev Ecol Syst 4(1):1–23
Jeanty PW, Partridge M, Irwin E (2010) Estimation of a spatial simultaneous equation model of population migration and housing price dynamics. Reg Sci Urban Econ 40(5):343–352
Jensen T, Deller S (2007) Spatial modeling of the migration of older persons with a focus on amenities. Rev Reg Stud 37(3):303
Knapp TA, Gravest PE (1989) On the role of amenities in models of migration and regional development. J Reg Sci 29(1):71–87
Lagravinese R (2015) Economic crisis and rising gaps North–South: evidence from the Italian regions. Camb J Reg Econ Soc 8(2):331–342
MacKinnon D, Derickson KD (2013) From resilience to resourcefulness: a critique of resilience policy and activism. Prog Hum Geogr 37(2):253–270
Martin R (2012) Regional economic resilience, hysteresis and recessionary shocks. J Econ Geogr 12(1):1–32
Martin R, Sunley P (2015) On the notion of regional economic resilience: conceptualization and explanation. J Econ Geogr 15(1):1–42
Martin R, Sunley P, Gardiner B, Tyler P (2016) How regions react to recessions: resilience and the role of economic structure. Reg Stud 50(4):561–585
McFadden D (1974) The measurement of urban travel demand. J Public Econ 3(4):303–328
McGranahan DA (1999) Natural amenities drive rural population change (No. 33955). United States Department of Agriculture, Economic Research Service
Miguélez E, Moreno R (2014) What attracts knowledge workers? The role of space and social networks. J Reg Sci 54(1):33–60
Molloy R, Smith CL, Wozniak AK (2014) Declining migration within the US: the role of the labor market (No. w20065). National Bureau of Economic Research
Ormerod P (2010) Risk, recessions, and the resilience of the capitalist economies. Risk Manag 12 (1):83–99
Partridge MD (2010) The duelling models: NEG vs amenity migration in explaining US engines of growth. Pap Reg Sci 89(3):513–536
Partridge MD, Rickman DS, Olfert MR, Ali K (2012) Dwindling US internal migration: evidence of spatial equilibrium or structural shifts in local labor markets? Reg Sci Urban Econ 42 (1):375–388
Quigley JM (1987) Interest rate variations, mortgage prepayments and household mobility. Rev Econ Stat 69(9):636–643
Rappaport J (2007) Moving to nice weather. Reg Sci Urban Econ 37(3):375–398
Reggiani A, De Graaff T, Nijkamp P (2002) Resilience: an evolutionary approach to spatial economic systems. Netw Spat Econ 2(2):211–229
Rupasingha A, Liu Y, Partridge M (2015) Rural bound: determinants of metro to non-metro migration in the United States. Am J Agric Econ 97(3):680–700
Saks RE, Wozniak A (2011) Labor reallocation over the business cycle: new evidence from internal migration. J Labor Econ 29(4):697–739
Sen A, Smith T (2012) Gravity models of spatial interaction behavior. Springer, Heidelberg